Garde Manger

The Art and Craft of the Cold Kitchen

The Culinary Institute of America

JOHN WILEY & SONS, INC.
New York • Chichester • Weinheim • Brisbane • Singapore • Toronto

This book is printed on acid-free paper. ♾

Published by John Wiley & Sons, Inc.
Published simultaneously in Canada.

Library of Congress Cataloging-in-Publication Data:

Garde manger: the art and craft of the cold kitchen / by The Culinary Institute of America.
p. cm.
Includes bibliographical references and index.
ISBN 0-471-32367-5 (cloth: alk. paper)
1. Cookery (Cold dishes) 2. Quantity cookery. I. Culinary Institute of America
TX830.G37 1999
641.7'9—dc21 98-29510

Printed in the United States of America.

10 9 8 7 6 5

The Professional Chef's™ Art of Garde Manger by Frederic H. Sonnenschmidt was one of the first books devoted solely to the contemporary practice of the garde manger. It has been the classic reference and teaching tool since it was first published in 1973. In preparing this new volume, The Culinary Institute of America has been the recipient of the author's treasure trove of practical and artistic knowledge that is the defining characteristics of one of this school's most appealing and appreciated chefs. "Fritz," as Chef Sonnenschmidt is known to his colleagues and students, has made an indelible mark as a chef, teacher, and administrator. Whether in the kitchen with a student learning a basic cooking skill, on the phone with an alumni needing guidance, or as a team member, captain, or international judge for The Culinary Olympics, Fritz is the essence of what is best about professional chefs.

• • •

As he is fond of saying, "Maybe in 50 years, we'll all be perfect." Fritz has spent a fruitful lifetime, worth 50 times over that of an ordinary lifetime, sharing both his knowledge and his passion for perfection. With a deep debt of gratitude, we dedicate *Garde Manger: The Art and Craft of the Cold Kitchen* to him.

EDITORIAL

Tim Ryan, *Executive Vice President*

Fred Mayo, *Associate Vice President*

Victor Gielisse, *Dean of Culinary and Baking and Pastry Arts*

Mary Cowell, *Director of the Food and Beverage Institute*

Mary Donovan, *Senior Editor for the Food and Beverage Institute*

Henry Woods, *Project Manager for the Food and Beverage Institute*

Jessica Bard, *Photo Editor for the Food and Beverage Institute*

Jennifer Armentrout, *Editor/Writer for the Food and Beverage Institute*

Terry Finlayson, *Recipe Editor*

PHOTOGRAPHY

Lorna Smith, *Photographer for the Food and Beverage Institute*

Elizabeth Corbett-Johnson, *Studio Manager/Photographer for the Food and Beverage Institute*

CONTRIBUTOR'S LIST—GARDE MANGER

The acts of making a book and of making a sausage have more in common than you might imagine. Both call for the careful assembly of a variety of ingredients, careful attention to proportion, and proper levels of scrutiny, testing, and adjustments to get it right.

Tim Rodgers, Associate Dean for the Meat and Garde Manger Department at the Culinary Institute of America, developed the original "formula." He and his team of instructors dedicated long hours to research the history of garde manger and its many traditions, develop and test recipes, write and review the methods and techniques contained in this book, and prepare the food for the book's inspiring photographs.

Tim Ryan, Executive Vice President, at the helm of the Food and Beverage Institute's editorial council, was a scrupulous critic. He spent hours leaning over a lightbox to be sure that the photographs were just right. He spent even more hours pouring over manuscript, red pen in hand, to ruthlessly exorcise the vague, the insupportable, and the boring from this book. His expertise as a chef and an educator greatly benefited this book.

This book was truly a "team effort." Everyone's enthusiasm for getting it right and keeping the focus on the food was an inspiration.

CONTENT LEADER

Timothy Rodgers

FACULTY TEAM

Chef Mark Ainsworth
Chef Ryan Baxter
Chef Catherine Brandel
Chef Lyde Buchtenkirk-Biscardi
Chef John DeShetler
Chef Eve Felder
Chef Mike Garnero
Chef Jim Heywood
Chef Tom Kief
Chef Pierre Leblanc
Chef Mike Pardus
Chef Henry Rapp
Chef John Reilly
Chef Kathy Shepard
Chef Rudy Smith
Chef Greg Zifchak
Chef Jonathan Zearfoss
Chef Corky Clark
Chef Tom Griffiths

Finally, we wish to especially thank two members of the team particularly—Chef Lyde Buchtenkirk-Biscardi and Chef Jim Heywood—for their insight, authority, and dedication to the craft of today's garde manger.

SUPPORTERS

No matter how many times we go over this list, we will always think of other names to add. To all those who helped in less tangible ways—an encouraging word, a ready hand, a thoughtful answer to a difficult question—we offer our sincere thanks. We especially wish to thank the following for their willingness to provide recipes, information, materials, foods, and the props used in our photographs: The associate deans and professors of The Culinary Institute, especially Chef Bob Briggs, Chef Shirley Cheng, Chef Corky Clark, Chef Markus Färbinger, Steven Kolpan, Chef John Kowalski, Chef Anthony Ligouri, Chef Bill Phillips, Chef Nick Rama, Chef Hans Sebald; members of the storeroom and administrative staffs: Gary Allen, Bettianne Runza and Janet Triolo; and also Brittany Hollow Farms, Arlene Chiaramonte, Chef Mark Erickson, Michael Ginor, Chef Dan Huglier, Chef Melissa Kelly; Erik Mahr, Chris Medley, Chef John Ohare, LeeAnn Rodgers, Jonathan White, and Izzy Yanay; Denise H. McMahon, Krista McKorkle, Lisa Becker, Bill Harris, Mary Ganchoff. Thanks to Villeroy and Boch; and to Apilco/Cuthbertson Imports of Connecticut for the terrines featured on the book's cover.

The Culinary Institute of America staff: (from left to right) Mary Deirdre Donovan, Senior Editor, Jennifer Armentrout, Editor/Writer (seated), Tim Ryan, Executive Vice President, Mary K. Cowell, Director of the Food and Beverage Institute, Lorna Smith, Photographer (seated), Henry Woods, Associate Dean for Faculty Development, Dawn Altomari-Rathjen, Kitchen Manager, Frederic B. Mayo, Associate Vice President and Dean of Liberal and Mangement Studies, Jessica Bard, Photo Editor, Elizabeth Corbett-Johnson, Studio Manager/Photographer.

Chef contributors: (top row from left to right) Eve Felder, Ryan Baxter, William Phillips, Tom Kief, Mark Ainsworth, John Reilly, Hans Sebald, Henry Rapp, Anthony Ligouri, Timothy Rodgers (bottom row from left to right) Nicholas Rama, Rudy Smith, Lyde Buchtenkirch-Biscardi, Jim Heywood, Pierre LeBlanc, Katherine Shepard, Morey Kanner.

Contents

Chapter 5
Cured and Smoked Foods 133

Chapter 6
Sausage 175

Chapter 7
Terrines, Pâtés, Galantines, and Roulades 221

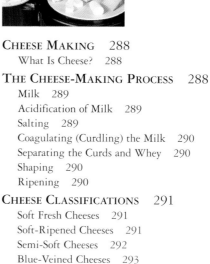

Chapter 8
Cheese 287

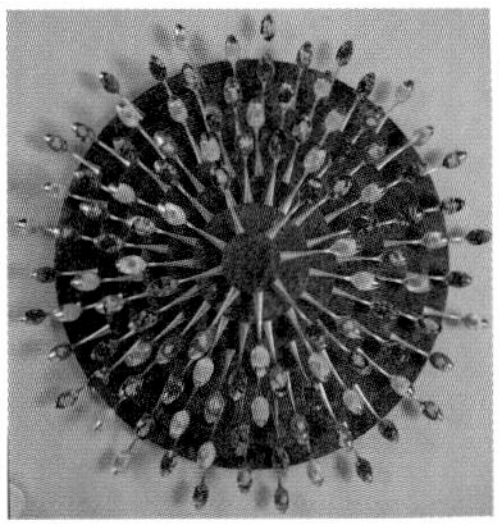

Recipe Contents

Chapter 3
Salads

Chapter 4
Sandwiches

Chapter 5
Cured and Smoked Foods

Chapter 6
Sausage

Chapter 7
Terrines, Pâtés, Galantines, and Roulades

Chapter 8
Cheese

Chapter 9
Hors d'Oeuvre

Chapter 10
Appetizers

Chapter 11
Condiments, Crackers, and Pickles

Preface

In writing *Garde Manger: The Art and Craft of the Cold Kitchen,* we have drawn widely from within the contemporary practice of garde manger, putting those skills and techniques into words, pictures, and recipes and gathering them into a single volume. This book is geared to meet the needs of students and seasoned practitioners alike, giving not only the basics of technique but the sound principles that result in the highest quality foods.

The book begins with a basic overview of the history of the garde manger and the charcutière. The traditional methods for preparing sausages and pâtés as well as modern ways with appetizers and hors d'oeuvre are explored with an eye toward basic methods, safe food handling techniques, and cutting edge approaches to combining flavors, colors, and textures in the foods prepared "on the cold side" of the kitchens in restaurants, hotels, banquet halls, and specialty food producers.

Beginning with cold sauces and soups, both traditional methods and newer adaptations of cold emulsion sauces (vinaigrettes and mayonnaise) are explained and illustrated. The recipes were selected to not only give a practical means of putting those techniques to use, but also to provide recipes for a cross section of cold sauces and soups found on menus worldwide.

Colds sauces and soups are followed by salads. The salad chapter discusses the proper selection of ingredients and their care, as well as some fundamental rules for preparing and presenting salads. Often, the care and handling of salad greens, herbs, and other salad components is the first assignment given to novice kitchen workers, regardless of whether they have their eyes set on the goal of becoming a line cook on the "hot side" or of pursuing a career dedicated to all that the cold side encompasses.

Sandwiches were not always the popular menu item they are today. But an increasing interest in healthful, satisfying, and unusual fare has prompted the garde manger to look beyond deli and diner specialties to embrace a variety of breads, fillings, and garnishes that make sandwich making more intriguing and challenging. Methods and practical advice for preparing sandwiches for an à la carte menu as well as for teas and receptions are provided. Recipes from classics to less widely known sandwiches drawn from the global scene are also included.

Sausages, pâtés, terrines, and cured and smoked foods were once the province of a group known as *charcutières.* The foods produced by the charcutières of days gone by are still familiar to us—from classic Andouilles Sausage and sugar-cured bacon to gravlax and duck confit. These foods are appreciated today for their satisfying flavors and textures. Chefs are finding that a thorough understanding of the hows and whys of curing and preserving meats, fish, and poultry is indispensable in the quest for healthier, lighter, and more contemporary approaches to these truly ancient practices. It is in these foods and their safe, wholesome preparation that the cold kitchen most clearly retains its original intent and purpose.

Cheeses have always had a place in the cold kitchen. Like other cured and preserved foods, cheeses are a time-honored, practical solution to the problem of keeping a constant supply of wholesome, nutritious foods on hand throughout the year. They are also the showcase for the talents and originality of their producers. Local and artisan cheeses are once more in the limelight, and the garde manger is faced with the challenge of learning to select, maintain, and present these complex and fascinating foods to an increasingly sophisticated audience. This chapter reviews the basics of cheese making, defines and describes various cheese "families," and provides guidelines for putting together a cheese selection. In addition, the basics of preparing fresh cheeses as well as some special preparations featuring those cheeses are included.

Hors d'oeuvre and appetizers represent an opportunity for the garde manger to pull together all the various skills and preparations of the entire discipline in a high-impact way. Just as hors d'oeuvre set the tone for a reception or banquet, so can a well-executed appetizer selection on a menu set the tone for the entire dining experience. There are a few classical standards to guide you in preparing and presenting appetizers and hors d'oeuvre. Many of the elements of these composed dishes are typically drawn from the chapters that precede this one. A perfect cold sauce provides the counterpoint to a silken pâté. A flourish of baby greens offers texture and color contrast to a luxurious slice of smoked salmon, and so forth.

Relishes, compotes, pickles, chutneys, mustards, ketchups, and crackers provide the little "something" that takes a presentation from run-of-the-mill to memorable. These finishing touches, offered as condiments and garnishes to bring out all the flavors and textures of a dish, are gathered together in a chapter that explores another time-honored realm of the cold kitchen. The book concludes with a chapter containing a variety of basic preparations, from stocks and aspics to marinades and spice rubs. The glossary provides thumbnail descriptions of a wide range of cooking terms and tools.

As I write this preface, I know that we can't look into a crystal ball to see how and where the instructions, photographs, and recipes will lead you. Perhaps you will choose to use them as a resource and a teaching tool. You may prefer to modify them to your particular needs by adjusting seasonings and garnishes to create signature dishes or scaling recipes up or down to match your production standards. One thing we do see in the future: a continued appreciation on the part of diners and chefs everywhere for the foods that are prepared by today's garde manger.

—Chef Timothy Rodgers

Garde Manger

ONE

The History of the Garde Manger

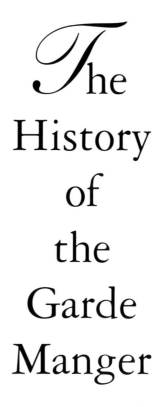

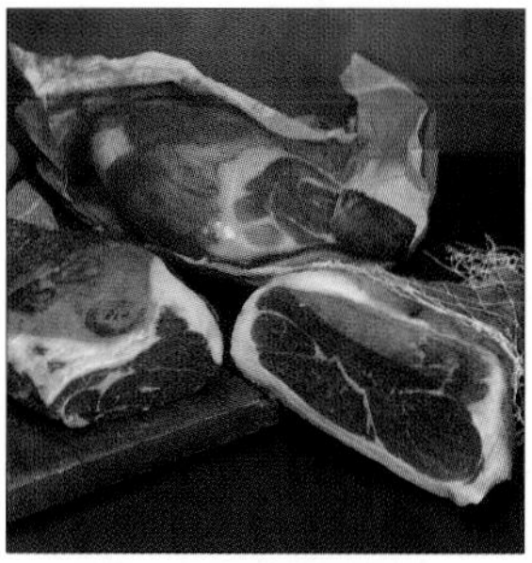

Smoked meats and fish. Sausages, pâtés, and terrines. Cheeses. Salads and salad dressings. Appetizers and hors d'ouevre. Pickles and condiments. These foods are part of the backbone of virtually every cuisine. Long before there was a person or a culinary specialty known as the garde manger, people were curing and preserving meats and fish, pickling vegetables and fruits, and making pungent sauces from vinegars and oils to give savor to their meals.

The term *garde manger* was originally used to identify a storage area. Preserved foods such as hams, sausages, and cheeses were held in this area. Cold foods were prepared and arranged for banquets there as well. Over time, the term has evolved to mean more than just a storage area or larder (see Figure 1-1). It also indicates the station in a professional kitchen responsible for preparing cold foods, the cooks and chefs who prepare these cold foods, as well as an area of specialization in professional culinary arts (see Figure 1-2). Members of today's garde manger share in a long culinary and social tradition, one that stretches back to well before the dawn of recorded history.

The Beginning of Garde Manger

As our ancestors became herdsmen and farmers, they developed the practical skills necessary to ensure a relatively steady food supply. This meant learning not only to domesticate animals and raise crops, but also to preserve those foods. The first preserved fish were most likely produced by accident. Fish were "brined" in sea water and left to dry on the shore, where they either fermented or dried. Meats were hung off the ground and near the fire. This kept them out of the reach of scavenging animals and insects. It also dried and smoked them.

Records of various curing methods have been tracked back as far as 3000 B.C.E., when it is believed the Sumerians salted meats as a way to preserve this valuable but perishable food. Historical evidence shows that the Chinese and the Greeks had been producing and consuming salted fish for many years before passing their knowledge on to the Romans.

In 63 B.C.E., the Greek writer Strabo detailed the importance of fish-salting centers in Spain and the exis-

Figure 1-1 Historical garde manger kitchen. *Source:* Revel, J. *La Sensibiliti Gastronomique.*

tence of salt producers in the Crimea. Salt cod, made in the same basic way as Strabo described, is still an important food in cuisines around the world.

The Gauls, in what became France, were considered successful hog domesticators and became experts at preserving hams and bacon. These products were regularly sent from Gaul to Rome and served at their legendary banquets.

Food preservation skills and the necessary ingredients, including salt, sugar, and spices, were greatly valued. Cities such as modern-day Rome and Salzburg were founded near a ready source of salt. As the Romans extended their empire, they conquered lands rich in a variety of resources, including foodstuffs. They brought with them their own recipes and formulas for a variety of preserved meats, fish, cheeses, wines, and cordials. They learned to appreciate some of the specialities already being produced locally. When the Romans were eventually overthrown, the great houses of the Catholic Church and the nobility kept both their own and their acquired food traditions alive.

The Growth of the Guilds

Into the twelfth century, approximately 80 to 90 percent of the world's population still fell into a category known as "rural peasants." These peasants worked the noble's lands to raise crops and farm animals. One of the most important activities of the year occurred in the fall, when cows, sheep, and other animals were butchered. Meats and other foods were then preserved by a variety of means: pickling, salting, brining, dry curing, drying, and/or smoking. Once the foods had been prepared, they could be held in storage.

The right to collect and keep these foods was a visible symbol of power, wealth, and rank. During the Middle Ages, this privilege belonged to the kings, lords, dukes,

Figure 1-2 Contemporary garde manger kitchen.

and other nobility, as well as to the monasteries and convents of the Catholic Church.

The castles and manor houses of the nobility each had an area devoted to food storage, typically located in an area below ground level to keep the foods cool. *Garde manger* (literally "keeping to eat") was the term used to identify this storage area. It is still used to indicate a larder or pantry—a place for cold food storage. The member of the household staff known as the *officier de bouche,* or steward, was responsible for managing this storeroom, dispensing foods as necessary.

Some of these special items, such as hams or cheeses, became part of the commerce and trade between towns and states. They were included as dowries and tributes, along with livestock, buildings, servants, and jewels, as well as a kind of currency, used to acquire other goods.

Eventually, rules were established governing how merchants prepared and sold these goods and services to prevent monopolies and pricing abuses. The work was divided into groups known as guilds. The guilds developed a training system for their members, taking them from an apprenticeship, to the journeyman stage, and finally, conferring the status of master.

By the end of the sixteenth century, there were approximately two dozen guilds dedicated specifically to food. They fell into two groups—those that provided raw materials and those that provided prepared foods. The guild that prepared and sold cooked items made from the pig was referred to as *charcuterie,* derived from French root words meaning cooked flesh. This guild kept the practical work of preserving meats alive and thriving, making bacons, hams, sausages, and pâtés.

Each individual guild was granted a charter, giving them some specific rights. The more essential the food, the more closely it was regulated. The guild permitted to sell bread, for example, provided one of the most basic of foods—the daily bread of peasants and nobles alike. In some instances, guilds abused their power, and sold adulterated or underweight loaves. When it became a severe enough problem, steps were taken to ensure that certain standards could be enforced. Other guilds faced similar regulation, and over time, the protocols of doing business in the middle ages evolved.

Progress and the lure of additional gain kept enterprising individuals pushing at limits imposed by the guild standards. Numerous strategies were taken to get around restrictions imposed on any given guild, and the charcutières were no exception. One of their tactics led to the development of terrines: charcutières were not permitted to sell foods baked in pastries. Making and selling forcemeat loaves baked in pastry, *pâté en croûte,* would not have been allowed, according to a strict reading of the charcutière's charter. Rather than stop making pâté en croûte, the charcutières baked the forcemeat in an earthenware mold instead of pastry—and so *pâtés en terrine* were created.

The more lucrative a guild's activities, the more likely it was that another guild might try to capture a piece of the action. Each guild tried to protect its individual rights. Several cases were brought before judges to determine if one guild's activities had crossed the line into the work of another's. One such case had a great and lasting effect on the business of preparing and serving food to paying customers.

Restaurants and the Role of the Garde Manger

There were no restaurants as we know them today until well into the 18th century. Inns and taverns (also operated within a guild) offered accommodations and drink to travelers, and at some establishments, a hot meal was also offered. The food was usually prepared by a separate guild and brought to the inn for sale to the travelers. Serving meals was not the primary business of inns. Guests had little, if any, choice about what, if anything, they were served.

In 1765, however, Monsieur Boulanger, a tavern keeper, hung out a sign offering a hot dish, known as a *restorante* (restorative) of sheep's trotters in a white sauce that had been prepared on the premises. There was a case brought against Boulanger by a guild that believed he had infringed on their exclusive rights to prepare and sell hot foods.

The judge in the case ruled that Boulanger had not broken any law by selling his *restorante.* This little tavern and its dish of sheep's trotters had opened a new type of business venture. From these beginnings, our modern-day restaurants have evolved. As restaurants and hotel dining rooms became more wide-spread, the opportunities for cooks grew, bit by bit.

When the French Revolution began in 1789, the upheavals in noble households were enormous. Noblemen left France to escape the guillotine, leaving their household staffs to look out for themselves. The garde manger, or steward, as well as chefs and cooks, were household employees, and as such did not have a formal guild of their own. These workers found their way into restaurants in increasing numbers throughout Europe and the British Isles.

When the guild system was officially abolished in 1791, some members of the charcutière's guild also found new occupations on restaurant and hotel kitchen staffs. Others continued to operate their businesses as before. The work of the charcutière and the garde manger has always been closely linked, since they are both founded on cold preserved foods. When the term garde manger is used today, it is often understood to include the work of the charcutière as well.

At first there was no widely recognized structure for kitchen workers. There were no established duties or areas of specialization. It took several years before a serious attempt was made to organize the kitchen workers. Eventually, the brigade system, recorded by Auguste Escoffier, detailed a logical chain of command that brought order to the unruly working arrangements of his day. We still use the brigade system, and refer to the various "stations" in the kitchen with the names assigned by Escoffier: saucier, rôtisseur, pâtissier, and garde manger.

The garde manger, recast in a restaurant setting, has retained its traditions of preparing a variety of preserved and cold foods. It has also expanded its scope to include appetizers, hors d'oeuvre, salads, sandwiches, and the accompanying cold sauces and condiments. Garde manger is involved in both à la carte service and banquets, as well as playing an important role in receptions and buffets.

Today's Garde Manger

The techniques required to prepare pâtés, terrines, sausages, and fresh cheeses are the particular domain of the garde manger. However, becoming a skilled garde manger also means learning a broad base of culinary skills, those directly related to handling basic cold food preparations, as well as those required to prepare hot foods: roasting, poaching, simmering, and sautéing meats, fish, poultry, vegetables, grains, and legumes.

It is precisely because the skills and responsibilities are so broad that many of today's most highly regarded chefs got their start in the garde manger as an apprentice or commis. In addition, recent years have seen a rebirth of the more traditional practices of charcuterie and cheese making, as purveyors with retail shops and wholesale businesses. Handcrafted foods such as country-style hams, sausages, pâtés, and fresh and aged cheeses are increasingly available to both the restaurant chef and the home cook.

The opportunities and challenges of the area of cooking known today as garde manger are fascinating. It is in this specialty that artistic sensibilities can find their outlet. The quality of the food is still the most important key to success. The visual appeal of the food is a close second. Presenting foods to look their best is a skill that you can spend a lifetime perfecting. Today's taste is for foods that look fresh and unfussy. The garde manger is like an artist, and the colors on his or her palate are the colors, textures, shapes, and height of the foods themselves.

Whether garde manger is your "entrée" into the culinary field, your lifelong passion, or a new challenge in your professional growth, the chapters that follow offer a wide-angle view of the foods that are prepared by today's garde manger.

TWO

Cold Sauces and Cold Soups

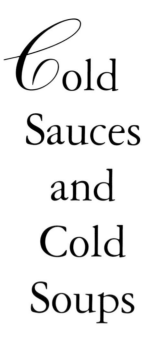

Sauces and soups are among the first true tests of a chef's skill. For the garde manger, the ability to produce perfectly balanced vinaigrettes, subtly flavored and creamy mayonnaise sauces, and cold soups of all varieties is a skill that should be constantly honed throughout a career.

Aïoli (above), page 29 and Chilled Tomato Saffron Soup with Shellfish (left), page 57.

Cold Sauces

The successful pairing of a sauce with any food demonstrates an understanding of the food and an ability to judge and evaluate a dish's flavors, textures, and colors. Evaluating why some combinations work well while others are less successful offers valuable lessons in composing a dish. What does the sauce bring to the dish? How does it function in the total composition? How does it taste? Sauces are not just an afterthought. They add flavor, color, texture, sheen, and moisture to a dish. In the cold kitchen, the chef's sauce repertoire includes:

- Cold emulsion sauces: vinaigrettes and mayonnaise
- Dairy-based sauces
- Salsas
- Coulis and purées
- Coating sauces
- Miscellaneous cold sauces such as Cumberland, horseradish, and mignonette

Cold Emulsion Sauces

Vinaigrettes and mayonnaise are made by combining two ingredients that would not otherwise blend into a homogeneous mixture. In order to understand how these sauces are prepared, we will first discuss what an emulsion is and how it is formed.

An emulsion consists of two phases, the dispersed phase and the continuous phase (see Figure 2-1). When making a vinaigrette, for example, the dispersed phase is the oil, meaning that the oil has been handled in such a way that it was broken up into very small droplets. Each oil droplet is suspended throughout the continuous phase, in this case, the vinegar.

Temporary emulsions, such as vinaigrettes, form quickly and require only the mechanical action of whipping, shaking, or stirring (see Figure 2-2). To make an emulsion stable enough to keep the oil in suspension, additional ingredients known as "emulsifiers" are necessary. The emulsifiers used to make cold sauces include egg yolks, mustard, and glace de viande. Starches such as those in garlic or modified starches such as cornstarch or arrowroot are also used. These emulsifiers are able to attract and hold both the oil and liquid (see Figure 2-3).

Stable emulsions, such as mayonnaise, are made by very carefully controlling the rate at which the oil is added to

Figure 2-1 Phases of an emulsion.

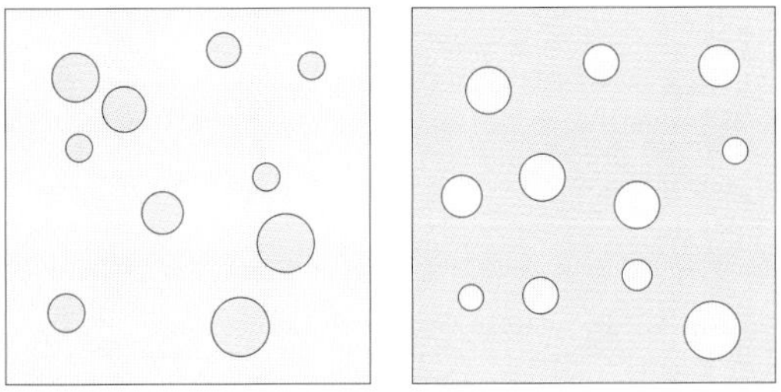

An oil-water emulsion *(left)* consists of oil in water. A water-in-oil emulsion *(right)* consists of water droplets in oil.

Figure 2-2 Temporary emulsions.

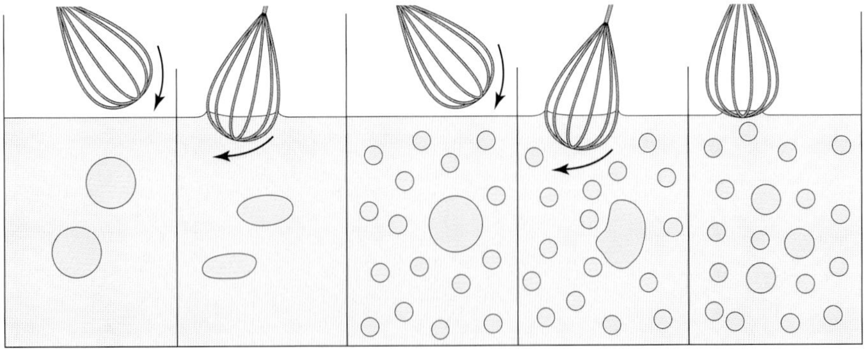

The droplet mill. When oil droplets are sparse *(left)*, they easily evade the whisk and are hard to divide. When after much work they are smaller and more numerous *(right)*, the droplets themselves become obstacles to new drops of oil, and help break them up.

Figure 2-3 Emulsifiers are able to attract and hold.

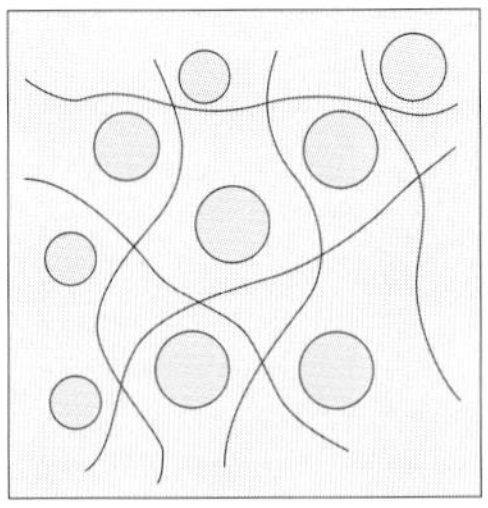

Long molecules like starch and proteins stabilize emulsions by getting in between droplets and interfering with coalescence.

the egg yolks. Egg yolks provide both the liquid that holds the oil droplets in suspension and a special emulsifier, known as lecithin. The oil is added very gradually at first so that the droplets can be made extremely fine. The more oil that is added to the yolks, the thicker the sauce will become. If the oil is added too rapidly, the emulsion cannot start to form properly. And if the emulsion becomes too thick early in the mixing process, the full amount of oil cannot be added, unless the sauce is thinned with a little water or an acid, such as vinegar or lemon juice.

Vinaigrettes

Vinaigrettes are closely associated with green salads, but they are used in other applications: as a marinade for grilled or broiled foods; to dress salads made from pastas, grains, vegetables, and beans; as a dip; as a sauce served with hot or cold entrées and appetizers; or brushed on some sandwiches.

It is interesting to note that while oil is the largest component by volume and weight of a vinaigrette, the sauce is most often named for the acid—red wine vinaigrette, balsamic vinaigrette, lemon vinaigrette, and tomato vinaigrette. (Blood orange juice is being used to prepare the vinaigrette shown in Figure 2-4.) The flavor of the acid dominates that of the oil. When an oil has a distinctive enough flavor, however, the vinaigrette may be called by the oil's name.

Oils for Vinaigrettes

A wide variety of oils are available to today's garde manger (see Figure 2-5). To make the most of this ingredient, select an oil with an eye to both its flavor and its cost. Oils used in salad dressings can be subtle or intensely flavored. They may serve simply to carry the other flavors in the vinaigrette, or they may have readily identifiable flavors of their own.

Fine-quality oils are often labeled "cold pressed" or "organic." These terms do not indicate any particular flavor in the oil. They are meant to define how the oil was extracted or the growing conditions of the base item: olives, nuts, seeds, corn, soybean, and so forth. Cold pressed refers to an extraction method that does not require heat or solvents. The oil is expressed by crushing, grinding, or pressing grains, seeds, nuts, or olives using traditional millstones or stainless-steel grindstones.

Olive oils may be further designated as extra-virgin, virgin, or pure. Extra-virgin oils are those made from the first pressing (either a mechanical press or a centifrugal extractor) of the best-quality olives. Once the oil has been

Figure 2-4 Adding oil to a Blood Orange Vinaigrette (page 23).

Figure 2-5 A selection of oils (from left to right): corn, sesame, extra virgin olive, white truffle, peanut, sweet almond, walnut.

filtered to remove any large particles, it is assessed on the basis of its flavor, color, aroma, and acidity. Free acids in an extra-virgin oil should total less than one percent. Extra-virgin oils are not refined, which means that each olive oil has a unique character. One producer's extra-virgin olive oil may be a crystal clear, deep green liquid with a pronounced flavor. Another's may be golden, slightly cloudy, with a milder flavor. Virgin olive oil, which may also be labeled as pure or ordinary, has a slightly higher level of acid, up to two percent.

Olive oil that does not have the attributes to merit the extra-virgin or virgin classification is refined, using heat or chemicals, to remove its color, flavor, and aroma, as well as any rancid or oxidized elements. This refined oil may be blended with virgin olive oil to give some color and aroma, and to replace the vitamin E that is lost during refining.

Vinegars for Vinaigrettes

A wide range of vinegar choices is also available. Made from wines, fruit juices, malted barley, and similarly acidic liquids (see Figure 2-6), vinegars each have a different level of tartness or acidity.

Good-quality vinegars are available for reasonable prices. Special vinegars, those made by the Orleans or batteria process, are more expensive. (A diagram of the batteria process is shown in Figure 2-7.) These vinegars are carefully aged in a series of wooden barrels made of different woods. Authentic balsamic vinegar can cost hundreds of dollars for a few ounces. These vinegars are savored on their own, and should not be used in a sauce where their special characteristics would be lost.

Making a Basic Vinaigrette

The challenge of making a good vinaigrette lies in achieving what chefs refer to as "balance," a point at which the acidity of the vinegar or juice is tempered but not dominated by the richness of the oil.

Many chefs know the standard vinaigrette ratio of three parts oil to one part acid. This works well as a starting point, but it is important to taste and evaluate the vinaigrette whenever a change is made in the type of oil, acid, or specific flavoring ingredients. Some vinaigrettes may require two parts oil to one part acid, when the oil is so strongly flavored that is could overpower the vinegar (walnut oil and red wine vinegar, for instance). Some vinaigrette formulas may call for either a quantity of water to

Figure 2-6 A selection of vinegars (from left to right): white wine, red wine, aged balsamic, rice, champagne, sherry, apple cider, verjus, malt.

Figure 2-7 Batteria vinegar production.

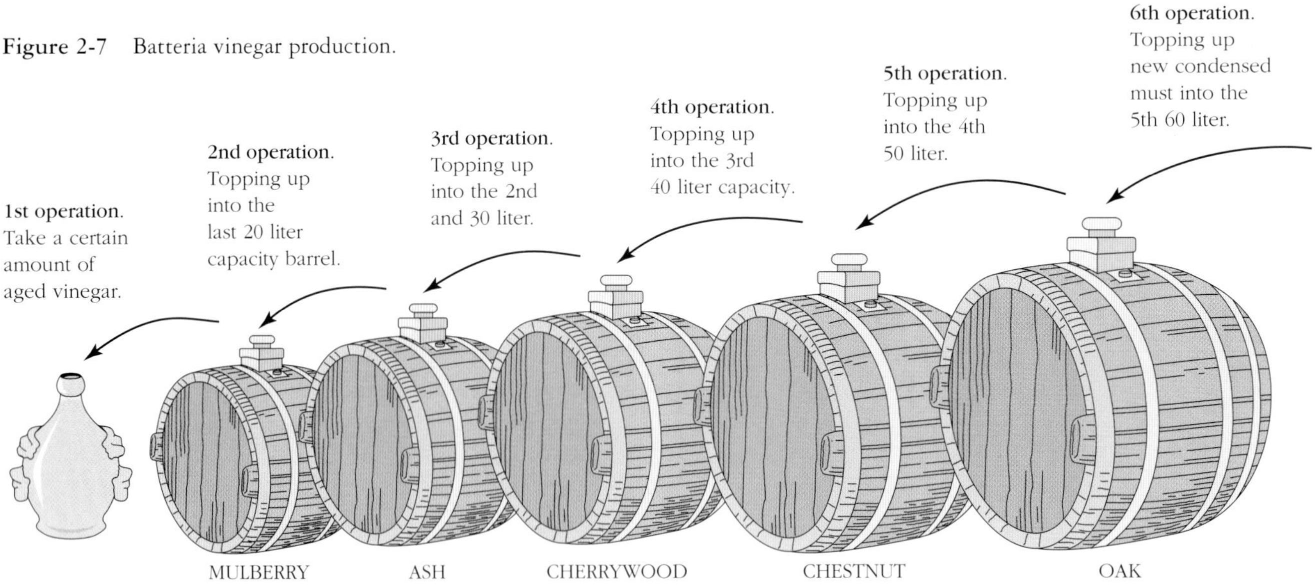
1st operation.
Take a certain amount of aged vinegar.
2nd operation.
Topping up into the last 20 liter capacity barrel.
3rd operation.
Topping up into the 2nd and 30 liter.
4th operation.
Topping up into the 3rd 40 liter capacity.
5th operation.
Topping up into the 4th 50 liter.
6th operation.
Topping up new condensed must into the 5th 60 liter.
MULBERRY
ASH
CHERRYWOOD
CHESTNUT
OAK

dilute very acidic vinegars, or a bit of sugar to soften the acidity, instead of calling for additional oil.

A basic vinaigrette is a temporary emulsion, made by blending the measured ingredients until they form a homogenous sauce (see Figure 2-8a and b). The sauce remains an emulsion for a only a short time, quickly separating back into oil and vinegar. To keep the sauce well balanced each time it is used, stir or whisk the vinaigrette each time it is served.

Figure 2-8 Balsamic Vinaigrette (page 22).

a. Adding balsamic vinegar to the seasonings.

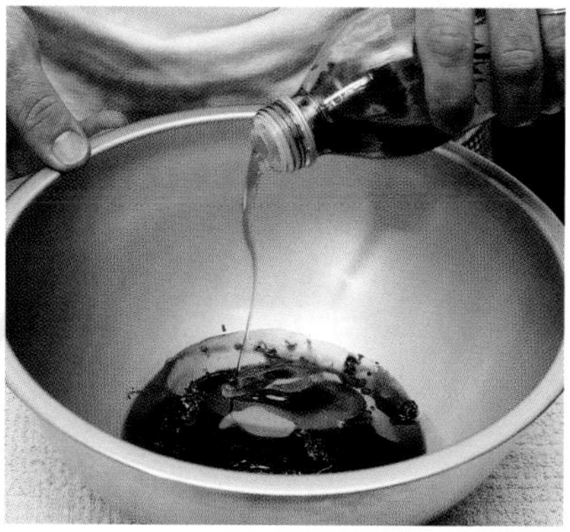

b. Adding the oil to the vinegar and herbs.

The best way to check for flavor and balance in a vinaigrette is to dip a piece of lettuce into it, shake off the excess, and then evaluate the taste of the sauce on the lettuce.

Making an Emulsified Vinaigrette

The ratio for an emulsified vinaigrette is the same as for a basic vinaigrette. To make these sauces, egg yolks, mustard, garlic, fruit or vegetable purées, or glace de viande are included in the formula, both to add flavor and to help stabilize the sauce.

1. *Combine the vinegar and all of the seasoning ingredients.*

   Add the salt, pepper, herbs, mustard, or other ingredients to the vinegar (see Figure 2-9a and b) to be sure that they are evenly dispersed throughout the sauce.

   Note: Fresh herbs give vinaigrettes a wonderful flavor and color. However, if they are added too far in advance, the vinegar can start to discolor their fresh green color and start to break down their lively flavors. When preparing a large batch of vinaigrette intended to last through several service periods, it may be preferable to add the fresh herbs to the sauce just before service begins.

2. *Add the oil gradually.*

   Slowly pour or ladle a few droplets of oil at a time into the bowl, whisking constantly. Once the emulsion has started to form, the oil may be added in a fine stream while whisking the sauce (see Figure 2-9c).

   Another way to create a stable vinaigrette is to use a blender, immersion blender, standing mixer with a whip, or food processor. Vinaigrettes made this way can hold their emulsion longer than those that are simply whipped together.

Figure 2-9 Emulsified Vinaigrette.

a. Making emulsified vinaigrette with mustard.

b. Adding the vinegar to the mustard.

c. Slowly whisking in the oil to create the emulsion.

3. *Add any garnish and check the seasonings at this point.*

Fresh or dried fruits and vegetables, crumbled cheese, or other garnishes can be added, if desired. Review the previous page for information about how to check the seasoning and serve this sauce.

Reduced-Fat Vinaigrettes

The total amount of oil in a vinaigrette can be greatly reduced by replacing up to two-thirds of the oil normally used with a lightly thickened stock or juice. Add enough diluted arrowroot or other modified starch to simmering stock or juice so that it will mimic the consistency of a salad oil once cooled.

Purées of fruits and vegetables can also be used in place of part of a vinaigrette's oil. Naturally thick purées such as tomato or red pepper purées may not need to be thickened further. Tomato Vinaigrette (page 27) is one such vinaigrette.

Store reduced-fat vinaigrettes as you would basic or emulsified vinaigrettes and follow the appropriate steps for recombining and adjusting seasoning before service.

Mayonnaise

Mayonnaise and dressings made with mayonnaise as a base can be used to dress salads, as a dip or spread, and to produce a coating sauce, such as Mayonnaise Collée (page 415). This sauce is made by combining egg yolks with oil so that a stable emulsion forms. Unlike vinaigrettes, this cold sauce should not break as it sits. Mayonnaise is a sauce that requires skill and finesse to prepare correctly. It also requires careful handling to avoid contamination.

1. *Select and prepare the ingredients for the mayonnaise.*

Classic recipes for mayonnaise-style dressing call for six to eight ounces of oil to each egg yolk. To avoid any possible food-borne illness (such as salmonella), professional chefs should use pasteurized egg yolks.

Since mayonnaise is often intended as a base sauce that can be used for a variety of purposes, it is usually best to choose an oil that does not have a pronounced flavor of its own. There are exceptions to this general rule. For example, a mayonnaise made with extra-virgin olive oil or a nut oil would be appropriate to serve as a dip with a platter of grilled vegetables or crudité.

Various acids may be used to prepare a mayonnaise, including lemon juice, wine, or cider vinegars. The acid is used both to give the sauce flavor, and along with water, to adjust its consistency.

2. *Blend the yolks with a bit of water.*

Whisk the yolks and water together to loosen the eggs and get them ready to absorb the oil (see Figure 2-10a). You may also wish to include lemon juice or vinegar and mustard at this point, if your formula calls for those ingredients.

3. *Add the oil a little at a time, whisking in the oil completely.*

It is important to proceed cautiously when the oil is first being added. The oil must be whipped into the egg yolks so that it is broken up into very fine droplets. This stage is where the emulsion first starts to form. If the oil is added too quickly, the droplets will be too large to blend into the yolks, and the sauce will appear broken. Adding the oil slowly allows eggs

Figure 2-10 Basic Mayonnaise (page 28).

a. Whisk the yolk mixture together to loosen the eggs.

b. Oil is being added to the yolk mixture.

c. The proper consistency for mayonnaise.

to absorb the oil properly, and the sauce will start to thicken. Once about one-fourth to one-third of the oil has been properly blended into the egg mixture, you may start to increase the amount you add (see Figure 2-10b).

When preparing a mayonnaise in a mixer, add the oil in a thin stream as the machine runs. It is still true that the oil should be added more slowly at the beginning than at the end.

4. *Adjust the thickness and flavor of the sauce by adding a bit more acid or water as you incorporate the oil.*

Additional lemon juice, vinegar, or a little water is added once the eggs have absorbed enough of the oil to become very thick. If this step is neglected, the sauce will become too thick to absorb any more oil.

Continue adding oil until the amount specified in the recipe has been added. A finished mayonnaise should be thick enough to hold soft peaks (see Figure 2-10c). However, depending upon your intended use, you may wish to thin the sauce with additional water to make it more pourable.

5. *Add any additional flavoring or garnish ingredients at the point indicated in the recipe.*

Aïoli (page 29), a garlic-flavored mayonnaise, calls for a good quantity of garlic to be included from the earliest stages of mixing. Other ingredients, such as vegetable purées or pastes, fresh herbs, chopped pickles, and so forth may be blended into the sauce once the oil is fully incorporated. Figure 2-11 shows two mayonnaise variations: Green Mayonnaise (Sauce Vert) (page 28) and Rémoulade Sauce (page 28).

When Mayonnaise Breaks

Mayonnaise and similarly prepared dressings may break for a number of reasons:

- The oil was added too rapidly for the egg yolk to absorb it.
- The sauce was allowed to become too thick.
- The sauce became either too cold or too warm as it was being prepared.

A broken mayonnaise can be corrected as follows (see Figure 2-12):

Figure 2-11 Mayonnaise-based sauces include Sauce Vert and Rémoulade Sauce (page 28).

Figure 2-12 Recombining the sauce to "fix" a broken emulsion.

1. Beat a pasteurized egg yolk until foamy.
2. Gradually incorporate the broken mayonnaise, whisking constantly.
3. The mayonnaise should recombine into a homogenous sauce.

Storing Mayonnaise

Mayonnaise should be kept refrigerated at all times once it is prepared. Transfer it to a storage container, cover it carefully, and label it with a date. Before using mayonnaise that has been stored, stir it gently and check the seasoning carefully. If the sauce needs to be thinned, add a bit of water.

Dairy-Based Sauces

Dairy-based sauces are used as salad dressings or dips. They are made from soft cheeses such as fraîche, quark, mascarpone, and cream cheese; cultured milks such as sour cream, crème fraîche, or buttermilk; cream; or low- or reduced-fat versions of ricotta, sour cream, or cottage cheese. (See Figure 2-13 for the *mise en place* of Ranch-style dressing made with buttermilk.) These dressings are generally white or ivory, so they can take on the color of purées or coulis of herbs, fruits, or vegetables.

Some typical additions to dairy-based dressings include cheeses (especially blue cheese, parmesan, or feta), fresh lemon, black pepper, and minced or puréed herbs. Diced, minced, or grated vegetables, pickles, capers, or olives add texture as well as flavor.

Creamy sauces can be prepared in a range of textures, from a relatively stiff sauce to serve as a dip or spread, to a pourable sauce that easily dresses a green salad. For a very light, almost mousselike texture, whipped cream can be folded into the sauce at the last moment.

Figure 2-13 Ranch Dressing (Reduced-Fat) (page 33).

Salsas

Salsas are typically made from uncooked fruits or vegetables. They often include an acid, such as citrus juice, vinegar, or wine, to add a sharp flavor. Spices, chilies, and herbs are sometimes added to these sauces to give them a potent flavor and a higher-than-average level of "heat."

Sauces made from vegetables and fruits have become increasingly popular. Both fresh (or raw) and cooked versions of salsas, chutneys, relishes, and compotes are found in cuisines from Mexico to India. While there will always be distinctions made by aficionados about when the term *salsa* is correctly used—versus *chutney, relish,* or even *compote*—in practical terms, the differences between them have more to do with their country or cuisine of origin than a difference in preparation method. (The recipes for a variety of chutneys, relishes, and compotes can be found in Chapter 11.)

Coulis and Purées

The classical definition of a coulis, written by Escoffier in *Le Guide Culinaire*, states that a coulis is the "well reduced, highly concentrated essential flavours of a food, in either purée or liquid form."

In the modern cold kitchen, coulis are made by puréeing raw or cooked fruits or vegetables to a saucelike consistency. The term *purée* may frequently be used interchangeably with *coulis.* The texture of these sauces can range from very light and smooth to coarse. They may be served "as is," or they may be adjusted by adding stocks, wines, infusions, oils, or cream.

Coulis or purées may begin to weep a clear liquid as they sit. To prevent this, bring the sauce to a simmer and add a small amount of diluted arrowroot or cornstarch. This is a helpful practice whenever advance plating is required, as might be the case for a banquet or reception.

Coating Sauces: Chaud-Froid and Aspic Gelée

Although these sauces are not as popular as they once were, they still have several applications for the garde manger. They can be used to coat canapés and other hors d'oeuvres, to prepare platters for display and service, and to coat various timbales and other appetizers.

Chaud-froids are made by adding gelatin to a warm sauce, such as demiglace, béchamel, or velouté. Clear coating sauces, known as aspic gelée or simply aspics, are made by clarifying stocks, juices, or essences and adding enough gelatin to achieve the desired strength. Techniques for working with gelatin are illustrated below.

Working with Gelatin

In order to achieve the correct results when preparing aspic or any other item including gelatin, you must be able to handle gelatin properly and incorporate it correctly. Ratios for producing aspic gelée in a variety of strengths can be found in Table 2-1 (page 18).

1. *Weigh the gelatin carefully.*

   Granulated or powdered gelatin, gelatin sheets, or instant gelatin can be used interchangeably (see Figure 2-14a).

2. *Add the gelatin to a cool liquid.*

   Rain the gelatin powder evenly over a cool liquid (see Figure 2-14b). If the liquid is warm or hot, the gelatin cannot soften properly. Scattering the gelatin over the liquid's surface prevents the gelatin from forming clumps.

3. *Bloom the gelatin.*

   As the gelatin absorbs the liquid, each granule becomes enlarged; this is known as blooming (see Figure 2-14c).

4. *Melt the gelatin enough to dissolve the granules.*

   Bloomed gelatin (or gelatin solution) can be dissolved in one of two ways: add it directly to a warm liquid (at about 100 to 110°F), or warm the mixture over a hot water bath (see Figure 2-14d). As the softened gelatin warms, the mixture will clear and become liquid enough to pour easily. Combine the gelatin thoroughly with the base liquid to be sure that it gels evenly.

   Note: In some kitchens, chefs prefer to have some of this bloomed softened gelatin on hand at all times, and refer to it as a *gelatin solution.* This mixture can be held for several weeks, and used as required to prepare aspics or other jellied sauces or soups.

5. *Test the gelatin strength.*

   To test the strength of both aspics and reduced stocks, chill a plate in the freezer. Ladle a small amount of the aspic or reduced stock on the plate, and chill under refrigeration until it gels. Adjust the strength by rewarming the aspic and then adding more gelatin or more base liquid as necessary.

Figure 2-14 Working with gelatin.

a. Weigh unflavored gelatin powder.

b. Rain gelatin evenly over the liquid.

c. Gelatin has fully bloomed.

d. Melt the gelatin over hot water.

Table 2-1 Ratios for Aspic Gelée

Ratio per gallon	Ratio per pint	Gel Strength	Possible Uses
2 oz	1/4 oz	Delicate gel	When slicing is not required. Individual portion of meat, vegetable, or fish bound by gelatin. Jellied consommés.
4 oz	1/2 oz	Coating gel	Edible chaud-froid. Coating individual items.
6-8 oz	1 oz	Sliceable gel	When product is to be sliced. Filling pâté en croûte, head cheese.
10-12 oz	1 1/4-1 1/2 oz	Firm gel	Coating platters with underlayment for food show or competition.
16 oz	2 oz	Mousse strength	When product must retain shape after unmolding. Production of a mousse.

The term *chaud–froid* means "hot and cold," a name that reflects the way in which the sauce is prepared for use. It is warmed over a hot water bath to the point at which it flows easily. Next, it is cooled over an ice water bath (see Figure 2-15) to the point at which the gelatin has thickened and the sauce starts to cling to the sides of the bowl. Chaud-froid is being used to prepare a platter in Figure 2-16. In Figure 2-17, port wine aspic gelée is being applied to an appetizer plate. It can also be used to coat individual slices of pâté en croûte (see Figure 2-18).

A quickly prepared substitute for chaud-froid, known as a mayonnaise collée, is made by thickening mayonnaise and/or sour cream with an appropriate amount of gelatin to produce a coating consistency.

Figure 2-15 Tempering the gelatin over an ice water bath.

Figure 2-16 Chaud-froid.

a. Pouring the liquid chaud-froid onto a polished silver serving platter.

b. Carefully laying down pluches of dill as decoration.

c. Sealing the chaud-froid with a layer of heavy-strength gelatin.

Figure 2-17 Port wine gelée.

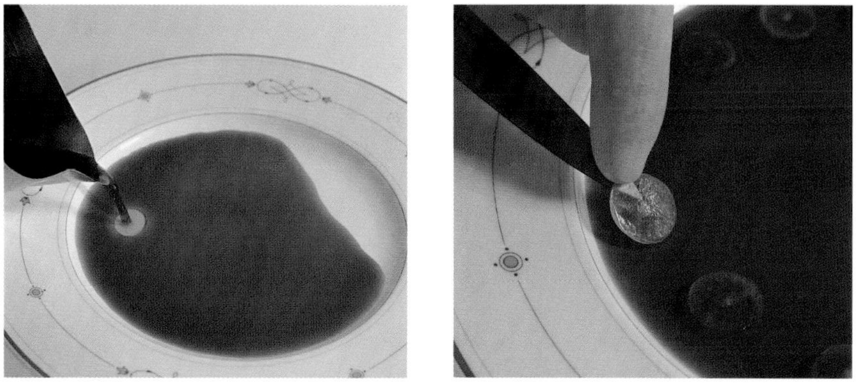

a. Pouring port-flavored aspic onto an appetizer plate.

b. Placing a grape slice onto the aspic before it congeals.

Figure 2-18 Aspic gelée coating slices of pâté en croûte.

Miscellaneous Sauces

In addition to the sauces discussed above, the garde manger may be called on to prepare some special sauces that do not necessarily fit into a single category. Cocktail, Cumberland, Oxford, mint, and horseradish sauces are among the basic repertoire of the cold kitchen. Dipping sauces, such as those served with satays and tempura, are also considered cold sauces. Consult specific recipes for information about preparing and serving these sauces. (Figure 2-19 shows chilled shrimp being served with cocktail sauce; recipe on page 37.)

Figure 2-19 Cocktail sauce may be served with chilled shrimp as an appetizer.

Cold Soups

Soups prepared by the garde manger are served chilled. They are found as first course offerings, as appetizer courses, or as desserts. They may be presented in a variety of ways—in chilled stemware, traditional soup plates or cups, or in tiny tasting portions served at stand-up receptions. Cold soups refresh the palate, regardless of what point in the meal they are served. They can be rich and suave, as in the case of cream based soups, or bold and robust. Whenever you intend to serve any food chilled, be sure to taste it carefully at the correct service temperature. Remember to allow soups sufficient time to develop their flavor; some soups are at their best and ready to serve as soon as they are prepared. Other soups will develop a more complex and satisfying flavor if they are allowed to mellow (under refrigeration) for several hours or overnight.

Cold soups may be prepared in one of three ways, depending on their type. Vegetable or fruit soups are made by puréeing or chopping fruits and vegetables finely enough to form a souplike consistency; cream soups are made from a thickened base such as a velouté, béchamel, or a potato purée; and clear soups are made by clarifying and fortifying a rich broth and, if desired, thickening the base with a little gelatin.

Vegetable and Fruit Soups

Cold vegetable and fruit soups are popular hot-weather offerings around the world. Many cuisines have special cold soups that feature a seasonal food—cherries, melons, tomatoes, peppers, and cucumbers. You will find an interesting range of soups in the following pages, as well as some unique garnishing and presentation ideas.

Cream-Style Soups

Cold cream soups should have the same velvety smooth texture as any hot cream soup. Taste and evaluate the flavor carefully, and give equal attention to the texture and consistency. Cold soups may thicken as they cool, so be certain that you have adjusted the consistency to make a soup that is creamy but not stiff. Good cold soups should not leave your mouth feeling coated with fat, so keep the amount of cream in good proportion to the other ingredients.

Vegetable or fruit soups range in texture from the appealingly coarse texture of a gazpacho to the velvety smoothness of a chilled melon soup. A broth or juice is often added to the fruits or vegetables to loosen the purée enough to create a good soup consistency. Other ingredients, such as cream, milk, buttermilk, garnish items, or granités, may also be added to the soup for additional interest.

Vichyssoise is a classic example of a cream-style soup. It is made by preparing a purée of potato and leek. Other cold soups are made by preparing a cream-style or velouté soup. They are typically finished by adding chilled cream, yogurt, or crème fraîche. The cold pea soup on page 54 is a good example.

Clear Cold Soups

Clear soups must have a deep and satisfying flavor in order to be successful. The body of the soup can be adjusted by adding gelatin, if you prefer to serve them as jellied soups. To review the information about working with gelatin, read page 17 earlier in this chapter. Not all clear soups are jellied, however, and some of the recipes included here are based on a delicious broth, garnished or left plain according to your intended presentation.

Clear cold soups require a rich, full-bodied, clarified broth or juice. Infusions, essences, or well-strained purées are often used to create the special character of the soup. Traditional clear cold soups such as jellied consommés are made by adding enough bloomed and dissolved gelatin to the soup to make it gel. Jellied clear soups should barely hold their shape, and should melt in the mouth instantly.

Basic Red Wine Vinaigrette

Yield: 1 quart

1 cup	red wine vinegar
2 tsp	mustard (*optional*)
2 each	shallots, minced
3 cups	mild olive oil or canola oil
2 tsp	sugar (*optional*)
2 tsp	salt
1/2 tsp	ground black pepper
3 tbsp	minced herbs, such as chives, parsley, tarragon, etc. (*optional*)

1. Combine the vinegar, mustard, and shallots.
2. Whisk in the oil gradually.
3. Adjust seasoning with sugar, salt, and pepper. Add the fresh herbs if desired.

Balsamic Vinaigrette

Yield: 1 quart

1/2 cup	red wine vinegar
1/2 cup	balsamic vinegar
2 tsp	mustard (*optional*)
3 cups	mild olive oil or canola oil
2 tsp	salt
1/2 tsp	ground black pepper
3 tbsp	minced herbs, such as chives, parsley, tarragon, etc. (*optional*)

1. Combine the vinegars and mustard.
2. Whisk in the oil gradually.
3. Adjust seasoning with salt and pepper. Add the fresh herbs if desired.

Tangerine-Pineapple Vinaigrette

Yield: 1 quart

$1\frac{1}{4}$ cups	tangerine juice
$\frac{2}{3}$ cup	pineapple juice
2 tbsp	lemon juice
2 tsp	balsamic vinegar
2 tsp	prepared Creole mustard
1 tsp	puréed roasted garlic
$1\frac{1}{4}$ cups	vegetable oil
$\frac{2}{3}$ cup	olive oil
2 tsp	salt
$\frac{1}{2}$ tsp	ground black pepper

1. Combine the juices, vinegar, mustard, and garlic.
2. Whisk in the oils gradually.
3. Adjust seasoning with salt and pepper.

Orange (or Blood Orange) Vinaigrette Substitute 2 cups orange (or blood orange) juice for the tangerine and pineapple juice. Reduce lemon juice to 1 tablespoon.
Lemon Vinaigrette Substitute $1\frac{1}{2}$ cups lemon juice and $\frac{1}{2}$ cup water for the tangerine and pineapple juice. Eliminate the garlic and mustard.

Vinaigrette Gourmande

Yield: 1 quart

4 oz/fl	sherry vinegar
3 oz/fl	lemon juice
2 tsp	salt
$\frac{1}{2}$ tsp	ground black pepper
2 cups	olive oil
$1\frac{1}{4}$ cups	vegetable oil
1 oz/wt	Fines Herbes (page 408)

1. Combine vinegar and lemon juice with salt and pepper.
2. Whisk in the oils gradually.
3. Add the herbs; adjust seasoning with salt and pepper.

Walnut and Red Wine Vinaigrette Substitute walnut oil for the vegetable oil and red wine vinegar for the sherry vinegar. Substitute parsley and chives for chervil and tarragon.

Truffle Vinaigrette

Yield: 1 quart

When fresh truffles are available, you can offer this dressing on Spring Herb Salad (page 72) topped with shaved truffles, prepared at table side.

1 1/2 cups	red wine vinegar
1/2 cup	balsamic vinegar
1/4 cup	water
2 tsp	Dijon mustard
2 each	shallots, minced
1 3/4 cups	mild olive oil
3 tbsp	truffle oil
2 tsp	sugar
2 tsp	salt
1/2 tsp	ground black pepper
1 each	black or white truffle, chopped (*optional*)

1. Mix together vinegars, water, mustard, and shallots.
2. Whisk in the oils gradually.
3. Adjust seasoning with salt, sugar, and pepper. Add the truffles just before serving if desired.

Apple Cider Vinaigrette

Yield: 1 quart

Use hard cider to replace the apple cider for a deeper, more complex flavor in the finished dressing.

2 cups	apple cider
3/4 cup	cider vinegar
1 each	Granny Smith apple, brunoise
3 cups	vegetable oil
2 tbsp	chopped tarragon leaves
2 tsp	salt
1/4 tsp	ground white pepper
1/2 tsp	sugar, as needed

1. Reduce the cider to 6 fluid ounces. Combine the cider reduction, the vinegar, and the brunoise apple.
2. Whisk in the oil gradually.
3. Add the tarragon and adjust seasoning with salt, sugar, and pepper.

Chef's Notes: Six ounces of apple juice concentrate may be substituted for the apple cider when it is not available. This dressing can be puréed in a blender for a smooth, creamier vinaigrette.

Curry Vinaigrette

Yield: 1 quart

3/4 cup	cider vinegar
1/2 cup	orange juice
1 each	lemon, juiced
3 tbsp	honey
2 tbsp	minced ginger
2 tbsp	minced lemongrass
2 1/4 cups	Curry-Infused Olive Oil (page 398)
2 tsp	salt
2 tsp	coarse ground black pepper

1. Combine the vinegar, orange and lemon juices, honey, ginger, and lemongrass.
2. Whisk in the curry oil gradually.
3. Adjust seasoning with salt and pepper.

Chipotle-Sherry Vinaigrette

Yield: 1 quart

7 oz/fl	sherry vinegar
2 tbsp	lime juice
4 each	chipotles in adobos, minced
2 each	shallots, minced
2 each	garlic cloves, minced
3 cups	extra-virgin olive oil
1/2 cup	chopped Fines Herbes (page 408)
1 1/2 tbsp	real maple syrup
1 tsp	salt
1/2 tsp	coarse ground black pepper

1. Combine the vinegar, lime juice, chipotles, shallots, and garlic.
2. Whisk in the oil gradually.
3. Add the fines herbes just before service, and adjust seasoning with maple syrup, salt, and pepper.

Roasted Shallot Vinaigrette

Yield: 1 quart

20 each	shallots, peeled
2 1/2 cups	extra-virgin olive oil
1 cup	sherry vinegar
1/4 cup	honey
2 tsp	chopped rosemary
2 tsp	chopped thyme
2 tsp	salt
1 tsp	cracked black pepper

1. Rub the shallots with a little oil and roast in a low oven (300°F) until very tender, well browned, and sweet-smelling. When cool enough to handle, cut into quarters.
2. Combine the shallots with the vinegar.
3. Whisk in the remaining oil gradually.
4. Add the herbs and adjust seasoning with honey, salt, and pepper.

Mustard-Walnut Vinaigrette

Yield: 1 quart

1 cup	champagne vinegar
1/4 cup	spicy brown mustard
1 tbsp	sugar
4 each	shallots, minced
2 1/2 cups	mild olive oil
1/2 cup	walnut oil
1/4 cup	chopped dill
1/4 cup	chopped flat-leaf parsley leaves
2 tbsp	minced chives
To taste	salt
To taste	coarse ground black pepper

1. Combine the vinegar, mustard, sugar, and shallots.
2. Whisk in the oils gradually.
3. Add the herbs and adjust seasoning with salt and pepper.

Hazelnut-Oregano Vinaigrette Substitute hazelnut oil for the walnut oil. Replace the dill and parsley with 1/2 cup chopped fresh oregano. Eliminate the chives if desired.

Tomato Vinaigrette

Yield: 1 quart

This nontraditional juice-based vinaigrette may be served with vegetable terrines or the Poached Salmon and Lemon Terrine on page 264.

1 lb	ripe tomatoes, seeded
2 tbsp	minced shallots
4 oz/fl	red wine vinegar
1 oz/wt	pasteurized egg yolks
8 oz/fl	mild olive oil
2 oz/fl	lemon juice
2 oz/fl	lime juice
2 tbsp	chopped basil
1 tbsp	chopped tarragon leaves
2 tsp	salt
1 tsp	ground white pepper

1. Purée the tomatoes, shallots, vinegar, and egg yolks in a blender or food processor. Add the olive oil slowly with the blender running to form a thick sauce.
2. Add the lemon and lime juices and seasonings, adjusting as desired.

Beet Vinaigrette

Yield: 1 quart

2 lb	beets
12 oz/fl	cider vinegar
6 oz/fl	extra-virgin olive oil
1 cup	chopped dill
2 tsp	salt
1 tsp	ground black pepper

1. Simmer the beets in acidulated water until tender. When the beets are cool enough to handle, peel and chop.
2. Place the beets and vinegar in a blender and purée until smooth. Whisk in the oil and season with the dill, salt, and pepper.

Chef's Notes: For a more intense color and flavor, use a juicer to juice the raw beets. Combine the juice and vinegar, whisk in the oil, and season with dill, salt, and pepper.

• • •

Acidulated water is made by combining 1 gallon of water with 2 tablespoons lemon juice or vinegar.

Basic Mayonnaise

Yield: 1 gallon

Sometimes referred to as the "mother sauce of the cold kitchen," mayonnaise can be seasoned to fit many needs. Variations can be made by adding purées of herbs, peppers, or tomatoes. Saffron can be infused in some of the oil to lend brilliant color; diced or chopped pickles, capers, or olives may also be added for additional flavor and texture.

12 oz/wt	pasteurized egg yolks
4 oz/wt	white vinegar
4 oz/wt	water
3 tbsp	dry mustard
3 qt	vegetable oil
3 tbsp	kosher salt
2 tsp	ground white pepper, or to taste
4 oz/wt	lemon juice, or to taste

1. Whisk the yolks, vinegar, water, and mustard until slightly foamy.
2. Add the oil gradually in a thin stream, whipping constantly, until all the oil is incorporated and the mayonnaise is thick.
3. Adjust seasoning with salt, pepper, and lemon juice.
4. Refrigerate the mayonnaise immediately. Use as desired.

Green Mayonnaise (Sauce Vert) Finely chop 4 ounces of cooked spinach. Squeeze it in a cheesecloth to extract the juice. Add the juice to the mayonnaise. Add additional chopped herbs to taste, such as parsley, basil, chives, and dill.

Rémoulade Sauce

Yield: 1 quart

3 cups	Basic Mayonnaise, recipe above
2 oz/wt	capers, drained, rinsed, and chopped
2 oz/wt	cornichons, chopped
3 tbsp	chives, chopped
3 tbsp	chervil, chopped
3 tbsp	tarragon leaves, chopped
1 tbsp	Dijon mustard
1 tsp	anchovy paste
To taste	salt
To taste	Worcestershire sauce
2 to 3 dashes	Tabasco sauce

1. Combine all ingredients thoroughly.
2. Hold the sauce under refrigeration.

Aïoli (Garlic Mayonnaise)

Yield: 1 quart

6 oz/fl	pasteurized egg yolks
1 tbsp	garlic paste
3 cups	vegetable oil
1 cup	extra-virgin olive oil
1/2 tbsp	red wine vinegar
2 tsp	lemon juice

1. Prepare as for Basic Mayonnaise (page 28), adding the garlic to the egg yolk mixture.

2. Hold the sauce under refrigeration.

Rouille Reduce 6 ounces of Red Pepper Coulis (page 43) to about 4 ounces. Add crushed cayenne pepper to taste. This sauce should have noticeable heat.

Saffron Aïoli Infuse 1/2 teaspoon of lightly crushed saffron threads in 2 tablespoons boiling water. Add this infusion to eggs along with the garlic paste.

Russian Dressing

Yield: 1 quart

In spite of its name, this dressing is all American. It is believed that its name was inspired by its resemblance to dressings first seen in Russia. By adding sweet pickles or pickle relish and hard cooked egg, Thousand Island dressing is made.

$2\frac{1}{2}$ cups	Basic Mayonnaise (page 28)
7 oz/fl	prepared chili sauce
2 oz/wt	prepared horseradish
1 tbsp	Worcestershire sauce
2 tsp	salt
1 tsp	ground black pepper

1. Combine all ingredients thoroughly.
2. Hold the sauce under refrigeration.

Thousand Island Dressing Add 1/2 cup pickle relish and 1/4 cup chopped hard-cooked egg to Russian Dressing.

Green Goddess Dressing

Yield: 1 quart

3 cups	Basic Mayonnaise (page 28)
1/4 cup	tarragon vinegar
1/2 cup	chopped flat-leaf parsley leaves
1/2 cup	chopped chives
3 tbsp	chopped tarragon leaves
2 tsp	kosher salt
1 tsp	anchovy fillets, made into a paste (1 to 2 fillets)
1 tsp	coarse cracked black pepper

1. Combine all ingredients thoroughly. This dressing may be puréed in a food processor if desired.
2. Hold the sauce under refrigeration.

Chef's Notes: If tarragon vinegar is unavailable, substitute white wine vinegar and add 2 tablespoons additional chopped fresh tarragon.

Creole Honey-Mustard Sauce

Yield: 1 quart

3 tbsp	minced shallots
3 tbsp	crushed green peppercorns (brine-packed)
1 tbsp	vegetable oil
3/4 cup	dry white wine
1 tbsp	coarse cracked black pepper
2 oz/fl	Dijon mustard
3/4 cup	Creole mustard
1 cup	Basic Mayonnaise (page 28)
1 cup	sour cream
2 tbsp	honey
To taste	kosher salt

1. Sweat the shallots and peppercorns in oil; do not brown.
2. Add the white wine and reduce until the wine has almost completely evaporated. Cool.
3. Add the remaining ingredients; mix well and check seasoning.
4. Hold the sauce under refrigeration.

Creamy Black Pepper Dressing

Yield: 1 quart

2 oz/fl	lemon juice
3 oz/wt	pasteurized egg yolks
2 tbsp	Dijon mustard
12 oz/fl	olive oil
12 oz/fl	vegetable oil
2 1/2 oz/wt	grated Parmesan cheese
1 tbsp	anchovy paste (3 to 4 fillets)
2 tsp	minced garlic
1 tbsp	salt
1 tbsp	coarse-ground black pepper

1. Whisk together the lemon juice, eggs, and mustard.
2. Add the oils gradually, whisking constantly.
3. Add remaining ingredients and mix well.
4. Hold the sauce under refrigeration.

Roquefort Dressing

Yield: 1 quart

This dressing can be made with other blue-veined cheeses such as Maytag, Danish Blue, or Gorgonzola.

6 oz/wt	crumbled Roquefort cheese
2 cups	Mayonnaise (page 28)
4 oz/fl	sour cream
6 oz/fl	buttermilk
1 tbsp	lemon juice
2 tsp	kosher salt
1 tsp	ground black pepper
1 tbsp	chopped flat-leaf parsley
2 tsp	Worcestershire sauce

1. Mix Roquefort, mayonnaise, sour cream, and buttermilk well, adjust seasoning with lemon juice, Worcestershire sauce, salt, pepper, and parsley. To thin, add more buttermilk.
2. Hold the sauce under refrigeration.

Chef's Notes: For a thicker sauce to use as a dip, add half of the cheese and purée the dressing until smooth. Fold in remaining crumbled cheese.

Maytag Blue Cheese Dressing (Reduced-Fat)

Yield: 1 quart

The Maytag Company of Iowa has been producing world class blue cheese since World War II. This reduced-fat dressing is based on a purée of ricotta cheese and buttermilk flavored with a moderate amount of this fully flavored blue cheese.

6 oz/fl	Maytag blue cheese
12 oz/wt	part-skim ricotta cheese
12 oz/fl	buttermilk
2 oz/fl	cider vinegar
1/2 oz/fl	Worcestershire sauce
1/2 tsp	roasted garlic (page 424)
2 tsp	kosher salt
2 tbsp	chopped chives
1 1/2 tsp	cracked black pepper

1. Combine all ingredients except chives and pepper and purée in food processor until smooth. Stir in chives and pepper.
2. Hold the sauce under refrigeration.

Ranch Dressing (Reduced-Fat)

Yield: 1 quart

12 oz/wt	part-skim ricotta cheese
8 oz/wt	nonfat yogurt
12 oz/fl	buttermilk
1 oz/fl	lemon juice
1 oz/fl	red wine vinegar
1 tsp	minced garlic
2 tbsp	minced shallots
1 tbsp	Dijon mustard
1/2 tsp	celery seed
3 tsp	kosher salt
1 tsp	ground black pepper
2 tbsp	Worcestershire sauce
2 tsp	chopped flat-leaf parsley leaves
1 tsp	chopped chives

1. Combine all ingredients except herbs and purée in food processor until smooth. Mix in the herbs and adjust seasoning.
2. Hold the sauce under refrigeration.

Salsa Fresca

Yield: 1 quart

$2^1/_2$ cups	seeded and diced tomatoes
$^1/_2$ cup	minced onion (1 each)
$^1/_2$ cup	diced green pepper (1 each)
2 each	garlic cloves, minced
$^1/_2$ cup	chopped cilantro
1 tsp	chopped oregano
2 each	limes, juice only
1 each	jalapeño
2 tbsp	olive oil
$^1/_4$ tsp	ground white pepper
2 tsp	salt

1. Combine all ingredients and adjust seasoning.

2. Hold the sauce under refrigeration.

Salsa Verde

Yield: 1 quart

2 each	shallots, finely diced
4 tbsp	red wine vinegar
To taste	salt
4 each	salt-packed anchovy fillets
2 cups	chopped flat-leaf parsley
1/2 cup	chopped chives
1/4 cup	chopped chervil
4 tbsp	chopped thyme
2 tbsp	chopped capers
1 tbsp	finely chopped lemon zest
1 cup	pure olive oil
1/4 cup	extra-virgin olive oil

1. Cover the shallots with the vinegar in a small bowl and season with salt. Let them macerate for about 20 minutes.
2. Rinse the anchovies well and remove their fins and back bones. Chop fine.
3. Combine the chopped herbs, capers, lemon zest, anchovies, and olive oils to make a saucy consistency. Add the shallots and vinegar. Adjust seasoning.
4. Transfer to a clean storage container. Hold the sauce under refrigeration.

Mango-Lime Salsa

Yield: 1 quart

1 lb	small-dice mango
3 oz/wt	small-dice red onion
2 tsp	minced jalapeños (or to taste)
2 oz/fl	lime juice
2 oz/fl	extra-virgin olive oil
3 tbsp	chopped basil
2 tsp	finely chopped lime zest
To taste	salt
To taste	pepper

1. Combine all ingredients.
2. Allow to sit one hour before service. Adjust seasonings.

Papaya and Black Bean Salsa

Yield: 1 quart

1 cup	cooked black beans
1 each	small dice ripe papaya
1 cup	small dice red pepper (2 each)
1/2 cup	small dice red onion (1 each)
2 each	minced jalapeños
1/4 cup	chopped cilantro
2 tsp	dried Mexican oregano
2 tbsp	minced fresh ginger
2 oz/wt	olive oil
2 each	limes, juice only
1 tsp	ground black pepper
2 tsp	kosher salt

1. Combine all ingredients and adjust seasoning.
2. Hold the sauce under refrigeration.

Cocktail Sauce

Yield: 1 quart

1 1/2 cups	prepared chili sauce
1 3/4 cups	prepared ketchup
1 each	lemon, juice only
2 tbsp	sugar
2 tsp	Tabasco sauce
2 tsp	Worcestershire sauce
1/4 cup	prepared horseradish

1. Combine all ingredients thoroughly.
2. Use the sauce immediately, or hold it under refrigeration. After storage, stir the sauce and adjust seasoning if necessary before serving.

Cumberland Sauce

Yield: 1 quart

2 each	oranges
2 each	lemons
2 1/2 tbsp	minced shallots
2 1/2 cups	currant jelly
1 tbsp	dry mustard
1 1/2 cups	ruby port wine
1 tsp	salt
Small pinch	cayenne pepper
Small pinch	ground ginger

1. Remove the zest from the oranges and lemons and cut into julienne. Juice the oranges and lemons.
2. Blanch the shallots and zest in boiling water; allow the water to return to a boil and strain immediately.
3. Combine all ingredients. Simmer for 5 to 10 minutes until syrupy.
4. Hold the sauce under refrigeration.

Asian-Style Dipping Sauce

Yield: 1 quart

2 cups	soy sauce
1 cup	white vinegar
1 cup	water
4 each	garlic cloves, minced
4 each	scallions, minced
2 tbsp	minced ginger
2 tsp	dry mustard
1 tsp	hot bean paste
1/4 cup	honey

1. Combine all ingredients thoroughly.
2. Use the dressing immediately, or hold it under refrigeration. After storage, stir the dressing and adjust seasoning if necessary before serving.

Orange-Jalapeño Sauce

Yield: 1 quart

2 1/2 cups	orange marmalade
1 cup	ruby port wine
1/2 cup	lemon juice
2 each	jalapeños, minced
2 tbsp	chili powder
2 tbsp	minced shallots
2 tsp	soy sauce
1 tsp	ground cumin
2 each	garlic cloves, minced

1. Simmer all ingredients for 10 to 15 minutes.
2. Cool to room temperature.
3. Use the sauce immediately, or hold it under refrigeration.

Yogurt-Cucumber Sauce

Yield: 1 quart

1 quart	plain yogurt, drained (see Chef's Notes)
6 each	cucumbers, peeled, seeded, and diced
1 tbsp	minced garlic
1 1/2 tbsp	ground cumin
1 tsp	ground turmeric
2 tsp	salt
1/4 tsp	ground white pepper

1. Combine the yogurt and cucumbers.
2. Add the garlic, cumin, turmeric, salt, and pepper to taste.
3. Serve the sauce chunky, or purée until smooth.

Chef's Notes: To drain yogurt, place it in a cheesecloth-lined colander. Set the colander in a bowl and drain at least 8 hours under refrigeration.

Roasted Eggplant Dip with Mint (Baba Gannouj)

Yield: 1 quart

4 lb	eggplants, cut in half (2 each)
To taste	salt
To taste	ground black pepper
2 oz/fl	olive oil
3 each	shallots, minced
3 oz/fl	lemon juice (about 2 each)
4 oz/wt	tahini paste
1 bunch	chopped flat-leaf parsley, leaves only (1/2 cup)
1/4 cup	chopped mint
2 each	garlic cloves, minced
To taste	Harissa Sauce (page 380)

1. Season the eggplant with salt and pepper and lightly coat the cut faces with olive oil. Roast cut side down on a sheet pan in a preheated 375°F oven until soft, about 30 to 40 minutes. Cool to room temperature; scoop out flesh and discard seeds.
2. While the eggplant is roasting, macerate the shallots in the lemon juice with 1/4 teaspoon of salt.
3. Combine the roasted eggplant with the olive oil, macerated shallots, tahini, and parsley.
4. Season with mint, garlic, salt, pepper, and Harissa Sauce. Chop the dip rough by hand or purée smooth.

Guacamole

Yield: 1 quart

The original Aztec name for the avocado, primary ingredient in guacamole, was ahuacatl.

10 each	avocados, halved, pitted, and peeled
2 each	limes, juice only
1 cup	diced tomato *(optional)*
1 each	jalapeño *(optional)*, seeded and minced
1 bunch	green onions, sliced
4 tbsp	chopped cilantro
1 tsp	Tabasco sauce
To taste	salt
To taste	ground black pepper

1. Push avocados through a medium-coarse screen as shown.
2. Combine all ingredients thoroughly. Taste for seasoning and adjust with lime juice and spices.
3. Hold the guacamole under refrigeration in a tightly covered storage container. It is best to make guacamole the same day it is to be served.

Hummus

Yield: 1 quart

1 1/2 lb	cooked chick-peas, drained
4 oz/wt	tahini (sesame paste)
1 1/2 oz/fl	lemon juice, or to taste
1/4 cup	extra-virgin olive oil
4 each	garlic cloves, minced
1 tbsp	salt
To taste	ground black pepper

1. Combine all ingredients. Purée in food processor (in batches if necessary), adding water to thin if needed. Adjust seasoning with lemon juice and garlic.

Chef's Notes: Hummus can be passed through a drum sieve for a very smooth texture.

Tapenade

Yield: 1 quart

12 oz/wt	Niçoise olives, pitted
8 oz/wt	black olives, pitted
8 oz/wt	salt-packed anchovy fillets, rinsed and dried
6 oz/wt	capers, rinsed
4 oz/wt	minced garlic
As needed	lemon juice
To taste	ground pepper
As needed	extra-virgin olive oil
As needed	chopped herbs, such as oregano or basil

1. In food processor, combine all ingredients except herbs, incorporating lemon juice and oil slowly. Blend until chunky and easily spread. Do not over mix; there should be texture, and identifiable bits of olive.

2. Adjust seasoning and finish with herbs.

Muhammara

Yield: 1 quart

This spicy-hot sauce made with peppers, walnuts, and pomegranate molasses, originated in Aleppo in Syria. Pomegranate molasses is produced by cooking ripe pomegranates and sugar to a thick, jamlike consistency. Muhammara is best when made 4 or 5 days in advance and held chilled to allow the flavor to fully develop.

1 1/2 lb	red peppers
1/2 cup	coarse-ground walnuts
3 tbsp	fresh white bread crumbs
1 each	lemon, juiced, to taste
4 tsp	pomegranate molasses
1/4 tsp	prepared red chili paste
To taste	salt
1 tbsp	olive oil
1/4 tsp	ground cumin

1. Roast the peppers, then peel, seed, and set aside to drain in a colander.
2. Process the walnuts and bread crumbs until finely ground. Add the peppers, lemon juice, and pomegranate molasses; purée until smooth and creamy. Add the chili paste and salt to taste. Chill at least overnight before serving.
3. When ready to serve, decorate with a drizzle of olive oil and a light dusting of cumin.

Hazelnut Romesco Sauce

Yield: 1 quart

This is a rich and flavorful sauce for use with a variety of foods, including fish, lamb chops, and such vegetables as beets, potatoes, asparagus, green beans, grilled baby leeks, and green onions.

4 each	dry anchos
4 each	Marinated Roasted Peppers (page 77)
1 1/4 cups	olive oil
6 each	garlic cloves, minced
1/4 cup	red wine vinegar
3 tbsp	Spanish paprika
1/2 tsp	cayenne pepper
1/4 cup	tomato paste
1 lb	ground hazelnuts
To taste	salt

1. Put the ancho chilies in a small saucepan and cover with water. Bring to a boil, then turn off the heat and let steep for 20 minutes.
2. Add Marinated Roasted Peppers and chilies to the olive oil, garlic, vinegar, paprika, cayenne, tomato paste, hazelnuts, and purée to a smooth consistency. Allow to rest overnight to develop full flavor. Adjust seasoning with salt before serving.

Chef's Notes: Hazelnut Romesco Sauce should be made the day before needed.

Red Pepper Coulis

Yield: 1 quart

4 to 4 1/2 lb	red peppers, diced (about 10 each)
1/2 cup	olive oil
2 oz/wt	minced shallots
12 oz/fl	dry white wine
12 oz/fl	Chicken Stock (page 410)
To taste	salt

1. Sauté the peppers and shallots in the olive oil until they are tender.
2. Deglaze with white wine.
3. Add the stock and reduce to approximately half the original volume.
4. Purée until smooth. Season with salt.

Roasted Red Pepper Coulis Roast, peel, and seed the peppers before preparing the coulis.

Apricot-Ancho Barbecue Sauce

Yield: 1 quart

6 oz/wt	bacon, diced
6 oz/wt	onion, diced
1 each	garlic clove, minced
1/4 lb	dried apricots
3/4 cup	ketchup
1/4 cup	malt vinegar
1/4 cup	orange juice
6 oz/wt	dark brown sugar
2 each	anchos, diced
1 tsp	paprika
1 tsp	dry mustard
1 tsp	Tabasco sauce
1 tsp	cayenne pepper

1. Sauté the bacon until almost crisp. Add the onions and sauté until browned. Add the garlic and sauté another minute.
2. Add remaining ingredients. Simmer until the apricots are soft. Purée in a blender; reheat and season as needed with salt and pepper.
3. Sauce can be used cold or warm and can be stored, covered, up to one week.

Chaud-Froid Sauce

Yield: 1 quart

2 cups	Ordinary Velouté (page 413)
12 oz/fl	Aspic Gelée, warmed to 110°F (page 45)
4 oz/fl	heavy cream
2 tsp	kosher salt
1/4 tsp	ground white pepper

1. Bring the velouté to a simmer and combine with aspic.
2. Add the cream and seasonings. Strain into a bowl set over an ice bath.
3. Cool to coating consistency and use as required.

Aspic Gelée

Yield: 1 gallon

The classic method for preparing an aspic gelée calls for a very strong and extremely gelatinous stock to be made by adding veal shank and calves' feet to a standard stock as it simmers. Today we use powdered gelatin or gelatin sheets, which act in the same way as the high percentage of cartilage in the shank and feet.

	Clarification
1 lb	Mirepoix (page 404)
3 lb	ground beef
10 each	egg whites, beaten
12 oz/wt	tomato concassé
1 gallon	stock (see Chef's Notes)
1 each	Standard Sachet d'Epices (page 405)
1 tsp	kosher salt
To taste	ground white pepper
As needed	gelatin powder (see Table 2-1, page 18)

1. Mix the ingredients for the clarification and blend with the stock. Mix well.
2. Bring the mixture to a slow simmer, stirring frequently until raft forms.
3. Add the sachet d'épices and simmer for 45 minutes, or until the appropriate flavor and clarity are achieved. Baste raft occasionally.
4. Strain the consommé; adjust the seasoning with salt and pepper to taste.
5. Soften the gelatin in cold water, then melt over simmering water. Add to the cooled clarified stock. Refrigerate until needed. Warm as necessary for use.

Chef's Notes: Choose an appropriate stock, depending upon the intended use. For example, if the aspic is to be used to coat a seafood item, prepare a lobster stock and use ground fish for the clarification.

Port Wine Gelée Replace half of the stock with ruby port wine.

Gaspacho Andalusia

Yield: 1 gallon; 20 portions (6 fluid ounces each)

"Of soup and love, the first is best."—Spanish proverb

1 1/2 lb	tomatoes, cored, diced
1 1/4 lb	cucumbers, peeled, diced
10 oz/wt	green peppers, seeded, diced
10 oz/wt	red peppers, seeded, diced
1 lb	onions, sliced
20 oz/wt	diced crustless white bread
24 oz/fl	tomato juice
1/4 cup	tomato purée
4 each	garlic cloves, mashed
1/2 tsp	minced jalapeño
2 1/2 oz/wt	olive oil
3 oz/fl	white wine vinegar
2 tsp	salt
1 tsp	ground black pepper
4 oz/wt	Garlic-Flavored Croutons, about 1/4 cups (page 428)

1. Reserve about 2 tablespoons each of the tomatoes, cucumbers, peppers, and onions for garnish.
2. Soak the bread cubes in the tomato juice.
3. Purée the soaked bread with the diced vegetables, tomato purée, garlic, and jalapeño.
4. Season with salt and pepper; chill.
5. Serve with garnish of diced vegetables and croutons on the side.

Gaspacho Southwest Style

Yield: 1 gallon; 20 portions (6 fluid ounces each)

1 lb	Vidalia onions, sliced thick, grilled
1 lb	green peppers, grilled, peeled, and seeded
1 lb	red peppers, grilled, peeled, and seeded
1 each	jalapeño, grilled, peeled, and seeded
1 lb	eggplant, peeled, sliced, and grilled
3 lb	tomatoes, halved and grilled
1 lb	tomatillos, peeled, halved, and grilled
1 lb	seedless cucumber, peeled
1 head	roasted garlic, flesh only (page 424)
2 tsp	chopped marjoram
6 tbsp	chopped cilantro
4 oz/fl	lime juice
12 oz/wt	olive oil
8 oz/fl	red wine vinegar
1 qt	tomato juice
2 tbsp	salt
2 tsp	Tabasco sauce

1. Put the grilled vegetables, cucumber, garlic, and herbs through the fine plate of a grinder.

2. Whisk together remaining ingredients and add to ground vegetables to taste.

3. Stir well, and keep chilled. Adjust seasoning before serving if necessary.

Presentation Ideas: Garnish with julienned corn or flour tortillas that have been baked or fried, and dusted with chili powder or ground toasted cumin seeds.

Cantaloupe Melon Soup with Lime Granité

Yield: 1 gallon; 20 portions (6 fluid ounces each)

3 lb	diced cantaloupe melon
4 each	oranges, juiced
3 each	lemons, juiced
$1\frac{1}{2}$ qt	sparkling water
2 tbsp	grated orange zest
2 tbsp	grated lemon zest
$1\frac{1}{4}$ oz/wt	cornstarch
5 oz/wt	sugar, as needed
	Garnish
12 oz/wt	small melon balls
1 qt	Lime Granité (recipe follows)

1. Purée melon and orange juice in blender and reserve under refrigeration.
2. Bring lemon juice, water, and zests to a boil. Thicken with cornstarch and chill.
3. Add melon purée and adjust seasoning with sugar to taste.
4. Add melon garnish to soup, and serve with approximately $1\frac{1}{2}$ ounces of lime granité.

Lime Granité

Yield: 1 quart

1 qt	water
2 cups	sugar
4 each	limes, zest only, minced fine
4 oz/fl	lime juice

1. Combine all ingredients in a shallow pan. Freeze mixture for 3 hours until firm, stirring every 25 minutes.

Chilled Cucumber Soup with Dill, Leeks, and Shrimp

Yield: 1 gallon; 20 portions (6 fluid ounces each)

1 1/4 lb	shrimp (26/30 count)
1/2 gallon	Shellfish Stock (page 411)
	Soup Base
1 lb	diced yellow onion
1 lb	diced celery
2 oz/wt	butter
6 lb	cucumbers, peeled, seeded, and diced
1 oz/wt	arrowroot
3 cups	sour cream
8 oz/fl	heavy cream
1 bunch	dill, chopped
1 1/2 tbsp	salt
1 tsp	ground white pepper
To taste	Tabasco sauce
3 each	lemons, juiced, to taste
	Garnish
2 each	cucumbers, peeled, seeded, and cut into fine dice
1/4 lb	leeks, julienned and fried until crisp
1/4 bunch	dill sprigs

1. Poach the shrimp in the stock and cut in half lengthwise and reserve for garnish. Reserve the stock.
2. Sauté the onions and celery in the butter until translucent.
3. Add the cucumbers and reserved stock and simmer 30 minutes.
4. Purée in a blender and strain through a sieve. Thicken with arrowroot. Bring back to a boil. Remove and cool to 40°F.
5. To finish the soup, blend 2 cups of the soup base with the sour cream, heavy cream, and dill.
6. Add this to the remaining soup base. Adjust seasoning with salt, pepper, Tabasco, and lemon juice.
7. Garnish individual portions of the soup with fine-diced cucumber, shrimp, fried leeks, and a sprig of dill.

Cold Roasted Tomato and Basil Soup

Yield: 1 gallon; 20 portions (6 fluid ounces each)

4 oz/wt	minced garlic
1 oz/fl	olive oil
1 lb	celery, chopped
$1\frac{1}{2}$ lb	onions, chopped
$1\frac{1}{2}$ cups	leeks, white part only, chopped
3 lb	Roasted Plum Tomatoes (page 425)
2 qt	Vegetable Stock (page 411) *or* Tomato Water (see step 1, page 57)
$\frac{1}{4}$ lb	basil
2 each	bay leaf
1 tsp	salt
$\frac{1}{4}$ tsp	ground black pepper
	Garnish
2 pt	yellow tomatoes, diced
1 oz/wt	basil chiffonade

1. Sauté garlic lightly in oil.
2. Add celery, onions, and leeks, and continue to sauté.
3. Add tomatoes, broth, basil, and bay leaf. Simmer 40 minutes or until vegetables are tender.
4. Remove the bay leaf and purée the soup in a blender; season with salt and pepper.
5. Chill soup.
6. Adjust seasoning before service if necessary. Garnish with yellow tomatoes and basil.

Cold Carrot Bisque

Yield: 1 gallon; 20 portions (6 fluid ounces each)

This brilliantly colored bisque calls for carrot juice. You can purchase carrot juice, or make your own using a juice extractor. There should be a strong fresh carrot flavor, enhanced but not overpowered by the orange juice.

1 oz/wt	minced shallots
2 each	garlic cloves, minced
3/4 oz/wt	minced ginger, or to taste
1/4 lb	minced onion
3 tbsp	butter
3 1/2 lb	carrots, sliced thinly
2 1/2 qt	Vegetable Stock (page 411)
2 oz/wt	white wine
1/2 tsp	ground cardamom
1 qt	orange juice
7 oz/wt	yogurt
2 cups	carrot juice
1 1/2 tbsp	salt

1. Sauté shallots, garlic, ginger, and onion in butter.
2. Add carrots, stock, wine, cardamom, and orange juice; simmer for 30 minutes or until carrots are tender.
3. Purée to a smooth texture; chill.
4. Finish with yogurt. Thin with carrot juice. Adjust seasoning before service.

Chef's Notes: Soup can be garnished with dollop of whipped cream, chives, and carrot chips. Fried ginger chips also make a spicy garnish.

Vichyssoise

Yield: 1 gallon; 20 portions (6 fluid ounces each)

Chef Loise Diat of the Ritz Carlton is credited with creating Vichyssoise. This recipe is adapted from one featured in Chef Diat's book, Cooking à la Ritz *(Lippincott, 1941).*

20 oz/wt	leeks, white part only, chopped fine
1 each	minced onion
3 tbsp	vegetable oil
1 each	sachet containing 4 whole cloves, 4 parsley stems, 3 peppercorns, 1 bay leaf
2 1/2 lb	diced potatoes
2 1/2 qt	Chicken Stock (page 410)
24 oz/wt	half-and-half, chilled
1 bunch	snipped chives
2 tsp	salt
1/4 tsp	ground white pepper

1. Sweat the leeks and onion in the oil until tender and translucent.
2. Add the sachet, potatoes, and stock. Bring to a full boil, then reduce heat and simmer until the potatoes begin to fall apart.
3. Remove and discard the sachet. Purée the soup. Cool rapidly.
4. To finish the soup for service, add cold half-and-half to the soup, fold in the chives, and season to taste with salt and pepper.

Chilled Potato Herb Soup with Lobster

Yield: 1 gallon; 20 portions (6 fluid ounces each)

Like the recipe for Vichyssoise, which inspired this elegant re-interpretation, a delicate purée of potatoes and leeks is the foundation of this soup. The lobster garnish could easily be omitted, or replaced by a scattering of finely julienned and fried leeks.

1/4 lb	medium diced leeks, light green and white parts
2 oz/wt	butter
1 1/4 lb	thinly sliced potatoes
3 qt	Shellfish Stock (page 411)
8 oz/fl	heavy cream
1 tsp	Worcestershire sauce
1 oz/wt	dry sherry
1 1/2 tsp	salt
	Garnish
1 lb	cooked lobster meat, cut into medium dice
1/4 cup	chopped chives
1/4 cup	chopped tarragon leaves
1/4 cup	chopped chervil
1/4 cup	chopped flat-leaf parsley leaves

1. Sauté leeks in butter until soft, about 5 minutes. Add potatoes and stock; simmer over low heat until tender, about 20 minutes. Purée through a food mill or in a blender.
2. Finish with heavy cream. Season to taste with Worcestershire, sherry, and salt.
3. Garnish with diced lobster and chopped herbs.

Fresh Spring Pea Purée with Mint

Yield: 1 gallon; 20 portions (6 fluid ounces each)

This soup has a delicate texture and flavor, making it suitable for elegant menus in the spring and early summer. Cook the soup just until the peas are tender for the freshest green color in the finished soup.

1/2 lb	minced leeks
1/2 lb	minced onions
1 oz/wt	vegetable oil
14 oz/wt	shredded green leaf lettuce
2 3/4 lb	fresh peas
2 1/2 qt	Vegetable Stock (page 411)
1 each	sachet containing 6 *each* chervil and parsley stems, 6 white peppercorns
10 to 12 oz/fl	light cream or half-and-half
1 tbsp	salt
1/4 tsp	ground white pepper
	Garnish
2 tbsp	fine chiffonade mint (or 20 each chervil plûches)

1. Sauté leeks and onions in oil.
2. Add lettuce and peas and smother briefly.
3. Add broth and sachet; bring to a boil.
4. Reduce heat and simmer until all ingredients are very tender.
5. Remove and discard sachet. Purée mixture in a blender until smooth. Chill thoroughly.
6. To finish for service, add chilled cream to cold soup. Season to taste with salt and pepper. Fold in mint chiffonade. Or garnish each portion with a chervil pluche.

Chilled Cauliflower Soup with Sevruga Caviar

Yield: 1 gallon; 20 portions (6 fluid ounces each)

In this presentation, cauliflower reveals its delicious nutty side, offering a perfect contrast to the slight "bite" of the crème fraîche and the briny savor of fine caviar. The caviar garnish can easily be omitted to make a more modest, but still delicious, soup.

6 lb	cauliflower, rough chopped (5 heads)
1 qt	half-and-half
1 qt	milk
pinch	ground nutmeg
1 tbsp	lemon juice
2 tsp	minced lemon zest
4 tsp	kosher salt
1/2 tsp	ground white pepper
	Garnish
4 oz/wt	Crème Fraîche (page 303), whipped
1 oz/wt	sevruga caviar
2 tbsp	minced chives

1. Place cauliflower in enough salted water to cover completely; simmer until tender, about 15 minutes.
2. Purée the cauliflower in a blender, adding cooking liquid as needed to assist in forming a thick purée.
3. Add half-and-half, milk, nutmeg, lemon juice, and lemon zest.
4. Blend well and chill. Adjust seasoning with salt and pepper after the soup is cold.
5. Garnish each portion with a dollop of crème fraîche, a bit of caviar, and a sprinkle of fresh chives.

Caribbean Coconut and Pineapple Bisque

Yield: 1 gallon; 20 portions (6 fluid ounces each)

6 cups	coconut milk
4 cups	milk
2 cups	heavy cream or half-and-half
	Liaison
2 cups	half-and-half
6 each	egg yolks
$1\frac{1}{2}$ tbsp	arrowroot
6 cups	pineapple juice
4 oz/fl	Simple Syrup (page 421), added to taste
2 tbsp	lime juice, added to taste
2 cups	diced pineapple, macerated in 2 ounces light rum

1. Simmer the coconut milk, milk, and half-and-half.
2. Combine the liaison ingredients and temper. Add to simmering mixture and continue to cook over low heat until thickened, about 4 to 5 minutes. Chill thoroughly.
3. Add pineapple juice, then adjust flavor with simple syrup and lime juice.
4. Garnish with macerated pineapple.

Presentation Ideas: Garnish with Plantain Chips (page 393) that have been fried or baked. Serve in a glass dish on shaved ice with a skewer of pineapple chunks alternating with sliced bananas rolled in toasted coconuts.

Chef's Notes: Rum may be reduced or omitted as desired.

Chilled Tomato Saffron Soup with Shellfish

Yield: 1 gallon; 20 portions (6 fluid ounces each)

9 lb	tomatoes
3 qt	Shellfish Stock (page 411)
3/4 tsp	saffron, crushed
3 each	oranges, zest and juice
3/4 tsp	salt
1/4 tsp	ground black pepper
	Garnish
1/2 lb	cooked lobster meat, diced
1/2 lb	cooked scallops, diced
2 oz/wt	cantaloupe melon, scooped into pea-sized balls
2 oz/wt	honeydew melon, scooped into pea-sized balls
4 oz/fl	diced yellow tomato
4 oz/fl	diced red tomato
1/4 cup	fine chiffonade basil
1/4 cup	fine chiffonade mint

1. Chop the tomatoes, salt well, and hang in cheesecloth overnight. Reserve the collected tomato water.
2. Combine stock with saffron, orange juice, and zest; bring to a simmer. Season with salt and pepper and strain through several layers of cheesecloth. Add tomato water and chill thoroughly.
3. Garnish with lobster, scallops, melon balls, tomatoes, basil, and mint.

Chef's Notes: Prepare the Shellfish Stock on page 411 using lobster shells. Be sure that the stock is very clear. If necessary, clarify it following the method outlined in the basic stock recipe.

• • •

Add 1 ounce gelatin solution (page 17) along with the tomato water in step 2 for a lightly jellied version of this soup as shown.

Chilled Clear Borscht

Yield: 1 gallon; 20 portions (6 fluid ounces each)

8 lb	raw beets, peeled and grated or chopped
1 1/4 gal	White Duck Stock (page 410)
2 1/2 oz/wt	red wine vinegar
1 tbsp	sugar
1 qt	sweet white wine, such as Reisling
1/2 tsp	ground white pepper
2 tbsp	kosher salt
	Garnish
1/2 lb	cooked beets, julienned
1/4 lb	Smoked Duck Breast (page 154), julienned
1/4 lb	radishes, julienned

1. Simmer the beets gently in the stock and vinegar for one hour.
2. Strain through doubled cheesecloth or a paper coffee filter; add sugar, wine, salt, and pepper to taste. Chill.
3. Garnish with julienned beets, duck, and radishes at service.

Chef's Notes: Smoked Ham (page 159) can be substituted for the Smoked Duck.

Fresh Infusion of Vegetables

Yield: 1 gallon; 20 portions (6 fluid ounces each)

Traditional French country cooking has a wealth of soups and stews that feature tender and succulent vegetables straight from the garden. Here, baby carrots, petit pois, fresh fava beans, and asparagus tips are presented in a subtly flavored and satisfying vegetable infusion based on leeks and celeriac.

3 lb	red tomatoes, quartered
	Infusion
2 lb	leeks, white and light green parts, sliced
10 oz/wt	sliced celeriac
5 oz/wt	minced shallots
3 oz/wt	minced parsley
1 oz/wt	sliced chives
1 gal	water, as needed
3 each	garlic cloves, minced
2 each	thyme sprigs
1 each	bay leaf
1 1/2 tbsp	salt
1/2 tbsp	ground black pepper
	Garnish
2 oz/wt	baby carrots, sliced on bias
2 oz/wt	petit pois, blanched
2 oz/wt	fresh favas, shelled and cooked
2 oz/wt	asparagus tips, parcooked
2 oz/wt	tomatoes, peeled, seeded, and cut into diamond shapes
10 each	chervil pluches

1. Make a tomato broth by combining the tomatoes with 3 cups of water. Simmer gently for 30 minutes, then strain through a fine sieve or cheesecloth. Chill thoroughly.
2. Make the vegetable infusion by simmering the ingredients in 3 quarts of water. Simmer gently, covered, for one hour. Add a little water to bring it back to its original level, return briefly to a boil, remove from heat, and allow to cool. Strain through a fine sieve or cheesecloth. Chill thoroughly.
3. Mix the tomato broth and the vegetable infusion; adjust seasoning.
4. Toss the garnish vegetables together. At service, garnish each portion with 1 ounce of the mixed vegetables and a chervil pluche.

THREE

Salads

Salads appear on the menu in so many different guises and are embraced by today's garde manger with such enthusiasm that one might imagine salads were invented by this generation of chefs. In fact, salads have played a key role throughout culinary history. Fresh concoctions of seasoned herbs and lettuces, known as *herba salata,* were enjoyed by the ancient Greeks and Romans alike. According to legend, the Greek philosopher Aristoxenus was so obsessed with freshness that while the lettuce was still growing he would sprinkle it with vinegar and honey the night before he planned to prepare a salad. We are indebted to the Romans for our very word *salad,* deriving as it does from their word for salt.

Figure 3-1 Mild Greens.

The early European settlers of America also valued salad greens. Thomas Jefferson recorded that the markets of his day supplied the cook with a variety of lettuces, endive, sorrel, corn salad (mâche), and cress. After a long absence from the market, the greens Jefferson favored are again appearing in salads served as appetizers, entrées, accompaniments to other items, or as intermezzos. This chapter will discuss three major salad categories:

- Green salads
- Side salads, made from vegetables, potatoes, grains, pastas, legumes, and fruits
- Composed salads

Green Salads

By selecting the appropriate greens and pairing them with properly chosen dressings, a wide range of salads suitable to several different menu needs can be created, from a delicate salad of butterhead with a light lemon vinaigrette served as a first course to an appetizer salad of bitter greens, walnuts, and blue cheese with a sherry vinaigrette.

Salad Greens

Commercially prepared salad blends are now available, but chefs can also create their own by combining lettuces from within one category or by selecting from among two or more categories. The greens that are selected will determine the character of the salad. Today's garde manger can choose from:

- Mild greens
- Spicy greens
- Bitter greens or chicories
- Prepared mixes of greens
- Herbs and flowers

Mild Greens

Mild lettuces can be grouped into four categories (see Figure 3-1):

- ***Iceberg/heading:*** Crisp heads have closely packed leaves and very mild flavor.

- ***Butterhead:*** Loose rosette of soft, thick leaves have a soft, delicate texture and mild flavor; includes Boston, Kentucky Limestone, and Bibb varieties.
- ***Loose-leaf:*** Open, deeply indented, loose leaves have a delicate flavor and a moderately soft texture; includes red and green leaf lettuce, oak leaf, and lola rosa. Baby varieties are often included in special salad blends.
- ***Romaine/Cos:*** This lettuce grows as a long cylindrical head, with the leaves joined to a core at the base of the head. The outer leaves are heavily ribbed, sometimes "savoyed" (crinkled). Leaves closer to the center have a milder, sweeter flavor than the outer leaves. The inner leaves, sometimes known as the heart, may be used exclusively in some salads. Baby romaine is also featured in mixed greens or specialty blends. The name *Cos* derives from the Greek island of the same name, where some believe this lettuce to have originated.

In addition to the lettuces described above, the mild greens also include mâche (a.k.a. corn salad or lamb's lettuce), some of the spicy greens when they are still young or immature, and baby varieties of various cooking greens and cabbages.

Spicy Greens

Spicy greens have a distinct pepperiness or assertive flavor, but are still delicate enough to eat in salads. The younger they are, the less spicy they will be (see Figure 3-2).

The spicy greens include, but are not limited to:

- ***Amaranth:*** Spinachlike in flavor, amaranth varies in color from green to purple to red.
- ***Arugula*** **(a.k.a. rocket or roquette):** Taste ranges from mild and nutty to peppery and pungent; best used when leaves are small and narrow.
- ***Watercress:*** With peppery, small leaves on tender branches, watercress is dark green.
- ***Mizuna:*** A Japanese mustard, mizuna has a mild flavor.
- ***Tat-soi:*** A flat black cabbage, the round leaves form an open rosette, with a faint but pleasant cabbagelike taste; used in its very young stages.

Figure 3-2 Spicy Greens.

Figure 3-3 Bitter Greens

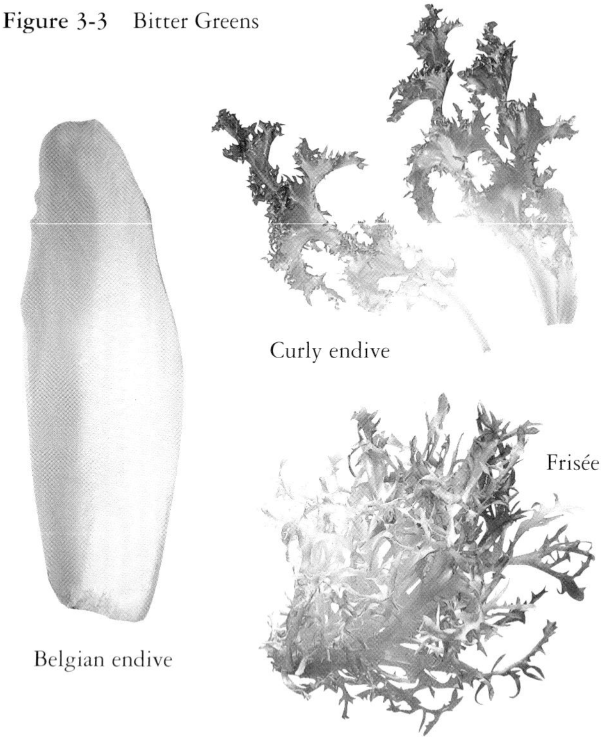

Figure 3-4 Mixed Greens.

Bitter Greens and Chicories

Chicories are heading-style or loose-leaf greens characterized by a distinctive bittersweet flavor (see Figure 3-3). When young, they may be used in salads. More mature chicories are considered cooking greens. This group includes:

- ***Belgian endive:*** As endive grows, soil is mounded over the heads to prevent them from turning green; this is known as "blanching" the endive. Belgian endive has white, tight heads with spearlike leaves and a succulent, very crisp texture. Red Belgian endive is a type of radicchio known as *treviso*.
- ***Dandelion, mustard, beet, Swiss chard, and collard greens:*** These distinctly bitter varieties have dark green, long, narrow leaves, some with white or red ribs. If they are overmature, they may give salads an unpleasant flavor. Beet greens have a tendency to bleed when combined with a dressing.
- ***Escarole:*** Large heads of greenish-yellow, slightly crumpled leaves are succulent and slightly nutty.
- ***Curly endive*** **(a.k.a. chicory):** This green has narrow leaves with deeply ridged edges, and an assertive flavor and texture. When very young it may be sold as frisée.
- ***Frisée:*** With fine white to pale green curly leaves, frisée is similar to chicory but with finer, smaller leaves. The flavor is slightly bitter, though generally less intense than curly endive.
- ***Radicchio:*** Sturdy purple-red leaves form a tight head. The flavor is bitter.
- ***Treviso radicchio:*** Resembling an elongated loose Belgian endive, this has red streaks or tips, and a succulent texture with a flavor similar to heading radicchio.

Prepared Mixes of Greens

The market also provides a number of specialty items for salad making. Among the most popular of these items are convenient, prewashed and trimmed mixes of greens. Their ready availability and ease of use have made them very popular, even to the point of indiscriminate use. The three most commonly available mixes are:

- ***Mesclun:*** This mix of small salad leaves is often found in combination with herbs or flowers (see Figure 3-4). Throughout Provence, where this mix is believed to have originated, seasonal greens of all sorts are paired with herbs and flowers. Today, commercially available mesclun mixes may contain blends of various mild, sweet, and peppery greens, with or without a flower or herb component. Different suppliers will offer different blends, so it is well worth the time to conduct a taste test.

Figure 3-5 Herbs.

- ***Oriental mix (OMX):*** This mix typically includes a combination of some or all of the following: tat-soi, lola rosa, red oak, arugula, beet greens, Swiss chard, sorrel, amaranth, dill, purslane, mizuna, red mustard, bok choy, red shiso, red fire, sierra, and shungi ku.
- ***Baby mix (BMX):*** A generic term for mixes of very young leaves of several varieties, colors, and textures, this is sold both in heads and prewashed leaves. A typical combination may include lola rosa, tango, baby red oak, baby romaine, and baby green oak.

Herbs and Flowers

Some varieties of herbs and flowers may also be used in salads. Herbs can range from pungent to lightly fragrant, and they can add a wonderful accent to a special dish. Herbs that have a naturally tender texture or soft leaves—young basil, chives, small mint leaves, pluches of chervil or flat-leaf parsley (see Figure 3-5)—are the ones to choose for salads. Flowers and herbs can turn an ordinary salad into something quite unique and beautiful, as long as they are not overdone.

Edible flowers are normally divided into two groups:

- ***Garden flowers:*** Bachelor's buttons, borage, calendula, carnations, fuchsia, geraniums, johnny jump-ups, marigolds, nasturtiums, pansies, primroses, roses, sunflowers, and violets (see Figure 3-6).
- ***Herb flowers:*** Anise hyssop, arugula, borage, chive, lavender, mustard, oregano, rosemary, sage, and thyme.

Caring for Salad Greens

Nothing is worse than a gritty salad. Salad greens should be kept properly chilled from the time they arrive until they are ready to be plated. The following guidelines should also be observed when handling salad greens.

1. *Rinse greens thoroughly in plenty of cool water to remove all traces of dirt or sand.*

   Sturdy greens may be able to hold up to a spray, but delicate greens, herbs, and flowers should be gently plunged into and lifted out of the water repeatedly to remove dirt or sand. The water should be changed as often as necessary until there are absolutely no traces of dirt, grit, or sand visible in the rinsing water.

Figure 3-6 Edible Flowers.

Figure 3-7 Lettuce in a salad spinner.

Figure 3-8 Storing lettuce.

2. *Dry greens completely.*

   Salad dressings cling best to well-dried greens. In addition, greens that are carefully dried before they are stored will last longer. Spinners are the most effective tools to use, either large-scale electric spinners for volume salad making, or hand baskets (see Figure 3-7). Spinners should be cleaned and sanitized carefully after each use.

3. *Store cleaned greens in tubs or other containers.*

   They should not be stacked too deep, since their own weight could bruise the leaves. They should be loosely wrapped or covered with dampened toweling to prevent them from wilting rapidly (see Figure 3-8). Once greens have been cleaned they should be used within a day or two.

4. *Cut or tear the lettuce into bite-sized pieces.*

   Traditional salad-making manuals have always called for lettuces to be torn to avoid discoloring, bruising, or crushing the leaf. Today's knives are not likely to discolor the leaves, and there is no reason to believe that properly sharpened knives could bruise the lettuce more than tearing. This is still a matter of personal style and preference, of course.

Dressing the Salad

Place the greens (about 2 ounces, or 3/4 cup, per serving) in a bowl and ladle a portion of salad dressing over them (2 to 3 tablespoons per serving). Use a lifting motion to toss the greens and dressing. Tongs, spoons, or, where appropriate, gloved hands can all be used to toss the salad (see Figure 3-9). Each piece of lettuce should be coated completely but lightly with the dressing. There should be just enough dressing for the greens; if the dressing pools on the plate, there is too much.

Vinaigrette recipes can be found on pages 22–26 and include the following options: Basic Red Wine Vinaigrette, Balsamic Vinaigrette, Vinaigrette Gourmand, Truffle Vinaigrette, Apple Cider Vinaigrette, Curry Vinaigrette, Chipotle-Sherry Vinaigrette, Roasted Shallot Vinaigrette, or Mustard-Walnut Vinaigrette. Two reduced-fat vinaigrettes, Tomato Vinaigrette and Beet Vinaigrette, can be found on page 27.

Creamy-style salad dressings can be used successfully with green salads. Recipes for these dressings can be found on pages 30–32 and include Russian Dressing, Green Goddess Dressing, Creamy Black Pepper Dressing, and Rouquefort Dressing. Two reduced-fat dressings, Maytag Blue Cheese Dressing and Ranch Dressing, can be found on page 33.

Figure 3-9 Tossing a salad with vinaigrette.

Garnishing the Salad

Choose from variety of vegetable garnishes according to the season and your desired presentation: slices or wedges of tomatoes, cucumbers, carrots, radishes, jícama, mushrooms (raw or marinated), olives, peppers, and so forth. In addition to these vegetable garnishes, the chef may also opt to use more unusual ganishes: raw or very lightly blanched asparagus, green peas or beans, pea shoots, sprouts of all sorts. These ingredients may either be tossed along with the greens as they are being dressed, or marinated separately in a little vinaigrette and used to top the salad.

Adding a crisp component to the salad gives another level of interest, both in terms of flavors and textures. There are several recipes included in the recipes throughout the book, such as the following: Assorted Vegetable Chips, page 393; Pepper Jack and Oregano Crackers, page 394; Cheddar and Walnut Icebox Crackers, page 395; Potato Crisps and Parsnip Crisps, page 396, toasted nuts, page 426, or a Parmesan Crisp, page 428.

Breads and breadsticks can be served with simple green salads to make them more interesting and satisfying as well: Olive Bread, page 422; Foccacia or Grissini, page 423. Sliced peasant-style breads can be served along with the salad, spread with a bit of Tapenade, page 41, or drizzled with one of the flavored oils found on pages 397-399.

Savory granités are another interesting way to garnish some salads. The granité may be based on a variety of fruit or vegetable juices. Cucumber and celery granité (pages 102 and 103) are good examples.

Side Salads

Vegetable Salads

Vegetables for vegetable salads are prepared as required by the specific recipes. Some are simply rinsed and trimmed; others may need to be peeled, seeded, and cut to the appropriate shape. Some vegetables may require an initial blanching to set colors and textures, while others must be fully cooked.

If the salad is to be served raw, the prepared vegetables are simply combined with a vinaigrette or other dressing and allowed to rest long enough for the flavors to "marry." When the vegetables are partially or fully cooked, there are two options for applying the dressing. In the first option, the vegetables are drained and combined with the dressing while they are still warm, for faster flavor absorption. This works well for root vegetables such as carrots, beets, parsnips, as well as leeks, onions, and potatoes. Some vegetables (especially green vegetables like broccoli or green beans) may discolor if they are combined with an acid in advance; in that case, the vegetables should be refreshed and chilled before being added to the dressing. In either case, the vegetables should be thoroughly drained and blotted dry to avoid watering down the dressing.

Potato Salads

Potatoes should be cooked completely, but not overcooked. Waxy potatoes (Yukon golds or Finnish) hold their shape better after cooking than starchy potatoes (Russets or baking potatoes).

The classic "American" potato salad is a creamy salad, typically dressed with mayonnaise. Other potato salads enjoyed around the world are often dressed with a vinaigrette. In some traditional European-style recipes, the dressing may be based on bacon fat, olive oil, stock, or a combination of these ingredients. The key to success with this style of potato salad is to combine the potatoes and dressing while the potatoes are still warm. The dressing is typically brought to a simmer before the potatoes are added, for the best finished flavor.

Pasta and Grain Salads

Grains and pastas for salads should be fully cooked, but care should be taken to avoid overcooking. Grains and pasta will still be able to absorb some of the liquid in the dressing, and can quickly become soggy.

If a pasta or grain salad is held for later service, be especially careful to check it for seasoning before it is served, because these salads have a tendency to go flat as they sit. Salt and pepper are important seasonings, of course, but others, such as vinegars, herbs, or citrus juices, can give a brighter flavor.

Legume Salads

Dried beans should be cooked until they are tender to the bite and allowed to cool in their own cooking liquid. The center should be soft and creamy, and it is even possible that the skins may break open slightly. If a salad is made from a variety of dried beans, it is important that beans with different cooking times be cooked separately to the correct doneness.

Unlike grains and pastas, which might become too soft as they sit in a dressing, beans will not soften any further. In fact, the acid in salad dressings will make the beans tougher, even if they are fully cooked. Bean salads, therefore, should not be dressed and allowed to rest for extended periods. If the salad is used within four hours of preparation, however, there is little significant texture change.

Fruit Salads

Fruits have a variety of characteristics, making some fruit salads fairly sturdy, while others lose quality very rapidly. Fruits that turn brown (apples, pears, and bananas) can be treated with fruit juice to keep them from oxidizing, as long as the flavor of the juice doesn't compete with the other ingredients in the salad. Dilute acidic juices, such as lime, with water.

Mixed fruit salads that include highly perishable fruits can be produced for volume operations by preparing the base from the least perishable fruits. More perishable items, such as raspberries, strawberries, or bananas, can then be combined with smaller batches or individual servings at the last moment, or they can be added as a garnish.

Fresh herbs such as mint, tarragon, basil, or lemon thyme may be added to fruit salads as a garnish. Experiment to determine which herbs work best with the fruits selected for the salad.

Composed Salads

Composed salads are made by carefully arranging items on a plate, rather than tossing them together. A "main item," such as grilled chicken or shrimp, a portion of cheese or grilled vegetables, and so forth, is often set on a bed of greens. The salad is garnished and dressed. Some composed salads feature foods that have contrasting colors, flavors, texture, heights, and temperatures. Others are based on a single motif that holds the plate's elements together.

Although there are no specific rules governing the requirements for a composed salad, the following principles should be kept in mind (see Figure 3-10):

- Consider how well each of the elements combine. Contrasting flavors are intriguing. Conflicting flavors are a disaster.
- Repetition of a color or flavor can be successful if it contributes to the overall dish. But generally, too much of a good thing is simply too much.
- All of the components on the plate should be capable of standing alone. However, the composition should be such that each part is enhanced by being in combination with the others. This produces a more intriguing eating experience than possible when one of the components is eaten alone.
- Components should be arranged in such a way that the textures and colors of the foods are most attractive to the eye. The appearance of the plate should be given careful thought.

Warm Salads

Warm salads, known in French as *salade tiède,* are made by tossing the salad ingredients in a warm dressing, working over moderate to low heat. The salad should be just warmed through. Another approach is to use a chilled crisp salad as the bed for a hot main items, such as grilled meat or fish.

Figure 3-10

BALANCING FLAVORS AND TEXTURES OF COMPOSED SALADS

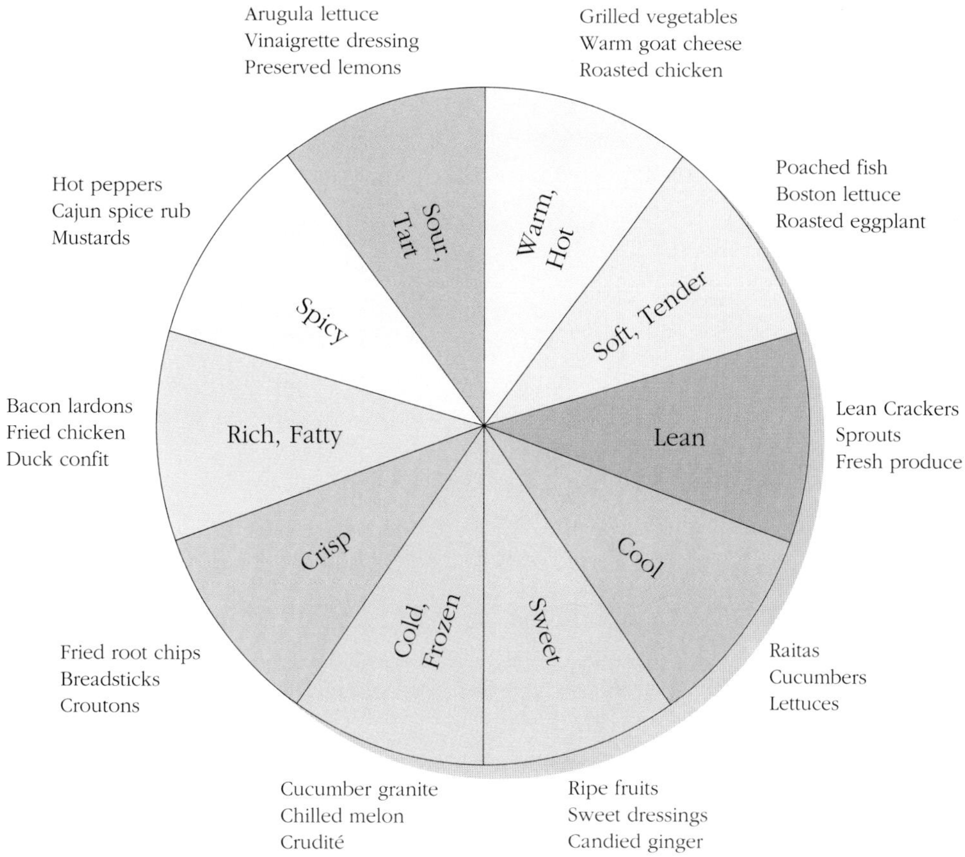

Spinach Salad with Tangerines and Pomegranate

Yield: 10 side salad portions

10 oz/fl	Tangerine-Pineapple Vinaigrette (page 23)
20 oz/wt	spinach, young tender leaves, stems removed
1 each	red onion, sliced into paper-thin rings
5 each	tangerines, segments only
1 each	pomegranate, seeds only

1. Prepare the vinaigrette.

2. Clean and thoroughly dry the spinach. Portion as necessary for single servings or larger batch salads. Hold under refrigeration until ready to serve.

3. ***Salad Assembly:*** Just before serving, whisk the vinaigrette vigorously and reseason. For each portion, toss 2 ounces of spinach with 2 tablespoons of vinaigrette. Arrange on chilled plates, top with onion rings, tangerine segments, and pomegranate seeds. Serve immediately.

Chef's Notes: Slice onion rings and place in a container of ice water for up to 24 hours to crisp them. This will also mellow the harsh bite of the raw onions that some people find offensive.

Parson's Garden Salad

Yield: 10 appetizer portions

This recipe is adapted from one featured on the menu of Michel Guerard, a famous French chef considered one of the great innovators in contemporary cuisine. This dish has been pleasing diners for more than twenty years.

10 oz/fl	Vinaigrette Gourmande (page 23)
5 oz/wt	mâche lettuce
5 oz/wt	frisée lettuce
5 oz/wt	red treviso radicchio
5 oz/wt	watercress leaves
2 cups	soy bean sprouts, blanched and chilled
6 oz/wt	shelled peas, blanched and chilled
2 tbsp	chopped chives
2 tbsp	chopped parsley
	Garnish
2 cups	olive oil
2 each	garlic cloves, crushed
8 each	whole black peppercorns
2 cups	julienne carrots
2 cups	julienne celeriac
To taste	salt
5 oz/wt	slab bacon, cut into medium dice, cooked crisp
30 each	quail eggs, poached in red wine and water (see Chef's Notes)

1. Prepare the vinaigrette.
2. Clean and thoroughly dry all the lettuces. Combine all mixed greens. Portion as necessary for single servings or larger batch salads. Hold under refrigeration until ready to serve.
3. Up to 2 hours before service, heat the oil, garlic, and peppercorns to 325°F. Add the carrots and celeriac and fry slowly until very crisp. Drain on absorbent toweling and hold warm. Salt to taste if desired.
4. ***Salad Assembly:*** Just before serving, whisk the vinaigrette vigorously and reseason. For each portion, toss 2 ounces of mixed greens with 2 tablespoons of vinaigrette. Arrange on chilled plates, top with bacon and fried vegetables. Add 3 warm poached quail's eggs. Serve immediately.

Chef's Notes: To poach quail eggs, combine 1 quart red table wine, 1 quart water, and a pinch of salt. Bring to 200°F. Carefully crack eggs into cups and add to poaching liquid. Reduce heat to 170°F and cook until eggs are set, approximately 2–3 minutes. Remove with a perforated spoon and blot dry before adding to salads.

Spring Herb Salad

Yield: 10 appetizer or side salad portions

10 oz/fl	Truffle Vinaigrette (page 24)
	Mixed Greens
10 oz/wt	baby arugula
5 oz/wt	mizuna
5 oz/wt	baby tat-soi
1/2 head	radicchio, cut into chiffonade
1 bunch	flat-leaf parsley, leaves only
2 bunches	chervil, separated into pluches
1 bunch	chives, sliced 1/2 inch long
To taste	truffle, shaved (*optional*)
To taste	salt
To taste	coarse ground black pepper

1. Prepare the vinaigrette.
2. Clean and thoroughly dry the mixed greens. Portion as necessary for single servings or larger batch salads. Hold under refrigeration until ready to serve.
3. ***Salad Assembly:*** Just before serving, whisk the vinaigrette vigorously and reseason. For each portion, toss 2 ounces of mixed greens with 2 tablespoons of vinaigrette. Arrange on chilled plates, top with shaved truffles if desired, and season with salt and pepper. Serve immediately.

Chef's Notes: Other herbs, such as dill, fennel, and tarragon, may be used in place of or in addition to the herbs listed.

Frisée with Walnuts, Apples, Grapes, and Blue Cheese

Yield: 10 appetizer portions

10 oz/fl	Apple Cider Vinaigrette (page 24)
20 oz/wt	frisée lettuce
2 each	apples (any tart apple)
5 oz/wt	green grapes, cut in half lengthwise
1/2 cup	toasted and coarse-chopped walnuts
5 oz/wt	blue cheese, crumbled

1. Prepare the vinaigrette.
2. Clean and thoroughly dry the frisée. Portion as necessary for single servings or larger batch salads. Hold under refrigeration until ready to serve.
3. Just before serving, slice the apples. If necessary, hold the apple slices in acidulated water.
4. ***Salad Assembly:*** Just before serving, whisk the vinaigrette vigorously and reseason. For each portion, toss 2 ounces of the frisée with 2 tablespoons of vinaigrette. Arrange on chilled plates, top with apple slices, grapes, walnuts, and blue cheese. Serve immediately.

Watermelon and Red Onion Salad with Watercress

Yield: 10 servings

A version of this salad was featured on the Institute's PBS series, Cooking Secrets of the CIA. *It was presented in the show by the Institute's Chef Tim Rodgers and offers a wonderful combination of sweet and hot flavors, layered textures, and beautiful colors.*

4 bunches	watercress
2 each	red onions, sliced paper thin
2 oz/fl	white wine vinegar
To taste	salt
To taste	cracked black pepper
4 oz/fl	vegetable oil
5 cups	seeded and cubed watermelon
5 tsp	toasted pine nuts (*optional*)

1. Trim the stems of the watercress. Rinse the watercress and dry thoroughly. Keep chilled until ready to assemble the salad.
2. Place the sliced onions in ice water and allow them to soak for at least 2 hours and up to 24 hours in advance.
3. Combine the vinegar, salt, and pepper. Gradually whisk in the oil. Adjust the seasoning with additional salt and pepper if necessary.
4. ***Salad Assembly:*** For each portion, toss 1 1/2 ounces of the watercress with 1 tablespoon of the dressing. Lift the watercress from the bowl, allowing the dressing to drain back into the bowl. Arrange on a chilled salad plate. Add the watermelon to the bowl and toss or roll until coated with the remaining dressing. Place the watermelon on top of the watercress. Garnish with a few slices of drained red onion, and 1/2 teaspoon pine nuts if desired. Top with a few turns of freshly ground pepper.

Caesar Salad

Yield: 10 appetizer portions

According to culinary lore, this salad was created by Caesar Cardini in 1924 at his restaurant in Tiajuana, Mexico. Today Caesar salads may be served as a salad buffet item, a plated first course or main-course salad garnished with smoked seafood, sliced grilled chicken, or duck breast.

20 oz/wt	romaine lettuce
1 1/2 cups	Garlic-Flavored or Plain Croutons (page 428)
	Dressing
1 tbsp	minced garlic
5 each	anchovy fillets
1/4 cup	pasteurized egg (whole or yolk only)
1/4 cup	lemon juice, or to taste
1/4 cup	water, or as needed
1 1/4 cups	extra-virgin olive oil
3/4 cup	finely grated Parmesan cheese, or to taste
3/4 tsp	salt, or to taste
1/2 tsp	ground black pepper, or to taste

1. Separate the romaine into leaves. Clean and thoroughly dry. Tear or cut into pieces if necessary. Hold under refrigeration until ready to serve.
2. Prepare croutons and hold until ready to serve.
3. To prepare the dressing, mash together the garlic, anchovy, salt, and pepper in a bowl to form a relatively smooth paste. Add the pasteurized egg, lemon juice, and water and blend well. Gradually add the olive oil, whisking as it is added to form a thick emulsion. Stir in the Parmesan. Adjust with salt and pepper if necessary.
4. Combine the 2 ounces of the greens with 2 tablespoons of the dressing, tossing gently until evenly coated. Garnish with a few croutons.

Marinated Tomatoes

Yield: 30 portions (3 ounces/1/2 cup each)

5 1/2 lb	tomatoes (such as plum, beefsteak, yellow, pear, currant, or cherry)
	Dressing
1 cup	extra-virgin olive oil
1/2 cup	red wine vinegar
1/4 cup	basil chiffonade
1/4 cup	chopped marjoram
1 tbsp	salt
1 1/2 tsp	coarse ground black pepper

1. Peel the tomatoes and cut into halves, quarters, or wedges, if necessary.
2. Combine the dressing ingredients.
3. Add the tomatoes to the dressing and let rest 2 hours before serving.

Chef's Notes: Use a single type of tomato or a combination of tomato varieties in this salad. If the tomato skins are thin and tender, peeling is optional.

Roasted Beet Salad

Yield: 20 portions (2 ounces each)

Use red or golden beets for this salad. The beets are roasted in this recipe, but could also be boiled or steamed. For a special presentation, alternate the sliced beets with orange slices.

8 each	beets, greens trimmed to 1 inch
To taste	kosher salt
	Dressing
2 1/2 oz/fl	extra-virgin olive oil
1 oz/fl	red wine vinegar
1 oz/fl	lemon juice
Pinch	ground cayenne pepper

1. Preheat the oven to 375°F. Arrange the beets in a 2-inch-deep hotel pan; add water just to cover the bottom of the pan. Season with salt. Cover with foil and roast until fork tender, approximately one hour depending on size.
2. While the beets are roasting, combine dressing ingredients.
3. Trim the beets, slip off the skin, and slice into rounds. Add to the dressing while still warm.
4. Let rest at room temperature for at least 30 minutes before serving or cooling for storage.

Roasted Pepper Salad

Yield: 15 portions (3 ounces/1/2 cup each)

This dish can be served as a salad or as a healthful alternative to traditional high-fat sauces with grilled meats, fish, and poultry.

12 oz/wt	roasted red peppers, peeled and seeded (4 each)
12 oz/wt	roasted green peppers, peeled and seeded (4 each)
12 oz/wt	roasted yellow peppers, peeled and seeded (4 each)
7 oz/wt	tomatoes, peeled and seeded
1/4 cup	golden raisins
1/4 cup	dry sherry wine
	Dressing
10 oz/fl	Balsamic Vinaigrette (page 22)
6 oz/wt	red onions, julienne
1/2 cup	black olives, cut in strips (20 each)
1/2 cup	chopped cilantro leaves
1 each	jalapeño, minced
2 each	garlic cloves, minced
	Garnish
1/4 cup	Parmesan cheese
1 oz/wt	toasted pine nuts

1. Prepare the vinaigrette.
2. Cut the roasted peppers into 1/2-inch-wide strips. Cut the tomatoes into strips. Plump the raisins in the sherry.
3. Combine the dressing ingredients and pour over the peppers, tomatoes, and raisins.
4. Toss to combine. Let the salad rest at room temperature for 30 to 45 minutes before serving at room temperature, or cool and store properly for later service.
5. ***Salad Assembly:*** Just before serving, shave Parmesan curls over each portion and top with toasted pine nuts.

Marinated Roasted Peppers Omit the tomatoes and plumped raisins. Dress with a plain Balsamic Vinaigrette, omitting olives, onions, cilantro, jalapeño, and garlic. Use as required in other recipes (see Roasted Chicken Sandwich, page 117).
Marinated Peppers and Mushrooms Prepare Marinated Peppers, adding 12 ounces julienned shiitake or white mushrooms.

Hearts of Artichoke Salad

Yield: 10 portions (3 ounces each)

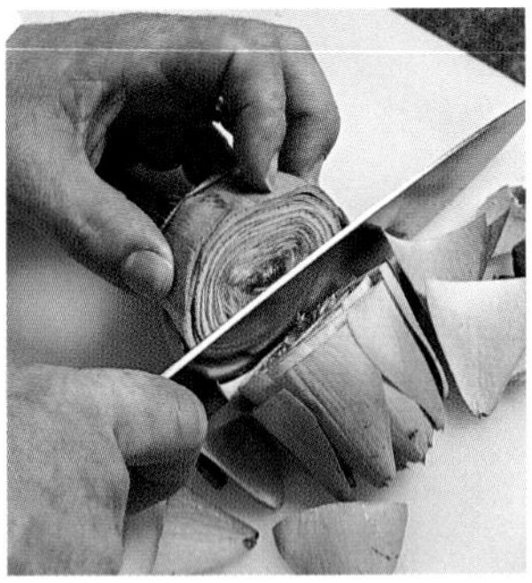

Cutting off the top leaves.

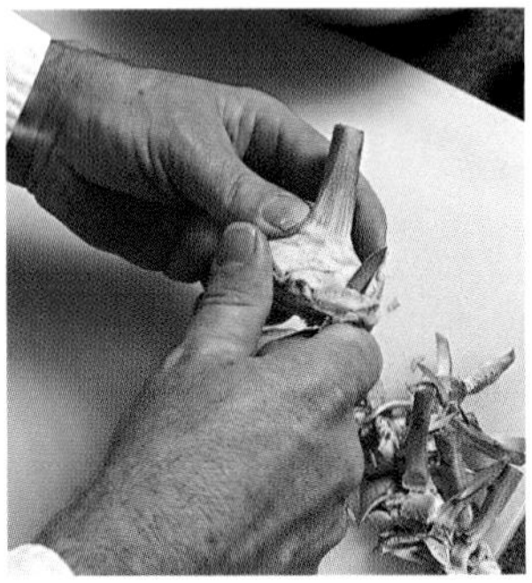

Trimming the choke.

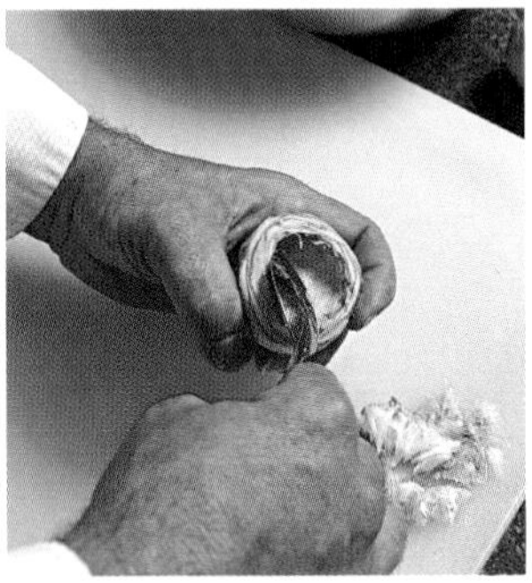

Scooping out the choke.

Artichoke hearts gently simmering.

10 each	artichoke hearts, quartered, or 30 baby artichokes
	Dressing
9 oz/fl	olive oil
3 oz/fl	balsamic vinegar
To taste	salt
To taste	ground white pepper
1/2 bunch	flat-leaf parsley, leaves only
1 cup	calamata olives, pitted (30 each)
1 each	red onion, sliced into thin rings or julienne
4 each	plum tomatoes, peeled, seeded, and quartered

1. Cut the ends off the artichokes and trim off the outer leaves. Scoop out the chokes and quarter each heart. Hold in acidulated water.
2. Simmer the artichoke hearts in a *cuisson* (see Chef's Notes) until tender, about 8 to 12 minutes. Drain and let dry on absorbent toweling while preparing the dressing.
3. Whisk together the dressing ingredients. Add the artichoke hearts, olives, onions, and tomatoes.
4. Let rest at room temperature for at least 30 minutes before serving or cooling for storage.

Chef's Notes: To prepare a cuisson, combine 1 gallon water with 4 ounces lemon juice, 4 whole cloves, 1 bouquet garni (page 411), and 2 teaspoons salt. Bring all ingredients to a simmer.

Poached Leek Salad

Yield: 10 portions (3 ounces each)

When ramps are available, they can be poached and served in this manner for a special springtime dish. If your leeks are large, they may be halved or quartered. Small leeks can be trimmed but left whole. Use the light and white green parts only; reserve the trimmings for use in stocks.

10 each	leeks (about 3 bunches or 4 1/4 pounds)
5 each	plum tomatoes, halved (1 1/4 pounds)
1 cup	Vinaigrette Gourmande (page 23)
To taste	salt

1. Rinse the leeks completely and cut as necessary. Cook in simmering salted water until almost tender, about 15 minutes. Drain the leeks and dry well on absorbent toweling. Reserve 2 ounces of the cooking liquid for the dressing.
2. Roast the tomatoes in a 375°F oven until dried and lightly browned, about 25 to 30 minutes. Cut into strips.
3. Add the reserved cooking liquid from the leeks to the vinaigrette and mix well. Adjust seasoning.
4. Pour the dressing over the warm or room-temperature leeks and tomatoes. Let the salad rest at room temperature 30 minutes before serving or storing.

Chef's Notes: Other vinaigrettes may be substituted, such as Mustard–Walnut Vinaigrette (page 26) or Truffle Vinaigrette (page 24) for a special occasion.

• • •

To work with leeks, first rinse away the dirt that clings to the roots and the exterior leaves. Next, trim away the root ends and the dark green outer leaves. Leave enough of the root end intact to prevent the layers of the leek from falling apart. If your leeks are large, split them into halves or quarters. Very small, baby leeks may not need to be split.

Thoroughly rinse the leeks once they have been trimmed and halved or quartered. Be sure to rinse them long enough to remove all traces of dirt. If your baby leeks are left whole, it is especially important to check that no dirt has been left trapped in the layers. Spread the leek layers out gently to permit the water to run through easily and flush out the sand or dirt.

Haricots Verts with Prosciutto and Gruyère

Yield: 10 portions (3 ounces/3/4 cup each)

This salad could be featured as a side salad for a pâté, terrine, or galantine. Or it could be served on its own or as part of a salad "sampler" appetizer plate. If haricots verts are unavailable, this salad is equally good prepared with regular green beans, asparagus, or leeks.

1 1/4 lb	haricots verts
5 oz/wt	prosciutto
5 oz/wt	Gruyère cheese
	Dressing
2 tbsp	lemon juice, or to taste
1 tbsp	white wine vinegar
1/2 tsp	salt
1/4 tsp	ground white pepper
2 tbsp	minced shallots
1/3 cup	vegetable oil

1. Trim the haricots verts and rinse. Cut the prosciutto and Gruyère into fine julienne.
2. Combine the lemon juice, vinegar, salt, pepper, and shallots. Gradually whisk in the oil to make a dressing.
3. Blanch the haricots verts in salted boiling water until barely tender to the bite. Refresh in cold water. Drain and blot dry.
4. Add the haricots verts, proscuitto, and Gruyère to the dressing. Toss to combine and let rest at room temperature for at least 30 minutes before serving or storing.

Haricots Verts with Walnut and Red Wine Vinaigrette (page 23) Paul Bocuse, the famous chef of Lyons, France, combines 3/4 pound haricots verts, 1/2 pound sliced white mushrooms, a few slivers of truffles, and a dressing made with walnut oil and Beaujolais wine vinegar for a simple but elegant salad.

Shaved Fennel and Parmesan Salad

Yield: 10 portions ($2\frac{1}{2}$ ounces each)

Slices of very fresh, raw cèpes (porcini or Boletus edulis) are superb in this salad.

20 oz/wt	fennel bulbs (about 2 large bulbs)
1/2–3/4 cup	extra-virgin olive oil
2 oz/fl	lemon juice
To taste	salt
To taste	pepper
1/2 cup	chopped flat-leaf parsley leaves
10 oz/wt	raw cèpes, sliced thin (*optional*)
	Garnish
3 oz/wt	Parmesan cheese
1–2 tbsp	white truffle oil *or* hazelnut oil

1. Trim, core, and shave the fennel very thin using a knife or mandolin.
2. Combine the olive oil, lemon juice, salt, and pepper thoroughly. Add the fennel, parsley, and sliced cèpes if desired; toss to coat evenly.
3. The salad is ready to serve now, or it may be refrigerated for later service.
4. ***Salad Assembly:*** For each portion, arrange 2 1/2 ounces of the salad on a chilled plate. Shave some Parmesan over the salad and drizzle with a little truffle or hazelnut oil.

Fennel and Persimmon Salad Prepare the salad through step 3. Garnish with shaved fuyu persimmon and finish with a few drops of balsamic vinegar.

Artichoke and Fennel Salad Replace half the fennel with cooked artichoke hearts (see page 78 for cooking instructions). Dress and finish as above.

Grilled Fennel Salad Slice the fennel 1/4 inch thick, brush with a little of the dressing, and grill until tender. Cool the fennel before combining with the remaining dressing in step 2.

Coleslaw

Yield: 30 portions (3 ounces/½ cup each)

A mixture of cabbages, peppers, carrots, and onions makes a colorful variation on the classic coleslaw. For a more traditional slaw, omit the peppers and onions.

3½ lb	green cabbage, cut into chiffonade
1 lb	red cabbage, cut into chiffonade
5 oz/wt	carrots, cut into julienne
5 oz/wt	red and yellow peppers, cut into julienne
5 oz/wt	red onions, cut into julienne
	Dressing
½ cup	sugar
2 tbsp	dry mustard
1 tbsp	celery seed
10 oz/fl	Basic Mayonnaise (page 28)
10 oz/fl	sour cream
3 oz/fl	cider vinegar
2 tbsp	prepared horseradish
1 tbsp	mild brown mustard
To taste	salt
To taste	ground white pepper
To taste	Tabasco sauce

1. Combine the cabbages, carrots, peppers, and onions. Reserve.
2. Stir together the sugar, mustard, and celery seed to work out lumps. Add the remaining dressing ingredients and stir to combine.
3. Fold the cabbages, carrots, peppers, and onions into the dressing. The salad is ready to serve now, or it may be held, covered, under refrigeration.

Roasted Corn and Tomato Salad

Yield: 30 portions (3 ounces/1/3 cup each)

	Dressing
2 cups	olive oil
1 1/2 cups	white wine vinegar
2 tbsp	roasted garlic paste
1 tbsp	salt
1 tsp	coarse ground black pepper
7 cups	roasted corn kernels (11 ears)
6 cups	tomato concassé (15 plum tomatoes)
1 cup	sliced scallions (8 each)
1/2 cup	chopped cilantro
1/3 cup	chopped flat-leaf parsley

1. Blend the oil, vinegar, and garlic paste. Season with salt and pepper.
2. Add the corn, tomatoes, scallions, and herbs. Toss to coat evenly. Adjust seasoning. The salad is ready to serve now, or it may be held, covered, under refrigeration.

Asian Vegetable Slaw

Yield: 10 side salad portions

20 oz/wt	savoy cabbage, cut into fine chiffonade
10 oz/wt	carrots, cut into julienne
1 cup	coarse-chopped cilantro
5 each	scallions, sliced thin on bias
	Dressing
1 cup	vegetable oil
1/4 cup	olive oil
1/4 cup	peanut oil
1 tsp	sesame oil
1/2 cup	Japanese rice wine vinegar
1 tbsp	soy sauce
1 tbsp	fish sauce
1/4 tsp	ground white pepper
Pinch	cayenne pepper
1/2 cup	chopped toasted peanuts
2 tbsp	toasted sesame seeds

1. Toss together the cabbage, carrots, cilantro, and scallions.
2. Blend the dressing ingredients and pour over the cabbage mixture. Adjust seasoning as necessary with pepper and cayenne. Garnish each portion with peanuts and sesame seeds.

Celeriac and Tart Apple Salad

Yield: 10 portions (3 ounces/$^1/_2$ cup each)

Both celeriac and apples will oxidize when exposed to air. This turns their creamy white flesh an unappetizing brown color. To prevent this, the celeriac is cooked in a blanc *(see Chef's Notes below). Although acidulated water containing lemon juice is often used to keep apples from browning, it might give the apples a strong lemon taste. We prefer to use apple juice combined with a few drops of apple cider vinegar. The acid in the juice and the vinegar will keep the apples from browning, and they add another "apple" flavor dimension.*

2 lb	celeriac
	Dressing
3 oz/fl	Crème Fraîche (page 303)
3 oz/fl	Basic Mayonnaise (page 28)
1 oz/fl	Dijon mustard
2 tbsp	apple cider vinegar
1 tbsp	sugar
To taste	salt
To taste	ground black pepper
3 each	Granny Smith apples

1. Cut away the outer rind of the celeriac and cut into allumette, about 1$^1/_2$ inches long. Hold in a *blanc* (see Chef's Notes) to prevent discoloring.
2. Combine the dressing ingredients.
3. Rinse the celeriac, boil until tender in acidulated water (add 1 tablespoon of lemon juice to each quart of water). Refresh in cold water; drain on absorbent toweling.
4. Peel and dice the apples. Fold the apples and the celeriac into the dressing. Adjust the seasoning with salt and pepper if necessary.
5. The salad is ready to serve now, or it may be held, covered, under refrigeration.

Chef's Notes: To prepare the *blanc*, whisk together 1 quart water with $^1/_4$ cup flour and 2 tablespoons lemon juice.

Waldorf Salad

Yield: 30 portions (3 ounces/$^{2}/_{3}$ cup each)

This classic fruit salad combining apples, celery, and walnuts in a mayonnaise-based dressing is credited to Oscar Tschirky, maître d' of the Waldorf Astoria Hotel in New York City. Since the early 1890s there have been a few modifications, but the essential salad has the same fresh taste and texture as the original.

5 each	Red Delicious apples
5 each	Golden Delicious apples
5 each	Granny Smith apples
	Dressing
1 cup	Basic Mayonnaise (page 28)
1 cup	sour cream
1 tsp	salt
$^{1}/_{2}$ tsp	ground black pepper
To taste	lemon juice
1 stalk	celery, peeled, cut into medium dice
1 cup	rough-chopped toasted walnuts

1. Cut the apples into medium dice.
2. Mix together all the dressing ingredients and season to taste. Fold in apples, celery, and walnuts.
3. The salad is ready to serve now, or it may be held, covered, under refrigeration for up to 8 hours. This salad should be made the same day it is to be served.

Chef's Notes: Peeling the celery removes the tough fibers and gives this salad additional refinement. Choose the most tender celery from the heart whenever possible. If your celery is very large and bitter, simply omit it from the salad.

Ambrosia Salad

Yield: 30 portions (3 ounces/$^1/_2$ cup each)

In Greek mythology, ambrosia was the food of the gods and was thought to confer immortality. Today, the word also refers to two distinct Southern specialties. The first is a cocktail created at the famed New Orleans restaurant Arnaud's. The second, and perhaps better-known, ambrosia is a chilled concoction of fruits (usually oranges and bananas) and flaked coconut. Originally served as a layered fruit dessert, this Southern classic also works quite well as a salad.

1 cup	whipping cream
1/4 cup	sugar, or to taste
12 each	oranges, segmented
1 each	pineapple, cubed
2 lb	bananas, sliced
1 lb	green grapes, halved
1/2 lb	unsweetened coconut flakes, toasted

1. Whip the cream to soft peaks and add sugar to taste.
2. Fold the fruits into the whipped cream.
3. Let the salad rest under refrigeration at least 30 minutes before serving.
4. *Salad Assembly:* Garnish each portion with toasted coconut.

Presentation Ideas: Serve this salad with turkey or chicken sandwiches, grilled or smoked shrimp or scallops, or to accompany hearty game or pork pâtés. This salad offers a refreshing counterpoint of sweetness and texture.

Chef's Notes: Make this and other fruit salads only when fruits are ripe and full flavored. This salad should be made just prior to service and should not be held overnight.

German Potato Salad

Yield: 10 portions (3 ounces each)

$2\frac{1}{4}$ lb	waxy potatoes (such as Yellow Finn or Yukon Gold)
	Dressing
2 oz/wt	diced bacon
$2\frac{1}{2}$ cups	Chicken Stock (page 410)
$\frac{1}{4}$ cup	white wine vinegar
4 oz/wt	diced onions
1 tsp	salt, or to taste
1 tsp	sugar, or to taste
To taste	ground white pepper
$\frac{1}{4}$ cup	vegetable oil
2 tbsp	mild brown mustard
$\frac{1}{2}$ bunch	chives, snipped

1. Cook the potatoes in simmering salted water until just tender. Drain and dry. While the potatoes are still hot, remove the peels and slice the potatoes $\frac{1}{3}$ inch thick.
2. While the potatoes are cooking, prepare the dressing: Render the bacon, remove it with a slotted spoon, and keep it warm.
3. Bring the chicken stock, vinegar, onions, salt, sugar, and pepper to a boil.
4. Combine the oil, rendered bacon fat, and mustard with the warm potatoes. Pour over the onions and then add the boiling stock-vinegar mixture. Add the rendered bacon and chives; toss the salad gently.
5. The salad may be served warm, at room temperature, or chilled.

Mediterranean Potato Salad

Yield: 10 portions ($3^1/_2$ ounces each)

$2^1/_2$ lb	waxy potatoes (such as Yellow Finn or Yukon Gold)
	Dressing
7 oz/fl	extra-virgin olive oil
3 oz/fl	red wine vinegar
2 tbsp	balsamic vinegar
3/4 cup	coarse-chopped flat-leaf parsley
4 tbsp	chopped capers
1 tbsp	chopped anchovies
1 tsp	minced garlic
1 tsp	salt
1/4 tsp	ground white pepper

1. Simmer the potatoes in salted water until just cooked through.
2. While the potatoes are cooking, mix the dressing ingredients.
3. Drain the potatoes and dry briefly to remove any excess moisture. Peel and dice while still very hot and place in a bowl.
4. Whip dressing to recombine, and pour over the potatoes. Let rest at room temperature for at least 30 minutes before serving or cooling for storage.

Chef's Notes: This salad can be served either warm or cold and works well as a component in the smoked duck appetizer on page 364. If the salad is to be served warm or at room temperature, it should be made just prior to service and held no longer than 3 hours. If the salad is to be held or served cold, cool it to room temperature once the potato salad has been assembled.

Mediterranean Potato Salad with Mussels This salad makes an interesting addition to a seafood buffet or antipasti and is a creative way to feature mussels. Steam or poach mussels or other shellfish until just cooked through. If the salad is being served warm, poach the seafood just before serving and fold into the salad while still warm. For a cold presentation, steam or poach the mussels, chill well, and add to the cooled salad. Store as described above.

Lentil Salad

Yield: 35 portions (3 ounces each)

Legumes will toughen if they are left in contact with an acid, such as this vinaigrette, for extended periods. Combine the lentil mixture with the dressing as close to service time as possible.

2 lb	French lentils
3 each	carrots, cut into small dice
2 stalks	celery, peeled, cut into small dice
1 each	leek, white part only, cut into small dice, blanched
1 lb	white mushrooms, sliced
10 oz/fl	Mustard–Walnut Vinaigrette (page 26)

1. Simmer the lentils in salted water until they are tender. Refresh in cold water and drain well. Drain, rinse until cold, and drain well again.
2. Combine the lentils, carrots, celery, leek, and mushrooms. Reserve until ready to serve.
3. ***Salad Assembly:*** Up to 4 hours before serving, combine the lentil mixture with the vinaigrette. Serve at room temperature or chilled. Adjust seasoning before serving.

Tabbouleh Salad

Yield: 10 portions (3 ounces/1 1/2 cups each)

This recipe offers a faithful rendition of a salad that, according to many authorities, is more a parsley salad with some bulgur than a bulgur salad with a little parsley!

1 lb	bulgur wheat
2 1/2 cups	chopped flat-leaf parsley (about 2 bunches)
2 cups	diced tomatoes (about 10 plum tomatoes)
1/4 cup	finely sliced scallions, white part only (about 5 each)
1/2 cup	chopped mint
	Dressing
1 cup	extra-virgin olive oil
1/2 cup	lemon juice
To taste	salt
To taste	ground black pepper

1. Place the bulgur in a bowl and cover with cold water. Soak for 30 minutes and drain well.
2. In a large mixing bowl, combine the bulgur with the parsley, tomatoes, scallions, and mint.
3. Whisk together the dressing ingredients, pour over the salad, and toss to coat evenly. The salad is ready to serve now, or it may be held under refrigeration.

Mixed Bean and Grain Salad

Yield: 30 portions (4 ounces each)

1 lb	chick-peas (garbanzos), soaked overnight
1 lb	green lentils
1/2 lb	acini de pepe pasta
1 lb	bulgur wheat
	Dressing
1 pt	Hazelnut–Oregano Vinaigrette (page 26)
10 each	sun-dried tomatoes, minced
To taste	salt
To taste	coarse ground black pepper

1. Cook the chick-peas, lentils, and pasta separately in salted water. Refresh in cold water and drain well. Combine.
2. Place the bulgur in a bowl and cover with cold water. Soak for 30 minutes and drain well. Combine with the chick-pea mixture.
3. Whisk together the dressing ingredients, pour over the salad, and toss to coat evenly. The salad is ready to serve now, or it may held under refrigeration.

Fattoush (Eastern Mediterranean Bread Salad)

Yield: 10 to 12 portions (1/2 to 3/4 cup each)

Sumac is a favored seasoning for Syrian, Lebanese, and other Middle Eastern cuisines. It is made from the berries of the sumac tree and it has a tart, slightly bitter flavor.

6 each	pita bread
3 tbsp	extra-virgin olive oil
To taste	salt
To taste	ground black pepper
	Dressing
2 oz/fl	lemon juice
1 tbsp	white wine vinegar
1 tbsp	ground sumac
2 each	garlic cloves, minced
4 oz/fl	extra-virgin olive oil
To taste	salt
To taste	ground black pepper
2 tbsp	chopped thyme
1/2 tsp	cayenne pepper
2 tsp	sugar
	Vegetables
1 bunch	chopped scallions
1 cup	chopped flat-leaf parsley
6 each	plum tomatoes, seeded and cut into medium dice
1 each	European cucumber, peeled, seeded, and cut into medium dice
8 oz/wt	radishes, brunoise or sliced thin
1 each	yellow pepper, cut into small dice

1. Cut the pita bread into small wedges. Toss with the oil, salt, and black pepper. Bake on a sheet pan in a 300°F oven for about 15 minutes, turning halfway through the baking. They should be crisp, but not crumbly.

2. Combine dressing ingredients thoroughly and adjust the seasoning if necessary. Reserve separately.

3. ***Salad Assembly:*** Combine the vegetables with the dressing and toss until coated. Fold in the pita bread. Adjust the salt and pepper. If the salad is too dry, sprinkle with a little water to moisten.

Panzanella (Bread Salad Tuscan-Style)

Yield: 30 portions (3 ounces/$^1/_2$ cup each)

Panzanella evolved as a thrifty way to use bread that had become too dry for slicing and eating. Combined with ripe tomatoes and fresh herbs, the stale bread was transformed into a luscious summer salad.

1 lb	country-style bread
3 lb	medium-dice plum tomatoes
1/2 lb	medium-dice European cucumbers
1/4 lb	medium-dice celery hearts
1/4 lb	thinly sliced red onions
1 cup	basil chiffonade
	Dressing
1/2 cup	extra-virgin olive oil
2 tbsp	red wine vinegar
3 each	garlic cloves, minced
To taste	salt
To taste	ground black pepper

1. Cut the bread into medium dice. Let dry for 8 to 12 hours.
2. Combine the bread with the tomatoes, cucumbers, celery, onions, and basil.
3. Blend the dressing ingredients and pour over the salad ingredients. Let rest for 30 minutes at room temperature before serving. Adjust seasoning if necessary.

Chef's Notes: To prepare this salad à la minute, keep the vegetables and bread separate. Toss together a spoonful of each for every portion, along with 1 ounce of the dressing for each portion.

• • •

Green olives or sweet peppers are sometimes added to this salad. For this recipe, use 1 cup pitted green olives or diced peppers.

• • •

This salad can be garnished with shaved Parmesan and drizzled with extra-virgin olive oil.

Tubettini Pasta Salad

Yield: 10 portions (3 ounces each)

1 lb	tubettini pasta
	Dressing
3 tbsp	white wine vinegar
1 tsp	salt
1/2 cup	olive oil
1/2 oz/wt	minced shallots
1/4 tsp	ground white pepper
1/4 cup	minced chives
2 oz/wt	brunoise sweet pepper (red, green, yellow, or combination)
To taste	salt
To taste	ground black pepper

1. Cook pasta in boiling salted water until al dente. Refresh in cold water; drain and dry.
2. To prepare the dressing, stir together the vinegar and salt. Whisk in the oil and remaining ingredients.
3. Pour the dressing over the pasta and adjust seasoning with salt and pepper. The salad is ready to serve now, or it may be held, covered, under refrigeration.

Asian-Style Buckwheat Noodles Prepare buckwheat noodles (sold as soba) according to the package directions. Drain well and dress sparingly with a little vinaigrette, made by combining 2 tablespoons safflower oil, 1 tablespoon dark sesame oil, 1 tablespoon rice wine, and very finely minced garlic and ginger to taste.

Avocado, Tomato, and Corn Salad with Aged Cheddar and Chipotle-Sherry Vinaigrette

Yield: 10 entrée portions

This salad highlights one of Vermont's famous culinary resources, aged Cheddar cheese, along with a variety of ripe tomatoes. It makes an excellent appetizer salad, or meatless main course for lunch menus.

3 each	red beefsteak tomatoes, sliced thin
3 each	yellow beefsteak tomatoes, sliced thin
1 cup	cherry tomatoes, halved lengthwise
1 cup	pear tomatoes, halved lengthwise
1 cup	currant tomatoes
5 ears	corn on the cob
20 oz/wt	mesclun lettuce mix, rinsed and dried
15 oz/fl	Chipotle-Sherry Vinaigrette (page 25)
5 each	ripe avocados, peeled and sliced at assembly
10 oz/wt	aged Vermont cheddar, crumbled
1 each	red onion, sliced thin, separated into rings
To taste	coarse ground black pepper

1. Portion the tomatoes for each salad as follows: 2 slices each red and yellow tomatoes, 1/3 cup combined cherry, pear, and currant tomatoes.
2. Roast the corn (see page 425) and cut the kernels away; you will use about 1/2 ear per salad.
3. ***Salad Assembly:*** For each portion, toss 2 ounces of the mesclun with 2 tablespoons of vinaigrette. Mound on a chilled plate. Slice or dice half an avocado and scatter over salad. Top with tomatoes, corn, cheddar, and red onion. Drizzle with an additional tablespoon of vinaigrette. Grind black pepper over salad. Serve at once.

Baked Goat Cheese with Garden Lettuces, Roasted Figs, Pears, and Toasted Almonds

Yield: 10 appetizer portions

This recipe, taught by Chef Eve Felder to her students, blends flavors and textures in an intriguing way. The cheese's texture is rich and creamy, contrasting its crust. Figs and almonds add deep rich flavors to the dish. The pungent backdrop of the mesclun mix pulls all the elements together.

20 oz/wt	Marinated Goat Cheese (page 307)
2 cups	dry bread crumbs
20 oz/wt	mesclun lettuce mix
15 oz/fl	Balsamic Vinaigrette (page 22)
2 each	pears, sliced into thin wedges
10 each	roasted figs (see Chef's Notes), halved
To taste	salt
To taste	ground black pepper
1/2 cup	Toasted Almonds (page 348)

1. Drain the goat cheese of excess oil. Gently dip the marinated goat cheese into the bread crumbs and place on sheet pans. Chill at least 2 hours and up to overnight.
2. ***Salad Assembly:*** For each portion, bake 2 rounds of cheese in a 450°F oven until lightly browned, about 10 minutes. Let the cheese cool while grilling the figs. Lightly grill figs to heat. Toss 3 ounces mesclun and 3 to 4 pear slices with 2 tablespoons of the vinaigrette; season with salt and pepper. Mound on a chilled plate. Top with goat cheese rounds, figs, and a few almonds.

Chef's Notes: To roast figs for this salad, remove the top portion of the stem. Season with salt and pepper, and put into a 2-inch-deep hotel pan. Add enough chicken stock to cover the figs halfway. Add a bay leaf and thyme sprig. Cover and roast at 350°F until tender and plump, about 20 minutes. Warm skin side down on a grill just before service if desired.

Buffalo Chicken Salad

Yield: 10 entrée portions

This salad is a variation on the popular appetizer "Buffalo Chicken Wings," which were created at the Anchor Bar in Buffalo, New York, in 1964 by owner Teressa Bellissimo. July 29 is Chicken Wing Day in Buffalo.

$2\frac{1}{2}$ lb	chicken wings, tips removed, disjointed
2 cups	flour (seasoned with salt and pepper) as needed for dredging
	Hot Sauce
1 cup	Frank's Hot Sauce
1 oz/wt	butter
To taste	Tabasco sauce
To taste	ground cayenne
To taste	lemon juice
20 oz/wt	mixed greens, washed, dried, and chilled
10 oz/fl	Basic Red Wine Vinaigrette (page 22)
$\frac{1}{2}$ bunch	celery, cut into 4-inch allumette strips
$\frac{3}{4}$ lb	carrots, cut into 4-inch allumette strips
1 each	seedless cucumber, peeled and sliced
20 pieces	Celeriac Chips (page 396) *(optional)*
15 oz/wt	Roquefort Dressing (page 32)

1. Dredge the chicken wings in flour and deep fry in 350°F oil until golden brown and crisp, about 12 minutes. Drain well.
2. Simmer the ingredients for the hot sauce. Pour over the warm chicken wings; hold in the sauce.
3. ***Salad Assembly:*** For each portion, warm 4 ounces chicken wings, if necessary. Toss 2 ounces mixed greens with 2 tablespoons vinaigrette. Arrange the mixed greens in a soup plate or salad bowl and top with the wings. Garnish with the celery, carrots, cucumbers, and celery chips. Serve with 3 tablespoons dressing.

Cobb Salad

Yield: 10 portions

Cobb salad was created at the Brown Derby Restaurant in Hollywood, California. Various interpretations may call for either chicken or turkey. The garnish suggestions here are typical, but some versions have included watercress, celery, Cheddar cheese, hard-boiled eggs, black olives, and alfalfa sprouts.

5 each	chicken breasts, on the bone
20 each	bacon slices
To taste	salt
To taste	ground black pepper
20 oz/wt	romaine lettuce, washed, dried, and torn into pieces
10 oz/fl	Basic Red Wine Vinaigrette (page 22)
10 oz/wt	medium-dice tomatoes, skin on
10 oz/wt	crumbled blue cheese
3 each	avocado, cut into medium dice
5 each	scallions, sliced on bias

1. Season (see Chef's Notes) and roast chicken breasts to an internal temperature of 165°F. Cool and remove from bone. Cut meat into 1/3-inch dice.
2. Bake, broil, or griddle the bacon until crisp. Drain on absorbent paper and keep warm.
3. ***Salad Assembly:*** For each portion, toss 2 ounces of romaine with 2 tablespoons of vinaigrette. Mound on a plate, top with 4 ounces chicken, 1/4 cup diced tomato, 1 ounce blue cheese, 1/3 cup avocado, 2 tablespoons scallions, and 2 bacon strips, crumbled.

Chef's Notes: If you use a spice rub on the chicken before roasting, you may opt to leave the skin on for additional flavor in the salad. Hot-smoked or smoke-roasted chicken breasts (pages 141 and 142) would also be good choices.

Mediterranean Salad with Tuna Confit

Yield: 10 entrée portions

This salad was composed by the late Chef Catherine Brandel to celebrate the grand opening of the Culinary Institute's California campus at Greystone in St. Helena. It combines a rich tuna confit with the fresh produce grown on campus.

	Vegetable Garnish
10 each	red potatoes
10 each	plum tomatoes, peeled and quartered
10 each	radishes, sliced thin
5 each	celery stalks, sliced
2 each	green peppers, cut into strips
1 each	Spanish onion, sliced
4 oz/wt	Niçoise olives (3 per portion)
1/4 cup	chopped basil
15 oz/fl	Lemon Vinaigrette (page 23)
20 oz/wt	mixed lettuces, washed and dried
30 oz/wt	Tuna Confit (page 172)
20 each	anchovy fillets
5 each	hard-boiled eggs, quartered
To taste	ground black pepper

1. Boil the potatoes in their skins until tender. Drain, dry, and slice thin while still warm. Combine the potatoes with the remaining vegetable garnish ingredients and pour 5 ounces of vinaigrette over the mixture. Toss gently until evenly coated. Let rest at room temperature 30 minutes before serving.

2. ***Salad Assembly:*** For each portion, toss 2 ounces of mixed greens with 2 tablespoons of vinaigrette. Mound on a chilled plate. Top with 4 tomato quarters and about 1/2 cup of the other vegetables. Top with 3 ounces of drained tuna confit, 2 anchovy fillets, and 2 hard-boiled egg quarters. Grind fresh black pepper over the salad just before serving.

Smoked Duck and Malfatti Salad with Roasted Shallot Vinaigrette

Yield: 10 entrée portions

Malfatti means something that is poorly made or irregularly shaped, so when making the pasta for this salad, exact dimensions are not important. This warm salad combines several flavors and textures that may appear to be unusual, but when this salad is executed properly, it is hard to find a more pleasing dish.

1/2 lb	Malfatti Pasta (page 421)
20 oz/wt	mixed bitter greens (such as arugula, frisée, and radicchio), washed and dried
10 oz/wt	chanterelles, halved or quartered if necessary
2–3 oz/fl	olive oil for sauté, as needed
1 lb	Smoked Duck Breast (page 154), cut into strips across the grain
15 oz/fl	Roasted Shallot Vinaigrette (page 26)
To taste	salt
To taste	ground black pepper
3 oz/wt	Parmesan cheese

1. Cook the pasta in boiling salted water until al dente. Refresh in cold water; drain and dry. Toss with oil if cooked in advance.

2. Wash and dry the greens; tear or cut into bite-sized pieces. Hold under refrigeration until needed.

3. ***Salad Assembly:*** For each portion, sauté 1 ounce (raw weight) of mushrooms in 2 teaspoons olive oil until tender. Add about 2 ounces of cooked pasta and 1 1/2 ounces of duck. Toss over high heat until hot. Add 2 ounces of the mixed greens and 1 ounce of the vinaigrette to the pan. Toss briskly and mound on a warm plate once the ingredients are just warmed through. Drizzle with an additional 1/2 ounce of the dressing. Season with salt and pepper and garnish with shaved Parmesan and some of the shallots from the dressing. Serve while still warm.

Chef's Notes: This salad is best made in a nonstick pan in small batches done at the very last minute before being served. Be certain to distribute shallots evenly over the salad.

Southern Fried Chicken Salad

Yield: 10 entrée portions

2 lb	chicken breasts (7 each)
1 cup	buttermilk
5 heads	butterhead lettuce (such as Boston, Bibb, or Kentucky Limestone)
30 each	cherry tomatoes
2 each	Vidalia onions
1 cup	flour, seasoned with black pepper and salt
1 1/2 cups	peanut oil
1 1/2 cups	white mushrooms, sliced
10 tsp	capers
5 tsp	minced shallots
2 1/2 oz/fl	white wine vinegar
5 tbsp	Dijon mustard
2/3 cup	chopped tarragon

1. Trim chicken breasts and cut into 1/2 ounce strips. Pour buttermilk over chicken and marinate under refrigeration until ready to assemble the salad.
2. Separate the lettuce into leaves; wash and dry. Core and quarter the tomatoes. Slice the Vidalia onion thinly and separate into rings. Hold all separately under refrigeration.
3. ***Salad Assembly:*** For each portion, remove 6 pieces of chicken from the buttermilk and dredge in the seasoned flour. Pan-fry in 1 1/2 ounces peanut oil. Remove and drain on absorbent toweling while finishing the dressing.
4. Add 2 1/2 ounces sliced mushrooms to the peanut oil along with 1 teaspoon capers and 1/2 teaspoon shallots; sauté until the mushrooms are tender. Add 1 tablespoon vinegar and 1 1/2 teaspoons mustard. Heat through, remove from heat, and stir in 1 tablespoon tarragon.
5. Arrange 2 ounces of lettuce on a chilled plate. Top with the chicken, tomato, and Vidalia onion. Pour the warm sauce over the salad and serve immediately.

Arugula Salad with Hot Italian Sausage, Cannelini Beans, and Roasted Peppers

Yield: 10 portions

	Salad Greens
1 lb	arugula (about 4 bunches)
1 head	frisée lettuce
20 leaves	red endive
$2^1/_2$ lb	hot Italian sausage
1 each	red onion, peeled
2 cups	Balsamic Vinaigrette (page 22)
2 each	roasted red peppers, cut into battonet
2 each	roasted yellow peppers, cut into battonet
2 cups	cooked cannelini beans
2 tbsp	capers, rinsed and drained
5 oz/wt	Parmesan cheese
To taste	salt
To taste	coarse ground black pepper

1. Rinse the salad greens, dry thoroughly, and tear or cut into pieces if necessary. Refrigerate until needed, keeping endive separate.

2. Grill the sausage to an internal temperature of 155°F. Let the sausages rest for 15 minutes before slicing into 4 or 5 pieces, cutting on the bias. Keep warm.

3. Slice the onion thinly across the grain and break into rings. Refrigerate until needed.

4. ***Salad Assembly:*** For each portion, toss 2 ounces of the combined arugula and frisée with 2 tablespoons of the vinaigrette. Mound on a chilled plate. Add 3 spears of endive. Top with a sliced sausage, about 1 tablespoon each of the red and yellow peppers, $1^1/_2$ ounces of the beans, and a few onion rings and capers. Drizzle with another tablespoon of vinaigrette. Shave parmesan over the salad; season with salt and pepper. Serve immediately.

Cucumber Granité

Yield: 2 quarts, or 16 portions (2 ounces each)

3 lb	cucumbers (about 6), peeled and seeded
3 oz/fl	white wine vinegar
3 tbsp	granulated sugar
$1\frac{1}{2}$ oz/wt	pasteurized egg white, lightly beaten

1. Purée the cucumber in a blender until very smooth.
2. Combine the cucumber purée with the vinegar, sugar, and egg white and stir until combined.
3. Pour the mixture into a hotel pan and allow it to freeze for at least 3 hours. To serve, scrape a kitchen spoon over the surface and shape into quenelles or balls. Serve at once.

Celery Granité

Yield: 2 quarts, or 16 portions (2 ounces each)

2 bunches	celery (about 4 pounds)
3 oz/fl	white wine vinegar
3 tbsp	granulated sugar
$1\frac{1}{2}$ oz/wt	pasteurized egg white, lightly beaten

1. Trim the celery, cut into dice, and juice or purée in a blender until liquid. Strain through a fine sieve to remove fibers.
2. Combine the celery with the vinegar, sugar, and egg white and stir until combined.
3. Pour the mixture into a hotel pan and allow it to freeze for at least 3 hours. To serve, scrape a kitchen spoon over the surface and shape into quenelles or balls. Serve at once.

FOUR

Sandwiches

Sandwiches have been part of virtually all cuisines since well before any written records were kept, though they have not always been called sandwiches. The honor of naming this favorite luncheon item goes to the infamous gambler John Montague, the fourth Earl of Sandwich. According to legend, this gentleman refused to leave the gaming tables because he didn't want to break his winning streak. He asked that some bread filled with meat be brought to him, and the rage for sandwiches was on.

Louis P. De Gouy published *Sandwich Manual for Professionals* in 1940. His approach to the assembly of sandwiches, based upon his work as the chef at New York's famous Waldorf Astoria Hotel, detailed hundreds of sandwiches organized into specific categories. This classic work has stood the test of time and is still a valuable resource of practical information and inspiration.

Sandwiches can range from delicate finger and tea sandwiches served on doilies to *pan bagnat,* traditionally served wrapped in plain paper from stalls in open markets in southern France. They may be an elegant bite-sized morsel of foie gras served on toasted brioche as an *amuse-gueule* or a grilled Reuben on rye, served with potato salad and a pickle. We can select from diverse culinary traditions, from Scandinavian smørrebrod to American regional favorites like the po'boy to Italian bruschetta and panini to Mexican tacos and burritos. What unifies the concept of the sandwich in all instances is a tasty filling served on or in bread or a similar wrapper.

In this chapter you will learn about handling and preparing ingredients to make the following styles:

- Cold sandwiches
- Hot sandwiches, including grilled
- Finger and tea sandwiches

Cold sandwiches include standard deli-style versions made from sliced meats or mayonnaise-dressed salads. Club sandwiches, also known as triple-decker sandwiches, could be included in this category as well.

Hot sandwiches may feature a hot filling, such as hamburgers or pastrami. Others are grilled, such as a Reuben sandwich. In some cases, a hot filling is mounded on the bread and the sandwich is topped with a hot sauce (Barbecued Pulled Pork, page 113, for example).

Finger and tea sandwiches are delicate items made on fine-grained bread, trimmed of their crusts and precisely cut into shapes and sizes that can be eaten in about two average bites.

Sandwich Elements

The garde manger may be called upon to prepare sandwiches for receptions and teas (see Figure 4-1), for lunch and bistro menus (see Figure 4-2), for special appetizers, and for picnics. In order to produce high-quality sandwiches, it is important to understand how basic filling, cutting, and holding techniques contribute to the overall quality of sandwiches.

Figure 4-1 Afternoon tea with finger sandwiches.

Figure 4-2 Volume sandwich production in a bistro setting.

Breads

Breads for making sandwiches run a fairly wide gamut, including many ethnic specialties. Sliced white and wheat Pullman loaves are used to make many cold sandwiches. The tight crumb of a good Pullman makes it a good choice for delicate tea and finger sandwiches, since they must be sliced thinly without crumbling. Whole-grain and peasant-style breads are not always as easy to slice thinly.

Special breads, buns, rolls, and wrappers are used to make special sandwiches. The characteristics of the bread and how they will fit in with the sandwiches should be considered. Bread should be firm enough and thick enough to hold the filling, but not so thick that the sandwich is too dry to enjoy.

Most breads can be sliced in advance of sandwich preparation as long as they are carefully covered to prevent drying. Some sandwiches call for toasted bread, which should be done immediately before assembling the sandwich. Bread choices include:

- Pullman loaves of white, wheat, or rye
- Peasant-style breads such as sourdough and miche
- Flatbreads including foccacia, pita, ciabatta, and lavash
- Rolls, including hard, soft, and Kaiser rolls
- Wrappers such as crêpes, rice and egg roll wrappers, and phyllo
- Flour and corn tortillas

Spreads

Many sandwiches call for a spread, applied directly to the bread. This element acts as a barrier to keep the bread from getting soggy. Spreads also add moisture to the sandwich and help it to hold together as it is held and eaten. Some sandwich fillings may include a "spread" directly in the filling mixture (for example, a mayonnaise-dressed tuna salad), so there is no need to add a separate one when assembling the sandwich.

Spreads can be very simple and subtly flavored, or they may themselves bring a special flavor and texture to the sandwich. The following list of spread options includes some classic choices, as well as some that may not immediately spring to mind as sandwich spreads.

- Mayonnaise (plain or flavored, such as aïoli or rouille) or creamy salad dressings
- Plain or compound butters
- Mustard or ketchup
- Spreadable cheeses, such as ricotta, cream cheese, mascarpone, or crème fraîche
- Tahini, olive, or herb spreads (hummus, tapenade, or pesto, for example)
- Nut butters
- Jelly, jam, compotes, chutneys, or other fruit preserves
- Avocado pulp or guacamole
- Oils or vinaigrettes

Fillings

Sandwich fillings may be cold or hot, substantial or minimal. In all cases, they are the focus of the sandwich. It is as important to properly roast and slice turkey for club sandwiches as it is to be certain that the watercress for tea sandwiches is perfectly fresh and completely rinsed and dried.

The filling should determine how all the other elements of the sandwich are selected and prepared. Choices for fillings include:

- Sliced roasted or simmered meats (beef, corned beef, pastrami, turkey, ham, pâtés, and sausages)
- Sliced cheeses
- Grilled, roasted, or fresh vegetables
- Grilled, pan-fried, or broiled burgers, sausages, fish, or poultry
- Salads of meats, poultry, eggs, fish, and/or vegetables

Garnishes

Lettuce leaves, slices of tomato or cheese, onion slices, or sprouts can be used to garnish many sandwiches. These garnishes become part of the sandwich's overall structure.

When sandwiches are plated, a variety of side garnishes may also be included:

- Green salads or "side" salads
- Lettuces and sprouts
- Sliced fresh vegetables
- Pickles spears or olives
- Dips, spreads, or relishes
- Sliced fruits

Presentation Styles

A sandwich constructed with a top and a bottom slice of bread is known as a closed sandwich. Some closed sandwiches have a third slice of bread, to create a club sandwich. Still other sandwiches have only one slice of bread, acting as a base; these are open-faced sandwiches (see Figure 4-3).

Finger and tea sandwiches (as well as canapé bases; see page 312) are cut into special shapes (see Figure 4-4). To prepare them, the bread is sliced lengthwise so that the greatest possible surface area is available. The bread is coated with a spread, filled, garnished if desired, then closed if desired, cut to shape, and served at once.

Straight-edged shapes give the best yield with the lowest food cost. These shapes are created by cutting with a sandwich knife or bread knife into squares, rectangles, diamonds, or triangles. Cutters in various shapes may be used to cut rounds, ovals, and other special shapes. The yield is generally lower when preparing these shapes, making them slightly more expensive to produce.

Time should be taken to cut shapes in an exacting and uniform fashion so that they will look their best when set in straight rows on platters or arranged on plates. It is best to cut tea sandwiches as close to service as possible. If these sandwiches must be prepared ahead of time, they can be held for a few hours, covered with damp cloths or in airtight containers.

Sandwich Production Standards and Guidelines

- Organize your work and your workstation carefully, whether you are preparing mise en place or assembling sandwiches for service. Everything you need should be within arm's reach. Write a list of tasks with a priority or time sequence assigned to each.
- Maximize your work flow by looking for ways to eliminate any unnecessary movements by rearranging the direction in which your work moves, or preparing larger (or smaller) batches of items (see Figure 4-5).

Figure 4-3 Curried chicken open-faced sandwiches.

Figure 4-4 Making specially shaped sandwiches.

Figure 4-5 Workflow for making open-faced sandwiches.

Spicy Catfish Sandwich

Yield: 10 sandwiches

2¾ lb	catfish fillets
As needed	oil for deep frying
1 tbsp	Cajun Spice Blend (page 407), to taste
1 cup	flour, or as needed for breading
6 oz/fl	egg wash, as needed for breading (2 eggs beaten with 2 tablespoons milk or water)
1 cup	cornmeal, or as needed for breading
10 oz/fl	Rémoulade Sauce (page 28)
10 each	soft sandwich rolls, split
3 to 4 each	slicing tomatoes, cut into 20 thin slices
2 each	red onions, cut into 10 thin slices
10 leaves	romaine lettuce (1 head)

1. Trim the catfish and cut into 4-ounce portions. Preheat deep fryer to 350°F.
2. Season the fillets with the Cajun spice blend. Dip the catfish into the flour, then the egg wash, and then the cornmeal.
3. Deep-fry the catfish until golden-brown and cooked through, 2 to 3 minutes. Drain on absorbent towels. Keep warm.
4. ***Sandwich Assembly:*** For each sandwich, spread 2 tablespoons of rémoulade sauce on a roll. Layer the tomatoes, onions, lettuce, and catfish on the bottom half. Close the sandwich and serve immediately.

Presentation Idea: Accompany the sandwich with Coleslaw (page 82).

Chicken Burger

Yield: 10 sandwiches

This alternative to beef hamburgers is very popular with guests looking for lower-fat, healthier fare.

2 tbsp	minced shallot (1 large)
2 tbsp	vegetable oil
1 1/2 lb	fresh white mushrooms, minced (6 1/2 cups)
3 oz/fl	dry white wine
1/2 tsp	salt, or to taste
1/4 tsp	ground black pepper, or to taste
2 1/2 lb	ground chicken
1 1/2 cups	dry bread crumbs
2 tsp	chopped fresh herbs (such as chives, oregano, and basil)
1/2 tsp	chopped fresh rosemary
1/2 tsp	poultry seasoning, or to taste
5 oz/wt	provolone cheese (10 slices)
10 each	soft sandwich rolls, split and toasted
3 cups	Tomato Ketchup (page 383)

1. Sauté the shallots in the oil over moderate heat. Increase the heat, add the mushrooms, and sauté until all the moisture has cooked off. Add the wine and continue to sauté until dry, as for duxelles.
2. Season to taste with salt and pepper. Remove from heat and chill thoroughly.
3. Combine the chicken with the bread crumbs, mushroom mixture, herbs, salt, pepper, and poultry seasoning.
4. Make a test as for forcemeat (page 181). Adjust seasoning as necessary.
5. Form the chicken mixture into patties, about 4 1/2 ounces each.
6. Sauté or griddle the patties until browned on both sides.
7. Transfer to a sheet pan or sizzler platter. Top each patty with a slice of provolone. Finish cooking the patties in a moderate (350–375°F) oven to an internal temperature of 165°F.
8. ***Sandwich Assembly:*** For each sandwich, place a patty on a roll, top with about 1 1/2 oz/fl (3 tablespoons) of tomato sauce, and serve at once.

Croque Monsieur

Yield: 10 sandwiches

Croque Monsieur is a classic French sandwich available almost anywhere in France, from the beach, to the train to sidewalk cafes. Muenster cheese is not a traditional ingredient, but it makes a nice addition. Croque *implies crisp or crunchy.*

20 slices	Pullman bread (about 1 loaf)
3 oz/fl	Dijon mustard
1/2 lb	Gruyère cheese (10 thin slices)
20 oz/wt	boiled ham (10 slices)
1/2 lb	Muenster cheese (10 thin slices)
4 oz/wt	soft butter

1. To assemble the sandwiches for grilling, spread the bread slices with mustard.
2. On 10 of the bread slices, layer one slice each of Gruyère, ham, and Muenster over the mustard.
3. Top the sandwiches with the remaining bread slices.
4. Griddle both sides of the sandwiches on a lightly buttered 325°F griddle until the bread is golden, the cheese is melted, and the sandwich is heated through.
5. Cut the sandwiches on the diagonal and serve immediately.

Croque Madame Some recipes simply add a fried egg to the Croque Monsieur. In the United States and England, the ham is usually replaced with sliced chicken breast. Use Emmenthaler instead of Gruyère. Grill as directed.
Monte Cristo Dip any of the variations in beaten egg and grill as you would French toast.

Oyster and Shrimp Po'boy

Yield: 10 sandwiches

The po'boy is a specialty of New Orleans. Some believe it to have been created in 1920 by Benny and Clovis Martin at Martin Brothers Grocery, and was offered to striking streetcar workers. Other sources believe the term relates to the French word pourboire, *meaning gratuity. Still other sources claim the term first appeared in writing in 1875—well before 1920. Like heroes, submarines, hoagies, and grinders, the po'boy can contain almost any ingredient, although seafood seems to be one of the most popular fillings.*

As needed	oil for deep frying
20 each	shrimp 16/20 count, peeled and deveined
30 each	oysters, shucked and drained
1 tsp	salt
1/4 tsp	ground white pepper
Pinch	cayenne pepper
1 cup	all-purpose flour, or as needed for breading
6 oz/fl	egg wash (2 eggs beaten with 2 tbsp milk)
1 cup	cornmeal, or as needed for breading
10 each	baguettes or hero rolls, split lengthwise
3 cups	Rémoulade Sauce (page 28)
1 head	green leaf lettuce, shredded
20 each	tomato slices (3 each)
20 each	red onion slices (2 each)
20 each	lemon wedges (*optional*)

1. Preheat oil for deep frying to 350°F.
2. Season the seafood with the spices. Dip the shrimp and oysters into the flour, then the egg wash, and then the cornmeal.
3. Deep fry the breaded shrimp and oysters in batches until golden and cooked through. Drain on paper towels and keep warm.
4. ***Sandwich Assembly:*** For each sandwich, spread each side of a baguette with 1 tablespoon rémoulade sauce. Fill the baguette with lettuce, tomato, and onion. Top with 2 shrimp and 3 oysters. Top the seafood with another teaspoon of rémoulade sauce, or serve with a portion of sauce on the side. Close the sandwich and serve at once with either sauce or lemon wedges on the side.

Barbecued Pulled Pork Sandwich

Yield: 10 sandwiches

$2^1/_2$ lb	Barbecued Pork Butt (page 169)
3 cups	Barbecue Sauce (recipe follows)
10 each	Kaiser rolls

1. Pull the meat off the pork butt and shred it. Remove and discard excess fat at this time.
2. Simmer the shredded pork meat with the barbecue sauce about 15 minutes.
3. Split the Kaiser rolls and grill or toast.
4. ***Sandwich Assembly:*** For each sandwich, mound approximately 4 to 5 ounces of the barbecued pork on the roll and serve immediately.

Presentation Idea: Accompany the sandwich with Coleslaw (page 82) and Assorted Vegetable Chips (page 393).

Barbecue Sauce

Yield: approximately 1 gallon

1/4 cup	vegetable oil
2 lb	minced onions (6 each or 5 cups)
7 each	garlic cloves, chopped (2 tbsp)
10 each	dry ancho chilies, chopped, stems and seeds removed
3 each	dry chipotle chiles, rough cut
3 each	ripe mangoes, peeled, seeded, and chopped (3 cups)
2 quarts	ketchup
2 cups	hoisin sauce
1 quart	Chicken Stock (page 410)
1 cup	bourbon
1 cup	cider vinegar
4 oz/wt	brown sugar
4 oz/fl	Worcestershire sauce
4 oz/fl	lemon juice (2 each)
2 tsp	ground black pepper

1. Heat the vegetable oil in a large saucepan; add the onions and caramelize. Add the garlic and cook until the raw aroma is gone.
2. Add the remaining ingredients and simmer for one hour.
3. Purée in a blender until smooth and reserve until needed. Adjust consistency with water as necessary.

Reuben Sandwich

Yield: 10 sandwiches

Mini open-faced versions of this sandwich make great hors d'oeuvre.

6 oz/wt	soft butter
20 slices	rye bread
15 oz/wt	Swiss cheese, sliced thin
$3^1/_2$ lb	corned beef brisket, sliced thin
$1^1/_2$ lb	Braised Sauerkraut (page 115)
5 oz/fl	Russian Dressing (page 30) (*optional*)

1. Butter each slice of bread. Lay slices butter-side down on a sheet pan, and top with a slice of Swiss cheese.
2. Place 2 ounces of beef on each bread slice. Top 10 sandwich halves with 2 ounces of sauerkraut, adding a tablespoon of Russian dressing if desired.
3. Preheat a sandwich griddle or frying pan to medium heat.
4. For each sandwich, transfer two sandwich halves (one with, one without sauerkraut) and griddle, butter-side down, until golden brown, and hot enough to melt the cheese.
5. Invert the sandwich half without sauerkraut top of the half with sauerkraut.
6. The sandwich may be placed in 350°F oven to heat through if needed. Cut sandwich diagonally in half and serve.

Braised Sauerkraut

Yield: 1 1/2 pounds

6 oz/wt	minced onions (5 each)
1 oz/fl	bacon fat
1 1/2 lb	prepared sauerkraut, rinsed and drained
2 tbsp	sugar
1 cup	Chicken Stock (page 410)
To taste	salt
To taste	ground white pepper

1. Sauté the onion in the bacon fat over low heat until tender and translucent. Add the sauerkraut, sugar, stock, salt, and pepper.
2. Simmer for 30 to 40 minutes, or until most of the liquid has been absorbed by the sauerkraut.
3. Check the seasoning, and adjust if necessary.
4. The sauerkraut is ready to serve now or may be refrigeraed until needed.

Pan Bagnat

Yield: 10 sandwiches

This tasty sandwich is built on excellent fresh, crusty bread. Without that key element, this recipe will produce only an ordinary sandwich.

	Dressing
3 oz/fl	red wine vinegar
1/2 oz/wt	chopped basil (1 bunch, 1/4 cup)
1/2 cup	rough-chopped Italian parsley (3/4 bunch, 1 1/2 ounces)
4 each	anchovy fillets (2 tbsp)
1 each	jalapeño, roasted, peeled, seeded, and chopped fine
1 cup	extra-virgin olive oil
10 each	hard rolls
1 lb	Tuna Confit (page 172) *or* drained oil-packed tuna, flaked
1 1/2 cups	tomato concassé (5 plum tomatoes or 10 ounces)
1 1/2 cups	Marinated Roasted Peppers (page 77)
3/4 cup	rough-chopped pitted black olives (3 ounces)
1 large	cucumber, peeled, seeded, and chopped (3/4 cup)
1/3 cup	minced red onion (2 1/2 ounces or 1 small)
2 each	hard-boiled eggs, chopped
3 tbsp	capers
4 tsp	minced garlic (4 cloves)
To taste	salt
To taste	ground black pepper

(continued on next page)

(continued from previous page)

1. Purée the vinegar, basil, parsley, anchovies, and jalapeño in a blender. With blender running, slowly pour in oil to emulsify.

2. Cut rolls in half lengthwise, and scoop out insides, leaving 1/2-inch-thick shell.

3. Crumble the removed bread and combine it with the tuna, tomatoes, peppers, olives, cucumber, onion, eggs, capers, and garlic. Add enough dressing to moisten and bind the filling. Season to taste with salt and pepper.

4. ***Sandwich Assembly:*** For each sandwich, brush a roll with some of the remaining dressing. Fill the roll with 5 ounces of the filling, and firmly press the sandwich closed. Wrap each sandwich tightly with deli paper and let rest at room temperature at least 1 hour before serving.

Pan Bagnat

Roasted Chicken and Peppers on Olive Bread

Yield: 10 sandwiches

2 1/2 lb	roasted chicken meat (two 3-pound chickens)
2 cups	Marinated Peppers and Mushrooms (page 77)
8 oz/fl	Whole-Milk Ricotta Cheese (page 299)
4 oz/fl	Mascarpone (page 298)
1 oz/wt	grated Parmesan cheese
To taste	ground white pepper
20 slices	Olive Bread (page 422)
1/3 cup	Basic Herb Oil (page 397), made with rosemary

1. Shred the chicken meat approximately batonnet size. Stir it into the peppers and mushrooms. Adjust seasoning as needed.

2. Mix together the ricotta, mascarpone, and parmesan. Season with white pepper.

3. ***Sandwich Assembly:*** For each sandwich, brush 2 slices of bread with rosemary olive oil and grill on both sides until toasted. Spread about 1 ounce cheese mixture on one slice of bread. Mound 5 ounces of chicken salad over the cheese spread and top with the second slice of bread. Cut the sandwich diagonally and serve immediately.

Presentation Idea: Accompany with a salad of tossed baby greens, fresh mozzarella cubes, diced tomato, and Basic Red Wine Vinaigrette (page 22).

Garlic-Roasted Leg of Lamb Sandwich

Yield: 10 sandwiches

3 lb	boneless leg of lamb (half a leg)
4 tbsp	olive oil
4 tbsp	slivered garlic (8 cloves)
1 tbsp	chopped fresh rosemary
$1\frac{1}{2}$ tsp	salt
$\frac{3}{4}$ tsp	coarse ground black pepper
10 each	focaccia, cut into 4-inch squares
5 oz/fl	Basic Mayonnaise (page 28) made with olive oil

1. Trim the roast and lay flat. Combine 2 tablespoons of the oil with the garlic, rosemary, salt, and pepper. Spread this mixture evenly over the roast, roll, and tie.
2. Rub roast with the remaining olive oil and marinate under refrigeration overnight.
3. Preheat the grill, and the oven to 375°F. Remove the roast from the refrigerator and let it warm slightly at room temperature for 25 to 30 minutes.
4. Sear the roast on a charcoal grill. Roast the lamb to an internal temperature of 130°F.
5. Rest the roast for 20 minutes in a warm place, then slice thinly.
6. ***Sandwich Assembly:*** For each sandwich, split a piece of focaccia horizontally and spread it with a tablespoon of the mayonnaise. Mound about 4 ounces of sliced meat on one piece of the focaccia. Close the sandwich and serve.

Presentation Idea: Hearts of Artichoke Salad (page 78) makes a great accompaniment for this sandwich, as does Mediterranean Potato Salad (page 88) and Artichoke Chips (page 393).

Salmon B.L.T.

Yield: 10 sandwiches

10 oz/fl	Basic Mayonnaise (page 28)
1 tbsp	chopped capers
To taste	salt
To taste	ground black pepper
2 oz/fl	olive oil
10 portions	salmon fillet (4 oz/wt each)
30 slices	Basic Bacon, cooked (page 163)
20 slices	bread
20 leaves	green leaf lettuce
30 slices	tomato (5 tomatoes)

1. Stir together the mayonnaise and capers. Season with salt and pepper.
2. Season the oil generously with salt and pepper.
3. ***Sandwich Assembly:*** For each sandwich, brush a salmon piece with the seasoned oil. Grill the salmon until cooked through, about 2 minutes on each side. Crisp 3 slices of bacon over medium heat, about 2 minutes. Drain briefly.
4. Toast 2 slices of bread and spread with caper mayonnaise. Place one lettuce leaf and the grilled salmon on one slice of toast. Layer it with the second lettuce leaf, bacon, and tomato. Top with remaining slice of toast. Secure sandwich with long toothpicks and cut in half.

Open-Faced Salmon B.L.T. with Aïoli Spread a toasted slice of whole-grain bread with 2 tablespoons Aïoli (page 29). Assemble the sandwich by layering the lettuce leaf, tomato, bacon, and salmon over the aïoli. Serve open-faced.

Grilled Chicken Sandwich with Pancetta, Arugula, and Aïoli

Yield: 10 sandwiches

2 1/2 oz/fl	olive oil
2 1/2 oz/wt	garlic, sliced (9 cloves)
1 tbsp	fresh thyme
3 tbsp	lemon zest (from 2 lemons)
Pinch	salt
Pinch	ground black pepper
10 each	boneless chicken breasts (4 oz/wt each)
30 slices	Pancetta (page 164), 1/8-inch thick
20 slices	sourdough bread
5 oz/fl	Aïoli (page 29)
6 oz/wt	arugula, washed and dried (1–2 bunches)

1. Combine the oil, garlic, thyme, lemon zest, salt, and pepper.
2. Pound the chicken breasts to an even thickness and marinate in the oil mixture overnight.
3. Preheat the grill, and the oven to 350°F. Lay the pancetta out on a sheet pan and place in the oven until crisp.
4. ***Sandwich Assembly:*** For each sandwich, lightly brush two slices of bread with the olive oil mixture and grill over moderate heat until golden and crispy on the outside but soft on the inside. Reserve. Grill a chicken breast until cooked through.
5. Spread some aïoli on the grilled bread. Place a few leaves of arugula, 3 slices of crispy pancetta and the chicken breast on one side of the bread. Top with the other half of bread and slice diagonally.

Presentation Ideas: In the summer serve with a Marinated Tomatoes (page 76) and in the winter with Celeriac and Tart Apple Salad (page 84).

Vegetable Burger

Yield: 10 sandwiches

1 1/2 lb	carrots
1/4 lb	celery
1/4 lb	onions
1/2 each	red pepper
1/2 each	green pepper
1/2 lb	fresh white mushrooms, chopped
1/4 lb	walnuts, ground
1/4 lb	scallions, chopped fine
2 each	eggs
To taste	sesame oil
To taste	soy sauce
To taste	Tabasco sauce
To taste	ground ginger
To taste	salt
To taste	ground black pepper
1/2 cup	matzo meal, or as needed
2 cups	cornflake crumbs, or as needed
As needed	oil for frying
10 each	soft hamburger rolls
5 oz/fl	Yogurt Sauce (see Chef's Notes)
2 cups	alfalfa sprouts

1. Preheat oven to 350°F. Grind carrots, celery, onions, and peppers through a medium die, and press out any excess liquid. Add mushrooms, walnuts, scallions, eggs, sesame oil, soy sauce, Tabasco sauce, ginger, salt, and pepper. Mix well.
2. Add enough matzo meal to firm up and bind the mixture.
3. Form a small test patty, coat in cornflake crumbs, and pan-fry. Adjust seasoning as necessary.
4. Form the remaining mixture into 10 patties of equal size. Roll in cornflakes to coat.
5. ***Sandwich Assembly:*** For each sandwich, pan-fry both sides of one vegetable burger, and finish in the oven until cooked thoroughly. Split and toast a bun; spread with sauce. Top with the vegetable burger and alfalfa sprouts. Serve immediately.

Chef's Notes: To make the Yogurt Sauce, add the juice of 2 lemons and 2 teaspoon finely minced garlic to 1 quart plain yogurt. Season with salt and pepper.

Turkey Club Sandwich

Yield: 10 sandwiches

30 slices	white Pullman bread
10 oz/fl	Basic Mayonnaise (page 28)
20 leaves	green leaf lettuce, washed and dried
20 oz/wt	roast turkey breast, sliced thin
20 oz/wt	Smoked Ham (page 159), sliced thin
20 slices	tomatoes, sliced thin (4 tomatoes)
15 strips	Basic Bacon (page 163), cut in half, cooked

1. ***Sandwich Assembly:*** For each sandwich, toast 3 pieces of toast and spread with mayonnaise. Top one piece of toast with a lettuce leaf and 2 ounces each of turkey and ham. Cover with a second piece of toast.
2. Top with 1 lettuce leaf, 2 tomato slices, and 3 half strips of bacon. Top with remaining toast, secure with 4 club frill picks, and cut into four triangles.

Soft-Shell Crab Sandwich with Rémoulade Sauce

Yield: 10 sandwiches

The crabs may be pan-fried to order, or they may be prepared in batches if necessary.

2 cups	flour
1 tbsp	Old Bay seasoning
1 tbsp	ground dry mustard
2 tsp	salt
1/4 tsp	cayenne pepper
1 qt	peanut oil, or as needed
10 each	jumbo soft-shell crabs, cleaned (page 429)
2 cups	milk
10 each	soft sandwich rolls, split
2 cups	Rémoulade Sauce (page 28)
20 each	lettuce leaves, shredded for garnish
10 each	lemon wedges

1. Combine flour, Old Bay, mustard, salt, and cayenne.
2. Heat 1 inch of peanut oil in a rondeau to 375°F.
3. ***Sandwich Assembly:*** For each sandwich, dip a crab into the milk and dredge it in the seasoned flour. Pan-fry the crab in the hot peanut oil until golden on both sides, 4 to 5 minutes total cooking time. Drain on paper towels.
4. Toast the roll and spread with 1 to 2 tablespoons of rémoulade sauce. Layer it with lettuce. Top with the crab, and close the sandwich with the top of the bun. Serve with lemon wedges.

New England Lobster Roll

Yield: 10 sandwiches

Lobster rolls are synonymous with summertime throughout New England and Long Island. The opening of roadside stands selling these luscious sandwiches is a seasonal highlight. It may seem incongruous to pair lobster with frankfurter rolls, but the combination is wonderful. Any other bread, no matter how wonderful, changes the entire character of the sandwich.

3 each	$1\frac{1}{2}$-lb Maine lobsters, cooked (page 427)
$1\frac{1}{2}$ cups	small-dice celery (3 to 4 stalks)
1 cup	Basic Mayonnaise (page 28)
1 tbsp	Dijon mustard
2 tsp	lemon juice
Pinch	salt
Pinch	ground white pepper
10 each	frankfurter rolls

1. Remove lobster meat from the shells and dice into $\frac{1}{2}$-inch pieces.
2. Combine all ingredients except rolls in a mixing bowl. Adjust seasoning.
3. ***Sandwich Assembly:*** For each sandwich, open a roll and toast on a griddle until golden brown. Fill immediately with some of the lobster salad and serve.

Eggplant and Prosciutto Panini

Yield: 10 sandwiches

This sandwich is delicious and can be easily adapted to a finger sandwich. Make sure to allow at least 3 days for the eggplant to marinate fully; it is well worth the wait.

20 oz/wt	Marinated Eggplant Filling (recipe follows)
1 cup	Ricotta Cheese (page 299)
2 tsp	chopped fresh basil
1 tsp	coarse ground black pepper
1 tsp	chopped fresh oregano
1 tsp	chopped fresh Italian parsley
1/2 tsp	salt
10 each	Italian hard rolls
5 oz/fl	oil from marinated eggplant
20 oz/wt	prosciutto, sliced thin

1. In a bowl combine ricotta cheese and seasonings and mix well. Cover and refrigerate overnight.
2. ***Sandwich Assembly:*** For each sandwich, split a roll lengthwise and brush the inside with oil from the marinated eggplant. Spread 1 ounce of herbed ricotta mixture on one half of the roll and top with 2 ounces each of eggplant and proscuitto. Top with the other half of the roll.

Marinated Eggplant Filling

Yield: approximately 1 pound

In this recipe the eggplant is not cooked, so it needs approximately three days to marinate. This allows the eggplant to completely denature and take on an almost cooked texture and flavor.

1 lb	Italian eggplant
1 tbsp	salt
2 cups	extra-virgin olive oil
3 each	garlic cloves, crushed
3 tbsp	red wine vinegar
2 tbsp	dried oregano
1 tbsp	dried basil
1 tbsp	coarse ground black pepper
Pinch	crushed red pepper flakes

1. Slice eggplant into 1/8-inch slices. Layer slices in a colander, salting each layer liberally. Let sit one hour.
2. Rinse off bitter liquid and blot slices dry with paper towels.
3. Mix remaining ingredients.
4. Toss eggplant slices in marinade; cover and refrigerate for 3 to 4 days. Stir every day.

Chef's Notes: The eggplant is ready when the flesh has become relatively translucent and no longer tastes raw.

Shrimp Open-Faced Sandwich

Yield: 30 open-faced sandwiches

30 each	shrimp (26/30 count), cooked, peeled, and deveined
3/4 cup	Green Mayonnaise (page 28)
30 slices	French bread, 1/4-inch thick, bias cut
30 each	mâche sprigs
10 each	radishes, sliced

1. Slice the shrimp in half lengthwise.
2. ***Sandwich Assembly:*** Spread 1 teaspoon green mayonnaise on each bread slice. Top with 2 shrimp halves. Garnish with a sprig of mâche, 2 radish slices, and a small dollop of green mayonnaise.

Tuna Salad Open-Faced Sandwich

Yield: 30 open-faced sandwiches

3/4 lb	Italian oil-packed tuna, drained
1/3 cup	extra-virgin olive oil
3 tbsp	balsamic vinegar
2 oz/wt	small-dice onion
3 oz/wt	small-dice celery
To taste	salt
To taste	ground black pepper
As needed	baby red leaf lettuce
As needed	baby romaine lettuce
30 each	whole wheat bread triangles
5 each	Kalamata olives, slivered
15 each	green olives, halved

1. Flake the tuna and combine with the oil, vinegar, onion, and celery. Toss lightly. Season with salt and pepper; set aside and keep cool.
2. ***Sandwich Assembly:*** Place a small piece of red leaf lettuce and a small piece of romaine on each bread triangle. Top with 1 tablespoon of tuna salad, 2 slivers of Kalamata olive, and 1 half green olive.

Curried Chicken Salad Open-Faced Sandwich

Yield: 30 open-faced sandwiches

1 lb	cooked chicken meat, cut into small dice
1 cup	small-dice celery
1 1/2 cups	Basic Mayonnaise (page 28)
2 tbsp	curry powder
To taste	salt
To taste	ground white pepper
1 head	Bibb or Boston lettuce, washed and dried
1/4 lb	butter, whipped
30 slices	French bread (1 loaf), bias cut into 1/4-inch thick slices
1/2 lb	cashews, toasted
2 each	apples, red delicious, peeled and sliced thin

1. Combine chicken, celery, mayonnaise, and curry powder; mix well. Season to taste with salt and pepper.
2. Cut the lettuce leaves to fit the bread slices.
3. ***Sandwich Assembly:*** Spread butter on the bread slices. Top with a piece of lettuce and 1 1/2 ounces chicken salad. Garnish with a cashew and 2 apple slices.

Egg Salad Tea Sandwich

Yield: 30 tea sandwiches

20 each	hard cooked eggs, chopped
1 cup	chopped celery
$1^{1}/_{2}$ cups	Basic Mayonnaise (page 28)
To taste	salt
To taste	ground white pepper
15 slices	pumpernickel bread, crusts removed

1. Combine the eggs, celery, and mayonnaise. Add salt and pepper to taste; mix well.
2. ***Sandwich Assembly:*** Spread the egg salad over half of the bread slices. Top with the remaining bread and slice each sandwich into 4 smaller square tea sandwiches.

Watercress Tea Sandwich

Yield: 30 tea sandwiches

1/2 cup	Crème Fraîche (page 303)
10 slices	white Pullman bread, 1/4-inch thick, crusts removed
3 bunches	watercress

1. ***Sandwich Assembly:*** Spread a thin layer of crème fraîche on one side of the bread slices. Place sprigs of watercress over half of the bread slices. Top with remaining bread and slice each sandwich into 3 smaller rectangular tea sandwiches.

Cucumber Tea Sandwich

Yield: 40 tea sandwiches

1 cup	Crème Fraîche (page 303)
3 tbsp	chopped dill
20 slices	white Pullman bread, 1/4-inch thick, crusts removed
4 each	European cucumbers, peeled, sliced 1/8-inch thick

1. Combine the crème fraîche and dill.

2. ***Sandwich Assembly:*** Spread one side of each bread slice with the dilled crème fraîche. Layer the cucumber slices over half of the bread slices. Top with the remaining bread and slice each sandwich into 4 smaller triangular tea sandwiches.

Deviled Ham Tea Sandwich

Yield: 40 tea sandwiches

1 lb	ham, cut into medium dice
1/2 cup	Basic Mayonnaise (page 28)
1 tbsp	prepared mustard
1 tbsp	dry mustard
1 tbsp	Worcestershire sauce
1/2 tsp	Tabasco sauce
1/4 tsp	cayenne pepper
20 slices	white Pullman bread, 1/4-inch thick, crusts removed

1. Combine all ingredients except bread in a food processor and purée until very smooth. Remove, adjust seasoning, and hold under refrigeration until ready to use.

2. ***Sandwich Assembly:*** Spread 10 bread slices with 2 ounces each deviled ham. Top with the remaining bread and slice each sandwich into 4 smaller triangular tea sandwiches.

Smoked Salmon Tea Sandwich

Yield: 40 tea sandwiches

1 cup	Crème Fraîche (page 303)
3 tbsp	chopped chives
20 slices	seedless rye bread, 1/4-inch thick
1 lb	Smoked Salmon (page 149), cut into thin slices

1. Combine the crème fraîche and chives.
2. ***Sandwich Assembly:*** Spread each slice of bread slice with the crème fraîche. Lay salmon slices over half of the bread slices and top each with the remaining bread. Using a 1 1/2-inch-diameter cutter, cut 4 rounds from each sandwich.

FIVE

Cured and Smoked Foods

The first preserved foods were most likely produced by accident. In fishing communities, fish were "brined" in sea water and left on the shore to either ferment or dry. Hunting communities and tribes hung meats near the fire to keep them away from scavenging animals, where they smoked and dried. Salted, dried, or smoked foods have added much-needed proteins and minerals to a diet that could otherwise have been woefully inadequate to keep body and soul together.

Preserved foods differ from fresh in various ways. They are saltier, dryer, and have sharper flavors. All of these attributes stem from the judicious application of some key ingredients: salt, curing agents, sweeteners, and spices.

Food preservation techniques from the most ancient to the most "high tech" are all intended to control the effects of a wide range of microbes, eliminating some and encouraging the growth of others. This is accomplished by controlling the food's water content, temperature, acidity levels, and exposure to oxygen.

Today's garde manger may be less responsible for ensuring a steady source of food intended to last from seasons of plenty through seasons of want, but the practical craft and science of preserving foods remains important, if only because we have learned to savor and enjoy hams, bacons, gravlax, confits, and rillettes. These same techniques are used to produce sausages (Chapter 6) and cheeses (Chapter 8).

This chapter explains the ingredients, methods, and processes for these preservation techniques:

- Curing and brining
- Smoking
- Drying
- Preserving in fat

The Ingredients for Preserving Foods

Salt

The basic ingredient used by the garde manger to preserve foods is salt. This common seasoning, found in virtually every kitchen and on every table, meant the difference between life and death to our ancestors, and it is still important to us from both a physiological and a culinary point of view.

Salt changes foods, by drawing out water, blood, and other impurities. In so doing, it preserves them, making them less susceptible to spoilage and rot. The basic processes in which salt plays an important role are:

- Osmosis
- Dehydration
- Fermentation
- Denaturing proteins

Osmosis

Osmosis happens without human intervention all the time, but to make use of osmosis for preserving foods, it is helpful to have a basic idea of how the process occurs. A simple definition states that osmosis is the movement of a solvent (typically water) through a semipermeable membrane (the cell walls) in order to equalize the concentration of a solute (typically salt) on both sides of the membrane. In other words, when you apply salt to a piece of meat, the fluids inside the cell travel across the cell membrane in an effort to dilute the salt on the other side of the membrane. Once there is more fluid outside the cell than in, the fluids return to the cell's interior, taking with them the dissolved salt. Getting the salt inside the cell, where it can kill off harmful pathogens, is the essence of salt-curing foods.

Dehydration

The presence of "free" water is one of the indicators of a food's relative susceptibility to spoilage through microbial action. In order to keep foods safe and appealing to eat for long periods of time, it is important to remove as much excess water as possible. Applying salt to foods can dry them effectively, since the salt tends to attract the free water, making it unavailable to microbes. Exposure to air or heat for controlled periods allows the water to evaporate, reducing the overall volume and weight of the food.

Fermentation

Substances known as enzymes feed on the compounds found in energy-rich foods, such as meats and grains. They ferment the food by breaking down the compounds in these foods into gases and organic compounds. The gases may be trapped, producing an effervescent quality in beverages, holes in cheeses, or the light texture of yeast-raised breads; or they may simply disperse, leaving behind the organic acid, as occurs when preparing sauerkraut or other pickles.

By increasing the acid levels in the food, enzymes also help to preserve foods, since most harmful pathogens can only thrive when the levels of acids are within a specific range (pH). Of course, a higher acid level also means that the food's flavor is changed, as well, making them sharper and tarter.

Left unchecked, the process of fermentation would completely break down the food. Salt is important to act as a control on this process, since it affects how much water is available to the enzymes. Like bacteria and other microbes, enzymes cannot live without water. Salt "uses up" the water and thereby prevents fermentation from getting out of hand.

Denaturing Proteins

Whenever you preserve foods, you will inevitably change the structure of the proteins found in the food. This change, known as "denaturing" the protein, involves the application of heat, acids, alkalis, or ultraviolet radiation. Simply put, the strands that make up the protein are encouraged to lengthen or coil, open or close, recombine or dissolve in such a way that foods that were once soft may become firm. Smooth foods may become grainy. Translucent foods may become cloudy. Firm foods may soften and even become liquid. Examples of these changes include preparing a ceviche from raw fish, blooming gelatin, and cooking meats.

Curing Salts: Nitrates and Nitrites

For thousands of years humans have been eating meat cured with unrefined salt. Those meats took on a deep reddish color. The reason for the color change was discovered at the turn of the twentieth century, when German scientists unlocked the mystery of how nitrates and nitrites—compounds already present in unrefined salts—cause cured meats to redden. Saltpeter, or potassium nitrate, the first curing agent to be identified as such, does not produce consistent results. And in fact, the use of saltpeter has been limited since 1975, when it was banned as a curing agent in commercially prepared cured meats.

Nitrates (NO_3) take longer to break down in cured foods than nitrites. For that reason, foods that undergo lengthy curing and drying periods must include the correct level of nitrates. Nitrites (NO_2) break down faster, making them appropriate for use in any cured item that will later be fully cooked.

The Nitrosamine Controversy

Today, we know that sodium nitrate and sodium nitrite are important elements in keeping meats safe from botulism infection. But we also know that when nitrates and nitrites break down in the presence of extreme heat (specifically, when bacon is cooked), potentially dangerous substances known as nitrosamines may form in the food.

The presence of nitrosamines in cured products has been a concern since 1956, when they were discovered to be carcinogenic. The amount of nitrosamine in any individual, like his or her cholesterol level, is influenced not only by the foods he or she eats but also the amount of nitrosamine produced by the salivary glands and in the intestinal tracts.

Bacon is a significant dietary source of nitrosamines, but bacon and other cured meats are not the only dietary source. In fact, most people ingest more nitrosamines from such items as celery, radishes, lettuce, zucchini, and potatoes. These vegetables contain a relatively higher concentration than most cured meats.

Although more than 700 substances have been tested as possible nitrate replacements, none has been identified as effective. Nitrites do pose some serious health threats when they form nitrosamines. There is little doubt that without nitrites, however, deaths from botulism would increase significantly and pose a more serious risk than the dangers associated with nitrosamines. The use of nitrates and nitrites is closely regulated. (See Table 5-1).

Table 5-1 USDA Regulations for Recommended Nitrite/Nitrate Levels in Various Meats

Product	Ingoing Nitrite Level ppm	Ingoing Nitrate Level ppm
Bacon, pumped	120 (with 550 ppm ascorbate or erythrobate)	None
Bacon, immersion cured	200 (2 lbs to 100 gal brine)	None
Cooked sausage	156 (1/4 oz to 100 lbs meat)	None
Dry and semidry sausage	625 (1 oz to 100 lbs meat dry cured)	1719 (2 3/4 oz to 100 lbs meat)
Dry cured meats	156 (1/4 oz to 100 lbs meat)	2188 (2 lbs to 100 gal brine at 10% pump)

Tinted Cure Mix, Pink Cure, and Prague Powder I

A blend of agents, also know simply as TCM, combines 94 percent sodium chloride (salt) and 6 percent sodium nitrite. It is tinted pink (by adding FD&C#3) to make it easily identifiable and thus help avoid its accidental use. When used at the recommended ratio of four ounces of TCM to each 100 pounds of meat, the meat is treated with only 6.84 grams of pure nitrite, or slightly less than .25 ounce.

Prague Powder II

Prague Powder II contains salt, sodium nitrite, sodium nitrate, and pink coloring. It is used to make dry and dry-fermented products. The longer curing and drying periods requires the presence of the nitrate in order to cure the meats safely.

Cure Accelerators: Sodium Erythorbate and Ascorbate

Both sodium erythorbate and ascorbate are cure accelerators and work together with the nitrite to enhance color development and flavor retention in cured foods. They have also been shown to inhibit nitrosamine formation in cooked bacon. Since the 1950s federal regulations have permitted a measured amount of either ascorbic acid, sodium ascorbate, or sodium erythorbate to be included in commercially prepared cured meat.

These cure accelerators do have some of the same reddening effects as nitrites and nitrates, though the effect is temporary.

More importantly, they cannot be used to substitute for nitrites or nitrates when those ingredients are called for in order to properly preserve or cure foods.

Seasoning and Flavoring Ingredients

Salt-cured foods have a harsh flavor unless some additional ingredients are added to the cure. Sugar and other sweeteners, spices, aromatics, and wines have all been used over time to create regional adaptations of hams, bacons, and preserved fish and poultry.

Sugar (Sweetener)

Sweeteners—including dextrose, sugar, corn syrup, honey, and maple syrup—can be used interchangeably in most recipes. Some sweeteners have very distinct flavors, so be certain that they will add the taste you intend. Dextrose is often called for in cures because it has the same ability to mellow the harsh salt and increase moisture as other sweeteners, without adding an extremely sweet flavor of its own. Sweeteners can:

- Help overcome the harshness of the salt in the cure
- Balance the overall flavor palette
- Counteract bitterness in liver products
- Help stabilize color in cured meats
- Increase water-retention (moisture) in finished products
- Provide a good nutrient source for fermentation

Spices and Herbs

A variety of spices and herbs are used in curing and brining processes to enhance a product's flavor and give it a particular character. Traditionally many of the sweet spices have been used, such as cinnamon, allspice, nutmeg, mace, and cardamom. These spices and spice blends are still used in many classic recipes.

In addition, ingredients such as dry and fresh chiles, infusions or essences, wines, or vinegars can be incorporated to give a contemporary appeal to cured meats, fish, and poultry. When you change a classic seasoning mix, make several tests to determine the best combinations and levels of intensity before putting anything new on your menu.

Cures and Brines

Cure is the generic term used to indicate brines, pickling or corning solutions, or dry cures. When salt, in the form of a dry cure or brine, is applied to a food, the food is referred to as cured, brined, pickled, or corned. The term *corned* is less familiar now, but derives from the fact that the grains of salt used to cure meats and other foods were likened to cereal grains, or corn, because of their size and shape. Salt brines may also be known as pickles; this is true whether or not vinegar is added to the brine.

Although unrefined salt or sea water were most likely the original cures or brines, we have learned more over time about how the individual components of cures and brines work. Refined and purified salts, sugar, and curing

Figure 5-1 Back: turkey in brine, corned beef in brine, ham in brine. Front: bacon in dry cure, pastrami in brine.

Figure 5-2 Spreading the cure on the bacon slabs.

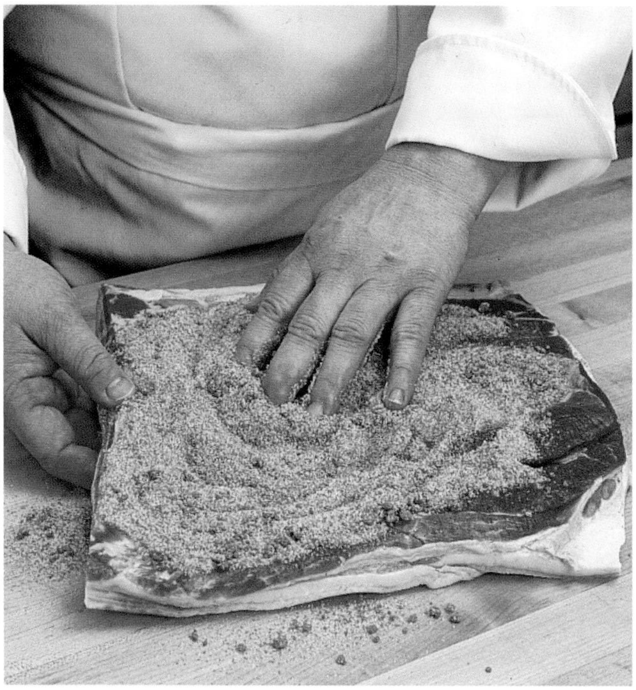

ingredients (nitrates and nitrites) have made it possible to regulate the process more perfectly. This means we can now produce high-quality, wholesome products with the best texture and taste.

Dry Cures

A dry cure can be as simple as salt alone, but more often the cure is a mixture of salt, a sweetener of some sort, flavorings, and, if indicated or desired, a commercially or individually prepared curing blend. (Brand names of some commercially prepared curing mixes include tinted curing mix, commonly referred to as TCM, and Prague Powders I and II; for resources, consult page 443.) This mixture is then packed or rubbed over the surface of the food (Figure 5-2).

Keeping the foods in direct contact with the cure helps to ensure an evenly preserved product. Some may be wrapped in cheesecloth or food-grade paper; others may be packed in bins or curing tubs with layers of cure scattered around them and in between layers. They should be turned or rotated periodically as they cure. This process is known as *overhauling.* Larger items such as hams may be rubbed repeatedly with some additional cure mixture over a period of days. (See Table 5-2 for a chart of dry curing times.) If there is an exposed bone in the item, it is important to rub the cure around and over the exposed area to cure it properly.

Table 5-2 Dry Cure Time for Meats

Item to be cured	Approximate curing time
1/4-inch-thick, approxiate	1–2 hours
1-inch-thick, approximate (lean meat)	3–8 hours
1 1/2-inch-thick pork belly	7–10 days
Ham, bone-in (15–18 lbs)	40–45 days

Brines

When a dry cure is dissolved in water, it is known as a wet cure, or a brine. As you make the brine, you may opt to use hot water, or even to bring the brine to a simmer to infuse it with spices or other aromatics. However, the brine must be thoroughly chilled before you use it to cure foods.

The brine may be applied in two different ways, depending upon the size and composition of the food you are brining. For small items such as quail, chicken breasts, or ham hocks, it is usually enough to submerge the food in the brine, a process sometimes referred to as brine-soaking.

These foods are placed in enough brine to completely cover the food, topped with a weight to keep them submerged as they cure, and allowed to rest in the solution for the required number of days (consult specific recipes for information).

Larger items, such as turkeys or hams, are injected with brine to ensure that the brine penetrates completely and evenly in a shorter period of time. (See Figure 5-3 for a diagram showing points of injection.) An amount of brine equivalent to 10 percent of the item's weight is injected into the meat. A turkey breast weighing 12 pounds, for example, requires 1.2 pounds of brine, or 19 ounces. Once the brine is injected, the product is generally submerged in a brine bath throughout the curing period. Figure 5-4 shows a turkey pumped with brine being submerged in a brine bath. See Table 5-3 for a chart of brining times.

A number of tools are used to inject brine. Syringe and continuous-feed pumps are the most popular tools for small operations. (Figure 5-5 shows a continuous-feed pump being used to brine a ham; a diagram of the pump is shown in Figure 5-6.)

Commercial operations use a variety of high-production systems. In some, vacuum pressure is used to force brine into the meat. Another process, known as artery pumping, was first introduced by a New Zealand undertaker named Kramlich in 1973. In this method, brine is injected through the arterial system. Stitch pumps inject brine by inserting a single needle into the meat at specific points. Multiple needle pumps rapidly inject meats through a large number of evenly spaced offset needles.

Table 5-3 Brining Time for Meats

Item	Not Pumped	Pumped (10% of Weight)
Chicken or duck breast	24–36 hours	Not recommended
Chicken, whole	24–36 hours	12–16 hours
Pork butt or loin (boneless)	5–6 days	2 1/2–3 days
Turkey, whole, 10–12 lbs	5–6 days	3 days
Corned brisket	7–8 days	3–5 days
Ham boneless	6 days	4 days
Ham, bone-in	20–24 days	6–7 days

Figure 5-3 Points of brine injection.

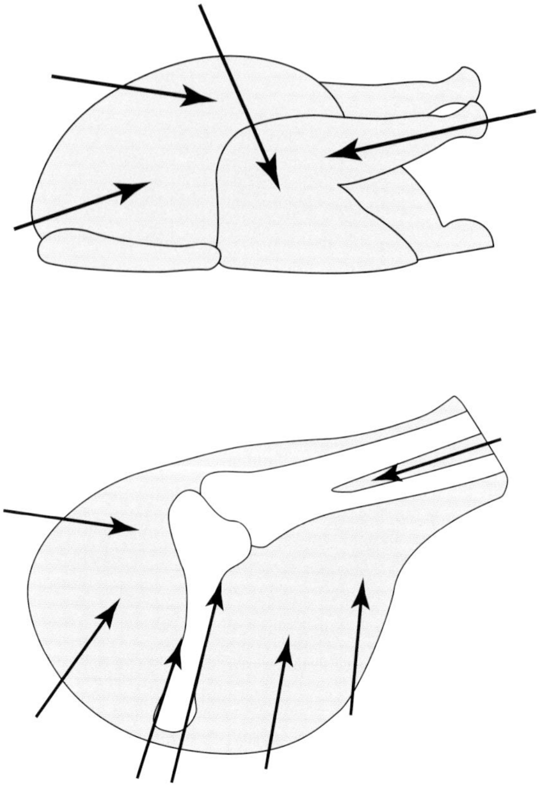

Figure 5-4 Submerging a whole turkey in brine.

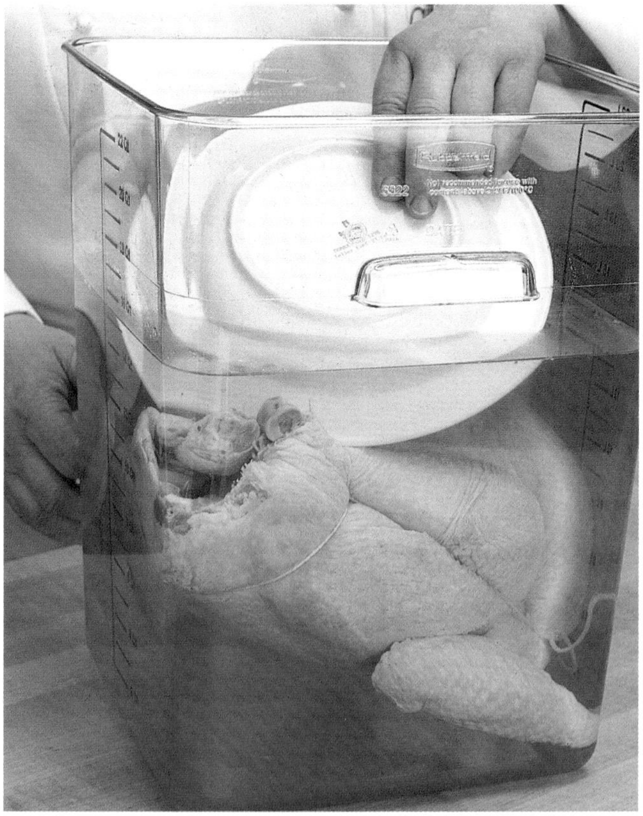

Figure 5-5 Using a continuous-feed pump to brine a ham.

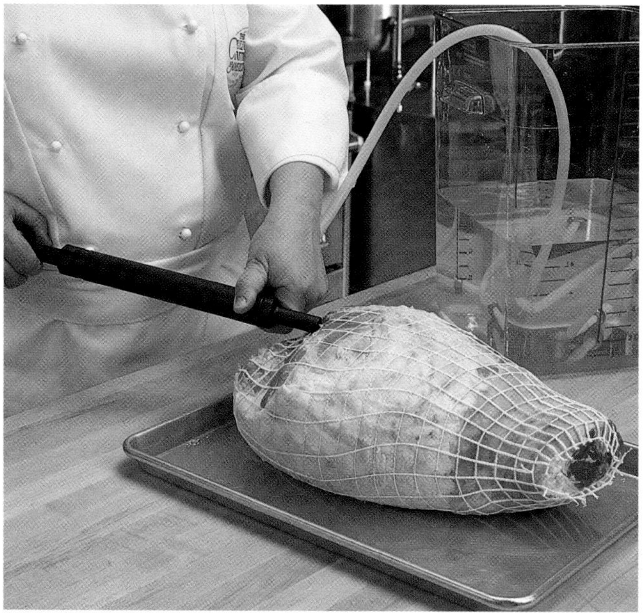

Figure 5-7 Sides of salmon in a Kookshack smoker.

Figure 5-6 The continuous-feed brine pump.

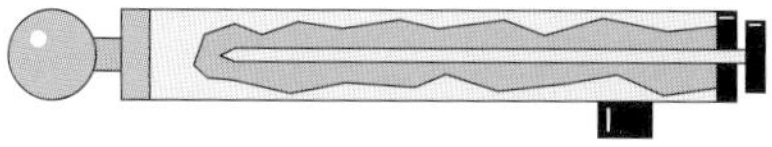

Diagram showing cutaway side view of brine pump with needle properly stored.

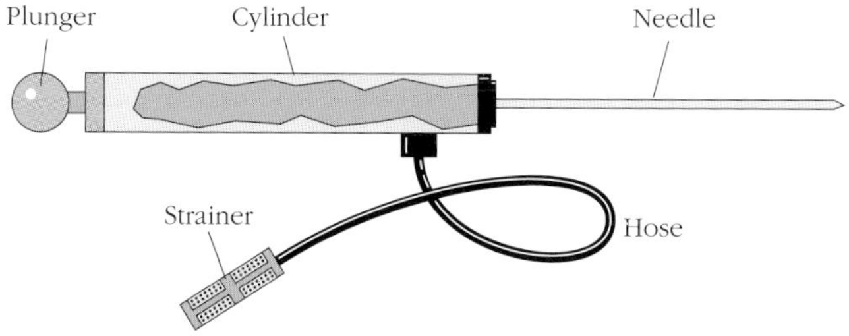

Figure 5-8 Diagram of a basic smoker.

Smoke is generated in the smoke house chamber and travels up a pipe into the smokehouse. The smokehouse has its own heating unit, air circulating fan and damper control.

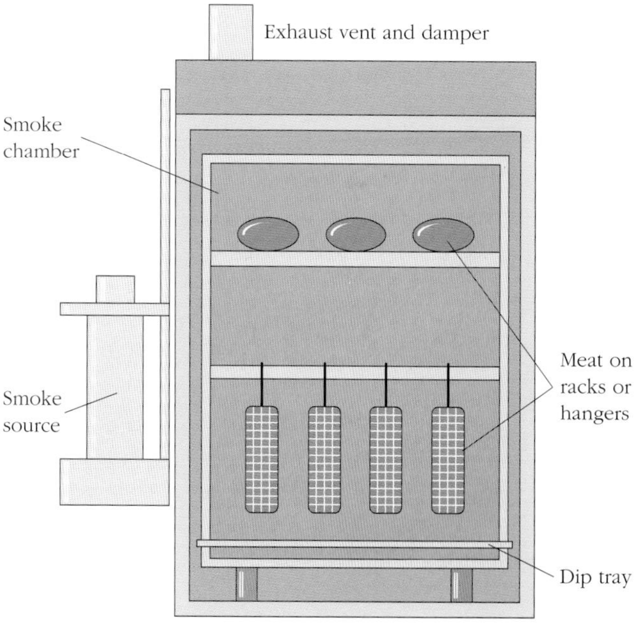

*S*moke

Smoke has been intentionally applied to foods since it was first recognized that holding meats and other provisions off the ground near the smoky fires did more than dry them more quickly or prevent animals from getting to them. The hanging foods, treated to a smokebath, took on new and enticing flavors.

Today we enjoy smoked foods for their special flavors. By manipulating the smoking process, it is possible to create a range of products, both traditional and nontraditional. Besides such perennial favorites as smoked salmon (see Figure 5-7), hams, bacon, and sausages, many unique smoked products are being featured on contemporary menus: smoked chicken salad, smoked tomato broth, even smoked cheeses, fruits, and vegetables.

Several types of smokers are available. The basic features shared by each type of smoker are a smoke source, a smoke chamber where the food is exposed, circulation, and ventilation (see Figure 5-8).

Hickory, oak, cherry, walnut, chestnut, apple, alder, mesquite, and wood from citrus trees are good choices for smoking. They produce a rich, aromatic smoke with proportionately few of the particles that make smoked foods taste sooty or bitter. Soft woods, such as pine, burn hot and fast with too much tar, making them unsuitable for smoking foods.

In addition to various hard woods, other flammable materials can be used. Teas, herb stems, whole spices, grapevine clippings, corn husks, fruit peels (such as orange and apple), and peanut shells can be added to the smoker to give a special flavor. A special smoking mixture is used to prepare Asian-Style Tea-Smoked Duck Breast (page 155).

Wood for smoking can be purchased in chunks or chips. If you use a wood-burning oven to create smoke-roasted specialties, you can use larger pieces of wood, available for purchase by the bundle, truckload, or cord. Make the effort to purchase woods from a reputable source. You should be certain that the wood is free of contaminants such as oil or chemicals. *Never* use pressure-treated wood under any circumstances—it is deadly poisonous.

Pellicle Formation

Before cured foods are smoked, they should be allowed to air-dry long enough to form a tacky skin, known as a pellicle. The pellicle plays a key role in producing excellent smoked items. It acts as a kind of protective barrier for the food, and also plays a role in capturing the smoke's flavor and color.

Most foods can be properly dried by placing them on racks or by hanging them on hooks or sticks. It is important that air be able to flow around all sides. They should be air-dried uncovered, in the refrigerator or a cool room. To encourage pellicle formation, you can place the foods so that a fan blows air over them. The exterior of the item must be sufficiently dry if the smoke is to adhere. (Figure 5-9 shows trout with the pellicle formed before smoking, and trout again after smoking.)

Figure 5-9 Smoked trout.

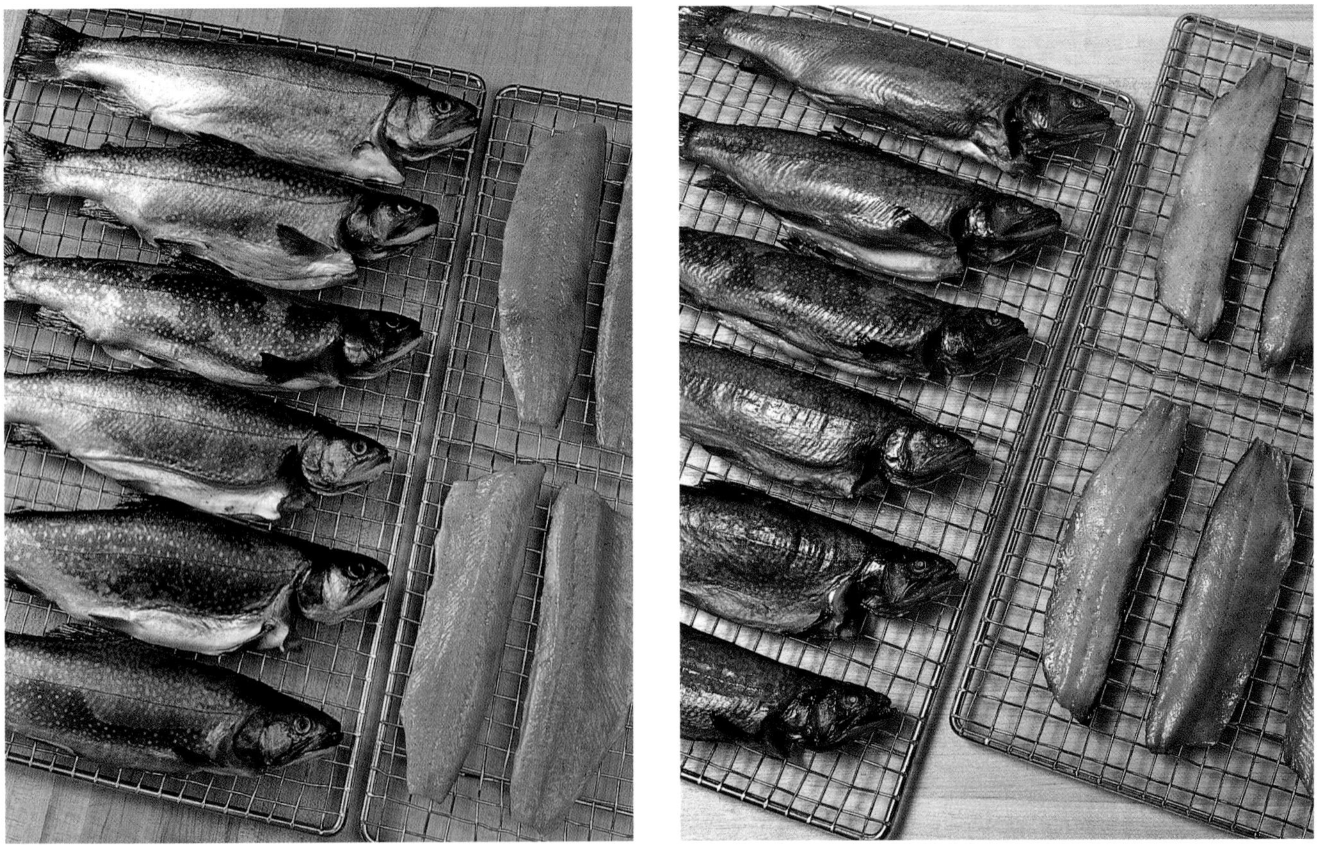

a. Pellicle has formed after curing whole and filleted trout. The fish is ready to be smoked.

b. Whole and filleted trout after smoking.

Cold Smoking

Some of the basic criteria used to determine which foods are suitable for cold smoking include the type and duration of the cure and whether or not the food will be air-dried after smoking. Smithfield hams, for example, are allowed to cold smoke for one week; after that, they are air-dried for six months to a year. But cold smoking need not be reserved just for hams that will be air-dried or salmon that has been rendered safe by virtue of the salt-cure. It can also be used to prepare foods that will be cooked by another means before they are served.

Cold smoking can be used as a flavor enhancer for items such as pork chops, beef steaks, chicken breasts, or scallops. The item can be cold smoked for a short period of time, just enough to give a touch of flavor. They are ready to be finished to order by such cooking methods as grilling, sautéing, baking, or roasting, or they may be hot smoked to the appropriate doneness for an even deeper smoked flavor.

Cheeses (see Figure 5-10), vegetables, and fruits can be cold smoked for extra and unique flavor. Typically a very small measure of smoke is best for these foods, just enough to produce a subtle change in the food's color and flavor.

Smokehouse temperatures for cold smoking should be maintained below 100°F. (Some processors keep their smokehouses below 40°F to keep foods safely out of the danger zone.) In this temperature range, foods take on a rich smoky flavor, develop a deep mahogany color, and tend to retain a relatively moist texture. They are not cooked as a result of the smoking process, however.

Keeping the smokehouse temperature below 100°F prevents the protein structure of meats, fish, or poultry from denaturing. At higher temperatures, proteins change and take on a more crumbly texture. The difference is easy to imagine: think of the difference in texture between smoked and baked salmon fillets.

Figure 5-10 Smoked cheeses: Colby, low-moisture mozzarella, and cheddar.

Figure 5-11 Top: cottage butts, pork loins. Bottom: ham hocks.

Hot Smoking

Hot smoking exposes foods to smoke and heat in a controlled environment. Although we often reheat or cook foods that have been hot smoked, they are typically safe to eat without any further cooking. Hams and ham hocks (see Figure 5-11) are fully cooked once they have been properly smoked.

Hot smoking occurs within the range of 165°F to 185°F. At this temperature, foods will be fully cooked and are moist and flavorful. If the smoker is allowed to get hotter than 185°F, your smoked foods will shrink excessively, buckle, or even split. Smoking at high temperatures will also reduce your yield, since both moisture and fat will be "cooked" away.

Smoke-Roasting

Smoke-roasting refers to any process that has the attributes of both roasting and smoking. This smoking method is sometimes referred to as barbecuing or pit-roasting. It may be done in a smoke-roaster, closed wood-fired oven or barbecue pit, any smoker that can reach above 250°F, or in a conventional oven (one you don't mind having smoky all the time) by placing a pan filled with hardwood chips on the floor of the oven so that the chips can smolder and produce a smokebath.

Pan-Smoking

It is possible to produce smoked foods even if you don't have a smoker or smokehouse. Pan-smoking is a simple and inexpensive method to give a smoke-enhanced flavor to foods in a relatively quick time. Pan-smoking requires two disposable aluminum pans, a rack, and some hardwood chips. (Figure 5-12 shows a diagram of a pan-smoker setup. Figure 5-13 shows trout in a pan-smoker.) The drawback of pan-smoking is that it is hard to control the smoke and products tend to get a flavor that is too intense and may be bitter.

Figure 5-12 Diagram of a pan-smoker setup.

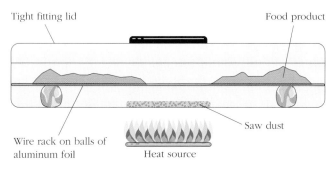

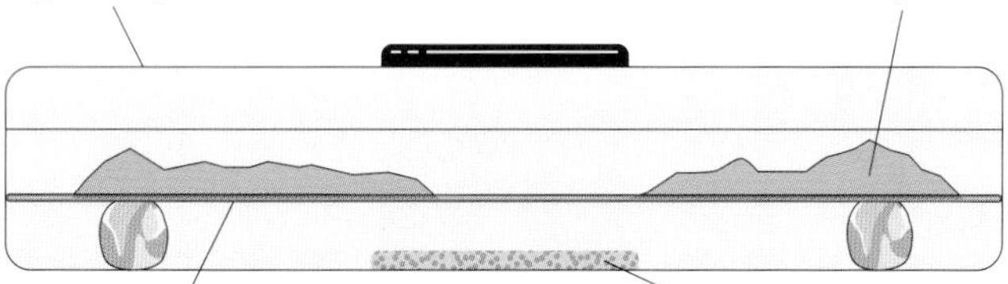

Figure 5-13 Brook trout in pan-smoker.

Drying

In addition to drying items before they are smoked to form a pellicle, you may also need to air-dry certain items in lieu of or in addition to smoking them.

Air-drying requires a careful balance of temperature and humidity control. It is important to place foods in an area where you can monitor both temperature and humidity, since dried hams may take weeks, months, or more to cure and dry properly. Be sure to learn and follow all the safe food handling precautions for foods that undergo extended drying periods. For a listing of information sources, see the Appendix on page 447.

Several world-famous hams, including Serrano ham from Spain, Smithfield ham from the United States, and prosciutto crudo di Parma from Italy, are cured, cold smoked, and then dried for an extended period, making them safe to store at room temperature and eat without further cooking (see Figure 5-14). Other products, including Roman-Style Air-Dried Beef (page 167), Bresealo, and Beef Jerky (page 166), are also preserved by drying as well (see Figure 5-15).

Figure 5-14 Air-dried hams: Serrano, Smithfield, Prosciutto di Parma.

Figure 5-15 Air-dried beefs: Roman-style, Bundnerfleisch, beef jerky.

Preserving in Fat: Confits and Rillettes

Confit and rillettes are classic methods of preserving foods. To prepare a confit of poultry or other small game animals such as rabbit and hare, the legs and other portions of the bird or animal are cured and then gently simmered in rendered fat, ideally fat from the animal itself. After this long cooking process is complete, the pieces are packed in crocks and completely covered with the fat. The fat acts as a seal, preventing the meat from being exposed to the air, which would turn it rancid.

Duck or goose confit is a traditional component of cassoulet and other long-simmered dishes based on beans. Today's chef has adapted this traditional dish to suit contemporary tastes. You will find confit prepared not only from ducks, geese, and rabbits, but also made from tuna (page 172) and red onions (page 389), allowed to stew gently in butter or oil to a rich, jamlike consistency.

Rillettes are made by stewing boned meats in broth or fat with vegetables and aromatics (see Figure 5-16). The thoroughly cooked meat is blended with fat to form a paste. This mixture is typically stored in crocks or pots, covered with a layer of fat to act as a seal, and served with bread or as a topping or filling for canapés and profiteroles.

Figure 5-16a Curing the duck with salt and spices.

Figure 5-16b Poaching cured duck in its own rendered fat.

*G*ravlax

Yield: 2 3/4 pounds; 12 to 14 servings (2 1/2 ounces each)

Fishermen in Scandinavia once prepared this salt-cured, unsmoked salmon by packing a dry cure of salt and sugar over freshly filleted salmon. They buried the fish near the stream or river, and continued in this way upstream.

Salmon fillet being covered with cure and dill.

1 each	salmon fillet, skin on (approximately 3 pounds)
2 oz/fl	fresh lemon juice (about 1/2 lemon)
1 oz/fl	Akavit or gin (*optional*)
	Cure Mix
6 oz/wt	salt
3-6 oz/wt	sugar (see Chef's Notes)
2 tbsp	cracked black pepper
3/4 oz/wt	rough chopped fresh dill (about 1 bunch)

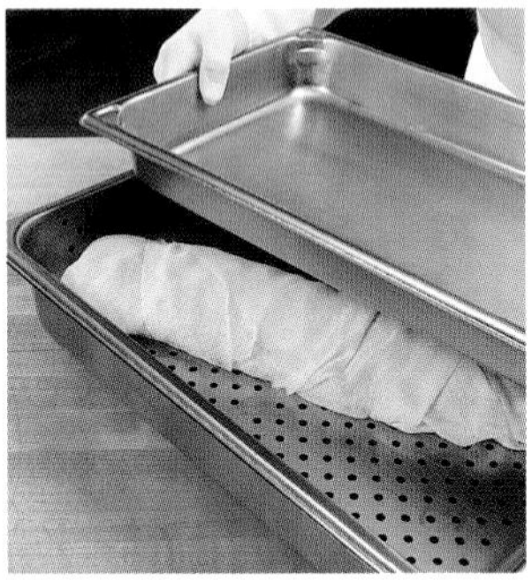

Perforated pan enables the juices to drip away from the fish.

1. Remove the pin bones from the salmon and center it skin side down on a large piece of cheesecloth. Brush the lemon juice (and Akavit or gin, if desired) over the salmon.
2. Mix the cure ingredients and pack evenly over the salmon as shown. (The layer should be slightly thinner where the fillet tapers to the tail.) Cover with chopped dill.
3. Wrap the salmon loosely in the cheesecloth and place it in a perforated hotel pan set in a regular hotel pan as shown. Top with a second hotel pan, and press with a 2-pound weight.
4. Cure the salmon under refrigeration for 3 days. After the third day, gently scrape off the cure. The salmon is now ready to slice as shown, or it may be held under refrigeration for up to 5 days.

Thinly slicing the cured salmon, holding the knife at a 30–degree angle.

Chef's Notes: Ratios of salt to sugar may range from two parts salt to one part sugar, to equal parts of each, or up to relatively sweet cures made with one part salt to one and a half to two parts sugar. Adding more sugar to any dry cure lends a moister texture and a sweeter flavor.

Southwestern-Style Gravlax Proceed as for Gravlax, substituting lime juice for the lemon juice and 1 ounce tequila for the Akavit or gin. Replace the dill with a equal amount of chopped fresh cilantro. This version can be served with Papaya Black Bean Salsa (page 36).

Norwegian Beet and Horseradish Cure

Yield: $2\frac{3}{4}$ pounds; 12 to 14 servings ($2\frac{1}{2}$ ounces each)

This is a vibrant, magenta-colored, spicy version of basic smoked salmon with a sweet-hot flavor.

1 each	salmon fillet, skin on (approximately 3 pounds)
	Cure Mix
3/4 lb	finely chopped or grated raw beets
1 lb	grated fresh horseradish
6 oz/wt	sugar
6 oz/wt	salt
2 tbsp	cracked black pepper

1. Remove the pin bones from the salmon and center it skin side down on a large piece of cheesecloth or plastic wrap.
2. Mix the cure ingredients and pack evenly over the salmon. (The layer should be slightly thinner where the fillet tapers to the tail.)
3. Wrap the salmon loosely in the cheesecloth or plastic wrap and place it in a hotel pan.
4. Cure the salmon under refrigeration for 3 days. After the third day, gently scrape off the cure.
5. The gravlax is ready for service now, or it may be wrapped and stored for up to 1 week.

Pastrami-Cured Salmon

Yield: 2 3/4 pounds; 12 to 14 servings (2 1/2 ounces each)

1 each	salmon fillet, skin on (approximately 3 pounds)
1/2 each	lemon, juice only (2 fluid ounces)
	Cure Mix
6 oz/wt	salt
3-6 oz/wt	granulated sugar
2 tbsp	cracked black pepper
1 bunch	rough chopped fresh cilantro
1 bunch	rough chopped fresh parsley
4 oz/wt	minced shallots
3 oz/fl	molasses
1 tsp	cayenne pepper
5 each	crushed bay leaves
2 tsp	crushed coriander seed
2 tsp	paprika
2 tsp	ground black pepper

1. Remove the pin bones from the salmon and center it skin side down on a large piece of cheesecloth. Brush with lemon juice.
2. Mix the cure ingredients and pack evenly over the salmon. Combine the cilantro, parsley, and shallots; pack evenly over the salmon.
3. Wrap the salmon loosely in the cheesecloth and cure under refrigeration for 3 days as shown on page 144. After the third day, gently scrape off the cure.
4. Bring the molasses, cayenne, and bay leaves to a simmer; remove from heat and cool. Brush evenly over the salmon. Blend the coriander, paprika, and black pepper. Press evenly over the salmon.
5. Rest uncovered under refrigeration for at least 12 hours before serving. The salmon may be wrapped and stored for up to 1 week.

Smoked Shrimp

Yield: $3^1/_2$ pounds

To prepare the shrimp for smoking, completely remove the shells, the tail section, and the veins. Even though it has been a standard practice to leave the tails on, removing them is more easily accomplished during kitchen preparation than by your guest. It is safer too, since there is no chance that someone might accidentally swallow a bit of shell.

5 lb	shrimp
	Basic Seafood Brine
3 1/2 oz/wt	salt
2 1/4 oz/wt	sugar
1/2 tsp	garlic powder
1/2 tsp	onion powder
1 tbsp	fresh lemon juice
2 qt	hot water

1. Peel and devein the shrimp. Place in a plastic or stainless-steel container.
2. Stir together the salt, sugar, garlic and onion powders, and lemon juice. Add the hot water and stir until the dry ingredients are dissolved. Cool.
3. Pour enough brine over the shrimp to completely submerge them. Use a plate or plastic wrap to keep them completely below the surface. Cure at room temperature for 30 minutes.
4. Remove the shrimp from the brine; rinse and blot dry. Cold smoke below 100°F for 45 minutes to an hour.
5. The shrimp are ready to grill, sauté, poach, stew in a sauce, or prepare according to other needs. Or they may be wrapped and stored for up to 1 week.

Chef's Notes: This brine can be doubled or tripled and used according to need. It can be held, covered, under refrigeration for up to two weeks. If preferred, the seafood may be pan-smoked to an internal temperature of 145°F, for about 6 to 8 minutes, and served hot, warm, or cold. This brine is also suitable for mussels, oysters, and eel.

Presentation Idea: These lightly smoked, sweet items can be used as a component of appetizers or composed salads. For an hors d'oeuvre they can be cut in half to garnish a canapé (page 327).

Smoked Scallops Four pounds of scallops may be substituted for the shrimp. The tough muscle tab should be removed before smoking.

Hot-Smoked Rainbow Trout

Yield: 30 whole trout ($6^1/_2$ ounces each after smoking)

Chef Jim Heywood, an instructor at the Institute, has been smoking fish for 20 years. He started as a hobbyist, smoking trout for himself and friends, but found that there was a market for his products. Today Jim produces his smoked trout for restaurants throughout the Hudson Valley.

30 each	rainbow trout, pan dressed (8 ounces each)
	Brine
2 gal	water
2 1/2 lb	salt
1/4 lb	dark brown sugar
1 1/2 tsp	garlic powder
1 tbsp	onion powder
1/4 cup	pickling spice
1/4 cup	honey

1. Place the trout in a deep plastic or stainless-steel container.
2. Combine water with remaining brine ingredients.
3. Pour enough brine over the trout to submerge them. Use a plate or plastic wrap to keep them completely below the surface. Cure the trout under refrigeration for 8 hours.
4. Rinse the trout in cool water and soak in fresh water for 10 minutes. Blot them dry with absorbent paper towels.
5. Hot smoke at 215°F to an internal of 145°F, or about 2 hours.
6. Cool the trout completely before serving. Smoked trout can be held covered under refrigeration for up to 2 weeks.

Presentation Idea: Fish should be filleted and boned and served 1 fillet per portion. Smoked trout fillets can be served whole as a cold appetizer with Swedish Mustard Sauce (page 383), or can be flaked into bite-sized pieces for tea sandwiches or canapés with a Horseradish Butter (page 415).

Smoked Salmon

Yield: $2\frac{3}{4}$ pounds; 12 to 14 servings ($2\frac{1}{2}$ ounces each)

Although imported smoked salmon carries a distinct cachet, there are many advantages to producing your own. With experience you can learn to control the subtleties and create a product that is not only tailored to your guests' taste, but also more profitable. Making your own can save you between 50 and 75 percent of the purchase cost of good-quality smoked salmon.

1 each	salmon fillet, skin on (about 3 pounds)
	Dry Cure
1/2 lb	salt
4 oz/wt	sugar
2 tsp	onion powder
3/4 tsp	ground cloves
3/4 tsp	ground or crushed bay leaf
3/4 tsp	ground mace
3/4 tsp	ground allspice
1/8 tsp	tinted curing mix (TCM) (*optional*)

1. Remove the pin bones from the salmon and center it skin side down on a large piece of cheesecloth.
2. Mix the cure ingredients thoroughly and pack evenly over the salmon. (The layer should be slightly thinner where the fillet tapers to the tail.)
3. Wrap the salmon loosely in the cheesecloth and place it in a hotel pan.
4. Cure the salmon under refrigeration 12 to 24 hours. Gently rinse off the cure with cool water and blot dry.
5. Air-dry uncovered on a rack under refrigeration overnight to form a pellicle.
6. Cold smoke at 100°F or less for 4 to 6 hours.
7. The smoked salmon is ready for service now, or it may be wrapped and stored for up to 1 week.

Presentation Ideas: Smoked salmon is an ideal carving item for a buffet or reception and can be served on brioche or pumpernickel croutons with a dollop of Crème Fraîche (page 303). Traditional accompaniments include capers, finely chopped onions, hard-cooked eggs, and parsley.

Basic Mayonnaise (page 28) or sour cream–based sauces flavored with caviar, mustard, or horseradish are often served with smoked salmon.

Chef's Notes: The dry cure can be doubled or tripled, if desired. Store, tightly covered, in a cool, dry area until ready to use.

•••

For additional flavor dimensions, brush salmon with a liquor such as brandy, vodka, or tequila before it is air-dried.

•••

Trim or end pieces can be used for rillettes, mousse, or cream cheese–based spreads for canapés, tea sandwiches, or bagels.

Southwest-Style Smoked Salmon

Yield: 2 3/4 pounds; 12 to 14 servings (2 1/2 ounces each)

1 each	salmon fillet, skin on (about 3 pounds)
	Southwest-Style Dry Cure
1/2 lb	salt
3 oz/wt	brown sugar
1 tbsp	dry mustard
2 tsp	ground cumin
2 tbsp	dried oregano leaves
1/2 tsp	ground allspice
1/2 tsp	ground ginger
1/2 tsp	ground nutmeg
3 tbsp	mild red chili powder
1 tbsp	paprika
2 tsp	ground white pepper
1 oz/wt	chopped fresh cilantro
2 tsp	onion powder
1 tsp	garlic powder
1/2 tsp	cayenne pepper
1/4 tsp	tinted curing mix (TCM) (*optional*)
2 oz/fl	tequila

1. Prepare the salmon and apply the cure as in step through 4 for Smoked Salmon (page 149).
2. Brush the salmon with tequila before air dry and smoking (steps 5 and 6).

Presentation Idea: This can be used as a pizza garnish with Lime-Flavored Crème Fraîche (page 303) or tossed with pasta. As an hors d'oeuvre, it can be served on tiny corn pancakes with cilantro cream.

Citrus-Scented Hot Smoked Sturgeon

Yield: 4 1/2 pounds; 24 to 30 portions (2 1/2 ounces each)

1 each	sturgeon fillet, skin on (approximately 5 pounds)
	Citrus Dry Cure
1 lb	salt
10 oz/wt	light brown sugar
1/4 cup	minced lime zest
1/4 cup	minced lemon zest

1. Remove the pin bones from the sturgeon and center it skin side down on a large piece of cheesecloth.
2. Mix the cure ingredients and pack evenly over the sturgeon. (The layer should be slightly thinner where the fillet tapers to the tail.)
3. Wrap the sturgeon loosely in the cheesecloth and place it in a hotel pan.
4. Cure the sturgeon under refrigeration overnight. Gently rinse off the cure with cool water and blot dry.
5. Air-dry uncovered on a rack under refrigeration overnight to form a pellicle.
6. Hot smoke at 160°F to an internal temperature of 145°F, or about 1 hour.
7. The smoked sturgeon is ready for service now, or it may be wrapped and stored for up to 1 week.

Chef's Notes: This sturgeon tastes great served warm right out of the smoker or at room temperature as a component of an appetizer or hors d'oeuvre. Sturgeon can be sliced thin and served warm or cold. Or substitute this for the salmon in the Smoked Salmon with Potato Galette (page 362).

Swiss-Style Smoked Salmon

Yield: 2 3/4 pounds; 12 to 14 servings (2 1/2 ounces each)

This recipe was brought to the Institute by one of our past chefs, who learned it while working at the Palace Hotel in Gstaad, Switzerland. Although it takes a little more time and is a little more expensive to produce than the basic smoked salmon, the smooth, buttery results speak for themselves.

1 each	salmon fillet, skin on (approximately 3 pounds)
	Dry Cure
1/2 lb	salt
4 oz/wt	granulated sugar
2 tbsp	coarse black pepper
1 bunch	dill, rough chopped
1 each	lemon, cut into five slices
1 each	orange, cut into five slices
1 qt	white wine, or as needed
1 qt	milk, or as needed

1. Remove the pin bones from the salmon and center it skin side down on a large piece of cheesecloth.
2. Mix the cure ingredients and pack evenly over the salmon. (The layer should be slightly thinner where the fillet tapers to the tail.) Cover the salmon with a layer of chopped dill. Lay alternating slices of lemon and orange over the dill.
3. Wrap the salmon loosely in the cheesecloth and place it in a hotel pan.
4. Cure the salmon under refrigeration 24 hours. Gently wipe off the cure and return the salmon to a clean container. Add enough cold white wine to completely cover the fillet. Marinate overnight.
5. The following day, remove the salmon from white wine. Add enough cold milk to completely cover the fillet. Marinate overnight.
6. Remove the salmon from the milk and air-dry uncovered on a rack under refrigeration for at least 8 and up to 14 hours to form a pellicle.
7. Cold smoke below 100°F for 4 to 6 hours.
8. The smoked salmon is ready for service now, or it may be wrapped and stored for up to 1 week.

Presentation Ideas: Smoked salmon should be sliced as thin as possible, as needed. This version can be used in the same manner as the basic version.

Smoked Turkey Breast

Yield: 7 pounds usable meat

2 each	turkey breasts, bone-in (12 pounds each)
	Basic Poultry Brine
$1^1/_2$ lb	salt
12 oz/wt	dextrose, honey, or white or light brown sugar
3 tsp	garlic powder (*optional*)
$1^1/_2$ tbsp	onion powder (*optional*)
7 oz/wt	tinted curing mix (TCM)
3 gal	warm water

1. Trim any excess fat from the turkey.
2. Stir together the salt, sugar, garlic and onion powders, and TCM. Add the water and stir until the dry ingredients are dissolved. Cool this brine completely.
3. Weigh the turkey breasts individually and pump 10 percent of its weight in brine evenly throughout breast as shown on page 138. Place in a deep plastic or stainless-steel container.
4. Pour enough brine over the turkey breasts to submerge them. Use a plate or plastic wrap to keep them completely below the surface. Brine 2 to 3 days under refrigeration.
5. Remove the turkey from the brine, rinse, and blot dry.
6. Hot smoke at 185°F to an internal temperature of 165°F, or about 4 hours.

Chef's Notes: Instead of hot smoking, you can opt to pan-smoke the turkey breast for approximately 1 hour and finish roasting the turkey in a 275°F oven to an internal temperature of 165°F, or about 30 minutes.

Presentation Ideas: Smoked turkey makes a great presentation on a buffet, especially if it is sliced to order in front of guests. It can also be sliced and arranged on a buffet platter with Cranberry Relish (page 387). Slice it for sandwiches or cube the meat for smoked turkey salad or Cobb Salad (page 97).

Bourbon Smoked Turkey Breast Prepare the Smoked Turkey Breast as directed above, pan–smoking the turkey for 1 hour as directed in the Chef's Notes. Bring to a simmer: 8 ounces bourbon, 4 ounces pure maple syrup, and 2 ounces brown sugar. Keep warm. Brush the turkey with this glaze two or three times during the final 30 minutes of roasting.

Smoked Duck

Yield: 6 ducks (about 85 percent of raw weight)

6 each	Pekin or Long Island ducks, 4 to 6 pounds each
	Duck Brine
12 oz/fl	Madeira
6 each	bay leaves
$1\frac{1}{2}$ tsp	fresh thyme leaves
$1\frac{1}{2}$ tsp	juniper berries
$1\frac{1}{2}$ tsp	chopped fresh sage
3 gal	Basic Poultry Brine (page 153)

1. Trim any excess fat from the ducks.
2. Combine Madeira, herbs, and spices with the basic brine.
3. Weigh each duck individually and inject with brine equal to 10 percent of its weight as explained on page 138. Place in a deep plastic or stainless-steel container. Pour enough brine over the ducks to submerge them. Use a plate or plastic wrap to keep them completely below the surface. Cure the ducks under refrigeration for 12 hours.
4. Rinse the ducks in cool water and soak in fresh water for 1 hour; blot dry. Air-dry uncovered under refrigeration for at least 8 hours or overnight.
5. Hot smoke at 185°F to an internal temperature of 165°F, or about $4\frac{1}{2}$ to 5 hours.
6. Cool the ducks completely before serving. Smoked ducks can be held, covered, under refrigeration for up to 2 weeks.

Presentation Ideas: Smoked duck can be used in numerous dishes, including hors d'oeuvre, salads, and main courses. It is featured in the Smoked Duck Malfatti Salad with Roasted Shallot Vinaigrette (page 26), Smoked Duck Mousse Canapé with Raspberry (page 329), Terrine of Foie Gras with Roasted Beet Salad and Smoked Duck Breast (page 371), and Smoked Breast of Duck Niçoise Style (page 364). It is also used as a garnish in Chilled Clear Borscht (page 58).

Asian-Style Tea-Smoked Moulard Duck Breasts

Yield: (about 90 percent of raw weight)

Asian flavors can be incorporated into duck breasts using an alternative smoke mixture that gives the duck an intriguing flavor.

6 each	boneless Moulard duck breasts, 3 1/2 lbs per double breast
1 recipe	Duck Brine (page 154)
	Smoking Mixture
1/2 cup	black tea leaves
4 oz/wt	light brown sugar
1/4 cup	dry jasmine rice
1 tbsp	Szechwan peppercorns
2 each	whole cinnamon sticks, crushed
1/2 each	orange, zest only

1. Submerge the duck breast in the brine and cure for 12 hours.
2. Combine the smoking mixture in the bottom of a disposable roasting pan. Set a rack over the smoking mixture, place the rinsed and dried cured breasts on the rack, and cover the pan tightly with a second roasting pan (see page 142).
3. Roast in a 275°F oven to an internal temperature of 165°F, or about 30 to 40 minutes.

Presentation Ideas: This style of duck can be served as part of an Asian-style appetizer platter, or served with Asian Noodle Salad (page 93) or Asian Vegetable Slaw (page 83).

Chef's Notes: The skin can be slowly rendered in a sauté pan with a few drops of water to help give a crisper finished product. For a lower-fat version, remove skin completely and reserve. Lay the reserved skin over the top during the final roasting to keep the duck from drying out.

Honey-Smoked Quail

Yield: 24 quails

These quail are flavored with a hint of honey, although they are not distinctly sweet. The quail are cold-smoked, so it is important to fully cook them by roasting, sautéing, or grilling before service.

24 each	quails ($3^{1}/_{2}$ ounces each), glove-boned (see Chef's Notes)
24 each	fresh sage leaf
24 sprigs	fresh thyme
As needed	cracked or coarse ground black pepper
	Honey Brine
1 gal	water
$^{1}/_{2}$ lb	salt
4 oz/fl	honey
4 oz/wt	dark brown sugar
$2^{1}/_{3}$ oz/wt	tinted curing mix (TCM)
2 tsp	onion powder
1 tsp	garlic powder
$^{1}/_{4}$ cup	pickling spice

1. Put 1 leaf of sage, 1 sprig of thyme, and a pinch of pepper into the cavity of each quail. Tie the quails' legs together with string to maintain shape. Place in a deep plastic or stainless-steel container.

2. Combine the water with the other brine ingredients.

3. Pour enough brine over the quail to submerge them. Use a plate or plastic wrap to keep them completely below the surface and cure under refrigeration for 8 hours or overnight. Rinse the quail and blot dry. Air-dry under refrigeration overnight to form a pellicle.

4. Cold smoke the quail at 100°F for 3 hours.

5. Grill, sauté, or roast the quail to an internal temperature of 165°F for service now, or wrap and store under refrigeration for 7 to 10 days.

Presentation Ideas: Honey-smoked quail can be used in salads, appetizers, or entrées. It is a featured garnish in Southwestern Quail Pâté en Croûte (page 268).

Chef's Notes: Glove-boned quail have the backbone, rib cage, and keel bone removed.

Smoked Ham Hocks

Yield: 35 pounds ham hocks (about 80 percent of raw weight)

The basic meat brine in this recipe may be used for all types of pork products, beef products, and other red meats. The recipes that follow show several uses for this brine.

45 lb	ham hocks
	Basic Meat Brine
3 gal	cold water
2 lb	salt
1 lb	dextrose
7 oz/wt	tinted curing mix (TCM)

1. Place the ham hocks in a deep plastic or stainless-steel container.
2. Combine the brine ingredients and mix until dissolved.
3. Pour enough brine over the ham hocks to submerge them. Use a plate or plastic wrap to keep them completely below the surface. Cure the ham hocks under refrigeration for 3 days.
4. Rinse the ham hocks in cool water and soak in fresh water for 1 hour; drain. Air-dry uncovered under refrigeration overnight.
5. Hot smoke at 185°F to an internal temperature of 150°F, or about 4 hours.
6. Cool the ham hocks completely before storing. Smoked ham hocks can be held, covered, under refrigeration for up to 6 weeks.

Chef's Notes: Smoked ham hocks are a staple in many kitchens and are a concentrated source of flavor for stews, soups, beans, braised greens, and sauerkraut.

Smoked Pork Loin

Yield: about 16 pounds (about 80 percent of raw weight)

3 each	boneless pork loins (about 7 pounds each)
1 recipe	Basic Meat Brine (page 157)

1. Cut the roasts in half if desired; tie or net them.
2. Weigh each pork loin roast individually and inject with brine equal to 10 percent of its weight. Place them in a plastic or stainless-steel container.
3. Pour enough brine over the pork loin roasts to submerge them. Use a plate or plastic wrap to keep them completely below the surface. Cure the pork loin under refrigeration for 3 days.
4. Rinse the pork loin roasts in cool water and soak in fresh water for 1 hour; blot dry. Air-dry uncovered under refrigeration for at least 16 hours.
5. Hot smoke at 185°F to an internal temperature of 150°F, or about 4 hours.
6. The pork loins are now ready for slicing and serving. They can be held, covered, under refrigeration for up to 2 weeks.

Presentation Ideas: Carve the smoked pork loin to order at a buffet station and offer it with an assortment of chutneys and relishes (see pages 384–389). It is also excellent in sandwiches and salads. Edible trim can be added to pâtés, terrines, soups, and stews.

Canadian Bacon Trim the roasts down to the eye muscle. Cut the roasts in half if desired and tie or net them. Pump with brine and cure, submerged in brine, for 2 days. Smoke and store as for smoked pork loin.

Whole Smoked Ham

Yield: 1 smoked ham, about 18 pounds (about 90 percent of raw weight)

1 each	fresh ham (pork leg roast, about 20 pounds)
1 recipe	Basic Meat Brine (page 157)

1. Trim the ham, leaving 6 inches of skin around the shank. Remove aitchbone and weigh the ham; inject with brine equal to 10 percent of its weight at the injection points illustrated below. Place it in a plastic or stainless-steel container.
2. Pour enough brine over the ham to submerge it. Use a plate or plastic wrap to keep it completely below the surface. Cure the ham under refrigeration for 7 days.
3. Rinse the ham in cool water and soak in fresh water for 1 hour; blot dry. Air-dry uncovered under refrigeration for 16 hours.
4. Hot smoke at 185°F to an internal temperature of 150°F, or about 12 hours.
5. The ham is now ready to be sliced for cold preparations, or reheated, sliced, and served hot. Ham can be held, covered, under refrigeration for up to 2 weeks.

Presentation Ideas: Smoked hams can be used in any number of ways. They can be carved on buffet lines hot, or wrapped in a brioche dough and baked for a more elegant presentation. Use smoked ham in any pâté or terrine recipes that call for ham, either as a liner or an internal garnish. The trim can be used in a variety of sandwiches and salads or used to flavor pasta dishes or soups.

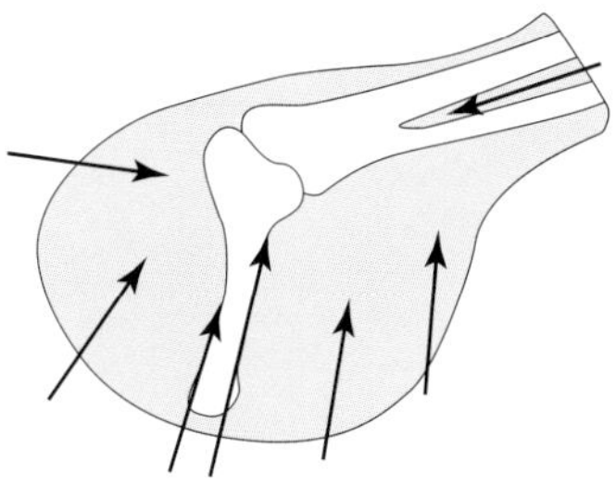

Corned Beef

Yield: 16–18 pounds fully cooked corned beef
(about 40–50 percent of raw weight)

Corned beef is a favorite slicing meat for deli-style sandwiches, and is essential to the Reuben Sandwich (page 114). Four briskets and the brine specified below will fit comfortably into a 10-gallon pail.

	4 briskets (10 to 12 pounds each)
	Corned Beef Brine
3 gal	cold water
2 lb	salt
10 oz/wt	dextrose
7 oz/wt	tinted curing mix (TCM)
6 cloves	garlic, minced to a fine paste
2 tbsp	pickling spices

1. Trim the fat cover on the briskets to 1/4 inch.
2. Combine 2 cups water with the remaining brine ingredients and purée in a blender until smooth. Combine with remaining water.
3. Weigh each brisket individually and pump brine equal to 10 percent of its weight evenly throughout the brisket (see photo).
4. Place the briskets in a deep plastic or stainless-steel container and add enough brine to submerge them. Cover with plastic wrap to keep them completely below the surface. Cure under refrigeration for 4 to 5 days.

Brining the beef with continuous pump.

Slicing the corned beef.

5. Rinse the briskets in cool water and drain thoroughly. Split along fat seam.
6. Place the briskets in a deep pot. Cover them with cool water and bring the water to a simmer. Continue to cook the brisket until fork-tender, approximately 3 hours.
7. Remove the brisket from the cooking liquid. Trim excess fat. It is now ready to carve or slice for hot or warm service (see Chef's Notes). Or cool the brisket, wrap, and hold under refrigeration for up to 2 weeks.

Chef's Notes: To rewarm cold corned beef for slicing warm, steam until heated through and slice on a machine or hand carve (see photo).

Pastrami Pastrami may be prepared from either the brisket or plate of beef. Trim exterior fat to 1/4 inch. Prepare a brisket as directed for the Corned Beef through step 5, but do not split. Mix 2 ounces *each* cracked coriander seed and black peppercorns, and coat the brisket. Cold–smoke at 100°F for 2 hours, then hot smoke at 185°F for 8 hours. The pastrami can be simmered as directed in steps 6 and 7 above, or it may be slow roasted at 300°F to an internal temperature of 150°F.

Packing on the pastrami cure.

Slicing the pastrami across the grain.

Kassler Ribchen

Yield: 2 roasts (about $7\frac{1}{2}$ pounds each)

The city of Kassel in Germany is famous for its smoked pork products. This specialty is made from the prized pork loin cut. It is one of the main components of choucroute garni, the famous dish of smoked meats and sauerkraut enjoyed throughout Germany and Alsace.

2 each	center-cut pork loins, with 10 to 11 rib bones (about 8 pounds each)
1 recipe	Basic Meat Brine (page 157)

1. Weigh each pork loin individually and inject with brine equal to 10 percent of its weight. Place them in a plastic or stainless-steel container.
2. Pour enough brine over the pork loins to submerge them. Use a plate or plastic wrap to keep them completely below the surface. Cure them under refrigeration for 3 to 4 days.
3. Rinse the pork loins in cool water and soak in fresh water for 1 hour; blot dry. Air-dry uncovered under refrigeration for 16 hours.
4. Hot smoke at 185°F to an internal temperature of 150°F, or about 5 hours.
5. The pork loins are ready now for roasting whole or slicing into individual chops for grilling, sautéing, or use in other preparations. They can be held, covered, under refrigeration for up to 2 weeks.

Basic Bacon

Yield: 45 pounds

Bacon is an example of a fully cooked smoked item that first undergoes a conventional dry curing method, based upon a standard ratio of 2 parts salt to 1 part sugar. For the most accurate results, weigh the fresh pork bellies and then determine how much of the cure mixture you will need. A useful ratio is 8 ounces of dry cure for every 10 pounds of fresh belly.

Spreading the cure on the bacon slabs.

5 each	fresh pork bellies, skin on (10 pounds each)
	Basic Dry Cure
$1\frac{1}{4}$ lb	salt
14 oz/wt	brown or white sugar
4 oz/wt	tinted curing mix (TCM)

Placing slabs in a container to marinate.

1. Weigh the pork bellies and adjust the basic cure as necessary.
2. Mix the cure ingredients thoroughly.
3. Rub the cure mix over the bellies, making sure to cover all areas. Stack in plastic or stainless-steel tubs, skin side down.
4. Cure under refrigeration for 7 to 10 days, overhauling them every other day during curing.
5. Rinse the bellies and soak them in cool water for 1 hour. Hang them on hooks and air-dry 18 hours.
6. Hot smoke at 185°F to reach an internal temperature of 150°F, or about $3\frac{1}{2}$ hours; cool. Remove rind.
7. The bacon is ready to slice or cut as required for baking, sautéing, or griddling, or for use as a flavoring in other dishes. It may be wrapped and stored under refrigeration for up to 2 weeks.

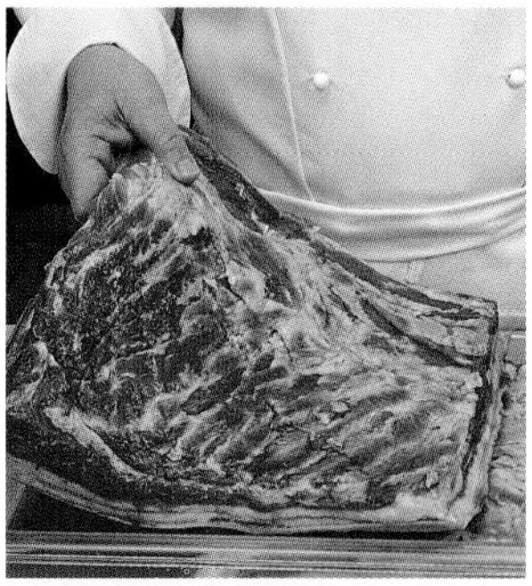

Overhauling the slabs.

Chef's Notes: Any cured belly will lose 7 to 8 percent of its water volume throughout curing and smoking.

Honey-Cured Bacon Substitute 2 cups honey for the white sugar in Basic Dry Cure (above).

Maple Sugar–Cured Bacon Substitute 2 cups maple syrup for the white sugar in Basic Dry Cure (above).

Brown Sugar–Cured Bacon Substitute brown sugar for the white sugar in Basic Dry Cure (above), and adjust salt-to-sugar ratio to 10 parts salt to 8 parts sugar.

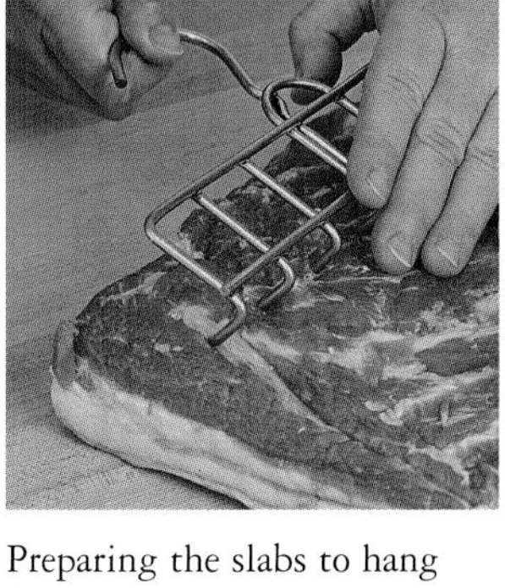

Preparing the slabs to hang dry.

Pancetta

Yield: 45 pounds

Pancetta can be prepared in a natural shape, known as stresa, *or it may be rolled into a cylinder and tied before air-drying, referred to as* arrotola.

5 each	fresh pork bellies, skin on (10 pounds each)
	Pancetta Dry Cure
2 1/2 lb	salt
10 oz/wt	brown sugar
10 oz/wt	cracked black pepper
5 oz/wt	juniper berries, crushed
20 each	bay leaves, crushed
5 tsp	grated nutmeg
5 tbsp	fresh thyme leaves
20 cloves	garlic, mashed
2 1/2 oz/wt	tinted curing mix (TCM)

1. Weigh the pork bellies and adjust the basic cure as necessary following a ratio of 8 ounces of cure for every 10 pounds of pork belly.
2. Combine the cure ingredients in a bowl and mix well.
3. Cure the bellies as for Basic Bacon (page 163) through step 4.
4. Rinse the bellies in cool water. Remove the skin.
5. Roll up into a cylinder and tie tightly if desired. Allow the pancetta to air-dry for 2 to 3 weeks in a dry, cool area.
6. The pancetta is now ready to slice as desired for sautéing or other preparations (see photo). It may be stored, well-wrapped, under refrigeration for 2 to 3 weeks.

Rolling the pancetta.

Tying the pancetta.

Pan-frying sliced pancetta.

Tasso (Cajun-Style Smoked Pork)

Yield: about 4 1/2 pounds

Tasso is a spicy cured and smoked pork butt used primarily as a flavoring ingredient in Cajun dishes such as gumbo and jambalaya. It also makes a zesty addition to pasta, rice, or forcemeats. It is featured as a flavorful garnish in the recipe for Southwestern Quail Pâté en Croûte (page 268).

1 each	pork butt (about 5 pounds)
4 oz/wt	Basic Dry Cure (page 163)
	Seasoning Mix
1/2 oz/wt	ground white pepper
1/4 oz/wt	cayenne pepper
1/2 oz/wt	ground marjoram
1/2 oz/wt	ground allspice

1. Cut cottage butt into 1-inch-thick slices across the grain.
2. Press pork pieces into the dry cure; cure for 3 hours at room temperature.
3. Rinse off the cure in cool water, drain the meat well, and blot dry.
4. Combine the ingredients for the seasoning mix, dredge the meat in it on all sides, and air-dry uncovered under refrigeration overnight.
5. Hot smoke at 185°F to an internal temperature of 150°F, or about 2 1/4 hours.
6. The tasso is ready to use now, or it may be wrapped and stored under refrigeration for up to two weeks.

Beef Jerky

Yield: 12 ounces (25 to 30 percent of raw weight)

Although once a necessary provision for those who needed lightweight, nutritious "road food," beef jerky is now enjoyed primarily for its intense, robust flavor. It makes a great snack food, and is wonderful pub or bar food. This version of beef jerky is tender enough to cut into a garnish or flavoring ingredient for sauces, pasta dishes, and salads.

3 lb	top round beef
	Jerky Cure
1/2 oz/wt	salt
1 tsp	tinted curing mix (TCM)
1 tsp	onion powder
1 tsp	garlic powder
1 tsp	ground black pepper
2 oz/fl	dark soy sauce
2 oz/fl	Worcestershire sauce

1. Cut the beef across the grain into thin strips, 1/4 × 2 × 8 inches.
2. Combine with remaining ingredients; cure meat 24 hours under refrigeration.
3. Place on lightly oiled racks and cold smoke for 2 hours at 100°F; continue to dry at 80°F for 24 hours.

Chef's Notes: Buffalo, venison, or other red game meat can be used instead of the beef. Most lean cuts, such as leg cuts, are appropriate.

Roman-Style Air-Dried Beef

Yield: 4 pounds

This mild cured beef is a specialty of Rome. It is less dry than the more traditional bresaola *of northern Italy. The following recipe was brought back to the CIA by Chef Tim Rodgers, who first sampled it in a restaurant in Rome. He noted that though it has some of the same characteristics as a cured ham, it has an unusual, mild flavor and a distinctive texture and color. (Roman-Style Air-Dried Beef is shown in Figure 5–15 on page 143.)*

5 1/2 lb	beef eye round or top round
	Marinade
3 qt	dry red wine, or as needed to cover beef
4 oz/wt	salt
1 tbsp	fresh cracked black pepper
1 tsp	red pepper flakes
2 each	bay leaves
1 sprig	fresh rosemary
1 oz/wt	Prague Powder #2
7 cloves	garlic, mashed to a paste

1. Trim the beef and place it in a deep hotel pan or other suitable container.
2. Combine all the ingredients for the marinade.
3. Pour enough marinade over the beef to submerge it. Use a plate or plastic wrap to keep it completely below the surface. Cure the beef under refrigeration for 8 days. Turn the beef at least once a day as it marinates.
4. Remove the beef from the marinade, blot dry, wrap in clean cheesecloth, and hang to dry in a cool, dry room for 4 to 5 days.
5. The beef is now ready to slice thinly and serve, or it may be properly wrapped and stored under refrigeration until ready to use. (Consult local health authorities if you have any concern about food safety and the service of this item to your guests.)

Presentation Ideas: This air-dried beef makes a great component of an antipasto or it can be served alone with crusty bread and good olive oil.

Smoke-Roasted Sirloin of Beef

Yield: 3 pounds

$3^{1}/_{4}$ lb	strip loin roast, oven-ready, tail removed
	Herb Mixture
3 cloves	garlic, minced
1 tbsp	chopped rosemary
1 tbsp	chopped thyme
2 tsp	salt
1 tbsp	ground black pepper

1. Trim roast's fat cover to $^{1}/_{8}$ inch; remove backstrap. Tie the roast to give a uniform shape.
2. Combine the ingredients for the herb mixture and spread evenly over the beef. Let the beef rest uncovered under refrigeration overnight.
3. Smoke-roast at 185°F to final internal temperature of 140°F, or about $3^{1}/_{2}$ to 4 hours.

Presentation Ideas: Smoke-roasting enhances the flavor of the meat and gives it chargrilled flavor. It can be served as an entrée or it can be cooled and sliced as a buffet item.

Chef's Notes: This dish can be pan-smoked if desired. Review the information about a pan-smoking set-up on page 142. Pan-smoke the beef for 20 to 30 minutes. Remove from the pan-smoker and finish roasting at 275°F and remove at an internal temperature of 130°F to reach a final temperature of 140°F. Since this preparation does not actually cure the meat, it should not be held for more than 3 to 4 days.

Carolina Barbecued Pork Butt

Yield: 8 to 9 pounds pulled meat

The barbecue rub given here can be used for other cuts of pork, including spareribs, loin roasts, or cottage butts. The pulled meat is featured in our BBQ Sandwich (page 113) and Carolina Barbecue Terrine (page 256).

2 each	pork butt (5 to 6 pounds each)
	Barbecue Dry Rub
1/2 cup	sweet paprika
1/4 cup	chili powder
1/8 cup	salt
1 tbsp	ground cumin
1/8 cup	sugar
1 tbsp	dry mustard
2 tsp	black pepper
2 tbsp	dried thyme
2 tbsp	dried oregano
1 tsp	cayenne pepper

1. Trim the pork butts of excess fat, leaving approximately 1/16 inch. Score the fat in a criss-cross pattern to allow spices to penetrate.
2. Combine the dry rub ingredients and rub well over all surfaces of the pork. Place on roasting racks.
3. Hot smoke at 185°F to an internal temperature of 150°F.
4. Pull meat off the pork bone and shred by hand. Remove any excess fat at this time as well.
5. The pork is ready to use in other dishes, or it may be cooled, wrapped, and stored under refrigeration for up to 7 days.

Duck Confit

Yield: 3 pounds

5–6 lb	duck legs (moulard)
	Confit Cure Mix
2–3 oz	kosher salt
1/4 cup	light brown sugar
1 tbsp	quatre épices
1 tsp	thyme leaves
2 each	garlic cloves, minced
10 each	peppercorns
1/2 tsp	tinted curing mix (TCM) (*optional*)
2 qt	duck fat
2 cups	water

Curing the duck with salt and spices.

Rinsing off the cure.

Poaching the cured duck in its own rendered fat.

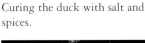

The duck confit is cooled in the fat. The excess fat is later wiped off.

1. Disjoint the duck; reserve any trim for stock or similar use.
2. Combine the cure mix ingredients; rub the duck pieces well with the cure mixture.
3. Place the duck in a stainless-steel pan, cover, and press with a weight. Let the duck cure in this manner under refrigeration for 2 to 3 days.
4. On the third day, rinse any remaining cure from duck pieces and blot dry.
5. Bring the duck fat and water to a simmer; add the duck pieces and simmer for 3 hours, or until very tender.
6. Allow the duck confit to cool to room temperature in the duck fat (see photo). Hold the confit in the fat under refrigeration. Remove it from the fat as needed and use as directed in other recipes.

Chef's Notes: The duck fat for this recipe can be the fat reserved from ducks, including the fatty skin, or you can purchase duck fat. Be sure to properly strain the duck fat so that it can be reused to make a second batch of confit.

Pork Rillettes

Yield: about 5 pounds

5 lb	pork butt, very fatty, cubed
1 lb	Mirepoix, large dice (page 404)
1 each	Standard Sachet d'Epices (page 405)
3 qt	White Beef Stock, as needed (page 410)
2 tbsp	salt, or to taste
2 tsp	ground black pepper, or to taste

1. Place the pork, mirepoix, and sachet in a heavy saucepan. Add stock almost to cover.
2. Simmer, covered, very slowly on the stove or braise in a 350°F oven until meat is cooked and very tender, at least 2 hours.
3. Lift out the pork, reserving stock and rendered fat. Discard the mirepoix and sachet. Let the meat cool slightly.
4. Transfer the meats to a chilled mixer bowl. Mix on low speed until meat breaks into pieces. Test for appropriate seasoning and consistency. Adjust consistency by adding back some of the fat and stock (consistency should be spreadable, not runny or dry). Make any adjustments before filling the mold. (Refer to seasoning and texture adjustment information on page 143.)
5. Place rillettes in a suitable mold, ladle some reserved fat over the rillettes, and allow to cool before serving. (The fat is scored for a decorative effect, as shown in the accompanying photograph.) Rillettes can be held under refrigeration for 2 to 3 weeks.

Smoked Chicken Rillettes Substitute 3 pounds cured, cold-smoked chicken leg meat and 2 pounds pork butt for the pork.
Smoked Ham Rillettes Substitute cured, cold-smoked pork butt for the fresh pork. Add mustard and cayenne pepper to the seasoning.
Duck Rillettes Substitute duck meat for the pork and add a small sprig of rosemary to the sachet.

Tuna Confit

Yield: 1 pound

2 tbsp	salt
$1^1/2$ lb	tuna (steak, belly strip, or good-sized trimmings)
	Herbed Oil
4 oz/wt	sliced yellow onion
4 each	garlic cloves, quartered lengthwise
1 each	1 fennel bulb, sliced thin
1 each	serrano chile, split lengthwise, seeded (*optional*)
4 each	basil stems, bruised
4 each	thyme sprigs, bruised
4 each	bay leaves, crushed
1 tsp	black peppercorns
3 to 4 cups	mild olive oil

1. Salt the fish liberally so there is a visible coating of salt on the surface. Small pieces should rest an hour, large pieces should rest under refrigeration overnight.
2. Put onion, garlic, fennel, chile, basil, thyme, bay leaves, peppercorns, and olive oil into a 2-quart saucepan and bring to 180°F for 20 to 30 minutes.
3. Add the salted fish and gently poach it in the oil. Watch the fish carefully; when it is barely pink in the center, remove from the vegetable oil. Adjust seasoning.
4. Cool the oil, strain if desired, and pour over the fish. Serve immediately, or hold under refrigeration.

Presentation Ideas: Use tuna confit on antipasto plates and in composed salads, such as Mediterranean with Tuna Confit Salad (page 98). It may also be eaten cold as a spread on toasted bread or crackers, or as canapés.

Chef's Notes: This is best if served immediately. It may be held under refrigeration for several days, but the delicate texture will be affected. The herbed oil mixture can be kept refrigerated for up to a week and used to flavor salads, for cooking, or to prepare more tuna confit.

Dilled Salmon Rillette

Yield: 2 pounds

1/2 lb	butter
1 lb	salmon, cut into 1-inch pieces
6 oz/fl	white wine
3 oz/wt	minced shallots
2 tsp	salt
1/4 tsp	ground white pepper
3 each	fresh dill sprigs, minced
1 tsp	lemon zest, finely chopped

1. Melt the butter in a saucepan over low heat.
2. Add the salmon, wine, shallots, salt, pepper, dill, and lemon zest; simmer slowly over very low heat for about 15 to 20 minutes.
3. Remove the pan from the heat and cool until butter begins to firm.
4. Transfer the mixture to a chilled mixer bowl. Mix on medium speed with a paddle until a smooth paste is formed.
5. Test for appropriate seasoning and consistency. Make any adjustments before placing in mold.
6. Fill desired mold(s) and store, covered, under refrigeration until needed.

Smoked Salmon Rillettes Half the salmon can be replaced with smoked salmon for a lightly smoke-flavored rillette.

SIX

Sausage

The word *sausage* comes from the Latin word *salsus,* meaning "salted," and it was in ancient Rome and Greece that some of the earliest sausages were created, from just about everything available—from nuts to dormice. In the ninth century B.C.E., Homer wrote about his famous hero Odysseus consuming sausages during his historic journey, and the ancient Egyptians were producing their own form of sausage by 641 C.E.

Lucanica sausages, produced in a part of Italy known today as Basiclicata, traveled with the conquering Romans into ancient France and whetted the Gauls' appetites for this versatile and useful food. These same long, nonsegmented, spicy smoked sausages are still eaten today, and have found a place in other cuisines as well. They are known in Portugal and Brazil as *lingucia,* and in Spain as *longaniza.*

By the Middle Ages, regional forms of sausage had begun to evolve into definite and unique forms all over Europe. Spices and herbs changed from region to region, as did the choice to smoke or dry the sausage, or leave it "fresh." Grains and potatoes were often added to extend expensive or scarce meat supplies, and some devout Christians made sausage from fish to enjoy on meatless fasting days. Even the variety of wood used to smoke sausages and other foods changed from area to area and gave subtle flavor characteristics.

The influence of nearby cultures gave further diversity to this important foodstuff. French- and German-influenced cuisines feature blood sausages, the addition of apples to flavor the sausage, and traditional "sweet" spices such as mace, allspice, and coriander. The sausages of the Mediterranean are more likely to be made from either pork or lamb, and are flavored with fennel, rosemary, and oregano.

Sausage Ingredients

Sausages are made by grinding raw meats along with salt and spices. This mixture is then stuffed into the natural or synthetic casings. The original "containers" were formed from intestines, stomachs, and other animal parts. In fact, the Italian word for sausages, *insacatta,* literally means "encased."

Main Ingredient

The sausages in this chapter are made with pork, veal, beef, lamb, venison, pheasant, chicken, and turkey. Traditionally, sausages have been made from the tougher cuts of meat from the leg or shoulder. The more exercised the muscle, the more highly developed the flavor. Any tendency toward toughness is eliminated by grinding the meat.

Meats for sausages should be trimmed, if necessary, and cut into dice or strips. When pork liver is called for in a sausage recipe, cut it into cubes before grinding. The seasonings or cure mix are tossed together with the meat before grinding.

Certified Pork

Pork sausages that undergo lengthy smoking or drying procedures but aren't cooked must be made with certified pork. This means that the pork has been treated in a way that destroys the pathogens responsible for trichinosis. You can purchase certified pork, or prepare it yourself by observing the appropriate freezing times and temperatures listed below:

Minimum temperature	Minimum freezing and holding time
5°F	20 days
-10°F	12 days
-20°F	6 days

Pack pork in containers to a depth of 6 inches.

Fat

Fat is an integral part of any delicious sausage. Today we are accustomed to foods with a reduced percentage of fat; this is true of our hamburgers and chops as well as our pâtés and sausages. While the percentage of fat considered appropriate for a forcemeat might have been as high as 50 percent in earlier formulations, today an average of 25 to 30 percent is generally preferred.

Reducing the amount of fat in a formula even further does require some additional understanding of the role each ingredient plays in a forcemeat, as well as a careful analysis of the reduced-fat version to be sure that it will fulfill your expectations as well as those of your guests. Three examples of lower-fat sausage recipes included in this book are Low-Fat Italian Sausage (page 192), Pheasant Sausage with Wild Rice (page 199), and Reduced-Fat Frankfurters (page 203).

Although all types of animal fat have been used at one time or another to produce a specialty product, you will find that most contemporary forcemeat recipes call for pork fat (jowl fat or fatback) or heavy cream.

Seasonings and Cure Mixes

The sausages in this chapter can be successfully prepared using ordinary table salt, but you can substitute other salts, such as kosher or sea salt. Be sure to weigh salt, since different salts have differing volume to weight relationships.

Sausages that are dried or cold-smoked must include either nitrate or a nitrite-nitrate combination in order to fully and safely cure the sausage. One such curing blend is available for purchase under the brand name of Prague Powder II. Hot-smoked sausages and fresh sausages do not require nitrite. If you prefer to blend your own curing agents, consult the Resource List (pages 447–449).

Sugar, dextrose, honey, and various syrups are added to the curing mixture to mellow the sausage's flavor and make the finished product moister. For more information about the role of sweeteners and curing agents, read page 136.

Spices

Spices are added to sausages as whole toasted seeds, ground, or in special blends, such as quatre épices and pâté spice. To get the most from your spices, purchase them whole whenever reasonable. Toast them in a dry pan or in the oven, and grind them just before you are ready to use them. Or, if you prefer, make larger batches of spice blends, and store them in airtight cans or jars, away from heat, light, and moisture.

Spice blend recipes can be found in Chapter 12.

Herbs

Sausage formulas often call for dried herbs. They should be handled in the same way as dried spices. When fresh herbs are necessary, be sure to rinse and dry them well before chopping. You may substitute fresh herbs for dried herbs, but the taste will be different and you must taste the sample carefully. As a general rule, you will need about 2 to 3 times more fresh herbs compared to dried herbs.

Aromatics

Many types of aromatic ingredients may be included in sausage recipes, including vegetables (especially the onion family, mushrooms, and celery), wines, and citrus zests.

Vegetables, though they may be left raw for some special formulas, are most often cooked. The cooking method and the degree of cooking has an impact on the finished flavor of the dish. Onions are generally cooked, but those cooked just until translucent and limp have a decidedly different flavor than onions that have been slowly caramelized to a deep mahogany color. Be sure to allow any cooked ingredient to cool completely before incorporating it into the sausage.

Additional aromatic flavorings and seasonings added to sausages include prepared sauces (such as Tabasco and Worcestershire), powdered onions and garlic, and stock. Highly acidic ingredients such as wines or vinegars should be added with care; too much can give the finished sausage a grainy texture.

Equipment Selection, Care, and Use

Electric meat grinders, food processors, choppers, mixers, and sausage stuffers have all but replaced the hand tools once used to make sausages and other forcemeats. These tools are certainly great for saving time and labor, but even more important, they produce sausages of superior quality to those made by the laborious process the original charcuterie and garde manger chefs knew.

Use the following guidelines:

Make sure the equipment is in excellent condition. Evaluate any machinery you use in the kitchen and consider its functionality and safety as part of a standard checklist. Are the blades sharp? Are all the safety features fully functional? Are the cords and plugs in good repair?

Make sure the equipment is scrupulously clean before setting to work. Every part of the equipment must be thoroughly cleaned and sanitized between uses. Cross contamination is a serious problem, especially for foods as highly processed and handled as sausages.

Chill any part of the machine that comes into direct contact with the sausage ingredients. Place parts into the freezer or refrigerator, or chill equipment rapidly by placing it in a sink or container of ice water (see Figure 6-1). Remember that if your sausage mixture becomes warm during production, you may need to cool both the mixture and the equipment before continuing.

Choose the right tool for the job. Do not overload your equipment. If you do not have equipment large enough to handle bulk recipes, then break the formula down into

Figure 6-1 Chilling grinder parts in ice water.

batches that your equipment can handle without straining.

Assemble the grinder correctly; novices often make the mistake of improperly setting up the blade and die assembly. Be certain that the blade is sitting flush against the die (see Figure 6-2). This cuts the food neatly, rather than tearing or shredding it.

Basic Grind Sausages

Sausages produced using the basic grind method have a medium to coarse texture. When left loose they are referred to as "bulk" sausages. Each of the following sausage types is made with the basic grind method:

- *Fresh sausages* are raw sausages that are typically pan fried, broiled, grilled, baked, or braised before serving.
- *Cooked sausages* are poached or steamed after they are shaped; they may be sliced and served cold or prepared by grilling, baking, or pan frying.
- *Smoked and dried sausages* are cold or hot smoked, then allowed to air-dry in a curing room to the desired texture; they may be prepared for service in the same way as cooked sausages. Sausages that are not fully cooked during smoking or are not fully dried must be fully cooked before serving.

Figure 6-2 Placing the blade onto the grinder with the flat part facing toward the die.

Figure 6-3 Meat-grinding dies.

a. Coarse die.

b. Medium die.

c. Fine die.

Figure 6-4 Grinding the meat.

Figure 6-5 Mixing the meat with spices and water.

1. *Grind chilled and diced meats, as well as other ingredients as required by recipe, to the desired texture.*

Meat or other foods should be cut into a size and shape that fits the feed tube (see Figure 6-4). You should not have to force foods through the tube with a tamper. When they are correctly cut, the worm will pull them evenly along without requiring you to exert undue pressure. If you have cut your food properly and it is still sticking to the sides of the feed tube, you may need to "coax" the pieces along.

If you discover that the products are not flowing smoothly through the grinder, stop immediately. This is a sign that the meat is being squeezed and torn, rather than cut cleanly. Disassemble the grinder unit, remove any obstructions, and reassemble the grinder properly.

2. *Mix the ground sausage meat(s) until it (they) become homogenous.*

Once the sausage is properly ground, it should be mixed long enough to distribute evenly the fat and lean components, as well as the spices and other seasonings. The process of mixing also continues to draw out the proteins responsible for the finished texture of the sausage.

Mixing may be done by hand with a wooden spoon. An ice bath under the mixing bowl helps keep the sausage properly chilled as you work. Add any liquids gradually, making sure that they are very cold when added.

If you are using an electric mixer, be certain that the parts that come in contact with the sausage are properly chilled. Do not overload the bowl; it is more efficient in both the short and the long run to work in smaller batches. Overloading the machine could cause an uneven mix, as well as unnecessary friction that will overheat the sausage. Depending upon the quantity of forcemeat being mixed, total mixing time should be about one to three minutes. The sausage is properly mixed when the ingredients become more homogenous. Look for a tacky appearance and a slightly sticky texture (see Figure 6-5).

3. *The sausage mixture is now ready to test, garnish, and shape (pages 181–186).*

Figure 6-6 Beef and turkey frankfurters and mortadella are divided for distribution.

Figure 6-7 Links of turkey and low-fat beef frankfurters are being poached.

Emulsion Sausages

Emulsion sausages such as frankfurters and mortadella (Figure 6-6) are made from a basic mixture referred to as 5-4-3 forcemeat, which reflects the ratio of ingredients: 5 parts trimmed raw meat to 4 parts fat (pork jowl fat) to 3 parts water (in the form of ice) by weight. Many emulsion-style sausages are poached before smoking (see Figure 6-7). If your production needs demand it, you can freeze uncooked emulsion-style sausages very successfully. Once finished, the sausages should be properly packaged, wrapped, and stored under refrigeration.

1. *Cure the meat and then grind through the fine die.*

   Meats should be trimmed of any gristle, sinew, or connective tissue. Add the cure mix (see Figure 6-8a), tossing to coat the meat evenly. The curred meat is ground through the fine plate of the meat grinder and must be kept very cold while grinding the fat. The meat and the fat should be kept separate at this point.

2. *Grind the chilled fatback through the fine grinder die.*

   The fat (jowl fat is typical) may be partially frozen after it is cubed. Grind it through a fine grinder plate and keep the ground fat well chilled until required.

3. *Chop together the ground meat and crushed ice and process until the temperature drops to below 30°F.*

   Place the meat in the bowl of a high-speed chopper or processor. Add the ice on top of the meat and start to process the mixture (see Figure 6-8b). Process until the temperature first drops below 30°F and then begins to climb up.

4. *Add the ground fat to the meat when the temperature reaches 40°F.*

   Check the temperature frequently to be sure that the mixture is within the desired temperature range (see Figure 6-8c). Add the ground fat and continue processing until the temperature is between 45°F and 50°F (see Figure 6-8d). The fat is added just at this point to form a good emulsion with the lean meat. The mechanical mixing action, as well as the friction created by the coarse ice and the effect of the salt, produces a light, almost spongy texture.

5. *Add the nonfat dry milk (and any remaining seasonings) when the temperature reaches 50°F.*

   Once the temperature nears 50°F, add the powdered nonfat dry milk. Continue to process the forcemeat until it reaches 58°F. This process requires the sausage to reach a higher temperature than other sausages and forcemeats so that the fat will liquefy enough to blend very evenly with the lean meat. The texture of an emul-

Figure 6-8 Emulsion sausage.

a. Tinted curing mixture (TCM) is essential to maintain a pink color in cured products.

b. Ice is added.

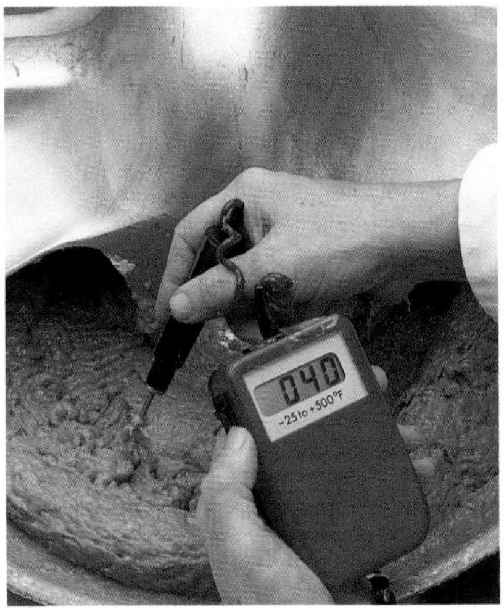

c. Temperature is carefully monitored.

d. Ground fat is added when the ground meat is 40°F.

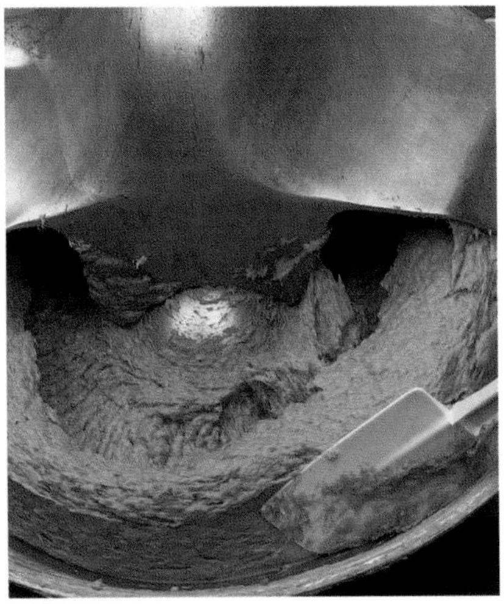

e. The edges are scraped down to ensure a homogeneous mixture.

sion sausage must be very even. To ensure the best results, scrape down the bowl as the sausage is mixed (see Figure 6-8e).

Make a test and evaluate the forcemeat before garnishing, shaping, and finishing the sausage.

Testing

You can't afford to wait until the entire batch has been made into sausage links to find out that your sausage is flavorless or has a poor texture. No matter how many times you have used a particular recipe, it is important to make a test each and every time. The quality of your ingredients, the temperature of the sausage mixture, and the condition of your equipment all play a big role in the final quality.

Test the sausage by making a small sample that has been cooked in the way that you intend the entire batch to be prepared. Taste the forcemeat test at the same temperature that you intend to serve it. Sausages in this chapter are:

- Sautéed
- Pan fried
- Oven-baked or roasted
- Grilled or broiled
- Poached in water
- Braised or stewed
- Served cold

Figure 6-9 Sausage Shaping.

a Rolling loose sausage into a cylinder with plastic wrap.

b Wrapping patties in caul fat.

Garnishing

Some sausage recipes may call for a garnish. Usually, the garnish item is diced and added to the forcemeat after it has been tested and adjusted. Cheeses, vegetables, cured or smoked meats, nuts, and dried fruits are all examples of garnishes that can be added to sausages. Add the garnish by folding it into the base mixture in the electric mixer, if desired, or working by hand over an ice bath.

Sausage Shaping

Sausage meat may be used either in bulk (loose) form, made into patties, or stuffed into natural or synthetic casings and then formed into links, loops, spirals, or other special shapes (see Figure 6-9a and b).

Loose or Bulk Sausages

To shape bulk sausage into a roll, place about 1 pound of the sausage on a square of plastic wrap. Roll it up, and twist the ends to form a solid log (see Figure 6-9a). Once rolled, the sausage can be sliced into patties. Bulk sausage can also be shaped into patties (see Figure 6-9b) and wrapped in caul fat if desired.

Sausages in Casings

Various types of casings, both natural and synthetic, are available today. Natural casings are made from the intestines and stomach of sheep, hogs, and cattle. Synthetic casings are made from a variety of food-grade materials, some edible and some not. They may be colored, lined with herbs, or netted (see Figure 6-10).

Figure 6-10 Assortment of synthetic casings.

Hog and sheep casings are shown in Figure 6-11a. Beef casings are made from various parts of the intestines: middle, round, and bung (see Figure 6-11b). The diameter of each type of casing varies. Individual links are typically made from lamb, sheep, or hog casings. Larger sausages are made using beef middles or bungs. (See Figure 6-12 for casing charts.)

Figure 6-11 Natural casings.

a. Left: hank of hog casings; right: hank of sheep casings.

b. Left: set of beef middles; right: hank of beef rounds; bottom: beef bung.

Figure 6-12 Casing charts.

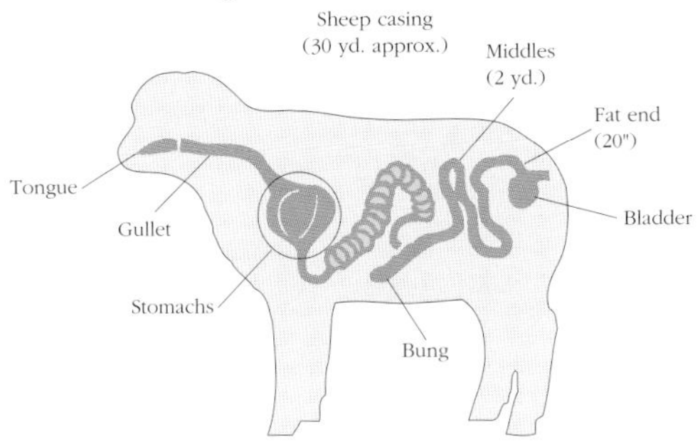

Items	Size	Length	Capacity	Comments/Uses
Sheep casing	18 mm and less	100 yds./hank	38-41 #	Cocktail franks
Sheep casing	24-26 mm	100 yds./hank	60-64 # (4 ft. per #)	Pork Sausage, Frankfurters Andouille
Sheep casing	28 mm and up	100 yds./hank	65-70 #	

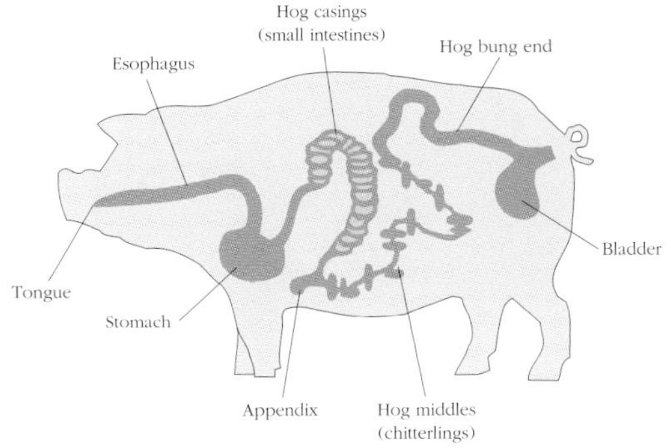

Items	Size	Length	Capacity	Comments/Uses
Hog casing (small intestine)	32-35 mm	100 yds./hank	105-115 # (2 ft. per #)	Country–style and Pork Sausage, Large Frankfurters, Pepperoni
Hog middles (middle of intestine)	4 in.	13 ft. 27 ft. set		
Hog bung end	2 in. and up	4 ft. long		
Sewed hog bungs	4 in. wide	36 inches long	$8^{1}/_{2}$-$9^{1}/_{2}$	Salami, Liverwurst Casings

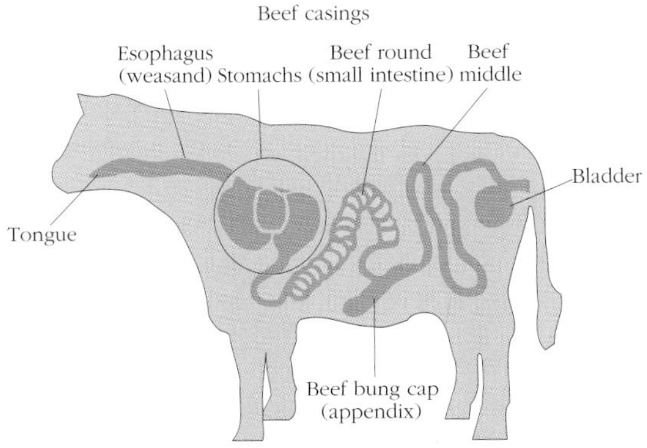

Items	Size	Length	Capacity	Comments/Uses
Beef round	43-46 mm (tight curl)	100 ft. per set	75-80 # (15"/per #)	Ring Liver, Ring Bologna, Sausage Kielbasa, Blood and Mettwurst Holsteiner
Beef middle (large intestine)	60-65 mm	57 ft. per set	70-80 # (9"/per #)	Lyoner–style Sausages and other types of Bologna, dry and Semi–dry Cervelats, Dry and Cooked Salami, Kishka (stuffed derma), and Veal Sausage
Beef bung cap (appendix)	120 mm	23-27 in.	17-20 #	Capicolla, Large Bologna Lebanon and Cooked Salami

Figure 6-13 Preparing natural casings.

a. Rewinding casings into smaller units.

b. Storing casings in salt.

c. Pushing water through the casing. The ends of each strand are hung over the edge of the bowl to help prevent tangling.

d. Casings are measured and cut into lengths. A bubble knot is tied.

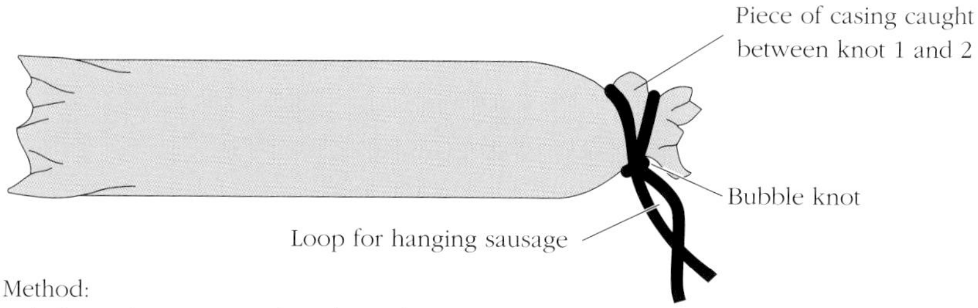

Method:

1. Cut casing to proper length, wash casing
2. Tie first knot (tight), tie second knot, catch a piece of casing in the knot
3. Tie third knot to lock first two knots, stuff and tie remaining end in same manner

e. Tying a bubble knot.

Preparing Natural Casings

1. Rewind the casings and store covered in salt. Lay out the casings and remove any knots. Form into bundles of the required length. If you will be holding the casings for a few days, store them covered with salt (see Figure 6-13a and b).

2. Before using the casings, rinse them thoroughly in tepid water, forcing the water through the casing to flush out the salt (see Figure 6-13c). Repeat this step as often as necessary to remove all traces of salt and any other impurities.

3. Cut the casing into lengths if necessary (consult specific recipes) and tie a bubble knot in one end of the casing (see Figure 6-13d).

Figure 6-14 Diagram of a sausage stuffer.

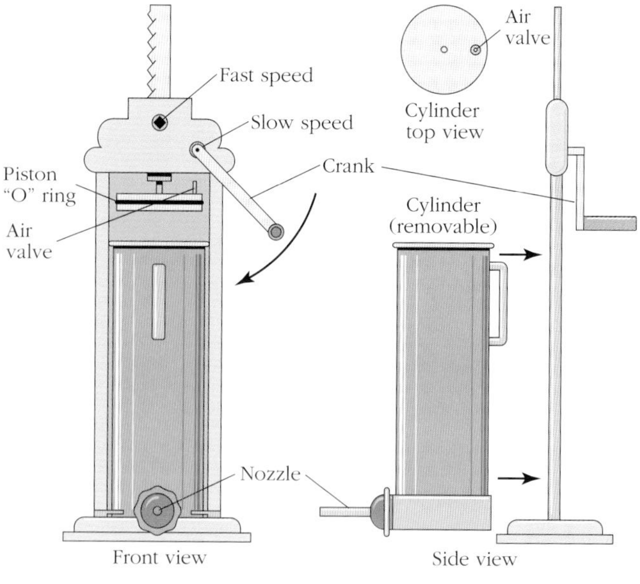

Figure 6-15 Stuffing the casing.

a. Casings are fitted on the end of the stuffer tube and gently drawn forward as they fill with sausage.

b. Pinching the links.

c. Twisting the links.

d. Tying links for smoked sausage.

Stuffing the Casing

The following method describes the procedure for filling sausage casings using a sausage-stuffing machine (see Figure 6-14).

1. Assemble and fill the sausage stuffer properly. Keep the nozzle of your stuffer as well as the work table lubricated with a bit of water as you work to prevent the casing from sticking and tearing.

   Be sure that all parts of the sausage stuffer that will come in contact with the forcemeat are clean and chilled. Fill the stuffer with the sausage meat, tamping it down well to remove any air pockets.

2. Press the sausage into the prepared casing. Gather the open end of the casing over the nozzle of the sausage stuffer. Press the sausage into the casing (if you are using a hand stuffer or piping the sausage into the casing, slide the open end over the nozzle of the hand stuffer or over the tip of the pastry bag). Support the casing as the forcemeat is expressed through the nozzle and into the casing (see Figure 6-15a).

3. Twist or tie the sausage into the appropriate shape. If the sausage is to be made into links, use either of the following methods: Press the casing into links at the desired intervals (see Figure 6-15b) and then twist the link in alternating directions for each link (see Figure 6-15c), or tie the casing with twine at the desired intervals (see Figure 6-15d).

Other typical sausage shaping methods are shown in Figures 6-16a and b. Larger sausages should be secured with a second bubble knot, to allow the sausage to expand as it cooks.

After the sausage has been formed into links, loops, or other shapes, pierce the casing with a teasing needle, sausage maker's knife, or similar tool (see Figure 6-17) to allow the air bubbles to escape.

Figure 6-16 More tying.

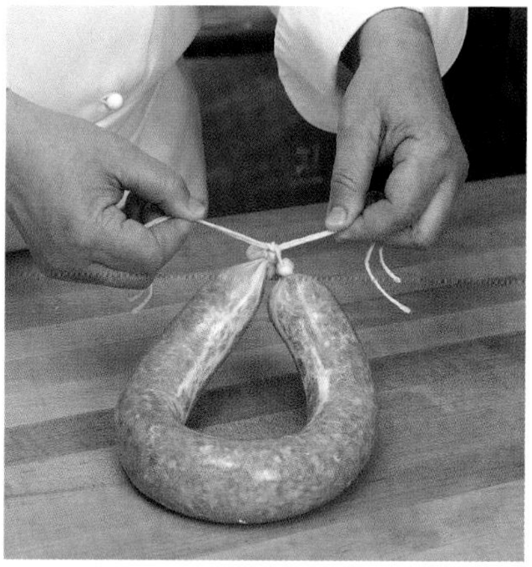

a. Tying the end of kielbasa.

b. Tying the end of a summer sausage.

c. Four types of sausages, clockwise from top right: beef middle for kielbasa, beef bung for summer sausage, sheep casings for Italian sausage, hog casings for bratwurst.

Figure 6-17 Poking air holes with a teasing needle.

Breakfast Sausage

Yield: 11 pounds bulk; 88 links (2 ounces each)

Breakfast sausage is a very basic fresh sausage, commonly shaped into bulk, 2-ounce patties, or links. Sheep casings are the most common choice for links, but they can be made in hog casings for larger sausages.

10 lb	boneless pork butt, cubed (70% lean, 30% fat)
	Seasonings
2 3/4 oz/wt	salt
2/3 oz/wt	ground white pepper
1/3 oz/wt	poultry seasoning
2 cups	ice-cold water
42 feet	sheep casings, rinsed *(optional)*

1. Toss the pork butt with the combined seasonings. Chill well.
2. Grind through the fine plate (1/8 inch) of a meat grinder into a mixing bowl over an ice bath.
3. Mix on low speed with mixer's paddle attachment for 1 minute, gradually adding water.
4. Mix on medium speed for 15 to 20 seconds, or until the sausage mixture is sticky to the touch.
5. Make a test. Adjust seasoning and consistency before shaping into patties, cylinders, or filling casings and shaping into individual 5-inch links.
6. The sausage is ready to prepare for service now by pan frying, baking, grilling, or broiling to an internal temperature of 150°F, or hold under refrigeration for up to 7 days.

Smoked Breakfast Sausage Add 1/3 ounce tinted curing mix to the seasoning mixture. Stuff into sausage casings; pinch and twist into 5-inch links. Dry overnight under refrigeration and cold smoke for 1 hour. Prepare for service as directed above.

Mexican Chorizo

Yield: 11 pounds bulk; 88 links (2 ounces each)

Mexican chorizo is often left loose and used as an ingredient in soups, bean dishes, or as a filling for omelets and soft tortillas.

10 lb	boneless pork butt, cubed (70% lean, 30% fat)
	Seasonings
2 1/2 oz/wt	salt
3/4 cup	ground dried chiles
1/4 cup	Spanish paprika
5 tbsp	minced garlic, sautéed and cooled
5 tsp	*each* ground cinnamon, oregano, thyme, cumin, black pepper
2 1/2 tsp	*each* ground cloves, ginger, nutmeg, coriander, bay leaf
6 oz/fl	red wine vinegar
42 feet	sheep casings, rinsed *(optional)*

1. Toss the pork butt with the combined seasonings. Chill well.
2. Grind through the medium plate (1/4 inch) of a meat grinder into a mixing bowl over an ice bath.
3. Mix on low speed for 1 minute, gradually adding red wine vinegar a little at a time.
4. Mix on medium speed for 15 to 20 seconds, or until the sausage mixture is sticky to the touch.
5. Make a test. Adjust seasoning and consistency before shaping into patties, or filling casings and shaping into individual 5-inch links.
6. The sausage is ready to prepare for service now by pan frying, baking, grilling, or broiling to an internal temperature of 150°F, or hold under refrigeration for up to 7 days.

Spanish Chorizo

Yield: 7 1/2 pounds; 46 links (4 ounces each)

This sausage is commonly used in paellas and to flavor other dishes. Like other dry sausage recipes in this book, certified pork (page 176) should be used. Although it is often used as an ingredient in cooked dishes, chorizo can be served cold as an appetizer or bar food. See Chapter 5, page 135 for the USDA regulations on dry-curing sausages.

10 lb	boneless certified pork butt, cubed (70% lean, 30% fat)
	Seasonings
3 1/2 oz/wt	salt
2 tsp	Prague Powder II
2 tbsp	dextrose
3 1/2 tbsp	sweet Spanish paprika
3 1/2 tbsp	chili powder
1 tbsp	cayenne pepper
6 oz/wt	Fermento
3 tbsp	garlic powder
23 feet	hog casings, rinsed

1. Toss the pork butt with the combined seasonings. Chill well.
2. Grind through the medium plate (1/4 inch) of a meat grinder into a mixing bowl over an ice bath.
3. Mix on low speed for 1 minute. Mix on medium speed for 15 to 20 seconds, or until the sausage mixture is sticky to the touch. Make a test. Adjust seasoning and consistency before shaping.
4. Stuff into prepared hog casings and shape into 4-inch links.
5. Hang on smoke sticks and dry 3 days at 70°F to 75°F with 70 to 80 percent humidity. Then dry for 15 to 18 days at 50°F to 55°F at 60 to 70 percent humidity.
6. The sausage may be served now, or wrap and hold under refrigeration for up to 3 weeks.

Green Chile Sausage

Yield: $11\frac{1}{2}$ pounds bulk; 46 links or patties (4 ounces each)

10 lb	boneless pork butt, cubed (70% lean, 30% fat)
	Seasonings
$3\frac{1}{2}$ oz/wt	salt
6 tbsp	chili powder
5 tsp	*each* cumin, sweet Spanish paprika, oregano, basil
$1\frac{1}{2}$ tsp	onion powder
6 each	garlic cloves, minced
5 tsp	Tabasco sauce
12 oz/wt	poblano chiles, roasted, seeded, peeled, and cut into $\frac{1}{8}$-inch dice (7 each)
3 each	jalapeños, seeded and minced
12 oz/fl	ice-cold water
21 feet	hog casings, rinsed

1. Toss the pork butt with the combined seasonings. Chill well.
2. Grind through the fine plate ($\frac{1}{8}$ inch) of a meat grinder into a mixing bowl over an ice bath.
3. Mix on low speed for 1 minute, gradually adding poblano chiles, jalapeños, and ice water. Mix on medium speed for 15 to 20 seconds, or until the sausage mixture is sticky to the touch. Make a test. Adjust seasoning and consistency before filling the prepared casings and shaping into 4-inch links.
4. The sausage is ready to prepare for service now by pan frying, baking, grilling, or broiling to an internal temperature of 150°F, or hold under refrigeration for up to 7 days.

Smoked Green Chile Sausage Add $\frac{1}{4}$ ounce tinted curing mix (TCM) to the seasonings. Cold smoke at 80°F for 2 hours, then cut apart into separate links.

Venison Sausage

Yield: 9 pounds bulk; 70 links (2 ounces each)

Venison sausage makes excellent use of less tender cuts and trim from the shoulder or leg. These sausages can be used to add another dimension to a main course featuring prime cuts such as loin or chops. This not only allows you to be more creative but lowers costs at the same time.

5 lb	boneless venison shoulder, cubed
1 1/2 lb	boneless pork butt, cubed
1 1/2 lb	fatback, cubed
	Seasonings
2 1/2 oz/wt	salt
1 1/4 oz/wt	dextrose
3 3/4 oz/wt	onion powder
2 3/4 tsp	ground black pepper
2 tsp	crushed juniper berries
1/2 tsp	garlic powder
2 tbsp	minced sage
12 oz/fl	Venison Stock (page 410), cold
32 feet	sheep casings, rinsed

1. Toss the venison, pork butt, and fatback with the combined seasonings. Chill well.
2. Grind through the fine plate (1/8 inch) of a meat grinder into a mixing bowl over an ice bath.
3. Mix on low speed for 1 minute, gradually adding cold venison stock a little at a time. Mix on medium speed for 15 to 20 seconds, or until the sausage mixture is sticky to the touch. Make a test. Adjust seasoning and consistency before filling prepared casings and shaping into 5-inch links.
4. The sausage is ready to prepare for service now by pan frying, baking, grilling, or broiling to an internal temperature of 150°F or hold under refrigeration for up to 7 days.

Smoked Venison Sausage Add 1/3 ounce tinted curing mix (TCM) to the seasoning mixture. Stuff into sausage casings and shape into 5-inch links. Twist them and cut into individual links. Dry overnight under refrigeration and cold smoke for 1 hour. Prepare for service as directed above.

Sweet Italian Sausage

Yield: 11 pounds bulk; 44 links (4 ounces each)

10 lb	boneless pork butt, cubed (70% lean, 30% fat)
	Seasonings
3 oz/wt	salt
1 oz/wt	dextrose
1 oz/wt	coarse ground black pepper
1 oz/wt	whole fennel seeds
1/4 oz/wt	sweet Spanish paprika
2 cups	ice-cold water
23 feet	hog casings, rinsed

1. Toss the pork butt with the combined seasonings. Chill well.
2. Grind through the coarse plate (3/8 inch) of a meat grinder into a mixing bowl over an ice bath.
3. Mix on low speed for 1 minute, gradually adding water.
4. Mix on medium speed for 15 to 20 seconds, or until the sausage mixture is sticky to the touch. Make a test. Adjust seasoning and consistency before shaping.
5. Stuff into prepared casings and twist into 5-inch links. Cut into individual links.
6. The sausage is ready to prepare for service now by pan frying, baking, grilling, or broiling to an internal temperature of 150°F, or hold under refrigeration for up to 7 days.

Hot Italian Sausage Replace the fennel seeds and sweet paprika with 4 ounces of the Hot Italian Spice Blend (page 409).

Italian Sausage with Cheese Grind 2 pounds cubed provolone cheese, 1 pound cubed Parmesan cheese, and 1 ounce chopped parsley along with the pork in step 2. This recipe makes approximately 50 links weighing 4 1/2 ounces each. Or cut the casings into 15-inch lengths and coil into a spiral as shown on page 186. Secure the spiral with a 6-inch skewer and bake or broil before serving.

Low-Fat Italian Sausage Trim all the exterior fat from the pork butt. Grind 4 cups of well-cooked rice pilaf along with the pork in step 2. May be seasoned as desired with sweet or hot spice blends.

Smoked Italian Sausage Add 1/3 ounce tinted curing mixture (TCM) to the cubed pork, before grinding. Cold smoke the sausages at 80°F for 2 hours. Since the sausages are cold smoked, they must be fully cooked before service as directed above.

Greek Sausage (Loukanika)

Yield: 12 pounds bulk; 64 patties (3 ounces each)

Traditionally made with lamb and scented with orange peel, this makes a wonderful grilled or roasted sausage. Pork can be substituted for lamb if desired.

10 lb	lamb shoulder, cubed
	Seasonings
3 oz/wt	salt
4 oz/wt	minced orange peel
1/4 oz/wt	ground black pepper
1 tsp	ground bay leaves
1 tsp	ground allspice
1 tsp	crushed red pepper
1 tsp	cayenne pepper
1/3 cup	chopped flat-leaf parsley
1 tbsp	chopped oregano
1 1/2 tsp	chopped thyme
20 oz/wt	minced onion, sautéed and cooled
1 1/2 tsp	minced garlic, sautéed and cooled
10 oz/fl	ice-cold water
2 1/2 lb	caul fat (*optional*)

1. Toss the lamb with the combined seasonings; chill well. Grind through the fine plate (1/8 inch) of a meat grinder into a mixing bowl over an ice bath.
2. Mix on low speed for 1 minute, gradually adding water. Mix on medium speed for 15 to 20 seconds, or until the sausage mixture is sticky to the touch. Make a test. Adjust seasoning and consistency before shaping.
3. Portion sausage meat into patties of approximately 3 ounces. *Optional:* Wrap each patty in a piece of caul fat and fold edges over sausage.
4. The sausage is ready to prepare for service now by pan frying, baking, grilling, or broiling to an internal temperature of 150°F, or hold under refrigeration for up to 7 days.

Merguez

Yield: 11 pounds bulk; 30 links (6 ounces each)

7 lb	lean lamb trim, cubed
3 lb	fatback, cubed
	Seasonings
3 oz/wt	salt
5 tsp	sugar
1 tbsp	Quatre Épices (page 406)
1 1/2 tsp	crushed red pepper flakes
1/4 cup	minced garlic, sautéed and cooled
1 1/2 lb	roasted red peppers, peeled, seeded, and cut into small dice
8 oz/fl	dry red wine
8 oz/fl	ice-cold water
38 feet	sheep casings, rinsed

1. Toss the lamb and fatback with the combined seasonings. Chill well.
2. Grind through the medium plate (1/4 inch) of a meat grinder into a mixing bowl over an ice bath.
3. Mix on low speed for 1 minute, adding red wine a little at a time. Mix on medium speed for 15 to 20 seconds, or until the sausage mixture is sticky to the touch.
4. Make a test. Adjust seasoning and consistency before shaping.
5. Stuff into prepared casings and twist into 15-inch links. Cut into individual links. Make a spiral with each link and secure with a 6-inch skewer.
6. The sausage is ready to prepare for service now by pan frying, baking, grilling, or broiling to an internal temperature of 150°F, or hold under refrigeration for up to 7 days.

German Bratwurst

Yield: 11 pounds bulk; 44 links (4 ounces each)

10 lb	boneless pork butt, cubed (70% lean, 30% fat)
	Seasonings
3 oz/wt	salt
1 1/2 oz/wt	rubbed sage
3/4 oz/wt	ground white pepper
1/8 oz/wt	ground celery seed (about 1/2 teaspoon)
1/8 oz/wt	ground mace (about 1/2 teaspoon)
2 cups	ice-cold water
22 feet	hog casings, rinsed and tied at one end

1. Toss the pork with the combined seasonings. Chill well.
2. Grind the pork through the fine plate (1/8 inch) of a meat grinder into a chilled mixing bowl.
3. Mix on low speed for 1 minute, gradually adding water. Mix on medium speed for 15 to 20 seconds, or until the sausage mixture is sticky to the touch. Make a test. Adjust seasoning and consistency before shaping.
4. Stuff into prepared casings and twist into 5-inch links.
5. Poach the sausages in simmering water (165°F) 15 to 18 minutes to an internal temperature of 150°F, then shock in an ice-water bath to an internal temperature of 60°F.
6. The sausage is ready to prepare for service now by sautéing, grilling, broiling, or baking just until hot, or wrap and hold under refrigeration for up to 7 days.

Chef's Notes: Smaller bratwurst may be made using sheep casings and twisting the sausages into 4-inch lengths.

Smoked Bratwurst Add 1/3 ounce (2 teaspoons) tinted curing mix (TCM) to the seasonings. Do not separate the sausages into links until after cold smoking at 80°F for 2 hours. Cook the sausage as directed above before serving.

Szechwan-Style Sausage

Yield: 8 pounds bulk; 46 links (4 ounces each)

See Chapter 5, page 135, for the USDA regulations for dry-curing sausages.

11 lb	boneless pork butt, cubed (70% lean, 30% fat)
	Seasonings
2 oz/wt	salt
2 tsp	Prague Powder II
4 oz/wt	sugar
2 oz/wt	chili powder
1 tsp	ground white pepper
2 tbsp	Chinese Five-Spice Powder (page 405)
1/2 oz/wt	Szechwan peppercorn powder
1/2 cup	soy sauce
2 1/2 oz/fl	white liquor or vodka
23 feet	hog casings, rinsed and tied at one end

1. Toss the pork butt with the combined seasonings, soy sauce, and liquor. Chill well.
2. Grind through the medium plate (1/4 inch) of a meat grinder into a mixing bowl over an ice bath.
3. Mix on low speed for 1 minute, then mix on medium speed for 15 to 20 seconds, or until the sausage mixture is sticky to the touch. Make a test. Adjust seasoning and consistency before shaping.
4. Stuff into prepared casings and twist into 8-inch links. Cut into individual links.
5. Dry for 3 days.
6. Poke small holes in the casing. Steam to an internal temperature of 150°F, about 15 minutes. The sausage is ready to prepare for service now by sautéing, grilling, broiling, or baking just until hot, or wrap and hold under refrigeration for up to 7 days.

Cajun-Style Sausage

Yield: 11 pounds bulk; 88 links (2 ounces each)

10 lb	boneless pork butt, cubed (70% lean, 30% fat)
	Seasonings
3 oz/wt	salt
2 1/2 tsp	tinted curing mix (TCM)
2 tbsp	onion powder
2 tbsp	hot Hungarian paprika
2 tbsp	dried oregano
4 tsp	coarse ground black pepper
4 tsp	ground white pepper
4 tsp	garlic powder
2 tsp	cayenne pepper
2 cups	ice-cold water
44 feet	sheep casings, rinsed

1. Toss the pork butt with the combined seasonings. Chill well.
2. Grind through the coarse plate (3/8 inch) of a meat grinder, then the fine plate (1/8 inch), into a mixing bowl over an ice bath.
3. Mix on low speed for 1 minute, gradually adding water.
4. Mix on medium speed for 15 to 20 seconds, or until the sausage mixture is sticky to the touch. Make a test. Adjust seasoning and consistency before shaping.
5. Stuff into prepared casings and twist into 6-inch links. Cut into individual links.
6. Refrigerate the sausages uncovered overnight on paper towel-lined trays to form a pellicle.
7. Cold smoke at 80°F for 4 to 5 hours.
8. The sausage is ready to prepare for service now by pan frying, baking, grilling, braising, or broiling to an internal temperature of 150°F, or hold under refrigeration for up to 7 days.

Kassler Liverwurst

Yield: 16 sausages (1 pound each)

6 lb	boneless pork butt, cubed
4 lb	pork liver
2 lb	jowl fat, cubed
	Seasonings
4 oz/wt	salt
1/2 tsp	tinted curing mix (TCM)
2 tsp	ground white pepper
2 tsp	Pâté Spice (page 408)
4 oz/wt	onions, minced
12 oz/wt	potato starch
8 oz/fl	dry white wine
12 each	whole eggs
1 lb	small-dice boiled ham
1 cup	pistachio nuts, blanched, peeled, and halved
16 pieces	beef middle casings, rinsed, cut in 12-inch lengths and tied at one end

1. Grind the pork through the coarse plate (3/8 inch) of a meat grinder.
2. Grind the pork with the liver through the medium plate (1/4 inch) of a meat grinder, then the fine plate (1/8 inch).
3. Grind the jowl fat through the fine plate (1/8 inch) of a meat grinder into a chilled mixing bowl.
4. Blend the meat, liver, and fat with the combined seasonings, onions, and potato starch in a mixer on low speed, about 1 minute.
5. Add the wine and eggs and mix on low speed for 1 minute, or until relatively homogenous. Mix on medium speed for 15 to 20 seconds, or until the sausage mixture is sticky to the touch. Make a test. Adjust seasoning and consistency before garnishing and shaping.
6. Fold the ham and pistachio nuts into the forcemeat by hand over an ice bath.
7. Stuff into prepared casings and tie ends with a bubble knot.
8. Poach at 165°F to an internal temperature of 150°F, then shock and blot dry.
9. Cold smoke at 80°F for 2 to 4 hours, or until desired color.
10. The sausage is ready to prepare for service now by poaching, sautéing, grilling, or baking, just until hot, or wrap and hold under refrigeration for up to 1 week.

Smoked Pheasant Sausage

Yield: 11 pounds bulk; 85 links (2 ounces each)

3 each	pheasants (3 pounds each)
3 lb	fatback, cubed
	Seasonings
3 oz/wt	salt
1 tbsp	tinted curing mix (TCM)
1 oz/wt	sugar
1/2 oz/wt	ground white pepper
1/2 oz/wt	poultry seasoning
1 tbsp	onion powder
12 oz/fl	ice-cold water or stock
44 feet	sheep casings, rinsed

1. Remove the meat from the breast and legs and cut into cubes. (You should have 7 pounds of meat.) Toss pheasant with the fatback and the combined seasonings. Chill well.
2. Grind through the medium plate (1/4 inch) of a meat grinder into a mixing bowl over an ice bath.
3. Mix on low speed for 1 minute, gradually adding water. Mix on medium speed for 15 to 20 seconds, or until the mixture is sticky to the touch. Make a test. Adjust seasoning and consistency before shaping.
4. Stuff into prepared casings and twist into 5-inch links. Cut into individual links.
5. Refrigerate uncovered overnight on paper towel-lined trays to form a pellicle.
6. Cold smoke at 80°F for 1 to 2 hours.
7. The sausage is ready to prepare for service now by poaching, sautéing, baking, or grilling to an internal temperature of 165°F, or wrap and hold under refrigeration for up to 2 weeks.

Pheasant Sausage with Wild Rice: Reduce the amount of fatback to 2 1/2 pounds. Add 1 cup cooked wild rice to the meat after it has been ground, before the second mixing in step 3.

Andouille Sausage

Yield: 8 pounds bulk; 25 links (8 ounces each)

6 1/4 lb	boneless pork butt, cubed (70% lean, 30% fat)
	Seasonings
2 1/4 oz/wt	salt
1/4 oz/wt	tinted curing mix (TCM)
1/2 oz/wt	dextrose
4 oz/wt	nonfat dry milk powder
2 1/2 tbsp	cayenne pepper
1 tsp	ground mace
1 tsp	ground allspice
1 tsp	ground marjoram
3/4 tsp	ground thyme
1/4 tsp	ground cloves
1 1/4 lb	onion, chopped coarse
1 1/4 oz/wt	minced garlic
32 feet	sheep casings, rinsed

1. Toss the pork butt with the combined seasonings. Chill well.
2. Grind through the fine plate (1/8 inch) of a meat grinder into a mixing bowl over an ice bath.
3. Mix on low speed for 1 minute or until the sausage mixture is sticky to the touch. Make a test. Adjust seasoning and consistency before shaping.
4. Stuff into prepared casings and tie into 10-inch links. Do not cut. Refrigerate uncovered overnight on paper towel–lined trays to form a pellicle.
5. Cold smoke at 80°F for 12 to 14 hours. Allow the sausages to dry in a cool, dry area or curing room for an additional 12 to 24 hours.
6. The sausage is ready to prepare for service now by poaching, sautéing, grilling, or baking just until hot to an internal temperature of 150°F, or wrap and hold under refrigeration for up to 2 weeks.

Summer Sausage

Yield: 7 pounds bulk; 6 links (18 ounces each)

3 1/2 lb	boneless beef shoulder clod, cubed
3 lb	boneless pork butt, cubed
	Seasonings
2 oz/wt	salt
3 oz/wt	Fermento
2 tsp	tinted curing mix (TCM)
1 1/4 oz/wt	dextrose
1/4 oz/wt	ground black pepper
1/4 oz/wt	ground coriander
1/4 oz/wt	ground mustard
1 tsp	garlic powder
6 pieces	beef middle casings, rinsed, cut in 10-inch lengths and tied at one end

1. Grind the beef through the medium plate (1/4 inch) of a meat grinder. Chill if necessary.
2. Toss the beef and pork with the combined seasonings and mix thoroughly. Transfer to a container, cover with plastic wrap, and cure in a 38°F to 40°F refrigerator for 2 to 3 days.
3. Grind the meat through the fine plate (1/8 inch) of a meat grinder into a bowl over an ice bath. Mix on low speed for 1 minute. Mix on medium speed for 15 to 20 seconds, or until the sausage mixture is sticky to the touch. Make a test. Adjust seasoning and consistency before shaping.
4. Stuff into casings, tying with bubble knot. Refrigerate uncovered overnight on paper-towel lined trays to form a pellicle.
5. Cold smoke at 80°F for 12 to 14 hours. Hot smoke at 160°F to an internal temperature of 150°F. Dry 1 to 2 hours in a smoker.
6. The sausage is ready to slice and serve now, or wrap and hold under refrigeration for up to 2 weeks.

Landjäger

Yield: 7 2/3 pounds bulk; 25 links (4 3/4 ounces each)

See Chapter 5, page 135, for the USDA regulations for dry-curing sausages.

7 1/2 lb	beef
5 lb	certified pork butt, trimmed (see Chef's Notes)
	Seasonings
4 1/2 oz/wt	salt
3 oz/wt	Fermento
1/2 oz/wt	Prague Powder II
2 tsp	ground caraway seeds
1 oz/wt	dextrose
3/4 oz/wt	ground black pepper
1 1/2 tsp	garlic powder
5 oz/fl	ice-cold water
12 feet	hog casings, rinsed and tied at one end

1. Toss the beef and certified pork with the combined seasonings. Chill well.
2. Grind through the fine plate (1/8 inch) of a meat grinder into a mixing bowl over an ice bath.
3. Mix on low speed for 1 minute, gradually adding water, until the sausage mixture is sticky to the touch. Make a test. Adjust seasoning and consistency before shaping.
4. Stuff into prepared hog casings and twist into 6-inch links. Cut at every other twist to separate into pairs of links.
5. Press in landjäger press (see Chef's Notes).
6. Place on a plastic sheet pan, cover with another plastic sheet pan, press with 2 cutting boards, and refrigerate for 2 to 4 days.
7. Cold smoke at 80°F for 12 to 24 hours, then dry until desired firmness, 3 to 4 days.

Chef's Notes: This is a dry-type sausage and is not cooked, so the pork used must be certified to prevent trichinosis. Certified pork may be purchased, or you can certify it yourself by freezing the pork at the appropriate temperature for a prescribed period (see page 176).

• • •

A landjäger press is used to shape the sausage. The press is typically made of a hard wood and is approximately 18 to 20 inches long. There is a rectangular well in the center of the mold, about 1 inch wide and 3/4 inch deep. Once the sausage is stuffed into the casing, the links are laid into the mold and then covered with plastic wrap. Weight the sausages by setting 2 wooden cutting boards on top of the press. This creates the typical rectangular shape of landjäger sausages.

Frankfurter

Yield: 12 1/2 pounds bulk; 80 links (2 1/2 ounces each)

"The noblest of all dogs is the hot-dog: it feeds the hand that bites it."—Laurence J. Peter

5 lb	boneless beef shoulder clod, cubed
4 lb	jowl fat cubed, partially frozen
3 lb	crushed ice
	Cure Mix
3 1/4 oz/wt	salt
2 tsp	tinted curing mix (TCM)
3/4 oz/wt	dextrose
	Spice Blend
1/2 oz/wt	onion powder
1/4 oz/wt	ground white pepper
1/4 oz/wt	ground coriander
1/4 oz/wt	ground nutmeg
1/2 tsp	garlic powder
5 1/2 oz/wt	nonfat dry milk powder
50 feet	sheep casings, rinsed

1. Toss the beef with the cure mix; chill well. Grind through the fine plate (1/8 inch) of a meat grinder.
2. Grind the jowl fat through the fine plate; reserve.
3. Transfer the ground beef to a chilled chopper bowl. Add the ice and the spice blend on top of the ground beef. Process the ingredients until the mixture drops to a temperature of 30°F. Continue running the machine until the mixture's temperature rises to 40°F.
4. Add the jowl fat and process until the mixture reaches 45°F. Add the milk powder and continue processing until the mixture reaches 58°F. Make a test. Adjust seasoning and consistency before shaping.
5. Stuff into prepared casings, twist and tie into 6-inch links. Refrigerate the frankfurters uncovered overnight on paper towel-lined trays to form a pellicle.
6. Hot smoke at 160°F until desired color is achieved, approximately 45 minutes. Poach in simmering water at 165°F to an internal temperature of 150°F, about 10 to 20 minutes, then shock in ice water to an internal temperature of 60°F. Blot dry.
7. The sausage is ready to prepare for service now by sautéing, grilling, broiling, or baking just until hot, or wrap and hold under refrigeration for up to 7 days.

Reduced-Fat Frankfurters For lower-fat frankfurters, increase the amount of meat by 2 pounds and decrease the amount of fat by 2 pounds. If desired, other combinations of pork, veal, or beef may be used.

Bologna

Yield: 12 1/2 pounds bulk; 16 links (1 1/2 pounds each)

5 lb	boneless beef shoulder clod, cubed
4 lb	jowl fat, cubed, partially frozen
3 lb	crushed ice
	Cure Mix
3 1/4 oz/wt	salt
2 tsp	tinted curing mix (TCM)
3/4 oz/wt	dextrose
	Spice Blend
1 1/2 oz/wt	onion powder
1/2 oz/wt	ground white pepper
2 tsp	ground caraway seeds
2 tsp	ground nutmeg
5 1/2 oz/wt	nonfat dry milk powder
1 piece	beef bung, or 8 pieces beef middle casings, 16-inch lengths, tied at one end with a bubble knot

1. Toss the beef with the cure mix. Chill well and grind through the fine plate (1/8 inch) of a meat grinder.
2. Grind the jowl fat through the fine plate; reserve.
3. Transfer the ground beef to a chilled chopper bowl. Add the ice and the spice blend on top of the ground beef. Process the ingredients until the mixture drops to a temperature of 30°F. Continue running the machine until the mixture's temperature rises to 40°F.
4. Add the jowl fat and process until the mixture reaches 45°F. Add the milk powder and continue processing until the mixture reaches 58°F. Make a test. Adjust seasoning and consistency before shaping.
5. Stuff into prepared casings and tie each end with a bubble knot. Refrigerate uncovered overnight on paper towel-lined trays to form a pellicle.
6. Hot smoke at 160°F until desired color is achieved, approximately 1 to 2 hours. Poach in simmering water at 165°F to an internal temperature of 150°F (10 to 30 minutes for beef round, 1 to 3 hours for beef bung), then shock in ice water to an internal temperature of 60°F. Blot dry.
7. The bologna is ready to slice and serve now, or wrap and hold under refrigeration for up to 2 weeks.

To each fully prepared basic bologna recipe, fold in the following garnish ingredients before shaping. Each variation will produce 11 sausages at 14 inches each using beef casing (casings should be precut 16 inches and tied) or one 16 1/2-pound sausage using beef bung.
Ham Bologna 4 pounds cured pork, cut into 3/4- to 1-inch cubes
Amish Bologna 4 pounds cured, cooked, diced pig head meat, cut into 3/4-inch cubes
Tongue Bologna 4 pounds cured, cooked beef tongue, cut into 3/4- to 1-inch cubes

French Garlic Sausage

Yield: 25 pounds bulk; 16 links (1 1/2 pounds each)

12 lb	boneless pork butt, cubed
5 lb	beef shoulder clod, cubed
4 lb	jowl fat, cubed and partially frozen
3 lb	crushed ice
	Cure Mix
3 1/4 oz/wt	salt
3/4 oz/wt	tinted curing mix (TCM)
2 oz/wt	dextrose
	Spice Blend
3 tbsp	chopped garlic
1 oz/wt	ground white pepper
1/2 oz/wt	dry mustard
5 1/2 oz/wt	nonfat dry milk powder
19 feet	beef middle casings, rinsed, cut in 14-inch lengths and tied at one end

1. Toss the pork with half the cure mix. Chill well and reserve for garnish.
2. Toss the beef with the remaining cure mix and the spice blend. Chill well and grind through the fine plate (1/8 inch) of a meat grinder.
3. Grind the jowl fat through the fine plate; reserve.
4. Transfer the ground beef to a chilled chopper bowl. Add the ice to the ground beef. Process the ingredients until the mixture drops to a temperature of 30°F. Continue running the machine until the mixture's temperature rises to 40°F.
5. Add jowl fat and process until the mixture reaches 45°F. Add the milk powder and continue processing until the mixture reaches 58°F. Make a test. Adjust seasoning and consistency before shaping.
6. Fold the pork garnish into the sausage in a mixer or by hand over an ice bath. Stuff into prepared casings and tie each end with a bubble knot. Refrigerate uncovered overnight on paper towel-lined trays to form a pellicle.
7. Hot smoke at 160°F until desired color is achieved, about 1 1/2 to 2 hours. Poach in simmering water at 165°F to an internal temperature of 150°F, then shock in ice water to an internal temperature of 60°F. Blot dry.
8. The sausage is ready to slice for service now, or wrap and hold under refrigeration for up to 7 days.

Chef's Notes: For more smoke color, cold smoke at 80°F for up to 12 hours, then finish cooking by poaching, as described in step 7 above.

Duck Sausage Substitute duck meat for all meats; instead of beef casings, substitute hog casings, cut into 5-inch lengths; follow the same method as above.

Kielbasa

Kielbasa is a smoked sausage originally made in Poland.

Yield: 22 pounds bulk; 21 links (1 pound each)

9 lb	boneless pork butt
5 lb	boneless beef top or bottom round
4 lb	jowl fat
3 lb	crushed ice
	Cure Mix
6 1/2 oz/wt	salt
4 tsp	tinted curing mix (TCM)
1 1/2 oz/wt	dextrose
	Spice Blend
1 oz/wt	ground white pepper
1/2 oz/wt	dry mustard
1/2 tsp	garlic powder
5 3/4 oz/wt	nonfat dry milk powder
21 pieces	beef round casings, rinsed, cut in 15-inch lengths and tied at one end with a bubble knot

1. Trim the pork and cube; reserve. Cube the beef; reserve. Cube the jowl fat; freeze until needed. Scale out the ice; keep frozen until needed.
2. Toss the pork with half of the cure mix. Chill well. Grind through the coarse plate (3/8 inch) of a meat grinder and reserve for garnish.
3. Toss the beef with the remaining cure and the spice blend. Chill well and grind through the fine plate (1/8 inch) of a meat grinder.
4. Grind the jowl fat through the fine plate; reserve.
5. Transfer the ground beef to a chilled chopper bowl. Add the ice on top of the ground beef. Process the ingredients until the mixture drops to a temperature of 30°F. Continue running the machine until the mixture's temperature rises to 40°F.
6. Add jowl fat and process until the mixture reaches 45°F. Add the milk powder and continue processing until the mixture reaches 58°F. Make a test. Adjust seasoning and consistency before shaping.
7. Fold the ground pork garnish into the sausage in a mixer or by hand over an ice bath.
8. Stuff into prepared casings and tie the open end with a bubble knot.
9. Refrigerate uncovered overnight on paper towel-lined trays to form a pellicle.
10. Hot smoke at 160°F until desired color is achieved, about 1 1/2 to 2 hours.
11. Poach in simmering water at 165°F to an internal temperature of 150°F, then shock in ice water to an internal temperature of 60°F. Blot dry.
12. The sausage is ready to prepare for service now by sautéing, grilling, broiling, or baking just until hot, or wrap and hold under refrigeration for up to 7 days.

Fine Swiss Bratwurst

Yield: 15 pounds bulk; 115 links (2 ounces each)

5 lb	boneless veal top or bottom round, cubed
5 lb	jowl fat, cubed and partially frozen
4 lb	crushed ice
	Cure Mix
4 oz/wt	salt
3/4 oz/wt	dextrose
	Spice Blend
1/2 oz/wt	ground white pepper
1/2 oz/wt	dry mustard
1/4 oz/wt	ground mace
1/2 tbsp	ground ginger
6 oz/wt	nonfat dry milk powder
60 feet	sheep casings, rinsed

1. Toss the veal with the cure mix. Chill well and grind through the fine plate (1/8 inch) of a meat grinder. Grind the jowl fat through the fine plate; reserve separately.
2. Transfer the ground veal to a chilled chopper bowl. Add the crushed ice and the spice blend on top of the ground veal.
3. Run the machine and process the ingredients until the mixture reaches a temperature of 30°F. Continue running the machine until the mixture's temperature rises to 40°F.
4. Add the fat and process until the mixture reaches 45°F. Add the milk powder and continue processing until the mixture reaches 58°F. Make a test. Adjust seasoning and consistency before shaping.
5. Stuff into prepared casings, twist, and tie into 5-inch links. Refrigerate uncovered overnight on paper towel-lined trays to form a pellicle.
6. Poach in simmering water at 165°F to an internal temperature of 150°F, about 10 to 20 minutes, then shock in ice water to an internal temperature of 60°F. Blot dry.
7. The sausage is ready to prepare for service now by sautéing, grilling, broiling, or baking just until hot, or wrap and hold under refrigeration for up to 7 days.

Turkey Bratwurst Replace veal with turkey thigh meat.

Chipolata Prepare as directed above, stuffing the sausage into sheep casings and shaping into 3-inch links.

Smoked Bratwurst Add 2 1/2 teaspoons tinted curing mix (TCM) to the cure mix. Stuff into casings and shape into 5-inch links. Twist and cut into individual links. Dry overnight under refrigeration and cold smoke for 1 hour.

Weisswurst Omit the ginger and mustard. Add finely chopped lemon zest to taste.

Mortadella

Yield: 14 pounds bulk; 14 links (1 pound each)

5 lb	boneless pork butt, cubed
4 lb	jowl fat, cubed
3 lb	crushed ice
	Cure Mix
$3\frac{1}{4}$ oz/wt	salt
$\frac{3}{4}$ oz/wt	dextrose
2 tsp	tinted curing mix (TCM)
$3\frac{1}{2}$ oz/fl	dry white wine
	Spice Blend
$\frac{1}{2}$ oz/wt	ground white pepper
$\frac{1}{4}$ oz/wt	ground mace
$\frac{1}{4}$ oz/wt	sweet Spanish paprika
$\frac{1}{4}$ oz/wt	ground nutmeg
$\frac{1}{4}$ oz/wt	ground coriander
1 tsp	ground cloves
1 tsp	ground bay leaves
$\frac{1}{2}$ tsp	garlic powder
7 oz/wt	nonfat dry milk powder
	Garnish
1 lb	pork fat, diced, blanched, cooled
7 oz/wt	pistachios, blanched and peeled
14 pieces	beef middles, rinsed, cut in 10-inch lengths and tied at one end

1. Toss the pork with the cure mix. Chill well and grind through the fine plate ($\frac{1}{8}$ inch) of a meat grinder.
2. Grind the jowl fat through the fine plate; reserve.
3. Transfer the ground pork to a chilled chopper bowl. Add the crushed ice and spice blend on top of the ground pork. Run the machine and process the ingredients until the mixture reaches a temperature of 30°F. Continue running the machine until the mixture's temperature rises to 40°F.
4. Add the fat and process until the mixture reaches 45°F. Add the milk powder and continue processing until the mixture reaches 58°F. Make a test. Adjust seasoning and consistency before shaping.
5. Working over an ice bath, stir in the garnish ingredients. Stuff into prepared casings and tie with a bubble knot.
6. Poach at 165°F to an internal temperature of 150°F, about $2\frac{1}{2}$ to 3 hours, then shock in ice water to an internal temperature of 60°F. Blot dry.
7. Refrigerate uncovered overnight on paper towel-lined trays to form a pellicle.
8. If desired, cold smoke at 80°F for 1 to 2 hours. The sausage may be sliced and served at this point, or wrapped and held under refrigeration for up to 3 weeks.

Presentation Ideas: For a nontraditional garnish, add 1 pound pork fat, cut into $\frac{1}{4}$-inch dice, blanched and cooled, and $1\frac{3}{4}$ ounces whole black peppercorns, soaked in hot water and drained.

Leberkäse (Bavarian Loaf)

Yield: 4 loaves (3 pounds each); 72–80 slices (1/4-inch thick, 2 1/2 ounces each)

Leberkäse is best when served warm, although it may be served at room temperature or chilled.

5 lb	boneless beef shoulder clod
4 lb	jowl fat
3 lb	crushed ice
	Cure Mix
3 1/4 oz/wt	salt
2 tsp	tinted curing mix (TCM)
3/4 oz/wt	dextrose
	Spice Blend
1/2 oz/wt	onion powder
1/2 oz/wt	ground white pepper
1/4 oz/wt	dry mustard
1 1/2 tsp	ground mace
1 tsp	ground ginger
5 3/4 oz/wt	nonfat dry milk powder

1. Cube the beef; reserve. Cube the jowl fat; freeze until needed. Scale out the ice; keep frozen until needed.

2. Toss the beef with the cure mix. Chill well and grind through the fine plate (1/8 inch) of a meat grinder.

3. Grind the jowl fat through the fine plate; reserve.

4. Transfer the ground beef to a chilled chopper bowl. Add the crushed ice and the spice blend on top of the ground beef.

5. Run the machine and process the ingredients until the mixture reaches a temperature of 30°F. Continue running the machine until the mixture's temperature rises to 40°F.

6. Add the fat and process until the mixture reaches 45°F. Add the milk powder and continue processing until the mixture reaches 58°F. Make a test. Adjust seasoning and consistency before filling the loaf pans.

7. Fill the loaf pans with the sausage and allow the leberkäse to rest under refrigeration overnight before baking.

8. Bake, covered with foil, in a 160°F water bath in a 325°F oven, for 1 3/4 to 2 hours or to an internal temperature of 145°F. Remove foil for last 1/2 hour to brown lightly.

9. The loaf may be sliced and served at this point, or wrapped and held under refrigeration for up to 1 week.

Chicken and Vegetable Sausage

Yield: 16 pounds bulk; 95 links (2 ounces each)

7 lb	chicken thigh meat, diced
2 lb	jowl fat, diced
3 lb	crushed ice
	Cure Mix
3 1/4 oz/wt	salt
3/4 oz/wt	dextrose
	Garnish
1 oz/wt	vegetable oil
8 oz/wt	small-dice carrots
8 oz/wt	small-dice celery
1 lb	small-dice onions
2 lb	small-dice mushrooms
8 oz/fl	dry white wine
2 tbsp	chopped flat-leaf parsley
	Spice Blend
3/4 oz/wt	ground white pepper
1/4 oz/wt	poultry seasoning
1 tsp	powdered thyme
6 oz/wt	nonfat dry milk powder
50 feet	sheep casings, rinsed and tied at one end

1. Toss the chicken with the cure mix and grind through the fine plate (1/8 inch) of a meat grinder. Grind the jowl fat and reserve, separate, under refrigeration.
2. Sauté the carrots, celery, and onions in oil, until cooked; add the mushrooms. Sauté until mushrooms release water, then add wine and reduce until almost dry. Chill.
3. Transfer the ground chicken to a chilled chopper bowl. Add the crushed ice and the spice blend on top of the ground chicken. Run the machine and process the ingredients until the mixture reaches a temperature of 30°F. Continue running the machine until the mixture's temperature rises to 40°F.
4. Add the fat and process until the mixture reaches 45°F. Add the milk powder and continue processing until the mixture reaches 58°F. Transfer to a bowl. Stir in the garnish, working over an ice bath. Make a test. Adjust seasoning and consistency before shaping.
5. Stuff into prepared casings and tie off into 5-inch links. Poach in simmering water at 170°F to an internal temperature of 165°F, then shock in ice water to an internal temperature of 60°F and blot dry.
6. The sausage is ready to prepare for service now by sautéing, grilling, or broiling just until hot, or wrapped and held under refrigeration for up to 3 days.

Braunschweiger

Yield: 12 pound bulk; 12 sausages (1 pound each)

5 lb	pork liver, cubed
3 lb	slab bacon, cubed
2 lb	boneless pork butt, cubed
18 oz/wt	crushed ice
	Cure Mix
3 1/2 oz/wt	salt
2 tsp	tinted curing mix (TCM)
1/2 oz/wt	dextrose
	Spice Blend
1/2 oz/wt	onion powder
1 tbsp	ground white pepper
1/2 tsp	ground allspice
1/2 tsp	ground cloves
1/2 tsp	rubbed sage
1/2 tsp	ground marjoram
1/2 tsp	ground nutmeg
1/2 tsp	ground ginger
2 cups	nonfat dry milk powder
12 feet	beef middles, rinsed, cut in 10-inch lengths and tied at one end

1. Toss the liver with the cure mix. Chill well and grind through the fine plate (1/8 inch) of a meat grinder.
2. Grind the slab bacon and pork butt separately through the fine plate; reserve separately.
3. Transfer the ground liver and pork to a chilled chopper bowl. Add the crushed ice and the spice blend on top of the ground pork. Process the ingredients until the mixture drops to a temperature of 30°F. Continue running the machine until the mixture's temperature rises to 40°F.
4. Add the slab bacon and process until the mixture reaches 45°F. Add the milk powder and continue processing until the mixture reaches 58°F. Make a test. Adjust seasoning and consistency before shaping.
5. Stuff into prepared casings and tie closed with a bubble knot. Refrigerate uncovered overnight on paper towel-lined trays to form a pellicle.
6. Hot smoke at 160°F until desired color is achieved, about 1 1/2 to 2 hours.
7. Poach in simmering water at 165°F to an internal temperature of 150°F, then shock in ice water to an internal temperature of 60°F. Blot dry. The braunschweiger is ready to slice and serve now, or wrap and hold under refrigeration for up to 2 weeks.

Seafood Sausage

Yield: 10 pounds bulk; 68 links (2 ounces each)

This mild seafood sausage can be served with sautéed Napa cabbage as an appetizer or it can used a part of a seafood medley in a number of dishes. If you wish, fold in up to 2 ounces of chopped black truffles as shown here.

	Mousseline
3 lb	sole fillet, diced
3 lb	sea scallops, muscle tabs removed
1/2 oz/wt	salt
3 tbsp	Old Bay seasoning
1 1/2 cups	fresh white bread crumbs
5 cups	heavy cream, cold
10 each	egg whites
	Garnish
1 lb	shrimp, peeled and deveined, cut into 1/4-inch dice
1 lb	crab or lobster meat, diced (from three 1 1/4-pound blanched lobsters)
1 lb	salmon meat, cut into 1/4-inch dice
1 lb	bay scallops, muscle tabs removed
2 tbsp	chopped fresh parsley
36 feet	sheep casings, rinsed, *or* 18 feet hog casings, rinsed

1. Combine the sole, scallops, salt, and Old Bay seasoning. Grind through the fine plate (1/8 inch) of a meat grinder. Chill in freezer 15 minutes.

2. Soak bread crumbs in half of the heavy cream to make a panada.

3. Pureé the seafood in food processor as smooth as possible. Add the egg whites and panada. Pulse in the remaining cream. Make a test. Adjust seasoning and consistency before shaping.

4. Fold in the garnish ingredients to coat evenly; refrigerate. Fold garnish into the forcemeat.

5. Stuff into prepared casings and twist into 5-inch links. Cut into individual links.

6. Poach in simmering water at 165°F to an internal temperature of 145°F. Shock in ice water to an internal temperature of 60°F. Blot dry.

7. The sausage is ready to prepare for service now by removing the strings and either sautéing the sausage in clarified butter until golden brown, or reheating in a 350°F oven for about 10 to 12 minutes. To store, wrap and hold under refrigeration for up to 3 days.

Smoked Foie Gras Sausage

Yield: 6 links (1 pound each)

Chef Rudy Smith developed this recipe when the Institute was asked to come up with a dish using foie gras. The only parameters were that it had to be able to be called a sausage and it needed to be smoked. The result was this fantastic sausage, suitable for hot or cold presentations.

	Garnish
3 lb	foie gras, cleaned and cut into large dice
1 oz/wt	salt
4 oz/fl	Armagnac
1 tsp	ground white pepper
1 tbsp	chopped fresh chives
1 tbsp	chopped fresh chervil
	Emulsion
1 1/4 lb	duck meat
1 lb	jowl fat
3/4 lb	crushed ice
	Cure Mix
2 tbsp	salt
1/2 tsp	tinted curing mix (TCM)
1/2 tbsp	dextrose
	Spice Blend
1/2 tsp	dry mustard
1 oz/wt	shallots, sautéed and cooled
1/8 oz	Pâté Spice (page 408)
1 1/2 oz	nonfat powdered milk
8 ft	beef round casings, cut in 15-inch lengths and tied at one end

1. Clean the foie gras and cut into 3/4-inch pieces. Combine with salt, Armagnac, pepper, chives, and chervil. Marinate 24 hours.

2. Combine the duck with the cure mix and chill well.

3. Grind the duck and the jowl fat separately through the fine plate (1/8 inch) of a meat grinder (keep separate).

4. Transfer the ground duck to a chilled chopper bowl. Add the crushed ice and the spice blend on top of the ground duck.

5. Run the machine and process the ingredients until the mixture reaches a temperature of 30°F. Continue running the machine until the mixture's temperature rises to 40°F. Add the fat and process until the mixture reaches 45°F. Add the milk powder and continue processing until the mixture reaches 58°F.

6. Transfer the sausage mixture to a bowl over an ice bath. Make a test and adjust if necessary. Fold in foie gras, making sure individual pieces are evenly coated in forcemeat.

7. Stuff into casings and tie.

8. Refrigerate uncovered overnight to dry.

9. Cold smoke at 80°F for one hour.

10. Hot smoke at 160°F for one hour.

11. Poach the sausages in simmering water (170°F) to an internal temperature of 165°F. Remove from the water and shock in an ice water bath to an internal temperature of 60°F. Wrap and hold under refrigeration for up to 3 days.

Blood Sausage with Apples

Yield: 6 pounds bulk; 44 links (4 ounces each)

Unlike other sausages, the blood sausage mixture is loose enough to pour through a funnel into the prepared casings.

3/4 cup	fresh white bread crumbs
1 1/2 cups	heavy cream
1 1/2 qt	beef blood
2 tbsp	salt
1/2 tsp	Quatre Épices (page 406)
1 tbsp	brown sugar
2 lb	fatback, diced
1 1/2 lb	fine-dice onions
1 1/4 lb	cored and peeled apples, sautéed and puréed
23 feet	hog casings, cut into 24-inch lengths and tied at one end

1. Soak the bread crumbs in the heavy cream to make a panada. Knead gently to moisten evenly.
2. Mix the blood with the salt, quatres épices, and brown sugar.
3. Render 1/2 pound of the fatback in a heavy sautoir.
4. Add the onions and sweat until translucent but not brown.
5. Mix in the rest of the diced fatback, the apples, panada, and seasoned blood, while stirring.
6. Gently heat while stirring until mixture reaches about 100°F. Remove from heat.
7. Tie a knot at one end of the hog casings. Fill the casings with the help of a funnel, making sure all the components are distributed evenly. Take care not to overstuff to prevent them from bursting when cooking.
8. Poach the sausages in 165°F water and cook for 20 minutes, then prick with a teasing needle. If brown liquid comes out, they are done; if blood comes out, let cook a few more minutes and check again.
9. When ready, shock sausages in ice water for 5 minutes, drain them, dry them with paper towels, lay them on a pan, and brush them with melted lard or duck fat. Place them in the refrigerator to finish cooling.

Presentation Ideas: To serve, cut the sausages into lengths, prick them all over with a fork, and sauté or grill them. Traditional accompaniments are mashed or home-fried potatoes, fried apple rings, and sauerkraut.

Southwest Dry Sausage

Yield: 6 pounds

3 1/4 lb	diced beef, chilled
2 1/4 lb	diced certified pork, chilled (see page 176)
1 1/2 tsp	garlic powder
2 1/2 oz/fl	cold water
2 tsp	chili powder
1 tsp	onion powder
1 tsp	ground cumin
4 tsp	coarse grind black pepper
1/2 tsp	Tabasco
1/4 oz/wt	Prague Powder #2
4 oz/wt	dextrose
2 oz/wt	salt
1 1/2 oz/wt	Fermento

1. Grind beef and pork through fine plate (1/8 inch) of meat a grinder into a mixing bowl over an ice bath.
2. Add all remaining ingredients to the ground meats; mix on low speed until meat feels sticky to the touch, about 15 to 20 seconds. Make a test. Adjust seasoning and consistency before shaping.
3. Place sausage meat into stuffer and tamp down to remove any air pockets.
4. Stuff into prepared hog casings and tie into 9-inch links.
5. Arrange on drying sticks and cure for 4 days. (See Chapter 5, page 135, for the USDA regulations for dry-curing sausages.)
6. Cold smoke at 80°F for 24 to 36 hours to the desired color. Allow the sausage to continue to dry until desired firmness.

SEVEN

Terrines, Pâtés, Galantines, and Roulades

The French are famous for their contributions to the world of terrines, pâtés, and other forcemeat specialties. From the rustic appeal of a peasant-style pâté grand-mère to a luxurious foie gras and truffle pâté, these dishes are part of the worldwide tradition of classic cold dishes.

In this chapter, we will look at the methods for preparing four basic forcemeat styles (straight, country, gratin, and mousseline) and the shaping methods to produce items from forcemeats (terrines, pâtés en croûte, galantines, and roulades), as well as a special commodity featured in the cold kitchen (foie gras). In addition, we will give several examples of nontraditional "terrines" made without forcemeats.

Forcemeats

One of the basic components of charcuterie and garde manger items is a preparation known as a forcemeat. A forcemeat is a lean meat and fat emulsion that is established when the ingredients are processed through together by grinding, sieving, or puréeing. Depending on the grinding and emulsifying methods and the intended use, the forcemeat may have a smooth consistency or may be heavily textured and coarse. The result must not be just a mixture but an emulsion, so that it will hold together properly when sliced. Forcemeats should have a rich and pleasant taste and feel in the mouth.

Forcemeats may be used for quenelles, sausages, pâtés, terrines, roulades, and galantines, as well as to prepare stuffings for other items (a salmon forcemeat may be used to fill a paupiette of sole, for example). Each forcemeat style will have a particular texture. The four basic forcemeat styles are:

- Straight
- Country-style or campagne
- Gratin
- Mousseline

Straight forcemeats combine pork and pork fat with a dominant meat in equal parts, through a process of progressive grinding and emulsification. The meats and fat are cut into cubes, seasoned, cured, rested, ground, and then processed.

A country-style forcemeat is rather coarse in texture. It is traditionally made from pork and pork fat, often with a percentage of liver and other garnish ingredients.

In a gratin forcemeat, some portion of the dominant meat is sautéed and cooled before it is ground. The term *gratin* means "browned."

A very light forcemeat, mousseline is based on white meats (veal or poultry) or fish. The inclusion of cream and eggs gives a mousseline its characteristic light texture and consistency.

Main Ingredients

Forcemeats, like sausages, are made from raw products, with the exception of the gratin forcemeat. Some classic choices for forcemeats include pork; fish such as pike, trout, or salmon; seafood such as shrimp and scallops; game meats such as venison, boar, or rabbit; poultry and game birds; and poultry, game, veal, or pork livers. When selecting cuts of red and white meat, opt for well-exercised cuts, since they have a richer flavor than very tender cuts, such as the tenderloin or loin. However, meats to be used as garnishes can easily be the more delicate portions: tenderloin of lamb, rabbit, or pork, or poultry breasts, for example. Often, recipes for shrimp or scallop mousseline call for a quantity of pike to ensure a good primary bind.

An adequate amount of fat is also important. Fatback is considered to have a neutral flavor and can be paired with most meats. Mousselines made from delicate white meats, fish, or shellfish generally call for heavy cream.

To prepare the meat and fatback for a forcemeat, it should first be trimmed of any gristle, sinew, or skin. The meat is then cut into dice, so it can drop easily through the feed tube of a grinder, or be quickly processed to a paste in a food processor.

Salt and Seasonings

Salt plays a vital role in producing good forcemeats. The salt acts to draw out the proteins in the meat (these proteins are the primary source of the forcemeat's "bind"), and it also adds its own unique flavor. Classic recipes often call for ground spices such as quatre épices, a combination of pepper, nutmeg, allspice, and cinnamon.

Herbs, aromatic vegetables such as onions or mushrooms, wines, cognacs, grain-based spirits, or vinegars may also be added. In some cases, a reduction of garlic or shallots, herbs, wines, glace de viande or volaille, and other flavoring ingredients may be made. This reduction should be thoroughly chilled before adding it to the meats.

It is always important to follow basic formulas carefully as you are learning to make forcemeats, and to properly test and taste forcemeats each time you make them.

Figure 7-1 Panadas: bread, milk, flour, rice, egg, nonfat dried milk.

Secondary Binders

The proteins in meats and fish are the basic source of the forcemeat's structure, texture, and bind. In some special cases, however, you may need to add a secondary binder, which is generally required for country-style and gratin forcemeats. There are three basic types of secondary binders: eggs, nonfat dry milk powder, and panadas. Panadas are made from starchy (farinaceous) items—well-cooked rice or potatoes, bread soaked in milk, *pâte à choux,* a cooked dough made from flour, water, butter, and eggs, or plain flour. (Figure 7-1 shows a variety of panadas.)

Garnish Ingredients

Garnishes give the chef an opportunity to add color, flavor, and texture to a basic formula. Some traditional garnishes include the poultry breast, pork, beef, veal, or lamb tenderloin portions, nuts (especially pistachios and pine nuts), mushrooms, truffles, and diced foie gras. The quantity of garnish added to a forcemeat can range from a few chopped nuts scattered throughout a pâté to a terrine in which there is a predominant garnish bound together with a small amount of forcemeat (for example, St. Andrew's Terrine, page 255).

You can add garnishes to a forcemeat in two ways. They can be simply folded into the forcemeat; in that case they are known as *internal* or *random* garnishes. The second means of introducing the garnish is to place it in the forcemeat as you are filling the mold or laying it out for a roulade or galantine. These garnishes are known as *inlays,* though you may also hear them called *centered* garnishes. Care should be taken to shape and place the garnish so that each slice will have a uniform, consistent appearance, whether the slice comes from the end or center of the pâté. Both styles of garnishing are illustrated in Figure 7-2.

Figure 7-2 Garnishes.

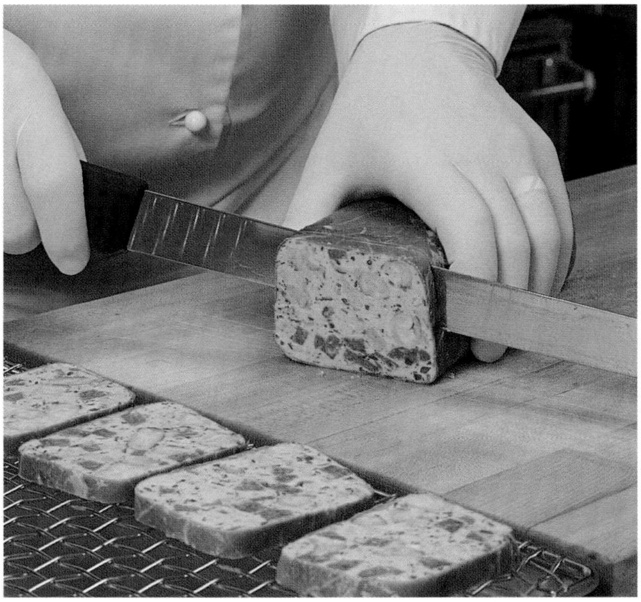

a. Slicing a terrine with random garnish.

b. Adding a placed garnish (duck breast shown here) to a pâté en croûte.

Figure 7-3 Ready to mix a forcemeat over an ice bath.

If you are preparing forcemeat items for display or competition, you may want to dust garnish items very lightly with a bit of powdered gelatin or albumen (dried and powdered egg whites) or a combination of these two items, to glue them into place. This will improve the adherence of the forcemeat to the garnish, making it less likely that they will separate when the item is cut into slices.

Making Forcemeats

Chill Ingredients, Chill Equipment

Maintaining both the ingredients and equipment used to prepare a forcemeat below 40 degrees keeps the food out of the danger zone, reducing the risk of food-borne illness. Temperature control is also the key to achieving the best results. When forcemeats are kept well chilled throughout processing, mixing, and cooking (see Figure 7-3), they require less fat, yet still have a smooth texture and an appealing mouthfeel. The flavor of the forcemeat itself is generally better, as well.

Progressive Grinding

The most common piece of equipment for grinding the meats for straight, country, and gratin forcemeats is a meat grinder. Review all the cautions and instructions found on page 177 in Chapter 6.

Some forcemeat formulas will call for some or all of the meats and fat to be ground through a succession of increasingly smaller grinder plates. This is known as *progressive grinding*. (Figure 7-4 shows how the texture of the meat changes as it undergoes progressive grinding.) Review the recipe to determine if you will need one or more grinding plates. Grind the meat directly into a well-chilled mixing bowl set over ice.

Mousseline forcemeats are typically made from start to finish in a food processor (see Figure 7-5), although some chefs prefer to grind the meat or fish before placing it in the bowl of the food processor. If you make a significant quantity of forcemeats using a food processor, it is a good idea to dedicate one very sharp blade to that purpose only.

Mixing and Processing

Once ground, the forcemeat is mixed in order to blend any seasonings, panadas, or other ingredients thoroughly and evenly. More importantly, an adequate mixing period is crucial to the development of the correct texture.

Mixing can be done by beating the forcemeat with a rubber spatula or wooden spoon over an ice bath, in a mixer, or in a food processor. Care should be taken not to overmix, especially when you use a machine. Be careful not to overload the bowl. Depending on the amount of product, one to three minutes at the lowest speed should be sufficient. The forcemeat's color and texture will change slightly when it is properly mixed.

Mixing in a food processor is very fast and provides a smoother texture. Most food processors handle relatively small batches. It is critical to keep an eye on the forcemeat as it processes. Your forcemeat can go from properly processed to overworked in a matter of seconds. This can cause pockets or bubbles to form in the item you are preparing, a distraction on a plated item presented to a guest and grounds for losing points in competition work.

Testing a Forcemeat

Forcemeats are prepared in the following two ways: poached directly in a liquid (as for galantines, roulades, or quenelles) or in a water bath (terrines), or baked in a crust (pâté en croûte). You can only be sure of the quality of the forcemeat after it is cooked, and the following method for testing a forcemeat will give you an opportunity to evaluate the quality, seasoning, and texture.

Figure 7-4 Progressive grinding.

a. Chunks of meat are ground using the coarse die first. Meat, containers, and equipment must be kept cold at all times.

b. Meat is ground through a medium-coarse die.

c. In the last step of a progressive grind, meat is passed through a small die.

This important step takes some time to do properly, but it can save you time and money. To make a test, wrap a one-ounce portion of the forcemeat in plastic wrap (see Figure 7-6) and poach it to the appropriate internal temperature (145°F for fish; 150°F for pork, beef, veal, lamb, or game; and 165°F for any item including poultry and poultry liver). Cool the forcemeat to the correct service temperature before you taste it. You will be checking for flavor, seasoning, and consistency.

The test portion itself will not taste or feel exactly the same as the finished product, since it is a general practice to allow forcemeat items to rest two or three days before they are served. However, with experience, you can train your palate to recognize the evidence of quality in a forcemeat, or to detect a flaw. This is the same "taste memory," built up through experience and practice, that permits a cellar master to foretell with some accuracy the qualities a wine will have when it is mature, even when the wine is far too young to actually drink.

If the texture is poor, evaluate just what kind of problem you have. Rubbery forcemeats can be improved by adding more fat or cream. Loose forcemeats, on the other hand, may be improved by adding egg whites or a bit of panada. Before you make a dramatic change, however, take into account whether the item will be pressed or coated with aspic.

Straight Forcemeat

This basic forcemeat is used to prepare pâtés, terrines, and galantines. It is generally made by grinding the meat and fat through a medium plate, then further processing it in a mixer or food processor.

Figure 7-5 Grinding salmon in a food processor.

Figure 7-6 Testing forcemeat.

Figure 7-7 Straight forcemeat.

a. Adding cream.

b. Keeping the mixture cold.

c. Filling a fatback-lined mode with forcemeat.

Process the ground meat with any additional ingredients. An egg may be added to the forcemeat to give a better bind. A quantity of heavy cream may also be included in some recipes to give the forcemeat a smooth texture and a richer flavor, if desired (see Figure 7-7a).

Once the forcemeat is tested and any adjustments to seasoning or consistency have been made, you may add garnish ingredients. This may be done in the mixer or by hand, working over an ice bath to keep the forcemeat properly chilled (see Figure 7-7b).

Straight forcemeats may be used to fill a pâté en croûte (see Figure 7-7c), or to prepare terrines and galantines. (For more information on preparing a pâté en croûte, terrines, and galantines, see pages 228–236.)

Country-Style Forcemeat

Country-style forcemeats are less refined in texture and heartier in flavor than others and are traditionally made from pork and pork liver.

The texture of this forcemeat is achieved by grinding the pork through a coarse die, then reserving most of this coarse grind. If desired, a portion of the ground meat may be ground again through a medium die before the forcemeat is blended with its panada and processed as for a straight forcemeat. The coarsely ground meat as well as the processed forcemeat is then combined, as shown in Figure 7-8. Because at least part of the forcemeat is left as a coarse grind, a panada is almost always included to help the finished product hold together after cooking.

Figure 7-8 Mixing garnish into forcemeat.

Gratin Forcemeat

A gratin forcemeat is similar to a straight forcemeat, with the exception of the way in which the main meat is handled. The meat is very quickly seared—just enough to enhance the flavor and color, but not enough to cook it through. The meat is changed enough by the searing that a panada is required to help produce the desired texture.

The first step is to sear the meat. Get the pan or grill very hot, sear the meat on all sides as quickly as possible, and just as quickly cool it down. The best way to accomplish this is to work in small batches, to avoid crowding the meat in the pan, as shown in Figure 7-9a. Remove it to a sheet pan, and cool it quickly in the refrigerator or

Figure 7-9 Gratin forcemeat.

a. Searing the meat.

b. The garnish may also be seared. Sherry is added to deglaze the pan.

c. The puréed ground meat is puréed with a panada. Shown here, milk-soaked bread and an egg.

d. The gratin forcemeat is puréed to a homogeneous mixture.

freezer. An optional step is shown in Figure 7-9b, preparing an aromatic reduction to flavor the forcemeat.

Follow the same procedure for grinding as for a straight forcemeat, and process it with a panada and any additional ingredients as suggested or required by the recipe (see Figure 7-9c). (The texture of a properly processed gratin forcemeat is shown in Figure 7-9d). Be sure to test the forcemeat properly before continuing on to add the garnish ingredients.

Gratin forcemeats can be used in the same general applications as a straight forcemeat.

Mousseline Forcemeat

Mousseline forcemeats are very light in texture and are typically made from either white meat, fish, or shellfish with the addition of heavy cream as the fat component of the forcemeat.

Although individual recipes will differ, the formula shown here works as an excellent starting point. The amount of cream indicated will produce a good texture for terrines and other forcemeat items that will be sliced. If the mousseline will be used to prepare a timbale or other similar applications, the quantity of cream can be increased by nearly double the amount indicated below:

Meat or fish	1 lb.
Salt	1 tsp
Egg (or egg white)	1 each
Cream	1 cup

When preparing a mousseline forcemeat, you may simply dice the main ingredients and proceed to grind them in the food processor, as shown on page 225, or you may wish to grind the main ingredient through a coarse or medium plate before processing it with an egg white (see Figure 7-10a).

Process the meat and salt just long enough to develop a paste with an even texture. Add the egg white, followed by the cream (see Figure 7-10b). In order to blend the mousseline properly, it is important to scrape down the bowl (see Figure 7-10c). Continue processing only until the forcemeat is smooth and homogenous, generally around thirty seconds (Figure 7-10d).

Optional: For a very light mousseline, you may prefer to work the cream in by hand (see Figure 7-11). This is more time-consuming and exacting than using a food processor,

Figure 7-10 Mousseline.

a. Adding egg whites to previously ground salmon.

b. As the mixture purées, cream is added slowly until just incorporated.

c. The sides of the processor should be scraped down.

d. The cream is fully incorporated.

e. A mousseline should be sieved through a tamis to ensure complete smoothness.

but the results are worth the extra effort. Both the base mixture and the cream must be very cold in order to add the cream in higher proportions than those suggested in the basic formula above. Work over an ice bath for the best results.

Fine forcemeats may be passed through a drum sieve (*tamis*) to be sure that a very delicate texture is achieved (Figure 7-10e). Be sure that the forcemeat is very cold as you work, and work in small batches to prevent the forcemeat from heating up as you work.

Mousseline forcemeats are often featured as appetizers, fillings, or stuffings, or to coat or wrap poached fish or poultry suprêmes (see Figure 7-12a–c). Another interesting way to use this forcemeat is to layer mousselines with different colors to create a special effect in a terrine (see Figure 7-12d).

Terrines

Terrines, the shortened name of a dish known classically as *pâté en terrine,* are traditionally understood to be forcemeat mixtures baked in an earthenware mold with a tight-fitting lid. This preparation gets its name from its association with the material used to make the mold, once exclusively earthenware of unglazed clay, or *terra-cotta.* Today, terrine molds are produced from materials such as stainless steel, aluminum, ceramic, enameled cast iron, ovenproof plastic, or glazed earthenware. These materials are more durable and more sanitary than the unglazed earthenware once favored by charcutières.

Some classic pâtés en terrine are still referred to simply as "pâtés." Pâté de campagne and pâté grand-mère are two examples. More often today, we tend to abbreviate the term to *terrine.* This may cause some initial confusion, so it is worth remembering that the word *pâté* does not, all by itself, automatically imply *en croûte.*

Traditionally, terrines were served directly from the mold. Now it is more common to present terrines in slices. This improves the chef's ability to control both the presentation and the portioning of the dish. This is clearly in the best interest of both the guest and the chef. In some special cases, however, terrines are still served in their

Figure 7-11 Cream worked in by hand.

Figure 7-12 Mousseline applications.

a. Quenelles of mousseline are poached and used as a garnish in fish consommé.

b. Mousseline may have a chunky garnish added as in this filling for tortelloni.

c. Salmon stays moist in a poached mousseline roulade.

d. Salmon and scallop mousselines are layered in a leek-lined terrine mold.

molds. A terrine of foie gras, for instance, may be presented in a small decorative mold, accompanied by toasted brioche. Guests use a special service spoon or knife to serve themselves.

Today, some non-traditional terrines are also made by binding items such as roasted meats or poultry, roasted or grilled vegetables, poached salmon, or seared lamb loins with a little aspic, making them similar to a head cheese. Examples from among the recipes in this chapter include Seared Lamb, Artichoke, Mushroom Terrine (page 258) and Terrine of Scallop and Salmon (page 254). Terrines made from layered vegetables can be bound with a custard or cheese. Roasted Vegetable Terrine with Fresh Goat Cheese (page 265) and Mozzarella, Prosciutto, and Roasted Tomato Terrine (page 266) are two examples. And while this book does not include dessert recipes, terrines made from sliced fruits bound in a sweet aspic or chocolate ganache terrines bound with a mousse or Bavarian cream have become part of the basic repertoire of the pastry chef.

Making Forcemeat Terrines

1. *Prepare the terrine mold by lining it.*

Terrine molds were traditionally lined with fatback, then filled with a forcemeat and any garnish called for by the recipe. This liner, also referred to as a *chemise* or

Figure 7-13 Terrines.

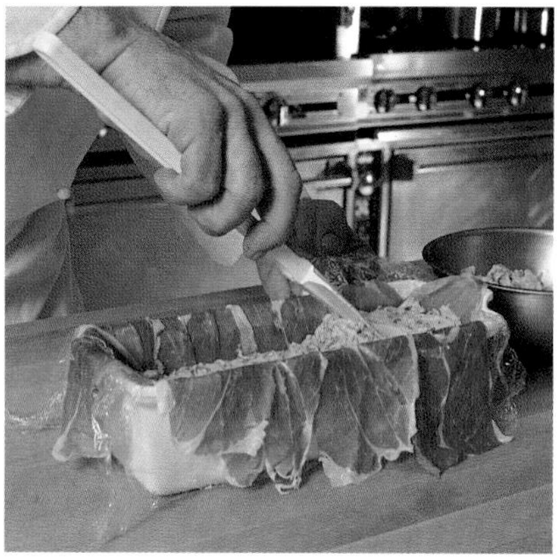

a. The terrine is lined with plastic wrap and prosciutto.

b. The terrine is in a water bath ready to go into the oven.

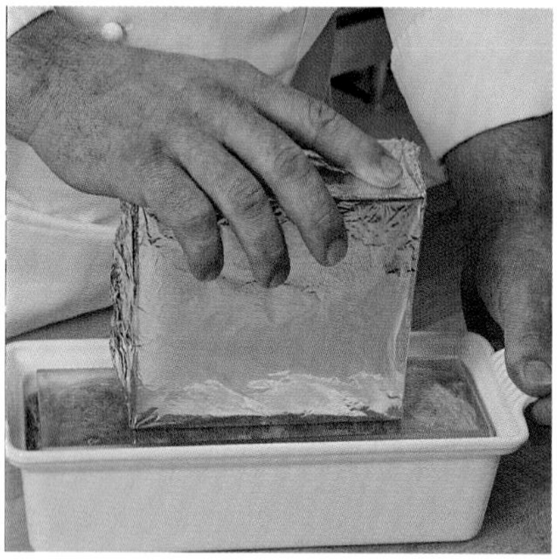

c. A terrine being weighted as it cools.

d. Aspic being added to the terrine.

jacket, is still used today, but fatback may be replaced today with proscuitto, bacon, caul fat, crêpes, leeks, spinach, or even seaweed. A liner is not always required, and may be replaced with plastic wrap; this makes it easy to remove the terrine neatly from the mold. Figure 7-13a shows a terrine mold lined with plastic wrap and prosciutto.

2. *Fill the prepared mold with forcemeat and any garnish required.*

Use a spatula to work the forcemeat into all corners and remove any air pockets. The liner is then folded over the forcemeat to completely encase it, and a lid or foil covers the terrine.

3. *Cook the terrine gently in a water bath (*bain marie*).*

Smooth, flavorful terrines must be properly cooked at a carefully regulated temperature. A water bath can insulate the terrine from temperature extremes. Set the filled, covered terrine mold in a baking pan on a clean side towel or several layers of paper towels. Add enough simmering water to come about two-thirds to three-quarters of the way up the mold's sides and monitor the water bath's temperature (see Figure 7-13b). It should be at a constant 170°F. An oven temperature of approximately 300°F should keep the water bath's temperature within a few degrees of that temperature, but if necessary, adjust the oven temperature.

4. *Cook to the correct internal temperature.*

Check for doneness by measuring the terrine's internal temperature with an instant-read thermometer. Remember to allow for carryover cooking when deciding whether the terrine is ready. The amount of carryover cooking will vary, depending upon the material used to make the mold, the forcemeat, and the overall shape and size of the mold.

5. *Cool, press, and store the terrine until ready to serve.*

Remove the fully cooked terrine from the water bath and allow it to rest at room temperature until the internal temperature drops to 90°F.

Set a press plate on the terrine. You can create a press plate by cutting Styrofoam, Plexiglas, or wood to the inside dimensions of the mold. Wrap the press plate in plastic wrap or foil to lengthen its useful life.

Place a two-pound mold on top of the press plate (see Figure 7-13c). Set this assembly in a hotel pan and let the terrine rest under refrigeration for at least two to three days to mellow and mature the flavor. If desired, coat the terrine with melted aspic (see Figure 7-13d). Techniques and ratios for aspic gelée can be found on page 45.

Aspic-Bound Terrines

To produce high-quality aspic-bound terrines, you should of course season and prepare the main ingredients with care; they are the foundation of the terrine. The aspic, though an important part of the dish, should be added only as needed to bind the major flavoring ingredients properly. Still, it is important to take the time to select a rich, full-flavored base liquid. Clear stocks, broths, consommés, juices, or wines can be used singly or in combination to prepare an aspic of slicing strength.

An alternative to an aspic is a reduced stock, glace de viande, or essence. The action of cooking the stock down drives off the water but leaves the gelatinous proteins in place.

The aspic can be prepared in advance and stored under refrigeration. In order to use it, warm the aspic over a hot water bath just enough to melt it. It should be incorporated while still warm, so that it will blend properly with the ingredients (see Figure 7-14).

Figure 7-14 Adding Warm Aspic the main Ingredients.

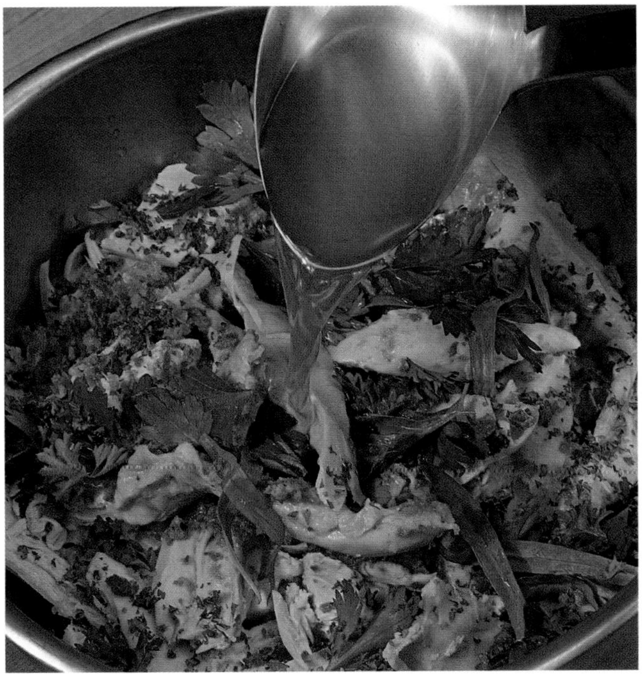

Figure 7-15 Molds for pâté en croûte and terrines.

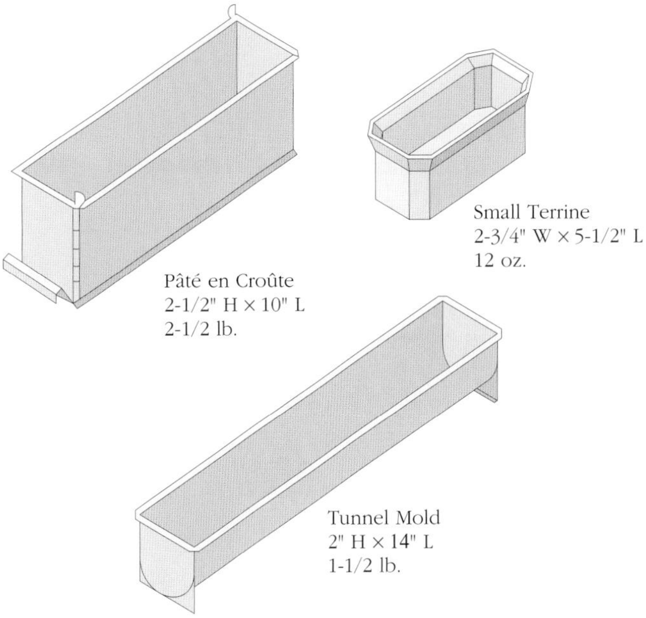

Pâté en Croûte

Making Pâté en Croûte

Today, pâtés en croûte are often made in rectangular molds. The advantage to these molds is that they have regular dimensions and straight sides. This encourages even baking and helps reduce the chances of undercooking the dough. Another reason to choose a rectangular mold is the ability to make uniform slices.

However, an oval pâté en croûte may be a more dramatic presentation if it is being served whole on a buffet or being displaying uncut, as a retail item for sale. (Various shapes for pâté and terrine molds are shown in Figure 7-15.)

1. *Line the pâté mold with dough.*

   First, roll out sheets of dough to approximately 1/4 to 3/16-inch thick. (Tip: use a piece of parchment paper as a template; the pâté dough recipe included in this book will roll out to the suggested thickness when it matches the dimensions of the parchment.) It is important to roll the dough evenly and to handle it gently to avoid tearing or stretching the dough as you line the mold (see Figure 7-16a).

   Now, mark the dough by pressing all sides of the mold very lightly into the dough. This will produce the

Figure 7-16 Pâté en Croûte.

a. Rolling the pâté dough.

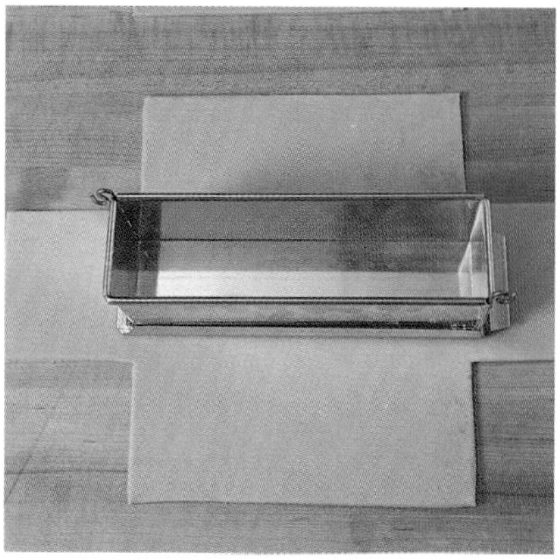

b. The dough is cut into the proper shape for lining the mold.

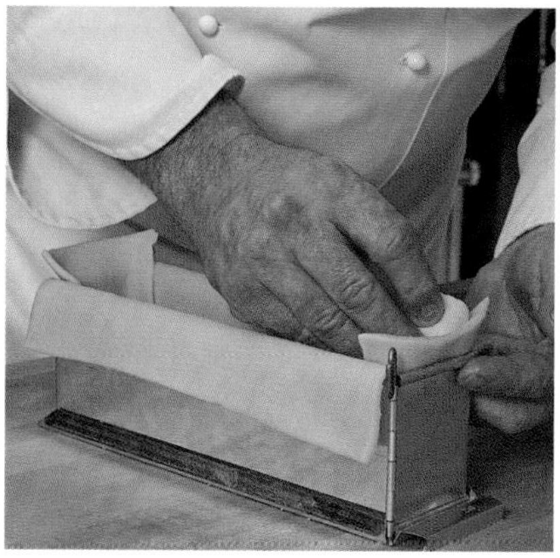

c. Pinching the seams at the corners.

d. Lining the dough with ham.

e. Tucking in the top.

appropriate pattern for the interior of the mold. To line a straight-edged terrine mold, allow an overhang of $\frac{1}{2}$ inch on one side piece as well as enough to fold over the mold's opening, plus $\frac{1}{2}$ inch to secure it into the sides (see Figure 7-16b). Allow an overhang of about 1 to $1\frac{1}{2}$ inches for oval or round molds.

The excess dough in the corners should be cut out before the dough is transferred to the mold. Reserve the excess dough to make the reinforcements for the vent holes you will cut in the top of the pâté, as well as any decorations you may wish to apply.

Set the dough in the mold so that the overhang on one side of the mold is enough to completely cover the top of the mold, and extend down into the mold on the opposite side at least $\frac{1}{2}$ inch. The overhang on the other side will be about $\frac{1}{2}$ inch. Use eggwash to "glue" the pastry together in the corners and pinch the seams (see Figure 7-16c).

If you wish, a second liner may be added at this time. Fatback is commonly used, but prosciutto and other thinly sliced cooked meats can be used to create a special effect (see Figure 7-16d).

At this point, the mold should be filled with the forcemeat and any inlay garnish. Fold the liner and then the dough over the top of the forcemeat. The dough should overlap itself along one side of the mold. Stretch the dough and push it down into the mold using a metal spatula (see Figure 7-16e).

A top crust, or cap, is the traditional way to finish enclosing the forcemeat in pastry. Straight-sided pâtés can be prepared without a separate cap piece as follows: Remove the pins of the mold, place the bottom of the mold on the top of the pâté, reinsert the pins and invert the entire assembly. This will give a smooth, neat top piece, without any extra layers of dough. It also allows the weight of the pâté and mold to hold the seams along the edges of the mold, preventing them from blowing out as the pâté bakes.

Oval pâtés or other shapes should have a separate cap piece. Cut a piece of dough large enough to completely cover the mold. Trim away any excess and tuck the edges down into the mold.

2. *Bake the pâté, adding the chimney and any additional dough garnishes as desired.*

The top crust of the pâté should be vented, to permit steam to escape during baking. If the vents are not cut, the pressure will cause the dough to burst. Be sure that the cut extends completely through every layer of dough and liner. Reinforce the vent's opening by gluing a ring of dough into place with some egg wash. Insert a tube of rolled aluminum foil, known as a *chimney,* to keep the hole from closing as the pâté bakes.

Any decorations made from dough scraps can be added now. (For more information about creating decorations with dough, refer to pages 418, 419.) You can complete these tasks before baking the pâté. Egg wash should be brushed over the entire surface for color and sheen, as well as to secure the reinforcing ring of dough and any decorations to the top crust.

An alternate method is to cover the pâté with foil and partially bake at 450°F for 15 minutes, or until the dough has a dry and light brown appearance. Remove the foil, and use round cutters to make one or two holes in the top piece and brush with egg wash.

Secure any additional decorative pieces to the cap piece, gluing them in place with egg wash. Finally, egg wash the entire top of the pâté. Return the uncovered pâté to the oven and finish baking at 350°F to the appropriate internal temperature.

3. *Cool the pâté en croûte and finish with aspic.*

Let the pâté cool for one or two hours. Insert a funnel into the foil chimney and ladle in melted warm aspic. Let the pâté rest under refrigeration at least twenty-four hours and up to three days before slicing and serving the pâté. Once a pâté en croûte is shaped, baked, and finished with aspic, it may be held for approximately five to seven days.

Galantines and Roulades

Galantines, as we know them, have been popular since the time of the French Revolution (1789–99). The chef from the house of marquis de Brancas, an M. Prévost, began producing the savory cold dish, made from boned poultry, sewn back into the bird's skin, poached in a rich stock, and preserved in the natural jelly. The origin of the dish appears relatively straightforward. The origins of the word, however, are less obvious.

According to *Larousse Gastronomique,* the term derives primarily from an old French word for chicken: *géline* or *galine.* According to this source, the association with chicken is so specific, in fact, that all by itself, galantine presumes chicken, unless it is specified otherwise in the title. Other experts have promoted the idea that galantine more likely comes from the word *gelatin,* with the current spelling gradually superseding other forms of the word, such as *galentyne, galyntyne, galandyne,* and *galendine.*

Two additional terms, *ballotine* and *dodine,* are occasionally used in the same way as *galantine.* Ballotines may be served hot or cold. Dodines, also normally made from poultry, especially duck and goose, are quite similar to galantines except that they are roasted rather than poached, and they are always served hot.

Roulades differ from galantines in that they are rolled in cheesecloth or plastic wrap, not in the natural skin "casing" featured in galantines. Another distinction between the two items is that, while galantines are firmly associated with poultry, roulades have no such identity. Instead, roulades are made from a wide range of base products, including foie gras or mousseline forcemeats made of fish or poultry.

Making Galantines and Roulades

1. *Carefully remove the skin and bone the bird for a galantine.*

The first step in preparing a galantine is to carefully remove the skin from the bird. Make an incision along the backbone, and carefully pull and cut away the skin from the meat (see Figure 7-17a). Keep the skin in a single piece and trim it to an even rectangle (see Figure 7-17b).

You may wish to save the breast portion or tenderloin to use as a garnish. These choice parts can be seared or cured, if desired. They may be used flattened to form the exterior of the galantine, or placed as a center garnish. Both options are shown in Figures 7-17c and 7-18a.

2. *Fill and roll the galantine or roulade.*

Lay out plastic wrap and/or cheesecloth, which should be several inches larger than the skin's dimensions. If

Figure 7-17 Galantine in cheesecloth.

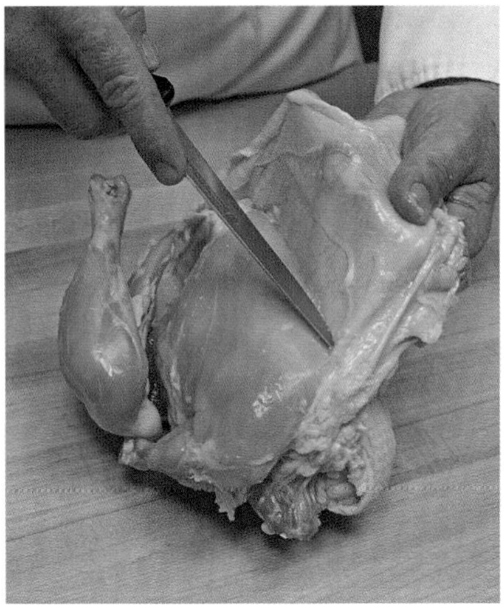

a. Removing the chicken skin in one piece.

b. Trimming the skin into a square.

c. Forcemeat is spread evenly over the skin. Seared chicken breast is placed in the middle.

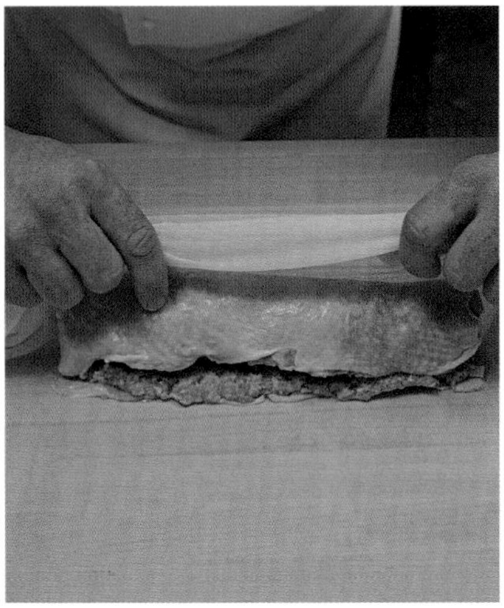

d. Cheesecloth is used to roll up the galantine.

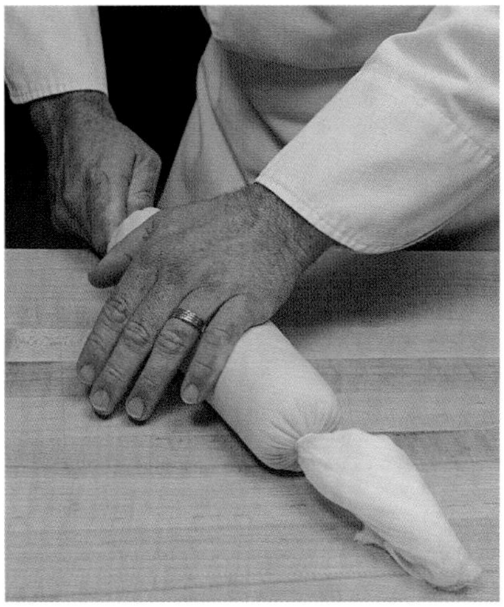

e. The galantine is rolled and tightly tied.

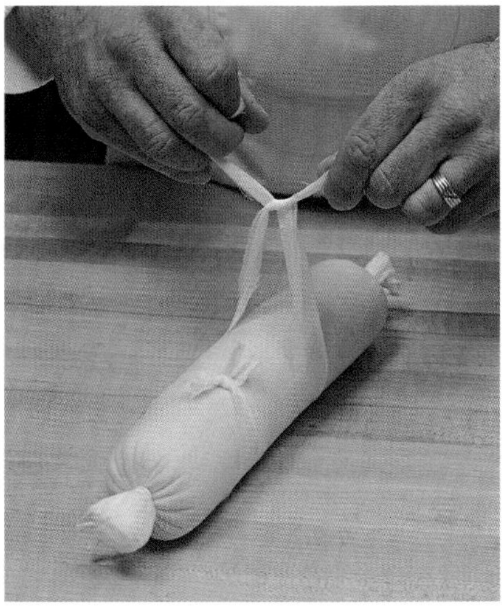

f. If using cheesecloth, two extra bands are tied to support the shape.

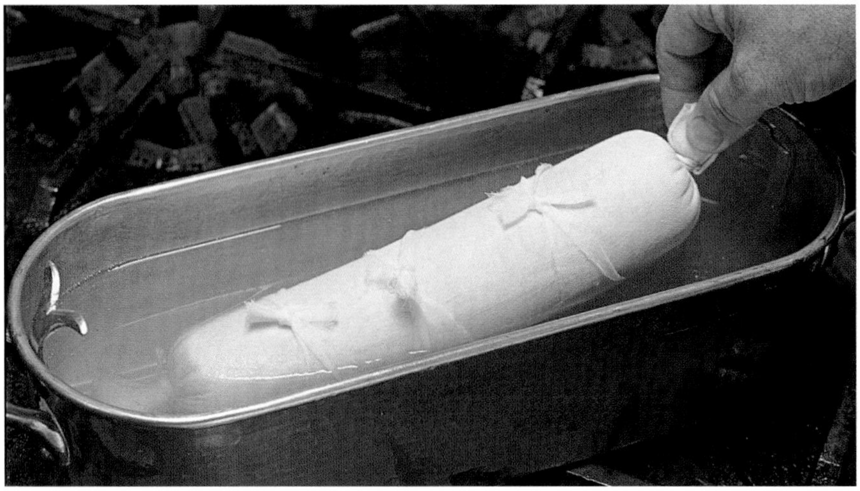

g. The galantine is poached in chicken stock.

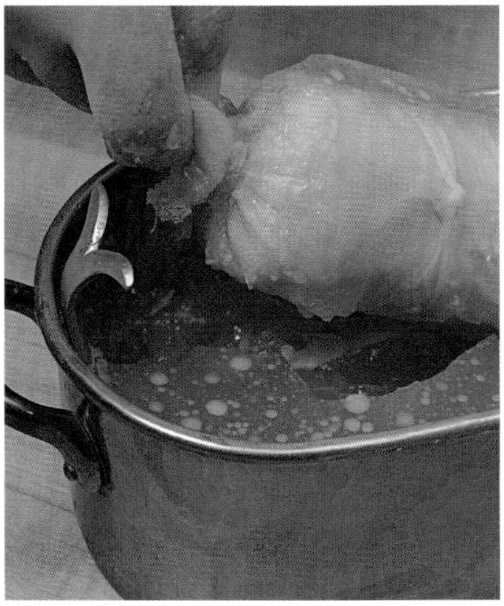

h. The galantine has cooled in the stock.

Figure 7-18 Galantine rolled in plastic.

a. Alternatively, pounded chicken breast is laid on the skin while the forcemeat is mounded in the center.

b. For a galantine rolled in plastic wrap, parchment paper is used to stabilize and support the shape.

Figure 7-19 Roasted galantine.

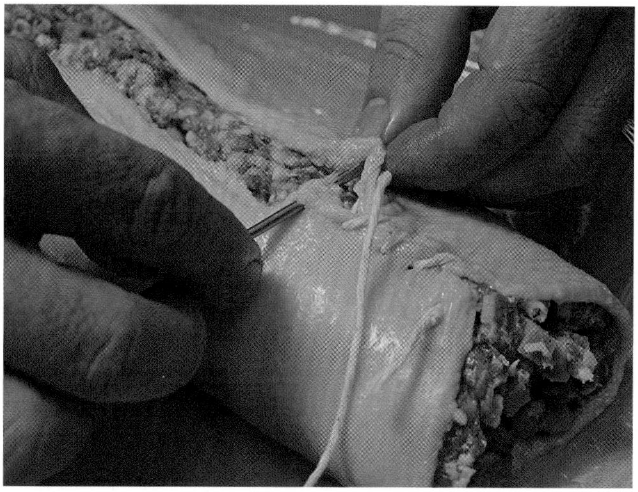

a. If a galantine is to be roasted, the skin must be sewn. Stitches should be small and tight without ripping the skin.

b. The sewn galantine is tied with string as with a roast. The galantine is seared and then roasted with mirepoix.

you are using cheesecloth, remember to rinse it well and wring it dry, until it is damp but not dripping wet.

Lay out the skin on the cheesecloth or plastic wrap and fill it with the forcemeat and any garnish. Roll the galantine or roulade carefully around the forcemeat. The skin should just overlap itself, forming a seam (see Figure 7-17d). A roulade can be rolled like a jelly roll to create a spiral effect, or as you would for a galantine to keep a centered garnish in place. Secure the galantine or roulade by crimping each end and smoothing the forcemeat away from the ends (see Figure 7-17e). You may need a pair of extra hands to maintain a compact shape while you tie the ends. Use butcher's twine to tie several knots to keep the roulade from unraveling as it poaches. Tie two cheesecloth bands or a paper sheath around the galantine (see Figures 7-17f and 7-18b).

In an alternative method for a roasted galantine or dodine, the skin is sewn together at the seam, then the entire galantine is tied as for a roast (see Figure 7-19a and b).

3. *Prepare the galantine or roulade by poaching or roasting.*

Galantines and roulades are commonly poached (see Figure 7-17g). Lower the galantine or roulade into a simmering pot of stock (water is fine if the roulade has been wrapped in plastic wrap rather than cheesecloth). To keep the galantine submerged, weight it down with small plates. This helps to cook the galantine evenly. A roasted galantine (see Figure 7-19b) is placed on a bed of mirepoix and cooked, uncovered, to the appropriate internal temperature.

Once properly cooked (check the internal temperature for accurate results), they should be completely cooled. Galantines may be cooled directly in the cooking liquid (see Figure 7-17h); roulades are generally removed from the poaching liquid and cooled. Galantines and roulades should be rewrapped to produce an even, appealing texture.

Foie Gras

Foie gras is one of the world's great luxury items. The earliest records of foie gras go back to 2500 B.C.E. The tombs dedicated to Ti, an Egyptian counselor to the Pharaoh, show scenes of Egyptians hand-feeding figs to geese.

The first published recipe for pâté de foie gras appeared in *Le Cuisiner Gascon,* a cookbook published in 1747. Jean-Pierre Clause developed another classic preparation in Strasbourg. He took a foie gras and truffles, wrapped them in a pastry case, and baked the dish. Escoffier included a version of this same dish, Pâté Strausbourgiose, in *Le Guide Culinaire.*

Today, foie gras is produced from both geese and ducks. Fresh foie gras is finally available to chefs in the United States (see Figure 7-20). Izzy Yanay, an Israeli who moved to the United States in 1981, is currently producing domestic foie gras from the moulard duck, a hybrid breed resulting from cross-breeding Muscovy (or Barbary) and Pekin ducks.

Working with Foie Gras

Grades

Foie gras may receive an A, B, or C grade (see Figure 7-21), based on the size, appearance, and texture of the liver. To receive a grade of A, the liver must weigh at least 1 1/2 pounds. It should be round and firm, with no blemishes. These livers are used for sautéing and grilling.

B-grade foie gras weigh between 1 and 1.2 pounds. They should have a good texture but are not necessarily as round in shape as foie gras graded A. This grade is a good choice for terrines and roulades.

Foie gras that weighs less than a pound, is slightly flattened, and has some visual imperfections will receive a grade of C. These livers may have some soft spots. They are used primarily for mousses.

Upon Arrival

1. *Inspect the foie gras.*

   This is an expensive product, whatever grade you buy. So take the time to be certain that you are getting the quality you are paying for. First, look to be certain that the packaging is still intact. Any rips or punctures may have damaged the foie gras. Weigh the foie gras yourself, and inspect it carefully for any unexpected imperfections.

2. *Prepare the foie gras for refrigerated storage.*

   Set the foie gras on a bed of crushed ice in a perforated hotel pan, set inside a standard hotel pan. Pack more ice around the liver and keep this assembly in the refrigerator until you are ready to prepare the foie gras.

Figure 7-20 Foie gras production. Freshly harvested livers on ice.

Figure 7-21 (From left to right) Grades A, B, C.

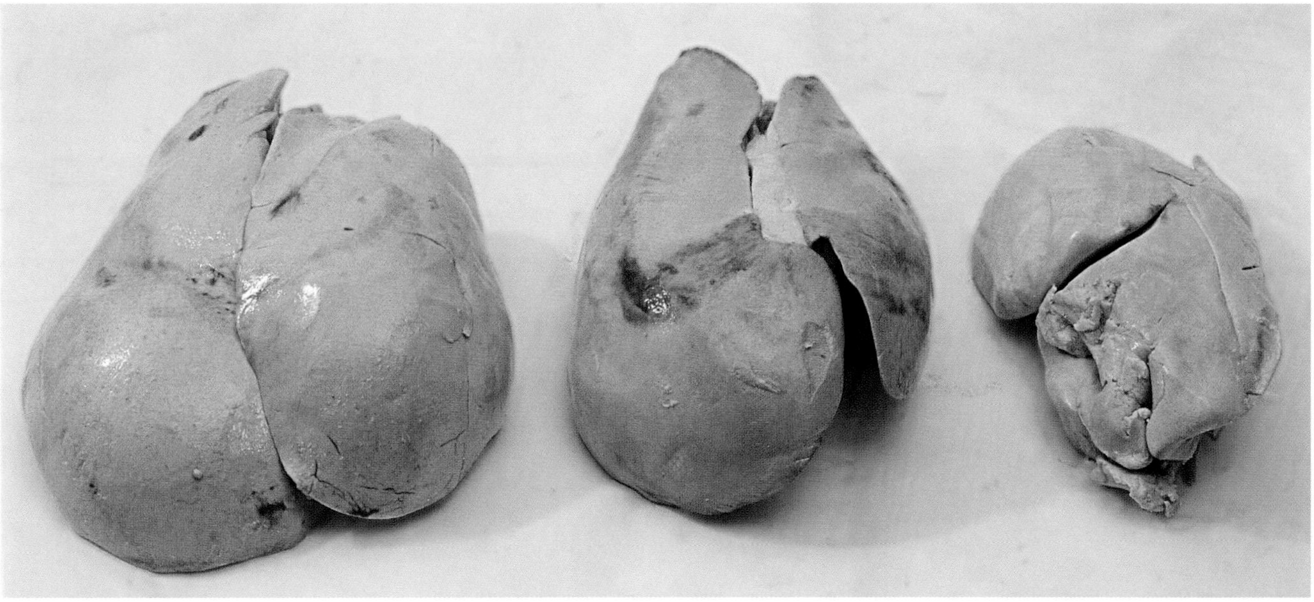

Figure 7-22 Veins of the foie gras.

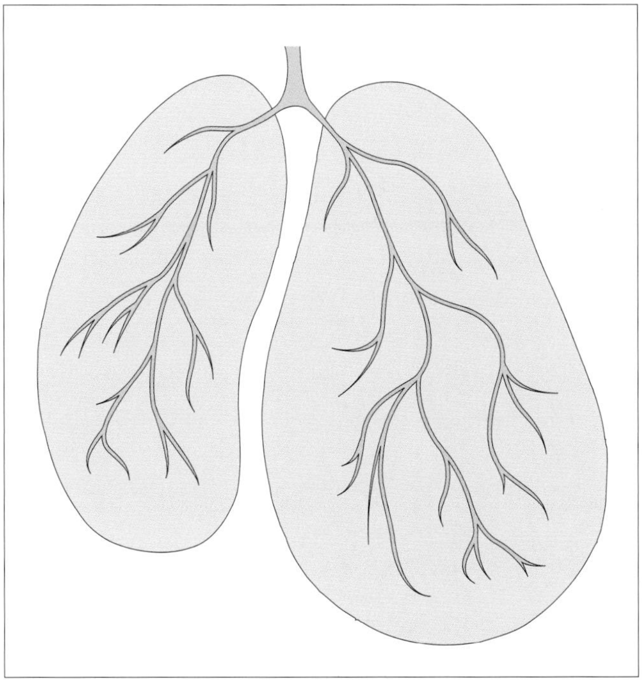

3. *Temper the foie gras before cleaning.*

Soak the foie gras in salted water at room temperature for at least two hours. This will temper the foie gras, making it easier to manipulate as you remove the veins. Inspect the surface and remove visible bruises or blemishes or traces of green bile with a sharp paring knife.

4. *Separate the foie gras into lobes and remove the veins.*

Holding the liver in both hands, gently pull the two lobes apart at their natural seam. Cut about one-third of the way into the lobe. Using a combination of pulling and loosening, expose the vein network (see Figure 7-22). Starting from the top of the lobe, where the veins are thickest, pull out the veins, using tweezers, the tip of a knife, and/or your fingertips (see Figure 7-23). Try to remove as much of the vein network in one piece as possible. Once the small vessels break, they are very hard to grip. Work carefully but quickly, to avoid overhandling the foie gras. You want to keep the lobes as intact as possible.

This procedure takes practice, but once mastered it should take only a few minutes to complete. If you are not ready to proceed with a recipe, be sure to store the cleaned foie gras, well wrapped in plastic, at approximately 34°F. It is important to keep the foie gras as cold as possible, both to keep it safe and wholesome and to keep it firm enough to slice or dice neatly.

Marinating Foie Gras

Foie gras terrines, pâtés, and roulades typically call for marinated foie gras (see Figure 7-24). Place the cleaned foie gras in a suitable container and add seasonings as indicated by the recipe. Sauternes, port, cognac, or Armagnac are among the classic marinade ingredients. You may also

Figure 7-23 Carefully pull the main vein from the liver.

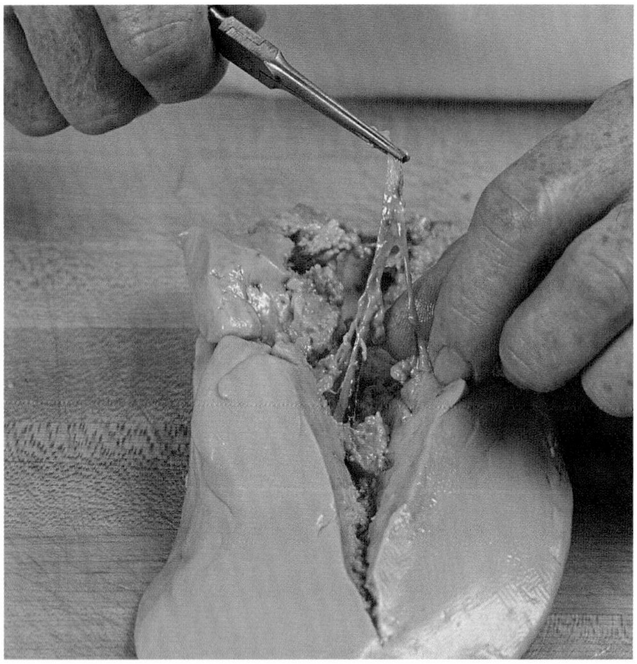

Figure 7-24 Marinate the foie gras in brandy and marsala, salt and pepper.

Figure 7-25 Sliced foie gras terrine.

wish to incorporate additional flavorings, such as quatres épices, cinnamon, or allspice, to give finished the dish a special flavor. Turn the foie gras to coat it evenly with the marinade, and let it rest, covered, under refrigeration for at least 12 and up to 24 hours.

Pâtés, roulades, and terrines of foie gras are still made according to time-honored methods (recipes for these items appear on pages 239, 250, 278, 370, and 371). Today they may be presented to the guest still in their ceramic crock, cut into slices (see Figure 7-25) or shaped into quenelles. A classic presentation, made famous by Fernand Point, features foie gras baked in brioche (see page 370 for recipe). Foie gras mousse is another popular item, and has been used with great effect to make special canapés and appetizers (see page 282 for mousse recipe).

Pâté Grand-Mère

Yield: 3-pound terrine; 18 to 20 servings (2 1/2 ounces each)

1 1/4 lb	chicken livers, sinew removed
17 oz/wt	pork butt, cubed
	Seasonings
1 1/2 oz/wt	salt
1 tsp	coarse ground black pepper (plus more as needed for liner)
2 each	bay leaves
1 sprig	thyme
1 tbsp	vegetable oil, as needed
1 oz/wt	shallots, minced
1 oz/fl	brandy
1 tbsp	chopped flat-leaf parsley
2 1/2 oz/wt	crustless white bread, cut into small dice
5 oz/fl	milk
2 each	eggs
3 oz/fl	heavy cream
1/4 tsp	ground white pepper
Pinch	freshly ground nutmeg
8 each	thin slices fatback (1/16 inch), or as needed for liner
6 to 8 oz/fl	Aspic Gelée, melted (page 45)

1. Combine the livers and pork butt with the seasonings; marinate overnight under refrigeration. The next day, remove and discard the bay leaves and thyme. Separate the chicken livers from the pork butt and dry well.
2. Sear the livers briefly in hot oil; remove them from the pan and chill. Sauté the shallots in the same pan; deglaze with the brandy and add to the livers. Chill thoroughly.
3. Grind the pork butt, liver and shallot mixture, and parsley through the fine plate (1/8 inch) of a meat grinder into a bowl.
4. Combine the bread and milk; let soak to form a panada. Add the eggs, heavy cream, pepper, and nutmeg. Mix with the ground meats on medium speed for 1 minute, until homogenous. Test the forcemeat and adjust seasoning if necessary before proceeding.
5. Line a terrine mold with plastic wrap and then the fatback slices, leaving an overhang. Sprinkle the fatback with the ground pepper, pack the forcemeat into the mold, and fold over the liners. Cover the terrine and poach in a 170°F water bath in a 300°F oven to an internal temperature of 165°F, about 60 to 75 minutes.
6. Remove the terrine from the water bath and allow it to cool to an internal temperature of 90°F to 100°F. Pour off the juices from the terrine, add enough aspic to coat and cover the terrine, and let it rest under refrigeration for 2 days. The terrine is now ready to slice and serve, or wrap and hold under refrigeration for up to 10 days.

Pâté de Campagne (Country-Style Terrine)

Yield: 3-pound terrine; 18 to 20 servings (2 1/2 ounces each)

2 1/2 lb	pork butt, cubed
8 oz/wt	pork liver, cleaned and trimmed
	Seasonings
2 each	minced garlic cloves, sautéed and cooled
4 oz/wt	onion, finely chopped
5 each	parsley sprigs, finely chopped
1 1/2 oz/wt	salt
3/4 tsp	tinted curing mix (TCM)
1/2 tsp	Pâté Spice (page 408)
1/2 tsp	ground white pepper (plus more as needed for liner
	Panada
4 oz/fl	heavy cream
2 each	eggs
2 1/2 oz/wt	flour
1 oz/fl	brandy
8 each	thin slices fatback (1/16 inch), or as needed for liner
6 to 8 oz/wt	Aspic Gelée, melted (page 45)

1. Grind the pork through the coarse plate (3/8 inch) of a meat grinder. Reserve 1 1/2 lb, then grind the remainder with liver and the seasonings through the fine plate (1/8 inch) of a meat grinder into a bowl.
2. Combine the panada ingredients in a bowl; whisk together until smooth; add to the ground meats. Mix on low speed for 1 minute, until homogenous. Then mix on medium speed until mixture feels sticky to the touch.
3. Test the forcemeat and adjust seasoning if necessary before proceeding.
4. Line a terrine mold with plastic wrap and then the fatback slices, leaving an overhang. Sprinkle the fatback with the pepper, pack the forcemeat into the mold, and fold over the liners. Cover the terrine and poach in a 170°F water bath in a 300°F oven to an internal temperature of 150°F, about 60 to 75 minutes.
5. Remove the terrine from the water bath and allow it to cool to an internal temperature of 90°F to 100°F. Pour off the juices from the terrine, add enough aspic to coat and cover the terrine, and let it rest under refrigeration for 2 days. The terrine is now ready to slice and serve, or wrap and hold under refrigeration for up to 10 days.

Pâté Maison Use 3 pounds pork butt and eliminate the liver, if desired.

Duck and Smoked Foie Gras Terrine

Yield: 2 1/2-pound terrine; 16 to 18 servings (2 1/2 ounces each)

1 lb	duck leg and thigh meat, skinned and boned
8 oz/wt	fatback
	Garnish
1 oz/wt	butter
8 oz/wt	smoked foie gras, cut into 1/2-inch dice (see Chef's Notes)
1 each	skinless duck breast, cut into 1/2-inch dice
4 oz/wt	smoked ham, cut into 1/2-inch dice
2 tbsp	minced shallots
1 tsp	minced garlic
2 oz/fl	port wine
1 tbsp	flour
1/4 tsp	tinted curing mix (TCM)
4 tsp	salt
1 each	egg
4 oz/fl	heavy cream
1 tsp	coarse ground black pepper
1/2 tsp	poultry seasoning

1. Cut the leg and thigh meat and the fatback into 1/2-inch dice. Reserve.
2. Prepare the garnish: Melt the butter in a sauté pan. Lightly and quickly sear the smoked foie gras; remove and chill quickly. In the same pan, brown the duck breast and ham; remove, chill, and add to the foie gras. Sweat the shallots and garlic. Add the port wine and reduce to a thick syrup; chill well. Combine with the duck leg meat and fatback; marinate 2 hours under refrigeration.
3. Combine the leg meat mixture with the flour, TCM, and salt, toss to coat evenly, and grind through the fine plate (1/8 inch) of a meat grinder.
4. Transfer the ground meats to a chilled mixing bowl. Add the egg and heavy cream. Mix on medium speed for 1 minute, until homogenous. Add the black pepper and poultry seasoning; mix to incorporate.
5. Test the forcemeat and adjust seasoning if necessary before proceeding.
6. Fold the garnish mixture into the forcemeat by hand over an ice bath.
7. Line a terrine mold with plastic wrap, leaving an overhang. Pack the forcemeat into the mold, and fold over the liner. Cover the terrine and poach in a 170°F water bath in a 300°F oven to an internal temperature of 165°F, about 60 to 75 minutes.
8. Remove the terrine from the water bath and allow it to cool to an internal temperature of 90°F to 100°F. Pour off the juices from the terrine and let it rest under refrigeration overnight. The terrine is now ready to slice and serve, or wrap and hold under refrigeration for up to 5 days.

Chef's Notes: To prepare smoked foie gras, soak and clean the liver as directed on page 237. Cold smoke at 80°F for about 20 minutes. The intention is simply to give a little smoke flavor to the foie gras; it should not be cooked through.

Southwest Chile-Chicken Terrine

Yield: 3-pound terrine; 18 to 20 servings (2 1/2 ounces each)

1 lb	diced chicken leg meat
2 each	whole chicken legs
8 oz/wt	fatback, cubed
	Seasonings
2 oz/wt	minced shallots, sautéed and cooled
1 tbsp	mild chili powder
2 tsp	minced jalapeño
2 tsp	minced garlic, sautéed and cooled
2 tsp	salt
1 tbsp	chopped oregano
1/2 tsp	ground white pepper
1 tsp	Tabasco sauce
2 oz/fl	heavy cream
	Garnish
12 oz/wt	chicken breast meat, 1-in. dice
1/4 cup	fine-dice ham, sautéed and cooled
1 cup	cooked pinto beans
1/2 cup	green chiles, roasted and diced

1. Debone the chicken and chicken legs. Dice the leg and thigh meat (you should have 1 pound). Cut the breast into 1-inch cubes (you should have 12 ounces). Reserve separately.
2. Toss the leg meat and fatback with the seasonings. Grind through the fine plate (1/8 inch) of a meat grinder into a chilled mixing bowl. Add the heavy cream and mix on medium speed for 1 minute, until homogenous. Chill.
3. Test the forcemeat and adjust seasoning if necessary before proceeding.
4. Fold the garnish ingredients mixture into the forcemeat by hand over an ice bath.

5. Line a terrine mold with plastic wrap, pack the forcemeat into the mold, and fold over the liner. Cover the terrine and poach in a 170°F water bath in a 300°F oven to an internal temperature of 165°F, about 60 to 75 minutes.
6. Remove the terrine from the water bath and allow it to cool to an internal temperature of 90°F to 100°F. Add enough aspic to coat and cover the terrine.
7. Let the terrine rest under refrigeration, covered with a 2-pound press plate if desired, for at least 24 hours and up to 2 days. The terrine is now ready to slice and serve, or wrap and hold under refrigeration for up to 7 days.

Venison Terrine

Yield: 3-pound terrine; 18 to 20 servings (2 1/2 ounces each)

2 lb	venison shoulder or leg meat
1 lb	fatback
	Seasonings
2 oz/fl	red wine
1/2 tsp	ground cloves
1 tbsp	crushed black peppercorns
1 tsp	tinted curing mix (TCM)
2 tbsp	minced onions, sautéed and cooled
1 1/2 tbsp	salt
2 tsp	ground black pepper
1 oz/wt	dried cèpes or morels, grounded to powder
3 each	eggs
6 oz/fl	heavy cream
1 tbsp	chopped tarragon
1 tbsp	chopped flat-leaf parsley
	Garnish
2 oz/wt	golden raisins, plumped in 4 oz/fl brandy
4 oz/wt	mushrooms, diced, sautéed, and cooled
8 each	thin slices ham (1/16 inch), or as needed for liner

1. Dice venison and fatback into 1-inch cubes. Marinate them with the seasonings and refrigerate overnight.
2. Prepare a straight forcemeat by grinding the marinated venison and fatback into a chilled mixing bowl. Mix in the eggs, heavy cream, tarragon, and parsley on medium speed for 1 minute, or until homogenous.
3. Line a terrine mold with plastic wrap and the ham, leaving an overhang. Pack the forcemeat into the terrine mold and fold over the ham and plastic. Cover the terrine.
4. Poach forcemeat in a 170°F water bath in a 300°F oven to an internal temperature of 150°F, about 60 to 70 minutes.
5. Remove the terrine from the water bath and allow it to cool to an internal temperature of 90°F to 100°F. Let the terrine rest under refrigeration overnight. The terrine is now ready to slice and serve, or wrap and hold under refrigeration for up to 10 days.

Duck Terrine with Pistachios and Dried Cherries

Yield: 3-pound terrine; 18 to 20 servings (2 1/2 ounces each)

1 3/4 lb	duck meat, trimmed and cubed (from 4- to 5-pound bird)
8 oz/wt	fatback
	Seasonings
1 tbsp	salt
2 tbsp	chopped sage
1 tsp	white pepper
1 tbsp	chopped flat-leaf parsley
1/4 tsp	tinted curing mix (TCM)
	Garnish
4 oz/wt	ham, cut into small dice
6 oz/wt	roasted and peeled pistachios
2 1/2 oz/wt	dried cherries
8 each	thin slices ham (1/16 inch), or as needed for liner

1. Combine 1 pound of the duck meat, the fatback, and the seasonings and grind through the medium plate (1/4 inch) and then the fine plate (1/8 inch) of a meat grinder.
2. Sear the remaining duck meat and the diced ham; let cool.
3. Test the forcemeat and adjust seasoning before adding garnish.
4. Fold in the duck, ham, pistachios, and cherries, working over an ice bath.
5. Line a terrine mold with plastic wrap and ham slices, leaving an overhang, then pack with the forcemeat. Fold the liners over the terrine and cover the mold. Poach in a 170°F water bath in a 300°F oven to an internal temperature of 165°F, about 50 to 60 minutes.
6. Let the terrine rest for 1 hour. Weight it with a 2-pound press overnight and up to 3 days under refrigeration. The terrine is now ready to slice and serve, or wrap and hold under refrigeration for up to 7 days.

Terrine of Wild Boar

Yield: 3-pound terrine; 18 to 20 servings (2½ ounces each)

1½ lb	boar meat (butt or leg), cubed
1 lb	fatback
4 oz/wt	pork liver
	Marinade
2 oz/wt	leek, white and light green parts, thinly sliced
1 oz/wt	white mushrooms, thinly sliced
3 oz/fl	gin
¼ tsp	tinted curing mix (TCM)
4 each	juniper berries, pulverized
4½ tsp	salt
½ tsp	ground black pepper
4 oz/wt	cooked long grain rice, cooled
2 each	eggs
4 oz/fl	heavy cream
½ tsp	ground coriander
1 bunch	savory, chopped
¼ lb	cèpes, sautéed and cooled
8 each	thin slices prosciutto (1/16 inch), or as needed for liner

1. Combine the boar meat, fatback, liver, and marinade ingredients. Marinate under refrigeration overnight. Drain and dry meat.
2. Sear boar meat and liver on both sides and allow to cool. Return the seared meats to the marinating fatback.
3. Grind the marinated meat and fatback, leeks, and mushrooms through the medium plate (¼ inch) of a meat grinder.
4. Combine ground meats and the rice; grind once more through the fine plate (⅛ inch) into a chilled mixing bowl.
5. Mix in the eggs, cream, coriander, and savory. Fold in the cèpes.
6. Test the forcemeat and adjust seasoning if necessary.
7. Line a terrine mold with plastic wrap and the prosciutto, leaving an overhang. Pack with the forcemeat, fold over the liners, and cover the terrine.
8. Poach in a 170°F water bath at 300°F to an internal temperature of 150°F, about 55 minutes.
9. Remove the terrine from the water bath and allow it to cool to an internal temperature of 90°F to 100°F. Let the terrine rest under refrigeration overnight. The terrine is now ready to slice and serve, or wrap and hold under refrigeration for up to 10 days.

Pork Tenderloin Roulade

Yield: $2^1/_2$-pound roulade; 16 to 18 servings ($2^1/_2$ ounces each)

1 each	pork tenderloin (about $1^1/_2$ pounds)
	Brine
1 pt	Basic Meat Brine (page 157)
3 each	star anise pods
2 oz/wt	ginger, roughly chopped
2 tsp	Szechwan peppercorns
	Mousseline
1 lb	ground chicken breast
2 tsp	salt
2 each	egg whites
10 oz/fl	heavy cream
2 tsp	minced garlic
2 tsp	minced ginger
1 tbsp	light soy sauce
1 oz/fl	sherry
3 each	scallions, minced
$^1/_2$ tsp	ground black pepper
2 tbsp	Glace de Volaille *or* Viande (page 412), warm

1. Trim the pork tenderloin; you should have 10 to 12 ounces after trimming.

2. Cover the pork with the brine ingredients; use small plates or plastic wrap to keep it completely submerged. Cure under refrigeration for 12 hours. Rinse tenderloin and dry well.

3. Prepare the chicken mousseline: Place the ground chicken and salt in the bowl of a food processor. Process to a relatively smooth paste. Add the egg whites. With the machine running, add the heavy cream and process just to incorporate. Pass the forcemeat through a drum sieve and fold in the remaining ingredients.

4. Test the forcemeat and adjust the seasoning if necessary before proceeding.

5. On a sheet of plastic wrap, spread half of the mousseline. Place the tenderloin in the middle and spread the other half of the mousseline evenly over the tenderloin. Roll tightly into a cylinder and secure ends with twine. Poach in a 170°F water bath in a 300°F oven to an internal temperature of 165°F, about 50 to 60 minutes.

6. Remove the roulade from the water bath and allow it to cool.

7. Let the roulade rest under refrigeration for at least 24 hours and up to 2 days. The roulade is now ready to slice and serve, or wrap and hold under refrigeration for up to 7 days.

Chef's Notes: If desired, line the plastic wrap with rough-chopped black pepper before spreading the mousseline and rolling the roulade to achieve the effect shown here.

Chicken and Crayfish Terrine

Yield: 2-pound terrine; 10 to 12 servings ($2\frac{1}{2}$ ounces each)

	Mousseline
1 lb	ground chicken breast
2 each	egg whites
2 tsp	salt
1/2 tsp	ground black pepper
6 oz/fl	Shellfish Essence, chilled (recipe follows)
2 oz/fl	heavy cream, chilled
	Garnish
1 lb	cooked crayfish tails, shelled and deveined
3 each	chipotles in adobo sauce, minced
6 each	shiitake mushrooms, cut into medium dice, sautéed, and chilled
2 tbsp	chopped cilantro
1 tbsp	chopped dill

1. Make a mousseline forcemeat: Process the ground chicken, egg whites, salt, and pepper. Add the shellfish essence and heavy cream with the machine running, and process just to incorporate. Pass the forcemeat through a drum sieve if desired.
2. Test the forcemeat and adjust the seasoning if necessary before proceeding.
3. Fold in the crayfish tails, chipotle, mushrooms, cilantro, and dill, working over an ice bath.
4. Oil a terrine mold and line it with plastic wrap, leaving an overhang. Pack the forcemeat into the lined mold, making sure to remove any air pockets. Fold the liner over the forcemeat to completely encase the terrine; cover.
5. Poach the terrine in a 170°F water bath in a 300°F oven to an internal temperature of 165°F, about 60 to 75 minutes.

6. Remove the terrine from the water bath and allow it to cool slightly.
7. Let the terrine rest at least overnight and up to 3 days under refrigeration, weighted with a 2-pound press plate if desired. The terrine is now ready to slice and serve, or wrap and hold under refrigeration for up to 7 days.

Chef's Notes: The Shellfish Essence can be prepared using the shells reserved from this recipe or from other uses. Be sure to freeze the shells if they cannot be used within 12 hours.

Shellfish Essence

Yield: 6 fluid ounces

1 lb	crayfish, shrimp, or lobster shells
1 tbsp	vegetable oil
2 each	shallots, minced
2 each	garlic cloves, minced
12 oz/fl	heavy cream
3 each	bay leaves
2 tsp	poultry seasoning
1 tbsp	chili powder
2 tbsp	Glace de Volaille *or* Viande, page 412

1. Sauté the shells in the vegetable oil until red. Add the shallots and garlic; sauté until aromatic.
2. Add the heavy cream, bay leaves, poultry seasoning, and chili powder; reduce to half of original volume. Add the glace and squeeze through a cheesecloth (final volume should be 6 fluid ounces); chill to below 40°F.

Lobster Terrine with Summer Vegetables

Yield: 2-pound terrine; 10 to 12 servings ($2^1/_2$ ounces each)

4 oz/wt	diced scallops
4 oz/wt	diced shrimp
	Seasonings
1 tbsp	Pernod
1 tsp	lemon juice
1 tsp	salt
1/2 tsp	ground white pepper
1/2 tsp	grated lemon zest
Pinch	cayenne pepper
1 each	egg white
5 oz/fl	heavy cream, chilled
	Garnish
10 oz/wt	assorted vegetables, cut into 1/4-inch dice, cooked, cooled, and drained (see Chef's Notes)
10 oz/wt	lobster meat, poached and cut into medium dice

1. Make a mousseline forcemeat by grinding the scallops, shrimp, and seasonings in the bowl of a food processor. Process to a relatively smooth paste. Add the egg white. With the machine running, add the heavy cream and process just to incorporate. Pass the forcemeat through a drum sieve if desired.
2. Test the forcemeat and adjust seasoning if necessary before proceeding.
3. Fold in the garnish by hand, working over an ice bath.
4. Oil a terrine mold and line it with plastic wrap, leaving an overhang. Pack the forcemeat into the lined mold, making sure to remove any air pockets. Fold the liner over the forcemeat to completely encase the terrine, and cover.
5. Poach the terrine in a 170°F water bath in a 300°F oven to an internal temperature of 145°F, about 60 to 75 minutes.
6. Remove the terrine from the water bath and allow it to cool slightly.
7. Let the terrine rest at least overnight and up to 3 days under refrigeration, weighted with a 2-pound press plate if desired. The terrine is now ready to slice and serve, or wrap and hold under refrigeration for up to 7 days.

Presentation Ideas: Serve with Basic Mayonnaise (page 28) flavored with chopped basil, and tomato concassé garnish.

Chef's Notes: For vegetable garnish, choose from broccoli, carrots, zucchini, squash, or shiitake or other mushrooms.

Mushroom Terrine

Yield: 2-pound terrine; 10 to 12 servings ($2\frac{1}{2}$ ounces each)

1 tbsp	powdered gelatin
4 oz/fl	Madeira wine
2 oz/fl	brandy
18 oz/wt	assorted mushrooms, cut into large dice
2 each	shallots, minced, sautéed, and cooled
3 each	garlic cloves, minced, sautéed, and cooled
2 tbsp	vegetable oil
2 tbsp	minced tarragon
2 tbsp	minced chives
2 tbsp	minced flat-leaf parsley
2 tbsp	Glace de Volaille (page 412), melted
2 tsp	salt
1/2 tsp	ground white pepper
12 oz/wt	chicken breast, raw, diced
1 each	egg
8 oz/fl	heavy cream

1. Sprinkle gelatin powder over the Madeira and brandy and let it bloom for 5 minutes.
2. Sauté the mushrooms, shallots, and garlic in the vegetable oil. Add the gelatin solution and reduce until 1 tablespoon of the liquid remains. Transfer to a bowl and add the tarragon, chives, parsley, glace, and half the salt and pepper. Chill.
3. Make a mousseline-style forcemeat by processing the chicken, the remaining salt and pepper, egg, and the cream until smooth.
4. Test the forcemeat and adjust seasoning if necessary before proceeding.
5. Fold in the mushroom and herb mixture, working over an ice bath.
6. Oil a terrine mold and line it with plastic wrap, leaving an overhang. Pack the forcemeat into the lined mold, making sure to remove any air pockets. Fold the liner over the forcemeat to completely encase the terrine, and cover.
7. Poach the terrine in a 170°F water bath in a 300°F oven until an internal temperature of 165°F is reached, about 60 to 75 minutes.
8. Remove the terrine from the water bath and allow it to cool to an internal temperature of 90°F to 100°F. Press with a 2-pound weight and let it rest under refrigeration overnight. The terrine is now ready to slice and serve, or wrap and hold under refrigeration for up to 3 days.

Chef's Notes: Raw turkey breast can be substituted for the chicken.

Sweetbread and Foie Gras Terrine

Yield: 2 3/4-pound terrine; 14 to 16 servings (2 1/2 ounces each)

1 lb	veal sweetbreads
1 cup	milk
2 qt	Court Bouillon (page 412)
3/4 lb	foie gras, B-grade
1 tbsp	albumen powder or powdered gelatin *(optional)*
	Mousseline
1 lb	turkey breast (or lean veal)
1 each	egg white
1 cup	heavy cream
1 1/2 tsp	salt
1/2 tsp	ground white pepper
1 tbsp	chopped chervil
1 tbsp	chopped chives
8 each	thin slices cooked smoked tongue (1/16 inch), or as needed for liner

1. Soak sweetbreads overnight in the milk. Drain and poach in the court bouillon at 170°F until just done and still pink inside. Cool and remove membranes. Break the sweetbreads into pieces approximately 1-inch square.
2. Cut foie gras into 1-inch cubes and sear in a hot sauté pan; cool quickly. Dust with the albumen powder (if using).
3. Make a mousseline-style forcemeat by processing the turkey, egg white, cream, salt, and pepper until smooth.
4. Test the forcemeat and adjust if necessary before proceeding.
5. Fold the sweetbreads, foie gras, and herbs into the forcemeat.
6. Line a terrine mold with plastic wrap and the sliced tongue, leaving an overhang.
7. Fill the mold with the forcemeat and smooth with a palette knife. Fold over the tongue and plastic wrap. Poach in a 170°F water bath in a 300°F oven until an internal temperature of 165°F is reached, about 60 to 70 minutes.
8. Remove the terrine from the water bath and allow it to cool to an internal temperature of 90°F to 100°F. Let the terrine rest under refrigeration overnight. The terrine is now ready to slice and serve, or wrap and hold under refrigeration for up to 3 days.

Mediterranean Seafood Terrine

Yield: 3-pound terrine; 18 to 20 servings ($2^1/_2$ ounces each)

This recipe was developed by Chef Mark Erickson to meet the special requirements of the Institute's nutritional cuisine restaurant. The vegetable and seafood garnish takes center stage, making this a dish that appeals to those concerned with nutrition as well as those concerned with the flavor and taste of a dish.

	Mousseline
4 oz/wt	shrimp, peeled, deveined, and diced
10 oz/wt	scallops, diced
2 tsp	salt
1/2 tsp	ground white pepper
2 each	egg whites
5 oz/fl	heavy cream, infused with saffron and chilled (see Chef's Notes)
	Garnish
1/2 lb	shrimp (16/20 count), split and cut into eighths
1/2 lb	sea scallops, quartered
1 tbsp	chopped parsley
2 tsp	chopped basil

1. Prepare a mousseline-style forcemeat by processing the shrimp, scallops, salt, pepper, egg whites, and saffron-infused cream until smooth.
2. Test the forcemeat and adjust if necessary before proceeding.
3. Fold the garnish ingredients into the forcemeat, working over an ice bath.
4. Line a terrine mold with plastic wrap, leaving an overhang, and fill it with the forcemeat. Fold over the plastic and cover the terrine.
5. Poach the terrine in a 170°F water bath in a 300°F oven to an internal temperature of 145°F, about 20 to 25 minutes.
6. Remove the terrine from the water bath and allow it to cool to an internal temperature of 90°F to 100°F. Let the terrine rest under refrigeration overnight. The terrine is now ready to slice and serve, or wrap and hold under refrigeration for up to 3 days.

Presentation Ideas: This terrine can be served with Red Pepper Coulis (page 43).

Chef's Notes: To make saffron-infused cream, heat 5 ounces of heavy cream to 160°F. Add a pinch of crushed saffron and allow the saffron to steep in the cream away from the heat until a brilliant yellow-gold color. Chill the cream well before using in the mousseline.

Terrine of Scallop and Salmon

Yield: 3-pound terrine; 18 to 20 servings ($2^{1}/_{2}$ ounces each)

12 oz/wt	salmon fillet
	Mousseline
1 lb 14 oz/wt	bay scallops, cleaned
2 tbsp	salt
4 each	egg whites
26 oz/fl	heavy cream
2 oz/fl	lemon juice
1/4 tsp	ground white pepper
2 oz/wt	truffle peelings
2 oz/wt	chives, minced

1. Cut the salmon fillet into 3 strips the length of the mold and about 1/2-inch square. Reserve.
2. Prepare a mousseline-style forcemeat by processing the scallops, salt, egg whites, cream, and lemon juice until smooth. Do not overmix. Season with pepper.
3. Test the forcemeat and adjust seasoning if necessary before proceeding.
4. Fold in the truffle peelings and chives, working over an ice bath.
5. Oil a terrine mold and line it with plastic wrap, leaving an overhang.
6. Pack half the forcemeat into the lined mold, making sure to remove any air pockets.
7. Lay the salmon strips on the forcemeat for the inlay garnish. Cover with the remaining forcemeat and smooth the surface.
8. Poach in a 160°F water bath in a 300°F oven to an internal temperature of 145°F, about 60 to 70 minutes.
9. Cool the terrine for 1 hour. Let it rest under refrigeration, covered with a 2-pound press plate if desired, at least 24 hours. The terrine is now ready to slice and serve, or wrap and hold under refrigeration for up to 4 days.

Saint Andrew's Vegetable Terrine

Yield: 3-pound terrine; 18 to 20 servings ($2^1/_2$ ounces each)

Saint Andrew's Vegetable Terrine, shown with Mediterranean Seafood Terrine (page 253)

3/4 lb	chicken breast, raw, cubed
1 each	egg white
6 oz/fl	heavy cream
2 tsp	salt, plus more to taste
To taste	ground white pepper
6 oz/wt	spinach, sautéed and rough chopped
1 each	roasted red pepper, cut into medium dice
8 oz/wt	fine-dice summer squash and/or zucchini, blanched
8 oz/wt	fine-dice carrots, fully cooked
2 oz/wt	fine-dice yellow turnip, fully cooked
1 tbsp	powdered gelatin
6 tbsp	minced fresh herbs (such as marjoram, dill, and/or chives)
Pinch	grated nutmeg
1 tsp	cardamom seeds, roasted

1. Make a mousseline-style forcemeat by processing the chicken, egg white, cream, salt, and pepper until smooth. Test the forcemeat and adjust seasoning if necessary before proceeding.
2. Toss the vegetables in a mixing bowl with salt and ground pepper. Add the gelatin powder and toss to coat evenly. Fold the vegetables with the herbs, nutmeg, and cardamom into the forcemeat, working over an ice bath.
3. Oil a terrine mold and line it with plastic wrap, leaving an overhang.
4. Pack the forcemeat into the lined mold, making sure to remove any air pockets. Fold over the liners.
5. Poach the terrine in a 170°F water bath in a 300°F oven until an internal temperature of 165°F is reached, about 60 to 75 minutes.
6. Let the terrine rest under refrigeration, weighted with a 1-pound press plate if desired, for at least 12 hours. The terrine is now ready to slice and serve, or wrap and hold under refrigeration for up to 4 days.

Carolina Barbecue Terrine with Apricot Barbecue Sauce

Yield: 3-pound terrine; 18 to 20 servings ($2\frac{1}{2}$ ounces each)

1 each	pork butt
	Dry Rub
1/4 cup	sweet Spanish paprika
2 tbsp	salt
2 tbsp	sugar
2 tbsp	dark brown sugar
2 tbsp	cumin
2 tbsp	chili powder
1 tbsp	finely ground black pepper
1 tbsp	cayenne pepper
	Spiced Vinegar
2 oz/fl	cider vinegar
1 tbsp	sugar
1 tbsp	crushed red pepper
1 tsp	salt
1/2 tsp	finely ground black pepper
1 lb	collard greens, cleaned, blanched, and rough chopped
1/2 cup	Chicken or Turkey Stock (page 410)
1/2 cup	Glace de Volaille, warmed (page 412)
2 each	pork tenderloins, brined overnight in Basic Meat Brine, and hot smoked (see page 157)

1. Trim pork butt of excess fat, leaving approximately 1/4 inch of fat cover. Score fat in criss-cross pattern.
2. Combine the spice rub ingredients and rub into the butt. Allow to sit overnight under refrigeration.
3. Combine the dry vinegar ingredients in a saucepan. Heat and allow to steep for 30 minutes.
4. Smoke-roast the pork butt at 225°F for 4 to 6 hours to an internal temperature of 150°F until tender, basting with the spiced vinegar. Remove from the oven and allow to rest until cool enough to handle.
5. Pull the meat from the bones, discarding any fat and gristle. Shred the meat into small pieces and combine with the collards, stock, and glace.
6. Oil a terrine mold and line with plastic wrap leaving an overhang. Pack the meat into the mold. Place the fully cooked pork tenderloins as center garnishes. Fold over liner.
7. Let the terrine rest under refrigeration for 2 to 3 days, weighted with a 4-pound press plate if desired. The terrine is now ready to slice and serve, or wrap and hold under refrigeration for up to 7 days.

Roasted Pepper and Eggplant Terrine

Yield: 3-pound terrine; 18 to 20 servings (2 1/2 ounces each)

1 lb	eggplant, sliced lengthwise 1/4-inch thick
3 lb	red peppers (about 6)
3 lb	yellow peppers (about 6)
3 lb	green peppers (about 6)
2 tsp	salt
1/2 tsp	ground black pepper
1/2 oz/wt	powdered gelatin
12 oz/fl	Basil Red Wine Vinaigrette (page 22)

1. Salt eggplant for 1/2 hour and let drain on toweling before grilling; peel eggplant. Grill eggplant and peppers on a hot grill. Peel and seed peppers; cool. Trim to fit a terrine mold. Season with salt and pepper.
2. Line the mold with plastic wrap, leaving an overhang (or see Presentation Ideas).
3. Dissolve the gelatin in the vinaigrette.
4. Layer the peppers and eggplant alternately with dressing to fill the mold; fold over the liner.
5. Cover the terrine with plastic and weigh down with a 2-pound weight overnight under refrigeration. The terrine is now ready to slice and serve, or wrap and hold under refrigeration for up to 7 days.

Presentation Ideas: Line the terrine mold with sliced, fully cooked carrots for the presentation shown in the photo.

Seared Lamb, Artichoke, and Mushroom Terrine

Yield: 2-pound terrine; 10 to 12 servings (2 1/2 ounces each)

1 each	whole lamb loin, bone-in
	Spices
1 1/2 tsp	curry powder
1/2 tbsp	celery seed
1 1/2 tbsp	whole coriander seed
1 tbsp	ground zaatar (see Chef's Notes)
1 tbsp	fennel seed
2 tbsp	salt
2 tbsp	cumin seed
1 tsp	anise seed
2 tbsp	olive oil
1 cup	cèpes, quartered
1 tbsp	olive oil
To taste	salt
To taste	ground white pepper
	Aspic
1 tbsp	tomato paste
4 oz/wt	Mirepoix (page 404)
2 cups	Chicken Stock (page 410)
3/4 oz/wt	powdered gelatin
3 each	artichoke bottoms, cooked and quartered
2 tbsp	chopped tarragon
2 tbsp	chopped parsley

1. Bone the loin, reserving the loins and tenderloins separately. Reserve the bones to prepare a stock.
2. Cut lamb loins lengthwise into two pieces, making 4 loin strips plus 2 tenderloin pieces.
3. Toast the spices; grind and rub over lamb. Marinate for 4 hours.
4. Sear the lamb to medium rare in a very hot sauté pan in olive oil. Cool and reserve.
5. Sauté the cèpes in hot oil, season with salt and pepper, and cook through. Cool and reserve.
6. Brown the lamb bones in the oven. Add the tomato paste and mirepoix; brown. Transfer bones and mirepoix to saucepan; add the chicken stock. Bring to a simmer and reduce by one third.
7. Strain through cheesecloth and cool. When cool, add the gelatin; bloom and heat to clear. Heat the aspic to 120°F.
8. Oil a terrine mold and line it with plastic wrap, leaving an overhang. Mix the lamb, artichokes, cèpes, and herbs. Mix in all but 1/2 cup of the aspic thoroughly and pack into the terrine mold. Pour the remaining aspic on top, spreading it over the entire length of the terrine. Use more stock if necessary.
9. Fold over liner and press with a 2-pound press plate. Chill the terrine for at least 24 hours before slicing and serving, or wrap and hold under refrigeration for up to 10 days.

Presentation Ideas: Serve this terrine with Hummus (page 41) and pita triangles.

Chef's Notes: One average bone-in lamb loin will yield approximately 1 pound of loin and tenderloin meat. Zaatar is a Middle Eastern spice blend made of ground sumac and thyme. It can be purchased or made as needed.

Terrine of Roasted Pheasant

Yield: 2 1/2-pound terrine; 14 to 16 servings (2 1/2 ounces each)

1 each	pheasant, about 3 pounds
2 qt	Basic Poultry Brine, chilled (page 153)
	Aspic
1 qt	Chicken Stock (page 410)
1/2 bunch	parsley stems
4 each	thyme sprigs
2 tsp	crushed juniper berries
1/2 cup	Madeira wine
1 tbsp	whole black peppercorns
4 oz/wt	baby braising greens, blanched and rough chopped
2 tbsp	chopped flat-leaf parsley
2 tsp	salt
1/2 tsp	coarse ground black pepper
1 tsp	Old Bay seasoning

1. Cover the pheasant with the brine and weight down with a plate to be sure it is completely submerged. Cure overnight. Remove the pheasant and rinse thoroughly.
2. Roast the pheasant to an internal temperature of 165°F, about 35 to 45 minutes. Remove the pheasant from the oven and allow to cool.
3. Pull the meat from the bones. Reserve the bones and discard the skin. Shred the meat coarsely, cover, and keep under refrigeration until ready to assemble the terrine.
4. Place the bones in a large pot and cover with the chicken stock. Bring to a slow, even simmer. Add the parsley stems, thyme, juniper, Madeira, and peppercorns; continue to simmer for at least 2 hours, or until the stock has a good flavor.
5. Strain the stock through a fine-mesh strainer, return it to the stove, and reduce it to 1 cup. Keep warm.
6. Line a terrine mold with plastic wrap, leaving an overhang. Combine the pheasant with the aspic, braising greens, chopped parsley, salt, pepper, and Old Bay. Pack into the mold. Fold over the liner.
7. Let the terrine rest under refrigeration for at least 24 hours and up to 2 days. The terrine is now ready to slice and serve, or wrap and hold under refrigeration for up to 7 days.

Chef's Notes: Do not use red beet greens or red Swiss chard; they will discolor the terrine. A julienne of vegetables can also be added.

Poached Chicken Terrine

Yield: 2-pound terrine; 10 to 12 servings (2 1/2 ounces each)

1 each	chicken (3 pounds)
1 gallon	Chicken Stock (page 410)
1 each	Standard Sachet d'Epices (page 405)
8 oz/wt	fine-dice zucchini, blanched
8 oz/wt	fine-dice yellow squash, blanched
8 oz/wt	fine-dice carrots, fully cooked
1 tsp	salt
1/2 tsp	ground white pepper
1 bag	cello spinach, cleaned, seasoned, and blanched
1/4 cup	Fines Herbes (page 408)

1. Skin the chicken and simmer in the chicken stock with the sachet d'épices until chicken is tender.
2. Shred the chicken meat into thick strips (about 1/4 × 3 inches) and combine with the vegetables.
3. Degrease and strain the stock; return to heat and reduce to approximately 1 1/2 cups. Season with the salt and pepper.
4. Line a terrine mold with plastic wrap and seasoned spinach and paint with a small amount of reduced stock. Sprinkle a thin layer of Fines Herbes over the painted spinach.
5. Mix the chicken and vegetables with the reduced stock and any remaining herbs. Pack this mixture into the mold. Fold over the liner.
6. Cover the terrine with plastic wrap and weight down with a 2-pound weight overnight under refrigeration. The terrine is now ready to slice and serve, or wrap and hold under refrigeration for up to 7 days.

Presentation Ideas: Serve two thin slices of the terrine with 2 ounces of Papaya and Black Bean Salsa (page 36) or Mango-Lime Salsa (page 35).

Chef's Notes: The vegetables should be blanched separately to ensure even coloring and to prevent color transfer.

Bouillabaisse en Terrine

Yield: 3-pound terrine; 18 to 20 servings ($2^1/_2$ ounces each)

	Vegetable Garnish
1/2 lb	medium-dice fennel
1/2 lb	medium-dice onions
1/2 lb	medium-dice celery
1/2 lb	medium-dice carrots
1 tbsp	minced garlic
2 oz/fl	olive oil
2 qt	Fish Stock (page 411)
1 tbsp	ground fennel seeds
1 tsp	ground anise seeds
6 each	parsley stems
1 tsp	chopped thyme
2 each	bay leaves
1 each	lemon, zest chopped, juice reserved
10 oz/fl	dry white wine
1/4 tsp	cayenne pepper
2 tsp	salt
	Seafood Garnish
1 lb	raw lobster meat, cut into medium dice
1/2 lb	shrimp, peeled and deveined, cut into medium dice
1/2 lb	scallops, cut into medium dice
1/2 lb	salmon fillet, skinless, cut into medium dice
1 lb	monkfish fillet, cleaned, cut into medium dice
	Aspic Gelée
5 each	egg whites, whipped to soft peak
1 1/4 lb	tomato concassé
1 each	lemon, juice only
2 tbsp	chopped flat-leaf parsley
1 tbsp	chopped tarragon
8 oz/wt	monkfish trim, ground
15 each	saffron threads
2 1/4 oz/wt	powdered gelatin, softened in 3 oz/fl cold water

1. Sweat the fennel, onions, celery, carrots, and garlic in the olive oil over low flame until vegetables are very tender; do not let them color. As the vegetables cook, occasionally add a small amount of fish stock to moisten. Remove and cool.

2. In a stock pot, place fennel and anise seeds, parsley stems, thyme, bay leaves, lemon zest, 8 ounces of the wine, the cayenne pepper, salt, and the remaining fish stock and bring to a boil. Simmer for 45 minutes then strain.

3. Poach fish and seafood at 170°F in the strained stock until just done, about 5 to 6 minutes. They must be cooked through but not overcooked. Remove from stock and refrigerate.

4. Strain the stock through a fine-mesh strainer into a soup pot and cool to 100°F.

5. Add the egg whites, tomato concassé, lemon juice, chopped parsley, tarragon, the remaining wine, monkfish trim, and saffron to the strained stock. Stir well.

6. Gradually bring to a simmer to form a raft over medium-high heat; simmer for 30 minutes without stirring.

7. Strain the clarified stock; adjust seasoning. Add the softened gelatin and stir to combine thoroughly. Test for gelatin strength (page 45) and add more gelatin if necessary. Cool this aspic.

8. Line a terrine mold with plastic wrap, leaving an overhang. Arrange the fish, seafood, and vegetables randomly in the mold, pour in enough aspic to cover, and refrigerate overnight. The terrine is now ready to slice and serve, or wrap and hold under refrigeration for up to 4 days.

Presentation Ideas: Bouillabaisse Terrine is classically served with Rouille (page 29). Or serve it with French bread toast topped with Tapenade (page 41) and Vinaigrette Gourmande (page 23).

Chef's Notes: Blanched spinach or savoy cabbage may be used as a liner, if desired. If preferred, replace the salmon fillet with mullet, rouget, bass, or snapper.

Poached Salmon and Lemon Terrine

Yield: 3-pound terrine; 18 to 20 servings ($2^1/_2$ ounces each)

This terrine is very flavorful and attractive, but requires particular attention when preparing and assembling.

2 lb	salmon fillet
2 qt	Court Bouillon (page 412), or as needed
To taste	salt
	Garnish
3 each	egg whites, poached, cut into small dice
4 each	lemons, sectioned and seeded
2 each	lemons, zest only, blanched and chopped fine
3 oz/wt	roasted red pepper, peeled, seeded, and cut into small dice
2 tbsp	rough-chopped flat-leaf parsley
1 tbsp	rough-chopped tarragon
2 tbsp	fine-dice shallots
1/2 tsp	white pepper
3 cups	Aspic Gelée (page 262), made with Fish Stock

1. Cut the salmon fillet into 5 strips the length of the terrine mold and about 3/4-inch square. Poach in the court bouillon until barely cooked, about 10 minutes. Drain and chill well.
2. Season the gelée with salt. Line a terrine with plastic wrap, leaving an overhang, then brush the sides and bottom with a thin layer of the gelée.
3. Working over an ice bath, fit the salmon and the combined garnish ingredients into the mold, covering each layer with fish aspic gelée. Make sure garnish is evenly distributed from end to end.
4. Fold over the plastic wrap, cover, and let rest at least 24 hours, weighted with a 2-pound press plate if desired. The terrine is now ready to slice and serve, or wrap and hold under refrigeration for up to 4 days.

Roasted Vegetable Terrine with Goat Cheese

Yield: 3-pound terrine; 18 to 20 servings (2 1/2 ounces each)

2 lb	zucchini (about 3)
2 lb	yellow squash (about 3)
1 1/4 lb	eggplant (about 1 large)
2 lb	tomatoes (about 4)
2 each	portobello mushrooms
	Marinade
1 oz/fl	olive oil
1 tbsp	Dijon mustard
1 tbsp	chopped flat-leaf parsley
1 tbsp	chopped chives
2 each	garlic cloves, minced, sautéed, and cooled
2 tsp	chopped rosemary
2 tsp	anchovy paste (about 4 fillets)
2 tsp	honey
2 tsp	salt
1/2 tsp	ground white pepper
8 oz/wt	fresh goat cheese
1 each	egg

1. Cut all vegetables lengthwise into 1/8-inch-thick slices.
2. Combine the marinade ingredients and add to the vegetables.
3. Line sheet pans with oiled parchment and lay out the vegetables in a single layer.
4. Dry in 200°F oven for 1 hour, or until dry but not brittle. Remove from oven and cool.
5. Mix the goat cheese with the egg to make the custard.
6. Line a terrine mold with plastic wrap, leaving an overhang, and assemble the terrine by alternating layers of vegetables and the cheese mixture until the terrine is filled. Fold over the liner.
7. Cover the terrine and poach in a 170°F water bath in a 300°F oven to an internal temperature of 145°F, about 60 minutes.
8. Remove the terrine from the water bath and allow it to cool slightly.
9. Let the terrine rest at least overnight and up to 3 days under refrigeration, weighted with a 2-pound press plate if desired. The terrine is now ready to slice and serve, or wrap and hold under refrigeration for up to 7 days.

Chef's Notes: Using a piping bag for the goat cheese custard makes it easier to distribute the custard evenly within the terrine. Vegetables can be marinated and grilled instead of dried.

Mozzarella, Prosciutto, and Roasted Tomato Terrine

Yield: $2^{1}/_{2}$-pound terrine; 14 to 16 servings ($2^{1}/_{2}$ ounces each)

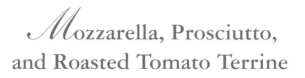

$^{3}/_{4}$ lb	Mozzarella Cheese (page 304)
$^{1}/_{2}$ lb	Spinach Pasta (page 421)
3 lb	ripe tomatoes
5 tbsp	basil chiffonade
4 tbsp	olive oil
2 tsp	salt
2 tsp	ground black pepper
8 oz	thin slices prosciutto ($^{1}/_{16}$ inch)

1. Prepare the spinach pasta as directed on page 421. Roll the pasta into thin sheets and trim as necessary to match the dimensions of your terrine mold. Cook the sheets until tender in simmering salted water. Drain, refresh in cold water, and drain again. Reserve.

2. Prepare the mozzarella as directed on page 304 through step 4. Roll and stretch the mozzarella into thin sheets ($^{1}/_{8}$-inch thick) and trim as necessary to match the dimensions of your terrine mold. *Or*, if using purchased mozzarella, cut into thin slices to layer into terrine.

3. Slice tomatoes 1/4 inch and season with basil, olive oil, salt, and pepper.
4. Lay tomatoes on a roasting rack and dry in a 200°F oven for 2 to 3 hours. Cool and reserve.
5. Cut the cooked pasta into 5 sheets to fit the inside dimensions of a terrine mold.
6. Line the terrine mold with plastic wrap, leaving an overhang.
7. Assemble the terrine by layering pasta sheets, prosciutto, mozzarella, and roasted tomatoes, creating layers that cover the entire surface of the mold. Repeat process until ingredients are used up and mold is filled, finishing with a layer of pasta. Fold plastic wrap over and smooth over the top.
8. Cover with a lid and place in a water bath in a 250°F oven for 30 minutes.
9. Cover with a 2-pound weight and let rest under refrigeration overnight. The terrine is now ready to slice and serve, or hold under refrigeration for up to 3 days.
10. For service cut into 3/16-inch slices, with plastic wrap still on. Remove plastic wrap after slices have been plated.

Presentation Ideas: This terrine may be served with a vinaigrette such as a tomato or balsamic, and a green salad. Grissini (page 423) or French bread slices topped with Tapenade (page 41) are also good accompaniments.

Southwestern Quail Pâté en Croûte with Tomato Cilantro Crust

Yield: $2^1/_2$-pound mold; 14 to 16 servings ($2^1/_2$ ounces each)

8 each	quails (3 to 4 ounces each)
2 cups	Honey Brine (page 156)
2 each	garlic cloves, minced
2 each	shallots, minced
1 tbsp	vegetable oil
3 oz/fl	tequila
6 oz/wt	pork butt, ground
6 oz/wt	fatback, ground
1/4 tsp	tinted curing mix (TCM)
2 tsp	salt
To taste	ground black pepper
2 tsp	chopped thyme
1 tsp	chopped oregano
4 each	scallions, minced
1/4 lb	Tasso, cut into small dice (page 165)
1 1/2 lb	Tomato Cilantro Pâté Dough (page 417)
8 each	thin-sliced ham (1/16 inch), or as needed for liner
2 oz/fl	egg wash (1 whole egg beaten with 1 tbsp milk)
8 oz/wt	Aspic Gelée, melted, or as needed to coat terrine (page 45)

1. Remove leg and thigh meat from quail and reserve. Submerge the bone-in breasts in the brine and cure for 4 hours. Dice leg and thigh meat; reserve. Debone the breasts; reserve.
2. Sweat the garlic and shallots in the vegetable oil; add tequila and reduce by three-forths. Cool.
3. Combine the quail leg and thigh meat, pork, fatback, TCM, salt, pepper, thyme, oregano, scallions, and garlic mixture in a chilled food processor bowl. Process until homogenous. Test the forcemeat and adjust the seasoning if necessary before proceeding. Fold the tasso into the forcemeat, working over an ice bath.
4 Roll out the pâté dough and line a hinged mold with it. Line the dough with the sliced ham, leaving an overhang.
5. Pack one-third of the forcemeat into the lined mold, making sure to remove any air pockets. Place 8 quail breasts on top, overlapping slightly. Add one-third more forcemeat and the remaining 8 quail breasts. Spread the remaining third of the forcemeat on top. Tap the terrine to settle the forcemeat.
6. Fold the ham and the dough over the forcemeat, cutting away any excess. Add a cap piece. Cut and reinforce vent holes; egg wash the surface.
7. Bake at 450°F for 15 to 20 minutes; reduce heat to 350°F and finish baking to an internal temperature of 165°F, about 50 minutes.
8. Remove the pâté from the oven and allow it to cool to 90°F to 100°F. Ladle the aspic through a funnel into the pâté. Chill for at least 24 hours. The pâté is now ready to slice and serve, or wrap and hold under refrigeration for up to 3 days.

Salmon Pâté en Croûte

Yield: 2 1/2-pound mold; 14 to 16 servings (2 1/2 ounces each)

1 lb	shrimp (16/20 count), peeled, deveined, and cut into medium dice
12 oz/wt	salmon, diced
4 tsp	salt
1/4 oz/wt	ground black pepper
2 each	egg whites
18 oz/fl	heavy cream
2 tbsp	Old Bay seasoning
8 drops	Tabasco sauce
6 oz/wt	crayfish tails, cleaned
2 tbsp	snipped chives
3 tbsp	chopped basil
1 each	truffle, cut into small dice (*optional*)
1 1/2 lb	Saffron Pâté Dough (page 417)
3 pieces	salmon fillet, cut into strips 1-inch wide and length of mold
2 oz/fl	egg wash (1 whole egg beaten with 1 tbsp milk)
6 to 8 oz/fl	Aspic Gelée, melted, or as needed to coat terrine (page 45)

1. Grind 12 ounces of the shrimp, the diced salmon, salt, and pepper through the medium plate (1/4 inch) of a meat grinder.
2. Make a mousseline-style forcemeat by processing the ground seafood, egg whites, cream, Old Bay seasoning, and Tabasco sauce until smooth. Test the forcemeat and adjust if necessary before proceeding.
3. Fold the remaining shrimp, the crayfish, chives, basil, and truffle into the forcemeat, working over an ice bath.
4. Roll out the pâté dough and line a hinged mold, leaving an overhang.
5. Pack half the forcemeat into the lined mold. Place the salmon strips down the center; cover with remaining forcemeat.
6. Fold the dough over the forcemeat, cutting away any excess. Add a cap piece (see Chef's Notes). Cut and reinforce vent holes; egg wash the surface.
7. Bake at 450°F for 15 to 20 minutes; reduce the heat to 350°F and finish baking to an internal temperature of 145°F, about 50 minutes.
8. Remove the pâté from the oven and allow it to cool to 90°F to 100°F. Ladle the aspic through a funnel into the pâté. Chill for at least 24 hours. The pâté is now ready to slice and serve, or wrap and hold under refrigeration for up to 3 days.

Presentation Ideas: Serve with Red Pepper Coulis (page 43).

Chef's Notes: Instead of making a separate cap piece, you may invert the pâté before cutting vent holes, as described on page 232.

Turkey Pâté en Croûte

Yield: $2^1/_2$-pound; 14 to 16 servings ($2^1/_2$ ounces each)

12 oz/wt	turkey leg and thigh meat, cleaned and cubed
6 oz/wt	pork butt, cubed
6 oz/wt	fatback, cubed
1/4 tsp	tinted curing mix (TCM)
2 tsp	salt
2 each	shallots, minced
2 each	garlic cloves, minced
1 tbsp	vegetable oil
3 oz/fl	brandy
6 each	juniper berries, crushed
2 tbsp	Dijon mustard
1 tbsp	chopped sage
1 tbsp	chopped thyme
Pinch	ground nutmeg
1/2 tsp	ground black pepper
2 tbsp	Glace de Viande or Volaille, melted (page 412)
1 each	egg
	Garnish
1 oz/wt	dried cherries, plumped in triple sec
1 oz/wt	dried apricots, quartered, plumped in triple sec
1 1/2 lb	Sweet Potato Pâté Dough (page 418)
8 each	thin-sliced ham (1/16 inch), or as needed for liner
3 pieces	turkey breast, cut into strips 1-inch wide and length of mold
2 oz/fl	egg wash (1 whole egg beaten with 1 tbsp milk)
6 to 8 oz/fl	Aspic Gelée, melted (page 45)

1. Combine the leg and thigh meat, pork butt, fatback, TCM, and salt and grind through the fine plate (1/8 inch) of a meat grinder.
2. Sweat the shallots and garlic in the oil; deglaze with the brandy. Cool.
3. Combine the ground meats, shallot mixture, juniper berries, mustard, sage, thyme, nutmeg, pepper, and glace; marinate 1 hour.
4. Transfer the ground meats to a chilled food processor bowl and add the egg. Process for 1 minute, or until smooth.
5. Test and the forcemeat and adjust seasoning if necessary before proceeding.

6. Drain the garnish ingredients and fold into the forcemeat, working over an ice bath.
7. Roll out the dough and line a hinged mold. Line the dough with the sliced ham, leaving an overhang.
8. Pack half the forcemeat into the lined mold. Lay in the turkey breast; cover with remaining forcemeat.
9. Fold the ham and the dough over the forcemeat, cutting away any excess. Add a cap piece (see Chef's Notes). Cut and reinforce vent holes; brush the surface with egg wash.
10. Bake at 450°F for 15 to 20 minutes; reduce the heat to 350°F and finish baking to an internal temperature of 165°F, about 50 minutes.
11. Remove the pâté from the oven and allow it to cool to 90°F to 100°F. Ladle the aspic through a funnel into the pâté. Chill the pâté for at least 24 hours. The pâté is now ready to slice and serve, or wrap and hold under refrigeration for up to 5 days.

Chef's Notes: Instead of making a separate cap piece, you may invert the pâté before cutting the vent holes, as described on page 232.

Rabbit Pie in Parmesan Prosciutto Crust

Yield: 10-inch tart; 16 servings (2 1/2 ounces each)

1 lb	lean rabbit meat (from a 3-pound rabbit)
8 oz/wt	fatback
2 oz/wt	minced shallots
1 each	garlic clove, minced
2 tbsp	butter
1/2 tsp	tinted curing mix (TCM)
2 tsp	salt
2 tbsp	sherry
1 each	egg
1/2 cup	heavy cream
1 tbsp	chopped flat-leaf parsley
1 tsp	poultry seasoning
1/2 tsp	ground white pepper
1 recipe	Parmesan Prosciutto Crust (recipe follows)

1. Cut the rabbit meat and fatback into medium dice.
2. Sweat the shallots and garlic in the butter until soft. Cool.
3. Combine the shallots and garlic with the rabbit meat, fatback, TCM, salt, and sherry; marinate 6 hours.

4. Grind through the medium plate (1/4 inch) of a meat grinder. Chill if necessary before grinding through the fine plate (1/8 inch).

5. Transfer the ground meat to a chilled mixing bowl. Add the egg and cream and mix on medium speed for 1 minute, until homogenous. Add the parsley, poultry seasoning, and pepper. Mix well.

6. Test the forcemeat and adjust seasoning if necessary before proceeding.

7. Place the forcemeat in the crust. Bake at 300°F to an internal temperature of 165°F, approximately 40 minutes. Chill 24 hours. The pie is ready to slice and serve or wrap and store under refrigeration for up to 5 days.

Presentation Ideas: Serve the pie garnished with quartered Seckel pears that have been poached in sweet wine and Orange–Jalapeño Sauce (page 38).

Parmesan Prosciutto Crust

Yield: Crust for one 10-inch tart

2 cups	fresh white bread crumbs
2 tbsp	flour
2 tsp	coarse ground black pepper
1 tsp	dried oregano
1 tsp	dried basil
1 tsp	dried thyme
1/4 cup	butter, melted
1 each	egg yolk
1/4 cup	grated Parmesan cheese
1/4 cup	fine-dice prosciutto

1. Combine bread crumbs, flour, pepper, oregano, basil, and thyme. Add the butter and egg yolk; mix well with kitchen fork. Mix in Parmesan cheese and prosciutto.

2. Press into a buttered 10-inch tart pan. Bake at 350°F until slightly brown, about 10 minutes. Cool. Fill and bake as directed.

Pheasant Galantine

Yield: 14 × 2-inch galantine; 10 to 12 servings (2 1/2 ounces each)

1 each	pheasant (about 3 pounds)
2 tbsp	vegetable oil
8 oz/wt	mirepoix (page 401)
1 cup	Madeira wine
3 qt	Chicken Stock (page 410)
10 each	whole black peppercorns
3 each	bay leaves, crushed
4 oz/wt	pork butt, trimmed of visible fat, diced
4 oz/wt	fatback, diced
1/4 tsp	tinted curing mix (TCM)
2 tsp	salt
2 tsp	chopped rosemary
2 tsp	chopped sage
2 tsp	chopped flat-leaf parsley
2 tsp	chopped thyme
3 each	juniper berries, crushed
1 each	egg
	Garnish
3/4 oz/wt	dried currants, plumped in Madeira
3/4 oz/wt	dried cherries, plumped in Madeira
3/4 oz/wt	dried apricots, quartered, plumped in Madeira
1 tsp	pink peppercorns, left whole

1. Debone the pheasant and remove the skin, keeping it intact. Dice the meat. Chop the carcass. Reserve the skin.

2. Brown the carcass in the oil; add the mirepoix and brown. Add the Madeira, 1 pint of the chicken stock, the peppercorns, and the bay leaves. Simmer for 3 hours. Strain, return to heat, and reduce to 2 ounces. Chill.

3. Combine the pheasant meat, pork, and fatback. Add the reduced pheasant stock, TCM, salt, rosemary, sage, parsley, thyme, and juniper. Mix well and marinate overnight under refrigeration.

4. Grind the meat through the medium plate (1/4 inch) of a meat grinder. Chill if necessary before grinding through the fine plate (1/8 inch).

5. Transfer the ground meats to a chilled food processor bowl. Process on medium speed for 1 minute, until homogenous. Add the egg and process until smooth.

6. Test and adjust the forcemeat if necessary before proceeding.

7. Drain the plumped fruit. Stir the garnish ingredients into the forcemeat, working over an ice bath.

8. Place damp cheesecloth on a work surface and lay the pheasant skin on top. Spread the forcemeat over the skin in an even layer. Use the cheesecloth to help roll the galantine. Carefully lap the skin over itself at the seam. Tie.

9. Heat the remaining chicken stock in a pot to 170°F. Place the galantine in the chicken stock and poach to an internal temperature of 165°F, about 45 to 50 minutes. Remove the pot from the heat and place over an ice bath. Let the galantine cool in the chicken stock. Refrigerate overnight. Rewrap the galantine and refrigerate at least 12 hours. The galantine is ready to slice and serve, or hold under refrigeration for up to 5 days.

Presentation Ideas: Serve with a classic Cumberland Sauce (page 37) or Cranberry Relish (page 387). Apricot-Cherry Chutney (page 385) or Dried Apricot Relish (page 389) would also be good accompaniments.

Chef's Notes: Replace the garnish ingredients with equal parts dried cherries and whole pistachios.

Chicken Galantine

Yield: 4-pound galantine;
28 to 30 servings (2 1/2 ounces each)

	Panada
2 each	eggs
3 tbsp	brandy
1 tsp	Pâté Spice (page 408)
3 oz/wt	flour
1 tbsp	salt
1/2 tsp	whole white peppercorns
8 oz/fl	heavy cream, heated
1 each	chicken (about 3 pounds), boned, wing tips removed, skin removed intact
2 lb	pork butt, cut into 1-inch cubes and chilled
6 oz/fl	Madeira wine
4 oz/wt	fresh ham *or* cooked tongue, cut into 1/4-inch cubes
2 tbsp	black truffles, chopped fine
4 oz/fl	pistachios, shelled, blanched, and chopped coarse
As needed	Chicken Stock (page 410)

1. Prepare the panada: mix the eggs with all the panada ingredients except the cream.
2. Temper the egg mixture with the hot cream. Add the cream to the egg mixture and cook over low heat until thickened.
3. Weigh the leg and thigh meat from the chicken. Add an equal amount of pork butt, or enough for approximately 4 pounds of meat. Grind the chicken leg and thigh meat and pork twice, using the fine plate (1/8 inch) of a meat grinder.
4. Cut the chicken breast meat into 1/2- to 3/4-inch cubes. Season it to taste. Marinate the meat in the Madeira under refrigeration for at least 3 hours.
5. Drain the chicken breast reserving the Madeira. Add the Madeira and panada to the ground meat mixture. Blend well.
6. Fold in the ham, truffles, and pistachios. Mix well.
7. Gently fold in the reserved chicken breast meat.
8. Lay out the reserved skin on cheesecloth or plastic wrap. Add the forcemeat and roll the galantine securely.
9. Poach the galantine at 170°F in enough simmering stock to cover, to an internal temperature of 165°F, about 60 to 70 minutes.
10. Transfer the galantine and the poaching liquid to a storage container. Chill quickly to 40°F and store under refrigeration overnight. Remove the galantine from the stock and wrap it in new cheesecloth to firm its texture; chill at least 12 hours. To serve the galantine, unwrap and slice it.

Chef's Notes: To reproduce the galantine as shown in the accompanying photograph, keep the breast of the chicken in large pieces as you bone out the bird. Butterfly or slice the breast meat and lay it out to make an even layer over the surface of the skin. Roll the galantine so that the skin and breast meat completely enclose the forcemeat without overlapping.

Roasted Asian Duck Galantine

Yield: 2-pound galantine; 10 to 12 servings (2 1/2 ounces each)

1 each	duck (4–5 lb)
2 cups	Poultry Brine (page 153)
	Marinade
2 each	minced shallots, sautéed and cooled
3 each	garlic cloves, minced
2 tsp	minced ginger
1 tbsp	vegetable oil
6 oz/wt	lean pork butt, cubed
6 oz/wt	fatback, cubed
1 tbsp	oyster sauce
1 tbsp	soy sauce
2 tsp	sesame oil
1 tbsp	minced thyme
1 tbsp	minced cilantro
1 each	jalapeño, stemmed, seeded, and chopped fine
1/2 tsp	Chinese Five-Spice Powder (page 405)
1 tbsp	honey
1/4 tsp	tinted curing mix (TCM)
6 each	shiitake mushrooms, stems removed, cut into fine dice
3/4 cup	fine-dice carrots, fully cooked
3 each	scallions, minced
2 tsp	powdered gelatin

1. Remove the skin from the duck in one piece, starting from the back. Debone the duck; reserve legs for forcemeat and breast for garnish. Square off the ends of the breasts and add the pieces of trim to the forcemeat.
2. Cover the duck breasts with the brine; cure under refrigeration for 4 hours.
3. Lay the skin out on a sheet pan lined with plastic wrap and freeze. When the skin has frozen, remove all the excess fat using a chef's knife in a scraping motion.
4. Sweat the garlic, shallots, and ginger in the vegetable oil and cool. Combine this mixture with the duck leg and thigh meat, trim from breasts, pork, fatback, oyster sauce, soy sauce, sesame oil, thyme, cilantro, jalapeño, five-spice powder, honey, and TCM; marinate for one hour.
5. Grind the meat through the medium plate (1/4 inch) of a meat grinder. Chill if necessary before grinding through the fine plate (1/8 inch).
6. Transfer the ground meats to a chilled mixing bowl. Mix on medium speed for 1 minute, until homogenous.
7. Test and adjust the forcemeat if necessary before proceeding.
8. Toss the mushrooms, carrots, and scallions with the gelatin. Fold the vegetables into the forcemeat, working over an ice bath.
9. Place the duck skin on a work surface. Pipe the forcemeat onto the skin and smooth with a pallet knife. Place the breasts in the middle and roll into a galantine. Sew or tie the galantine securely with butcher's twine.
10. Place the galantine on a sheet pan and roast in a 300°F oven to an internal temperature of 165°F, about 50 to 60 minutes.
11. Remove the galantine from the oven and allow it to cool to an internal temperature of 90°F to 100°F. Let it rest under refrigeration overnight. The galantine is ready to slice and serve, or wrap and hold under refrigeration for up to 5 days.

*F*oie Gras Terrine

Yield: 2-pound terrine; 10 to 12 servings ($2^{1}/_{2}$ ounces each)

Foie gras terrines are traditionally served directly in the mold used to prepare them. A layer of fat is allowed to remain in place, acting as a protective barrier, slowing down the deterioration of quality that occurs when the terrine is exposed to air, moisture, or flavor transfers from strongly flavored foods such as cheeses, certain fruits, or vegetables. Alternative presentation methods can of course be used.

$2^{3}/_{4}$ lb	foie gras, grade A
2 tbsp	salt
2 tsp	ground white pepper
1 tbsp	sugar
$^{1}/_{4}$ tsp	tinted curing mix (TCM)
2 cups	white port wine

1. Clean the livers, remove all veins, and dry well. Combine 1 tablespoon of the salt, 1 teaspoon of the pepper, the sugar, TCM, and port wine and marinate the livers in the mixture overnight under refrigeration.

2. Line a 2-pound terrine mold with plastic wrap.

3. Remove the marinated foie gras from the refrigerator, place it on a cutting board, and slice into large pieces that will fit snugly into the mold. Place them into the mold so that the smooth sides of the foie gras pieces form the exterior of the terrine; season as needed with the remaining salt and pepper. Fill the mold up to the inner lip and press the pieces down tightly to remove any air pockets. Cover the terrine mold.

4. Poach the terrine in a hot water bath, maintaining it at a constant 160°F, for 45 to 50 minutes. The oven temperature may need to be adjusted to keep the water at a constant temperature. If it gets too hot, add cold water immediately to lower the temperature. Foie gras has the best texture and flavor when cooked to an internal temperature of 135°F. (Be sure to check with your local and state health authorities, however.)

5. Remove the terrine from the water bath and rest for 2 hours at room temperature, then pour off the fat (see photo). Cover the terrine with a press plate and top with a 1- to 2-pound weight. Let the terrine rest under refrigeration for at least 24 hours and up to 48 hours to mellow and mature.

6. Remove the plastic wrap and carefully remove the congealed fat. Then tightly rewrap in fresh wrap. Refrigerate until ready to slice and serve the terrine. Hold under refrigeration for up to 3 days.

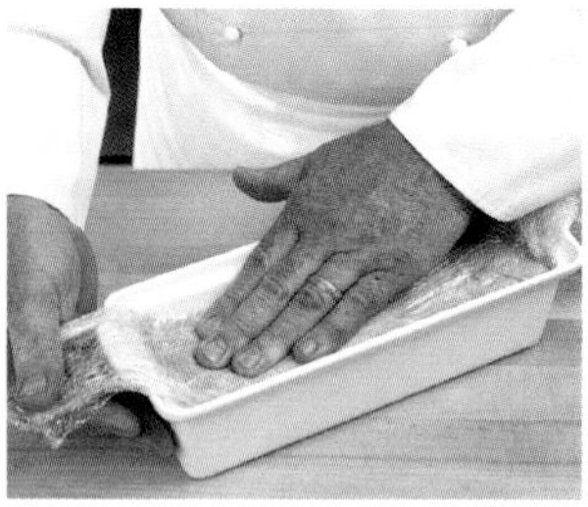

Pack the foie gras into the plastic wrap-lined terrine mold.

The excess fat is poured off.

The terrine will be ready to unmold after 24 to 48 hours.

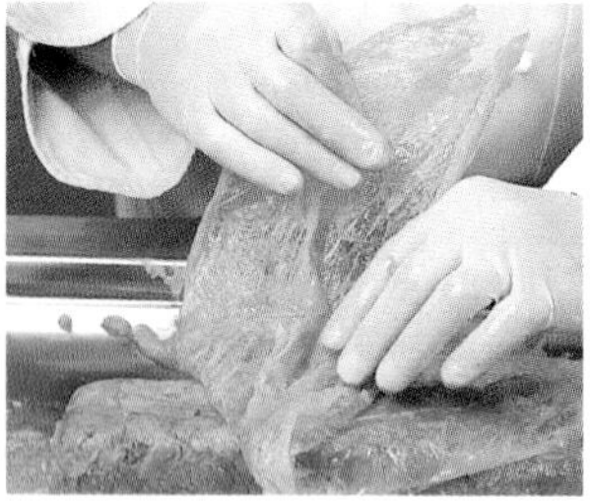

Pull the plastic wrap off the unmolded terrine.

Leave the plastic wrap on to help keep slices as neat as possible.

Presentation Ideas: Foie gras terrines may be sliced for plated presentations, shaped into quenelles, or served directly in the terrine.

Take the time to select the most appropriate accompaniments. You may want to consult with your sommelier or make suggestions yourself to the dining room staff so that they can help guests choose the most appropriate wine or other beverage to enjoy with the terrine.

When you are ready to serve the terrine, remove the weight and carefully pull off the press plate. To neaten up the appearance, smooth out the top with a small knife and clean the edges of the terrine with a towel. Or you may wish to score the top of the terrine in a cross-hatched pattern if it is to be served directly in the terrine.

Chef's Notes: To determine the amount of foie gras needed to fill any size terrine mold, simply measure the volume of water the terrine can hold. The number of ounces in volume will correlate to the number of ounces in weight of foie gras necessary to fill the mold.

• • •

For easier service, slice the terrine with the plastic wrap on. Remove the plastic after the slices have been plated. A warm beveled knife works best. Save any fat removed in step 5 to use to sauté vegetables or potatoes.

Foie Gras Roulade Prepare the foie gras as directed for the terrine. Arrange the marinated foie gras on a large sheet of plastic wrap; wrap tightly around the foie gras to form a roulade. If desired, insert whole truffles into the foie gras lobes before rolling the roulade. Poach in a 160°F water bath to an internal temperature of 118°F. Remove from the water, cool, and rewrap. Let the roulade rest under refrigeration for at least 24 hours before slicing. This roulade may also be baked in brioche (see page 370) and served as an appetizer.

Foie Gras Mousse

Yield: 2-pound terrine; 10 to 12 servings ($2^{1}/_{2}$ ounces each)

$1^{1}/_{2}$ lb	foie gras, cleaned and veins removed
2 tsp	salt
$^{1}/_{2}$ tsp	ground white pepper
2 oz/fl	Sauternes wine
2 oz/wt	minced shallots
1 each	garlic clove, minced
4 oz/wt	butter
6 oz/fl	heavy cream, whipped to medium peak

1. Marinate the foie gras in the salt, pepper, and wine overnight.
2. Drain foie gras and cut into 1-inch chunks.
3. Sauté the shallots and garlic in the butter until soft; do not brown.
4. Add the foie gras and cook over high heat, stirring continuously, until foie gras is cooked through, about 4 to 5 minutes.
5. Cool mixture to 90°F and purée in a food processor. Pass this mixture through a drum sieve into a 2-quart bowl set over an ice bath.
6. Stir mixture continuously until it begins to thicken. Fold the whipped cream into the mixture, and adjust seasoning.
7. Line a 2-pound terrine mold with plastic wrap, leaving an overhang. Fill with the foie gras mousse and smooth the top. Chill overnight before serving. Wrap and hold under refrigeration for up to 3 days.

Presentation Ideas: Foie gras mousse is best enjoyed on simple toasted croutons, but it can be used to embellish other hors d'oeuvre, such as prunes soaked in Armangac and then filled with this mousse.

Chicken Liver Pâté

Yield: 2-pound terrine; 18 to 20 servings ($2\frac{1}{2}$ ounces each)

$1\frac{1}{2}$ lb	chicken livers, cleaned, sinew removed
2 cups	milk, or as needed for soaking
$\frac{1}{4}$ tsp	tinted curing mix (TCM)
$4\frac{1}{2}$ tsp	salt
$\frac{1}{4}$ cup	minced shallots
2 each	garlic cloves, minced
$\frac{1}{2}$ lb	fresh fatback, cut into medium dice
1 tsp	ground white pepper
$\frac{1}{2}$ tsp	ground allspice
$\frac{1}{2}$ tsp	dry mustard
$\frac{2}{3}$ cup	fresh white bread crumbs
1 oz/fl	sherry wine
$\frac{2}{3}$ cup	bread flour
2 tsp	powdered gelatin
3 each	eggs
6 oz/fl	heavy cream

1. Soak the chicken livers in the milk with $1\frac{1}{2}$ tsp salt and the TCM for 12 to 24 hours. When ready to use, drain well and pat dry with paper towels.
2. Purée all ingredients except the cream in a blender to a smooth, loose paste.
3. Pass through a wire-mesh strainer into a stainless-steel bowl.
4. Stir in the cream.
5. Let mixture rest under refrigeration for 2 hours.
6. Pour into a terrine mold lined with plastic wrap, cover, and poach in a 170°F water bath in a 300°F oven to an internal temperature of 165°F about 45 minutes to 1 hour.
7. Remove from the oven and let cool at room temperature for 30 minutes.
8. Press with a 1-pound weight and chill overnight under refrigeration before unmolding and slicing.

Smoked Chicken Liver Pâté Cut 8 ounce of the livers into medium dice and pan-smoke (see page 142) for a flavorful contrasting garnish. For even more flavor, the terrine can also be lined with sliced ham.

Duck Liver Terrine

Yield: 2-pound terrine; 18 to 20 servings (2 1/2 ounces each)

The next best thing to foie gras! This recipe combines the richness of butter with the flavor of duck livers in proportions that create a wonderful, smooth, rich terrine.

1 1/4 lb	duck livers, cleaned, soaked in milk overnight, and dried
2 oz/fl	Madeira wine
1 1/2 oz/wt	minced shallots, sautéed and cooled
1 tsp	salt
1/4 tsp	ground white pepper
1/8 tsp	tinted curing mix (TCM)
1 1/4 cups	heavy cream
	Beurre Manié
1 lb	butter, softened
1/4 cup	flour, sifted
2 each	eggs, beaten

1. Combine the livers, wine, shallots, salt, pepper, and TCM. Grind through the fine plate (1/8 inch) of a meat grinder into a chilled bowl.

2. Reduce the cream by half and keep warm.

3. Knead the butter and flour together to make a beurre manié.

4. Transfer the liver mixture to a food processor and process until smooth. Add the eggs and blend to incorporate.

5. With the processor running, carefully add the beurre manié to the liver mixture a little at a time until completely incorporated. Scrape down the sides of the processor.

6. Add the warm cream to the liver mixture and combine until homogenous. (It will look very grainy.) Pass the forcemeat through a fine drum sieve.

7. Test and adjust the forcemeat if necessary before proceeding.

8. Oil a 2-pound terrine mold and line with plastic wrap. Pour the forcemeat into the lined mold and tap the mold on the table to remove any air pockets. Fold the liner over the forcemeat to completely encase the terrine, and cover.

9. Poach the terrine in a 170°F water bath in a 300°F oven to an internal temperature of 165°F, 60 to 75 minutes.

10. Remove the terrine from the water bath and allow it to chill at least overnight or up to 3 days under refrigeration, weighted with a 2-pound press plate if desired. The terrine is now ready to slice and serve, or wrap and hold under refrigeration for up to 7 days.

Chef's Note: If desired, line the mold with fatback, prosciutto, or ham before filling with forcemeat. An internal garnish of diced truffles or truffle peelings may be folded into the forcemeat before baking.

TAYLOR FLADGAT
10 Years
PORTO

EIGHT

Cheese

Wines, sausages, dried foods, and cheeses are all the fruits of preservation practices known to ancient humankind, then refined, recorded, and evolved over time. We know that cheeses were enjoyed by the ancient Sumerians, whose writings about many aspects of daily life are believed to date from 3000 B.C.E. Early records of cheese have been found on earthenware vessels from Egyptian tombs dating as far back as 2300 B.C.E. The Bible includes numerous references to cheese, beginning with Genesis. Later in the Bible, David is said to have carried ten cheeses to the troops just before slaying the giant Goliath.

The Romans were the first to mass-produce cheese to be carried on long journeys and used by their armies as a convenient form of concentrated nutrition. They carried their formulas into conquered lands as their empire expanded, marrying them with indigenous cheeses in Europe. During the period of European history known as the Dark Ages, the traditions of cheese making were preserved and refined by religious houses and monasteries, as were the traditions of wine and spirit making. Some of these religious orders are still creating handmade cheeses using the same original formulas and methods.

Until the early to mid-1800s, cheese production continued on an individual home or cottage level, by families who were fortunate enough to own sheep, goats, and cows. As farms grew in size and were able to supply communities with agricultural products, so the cheese business grew as well, although the cheese-making process continued to be both painstaking and time-consuming.

This chapter explores the basic cheese-making process in order to provide a better understanding of the special characteristics of the cheeses and why some special cheeses are so highly prized. Also discussed are the basic cheese categories—fresh, rind-ripened, semi-soft, blue cheeses, pasta filata, hard, and very hard—and the basic principles used to select cheeses for a cheese course offered on the menu, a cheese platter or tray for buffets, or a cheese cart for the dining room.

Fresh cheeses can be produced with relatively little in the way of special equipment. These cheeses are served very fresh and can easily become a signature piece in an appetizer, salad, sandwich, entrée, or dessert item. Mozzarella, mascarpone, ricotta, and other cultured dairy items such as crème fraîche and yogurt are among the recipes and techniques included in this chapter.

Cheese Making

The techniques used today to produce cheese have changed little since the times of the Romans and the medieval monasteries, but scientific discoveries have led to better control of the natural processes involved in cheese making: acidification and coagulation of the milk, salting, cutting and draining the curds, shaping the cheese, and finally, ripening.

In the nineteenth century, scientists were able to identify the many bacteria present in the milk, the air, and the caves used for ripening. Bacteria that would interfere with the process could be eliminated, and the individual strains that contribute to the desirable character of individual cheeses could be cultivated and standardized. By the turn of the century, "pure cultures" were made available and allowed for more uniform results from cheese maker to cheese maker when producing cheese within a single variety.

In 1851, the first real cheese factory in America was established in Rome, New York, by Jesse Williams. It was obvious that the market for cheese was ready, because within the next fifteen years there would be five hundred more of these operations established in New York alone. In 1990, over eight billion pounds of cheese and cheese-related products were produced in the United States, and today, the United States is the largest producer of cheese as well as the largest importer.

Increasing renown is being accorded to today's high-quality, hand-crafted cheeses. These artisanal cheeses are being produced all over the country, on the same small scale and with the same high standards of years ago. Familiar varieties as well as brand new cheeses are becoming available on the local level, making the opportunity for the garde manger to feature excellent and unusual cheeses better all the time.

What Is Cheese?

Cheese is defined as a food product made from the pressed curd of milk. Like wine, cheese is thought of as a living food because of the "friendly," living bacteria that are continually changing it. You may hear cheeses referred to as "natural" to distinguish them from highly processed cheeses that are not expected to ripen.

It is believed that sheep's and goat's milk were first used to make cheese, as these were probably the first domesticated animals appropriate for milking. Today, cow's milk is the base for many cheeses, followed by goat's and then sheep's milk. The milk of water buffalo, yak, camel, llama, and mare are also used to create the special cheeses of the societies where these animals were domesticated.

The Cheese-Making Process

For the most part, the only changes in cheese making since the early days have been in understanding how we can control the complicated interaction of various biological agents and processes, all integral to cheese making. The basic stages in the modern production are:

- Milk and its pretreatment, including homogenizing, pasteurizing, or heating
- Acidification of milk, to change the pH level
- Salting the curds
- Coagulating (curdling) the milk to create curds
- Separating the curds and whey
- Shaping, cutting, or molding less the curds into their appropriate shapes
- Ripening

Considering how few ingredients are needed to make cheese, there is astonishing variety in the types of cheeses that can be produced. Hundreds of distinct cheeses can be made by introducing only slight modifications: Choosing sheep's milk instead of cow's, using a different starter culture, draining the cheese a little more or less, cutting the curds very fine or leaving them whole or in slabs, rubbing the cheese with salt at a different point in the process, and shaping it into a disk, a wheel, or a round will produce different cheeses, with unique textures, flavors, and aromas.

Different steps applied during the ripening process can play a critical role as well: The rind may be washed with a brine or coated with wax, additional molds or cultures can be introduced directly to the cheese or applied to the surface, and so forth.

Milk

The type of milk the cheese maker chooses is critical to the development of the cheese. Not only are there different milks (cow, sheep, goat, yak, llama, buffalo, mare, and others), there are also various ways to collect, combine, and treat milk. One famous cheese, Parmigiano Reggiano, for instance, is traditionally made by combining the richer milk collected in the evening with the leaner milk of the next day's first milking.

In large-scale cheese production, milk is routinely handled as follows: it is tested for quality, pasteurized, homogenized, and the milk fat content is standardized. Although cheeses aged more than sixty days may be made from raw milk, the majority of cheeses in this country are produced from pasteurized milk.

Pasteurization is the process by which a liquid, in this case milk, is heated to a particular temperature and held there for a specific period of time to destroy the naturally occurring bacteria in the milk. This landmark discovery in food safety came at a price for cheese makers. The down side is two-fold. First, the process destroys not only pathogens but also the "friendly" bacteria, which are not only safe but also play an important role in producing cheeses. Second, heating the milk gives it a "cooked" flavor.

The importance of food safety outranks the changes to the flavor and quality of the cheese, however, and cheese makers have worked to compensate for the loss of naturally present bacteria and changes in flavor.

Acidification of Milk

The serious business of cheese making gets underway when the milk is acidified, or soured. The milk is heated to a specific temperature and a starter is added that contains either an acid or an organism that produces lactic acid.

To produce many of the soft fresh cheeses featured in this chapter, lemon juice, vinegar, or citric or tartaric acid—the acid starters—can be used. Mozzarella and provolone (known as *pasta filata*) as well as most ripened cheeses are produced by souring the milk with a culture composed of a lactic acid-producing organism—the enzyme starters. Acid development is critical in order to control the growth of undesirable organisms and the rate of coagulation.

The starter is added at a ratio that will produce the appropriate level of acid. If there is too much acid, the curd may take several days to release the whey. If there is too little, a seemingly dry cheese may begin to leak whey several weeks after it has been shaped and pressed.

Salting

Salt may be added at various points in the cheese-making process. It may be stirred into the milk along with the starter or shortly after the starter is added. Coarse salt may be spread over the surface of the curd, or the cut and drained curd may be submerged in or rubbed with a salt brine.

Salt is important to cheese making in a number of ways. In addition to adding its own flavor, salt affects the cheese's flavor because of its role in controlling fermentation. The quantity of carbon dioxide and alcohol produced as a by-product of this bacterial activity gives each cheese its unique flavor. Salt controls spoilage by creating an inhospitable environment for the organisms that cause spoilage. It also affects the finished texture of the cheese, acting to dry the cheese. The dryer the cheese, the longer its useful life. Very dry grating cheeses, such as Pecorino Romano, are so salty they can be used as a substitute for some of the salt added in a dish.

Coagulating (Curdling) the Milk

Acid starters will change the milk rapidly, souring the milk as well as forming curds. The effect of any acid on a protein is to tighten it. This is the basic action in curdling milk. Enzyme starters, including rennet, result in a sweeter curd. The action of the so-called friendly bacteria (either in the milk or in the starter) produces lactic acid, resulting in a sweeter-tasting curd since less overall acid is required.

Rennet was originally obtained from the fourth stomach of young ruminant animals such as cows, sheep, and goats. It can also be derived from certain plants. Today both animal- and plant–based forms are available, as well as a genetically engineered substitute called chymosin.

Separating the Curds and Whey

When the milk coagulates, it generally forms a soft mass curd that must be broken up to allow the noncoagulated portion of the milk, known as the *whey,* to drain off. Figure 8-1 shows fresh lemon cheese being hung to drain. If the curd is cut only a little, you can create soft, creamy cheeses.

When the curd is cut quite small, more of the whey will drain away, and the cheese will have a drier texture. For some very dry cheeses, the curds and whey are even cooked to further shrink the curds and allow even more moisture to escape.

Shaping

There are a number of methods for draining and shaping cheeses, each specified both by tradition and by the role that those methods play in producing the desired flavor and texture in the finished cheese. After the curds are drained of the freed whey, some are placed in cheesecloth bags, baskets, or molds, and set on racks or hung and allowed to drain and dry for the prescribed time. For fresh and soft cheeses, draining and shaping is accomplished simultaneously. Some cheeses—notably Cheddars—are shaped into thick slabs and then stacked, so that the weight of the cheese itself presses out the whey.

Figure 8-1 Fresh Lemon Cheese (page 300).

Ripening

The last stage of cheese making is ripening, also known as aging or curing. This is where the "magic" of flavor development takes place. The ripening process may take anywhere from thirty days to several years, depending upon the cheese being made. During that time, the cheese undergoes changes that will affect its flavor, body, texture, and occasionally its color. What began as rubbery fresh cheese curd is transformed into smooth and mellow ripened cheese.

Originally cheeses were aged in caves, where conditions were perfect for the magic of ripening to take place. Today, most cheeses are aged in temperature- and humidity-controlled environments that simulate caves.

Cheeses may be ripened in leaves, ashes, wax rinds, or no rind at all. Some are rubbed or washed, and some are simply left to cure naturally. In some cases, holes are made in the cheeses to allow gases produced by bacteria to escape; in others, the gases are confined to form a variety of holes ranging in size from tiny to the size of a quarter, as in Swiss cheese. Special additional bacteria cultures or molds are introduced in many cheeses by injecting, spraying, or washing them. Once these steps are done, the rest of the work is left to nature.

Cheese Classifications

With so many cheeses available today, there are several categories by which they can be referenced. Milk type, country of origin, region, handling, aging, and texture are some of the various classification strategies that have been used. Although most experts agree that none of these classifications are completely adequate, so far no one has been able to come up with one that really covers all the variables. Even when two experts agree on which method to use, they do not necessarily agree on which cheeses fall into which categories.

For the sake of discussion, this section presents several broad groups of cheese that have been loosely categorized according to texture.

Soft Fresh Cheeses

Soft fresh cheeses are those cheeses that are unripened and generally have a fresh, clean, creamy flavor. These cheeses are typically the most perishable and are sometimes held in brines. Examples of soft fresh cheeses are cottage cheese, pot cheese, queso blanco, and cream cheese.

Ricotta cheese, made from recooking whey, actually began in Italy as a by-product of the cheese-making industry. (The name literally means "recook.") When whey is heated, the proteins fuse together and create a new curd that, when drained, becomes a snowy white ricotta high in moisture and naturally low in fat. It is commonly used in Italian cooking as a filling for pastas or as a base for cheesecakes. Today, some ricottas are made with added part-skim or whole milk for a richer flavor.

Mascarpone is a fresh cheese made by curdling heavy cream with citric acid. The process releases excess moisture and yields a rich creamy cheese that is mildly acidic and adapts to both sweet and savory preparations. One of the most famous uses of mascarpone is in the dessert tiramisu, in which the rich cheese is layered with sponge cake or ladyfingers that have been dipped in espresso and Marsala wine. Savory mascarpone dishes such as dips and spreads may also include herbs and spices.

In the United States, fresh goat's milk cheeses have become very popular of late and are being produced in many parts of the country. They can be found in a variety of shapes and may be coated in herbs or edible ash.

Recipes for fresh cheeses appear on pages 298-300.

Soft Ripened Cheeses

Soft ripened cheeses are those that have typically been sprayed or dusted with a mold and allowed to ripen. The two most popular varieties are probably Brie and Camembert. Neither name is protected by law, so both have been counterfeited in many places with vast differences in quality.

Soft ripened cheeses (see Figure 8-2) are available in varying degrees of richness. For example, single, double,

Figure 8-2
Soft ripened cheeses from left to right: Brie, Camembert, Pyramids.

and triple cream cheeses have 50, 60, and 70 percent butterfat, respectively.

Soft ripened cheeses should be eaten only when properly ripened. An underripe cheese is firm and chalky, an overripe cheese will run when cut, and a cheese ready for eating will "bulge" when cut and barely hold its shape. Soft ripened cheeses will ripen only until they are cut into. After that they will begin to dry and deteriorate. To check for ripeness before cutting, press firmly but gently in the middle of the cheese. It should have some feel of softness to the center. An overripe cheese can be identified by an ammonia odor.

Soft ripened cheeses can be served at room temperature as a dessert cheese or as an appetizer. For those who are not purists, these cheeses can also be served warm by baking them in a crust of flaky dough or toasted almonds.

It still remains a matter of taste as to whether soft ripened cheeses should be eaten with the rind. Even the "experts" don't agree on that age-old discussion, so it should be left up to the individual.

Semi-Soft Cheeses

Semi-soft cheeses include a wide variety ranging from mild and buttery to very pungent and aromatic (see Figure 8-3). They are allowed to ripen in several ways.

Rind-Ripened Cheeses

Wash-rind cheeses are periodically washed with brine, beer, cider, wine, brandy, or oils during the ripening period. This remoistening encourages bacterial growth, sometimes know as a "smear," which allows the cheese to be ripened from the outside in. Popular examples of this type of cheese include Limburger and its famous American counterpart Liederkranz, both of which are intensely pungent, as well as Muenster, Saint Paulin, and Port-Salut.

Dry-Rind Cheeses

Dry-rind cheeses are those that are allowed to form a natural rind during ripening. Bel Paese ("beautiful country") is a cheese of Italian origin that has become quite popular since it was first made in 1929. Its soft texture and very mild flavor have contributed to its popularity. Havarti, another popular dry-rind cheese, has a buttery flavor that is often enhanced with herbs or spices such as dill, caraway, and basil.

Waxed-Rind Cheeses

Gouda and Edam are semi-soft cheeses that are sealed in wax prior to the aging process. These cheeses, which get their names from two towns in Holland, have been made

Figure 8-3
Semi-soft cheeses from left to right: Edam, Fontina, Port-Salut.

for eight hundred years. Gouda is made from whole milk and tends to be softer and richer than Edam, which is made from part-skim milk and is firmer in texture. These cheeses may be either flavored or smoked, and are available in mild and aged varieties.

Blue-Veined Cheeses

Blue or blue-veined cheeses are thought to have been among some of the first cheeses produced. Although there is no specific research to prove the theory, it is believed that the mold was first introduced to cheese from moldy bread that had come in contact with the cheese.

In the modern production of blue cheeses, needles are used to form holes that allow gases to escape and oxygen to enter to support mold growth within the cheese. The cheese is then salted or brined and allowed to ripen in caves or under "cavelike conditions." Some of the most famous blue cheeses are the French Roquefort, Italian Gorgonzola, English Stilton, and American Maytag blue (see Figure 8-4).

Roquefort is made strictly from raw sheep's milk and has been made since ancient times in the Rouergue area of southern France. The Roquefort Association, Inc., ensures that quality standards and name integrity are protected. Today the cheeses are still ripened in the caves of Cambalou for three months to develop their unique character. They may be eaten after the initial ripening but are more typically stored for an additional three to twelve months as the market allows.

One of the things that makes Roquefort unique is the fact that the mold is not grown in a laboratory, as are molds for many other blue cheeses. Instead, Roquefort mold is developed naturally from rye bread. Roquefort should therefore be highlighted for what it is, and when used in dips or dressings should be clearly identified on the menu.

Gorgonzola is another special blue cheese. Unlike Roquefort, Gorgonzola is made from cow's milk, and its mold is from a completely different strain, which is now commercially produced. Gorgonzola is made with evening milk and the following day's morning milk. There are two varieties available: "sweet," which is aged three months, and "naturale," which is aged further and has a fuller, more robust flavor.

Pasta Filata Cheeses

Pasta filata literally means "spun curds" or "spun paste." During manufacture, the curds are dipped into hot water and then stretched or spun until the proper consistency and texture is achieved. They are then kneaded and molded into the desired shapes.

Figure 8-4
Blue-veined cheeses from left to right: Maytag blue, Roquefort, Stilton, Gorgonzola.

Figure 8-5 Pasta filata: Shaping Mozzarella curd into balls.

Pasta filata cheeses are a group of cheeses that are related by the process used in their manufacture, rather than by their textures. In fact, the textures of pasta filata cheeses run the gamut from soft to hard, depending upon how they are aged, if at all.

The most common cheese of this category is mozzarella. In 1990, over 1.5 billion pounds of mozzarella were produced in America alone. Today there are two types of mozzarella available: the traditional fresh style, which is available in a variety of shapes and sizes, and the newer American invention of low-moisture mozzarella, which has a longer shelf life than the fresh style. Both whole milk and part-skim varieties are available. The recipe for making fresh mozzarella appears on page 304 (see Figure 8-5).

Provolone is another popular pasta filata cheese that is similarly handled but is made with a different culture. Once the curd is stretched and kneaded, it is rubbed with brine and tied into shape. It is then hung and left to dry in sizes ranging from 250 grams to 200 pounds. Provolone is often smoked and/or aged for additional character and firmer texture.

Hard Cheeses

A variety of hard cheeses are produced throughout the world (see Figure 8-6). Cheddars and Swiss-style cheeses are among the most well known.

Originating in England, Cheddar has become the most popular hard cheese in the United States. The Pilgrims brought Cheddar formulas to the United States, and by 1790, it was produced in such quantities that it was exported back to England.

Cheddar derives its name from the process used in its manufacture. The "cheddaring" process involves turning and stacking the slabs of young cheese to extract more whey and give the cheese its characteristic texture. The yellow color of some Cheddars is achieved through the addition of annatto seed paste and has nothing to do with the flavor.

Once the cheddaring process is complete, the cheeses are wrapped in cheesecloth dipped in wax and allowed to ripen. Cheddars are categorized by age. Current Cheddar is aged for thirty days, mild for one to three months, medium for three to six months, sharp for six to nine months, and extra sharp for nine months to five years.

Many cheeses that originated in the United States are produced using the cheddaring method. American cheese is said to have gotten its name after the American Revolution when the proud producers of Cheddar in the United States did not want their cheeses to be mistaken for anything that might have originated in England, and aptly labeled them "American cheese."

Colby is another truly American cheese that was invented in the town of Colby, Wisconsin, in 1874. When Colby slabs are cut in half they are popularly known as longhorns.

Monterey Jack is also an American original produced in the style of Cheddar. It was first made by David Jacks in Monterey, California, in 1849 and has remained popular to this day. Aged Monterey Jack cheese, known as dry Jack, makes an excellent grating cheese.

The family of cheeses generically referred to as Swiss are also hard cheeses. These cheeses are characterized by holes, sometimes called eyes, that range in size from tiny to the size of a quarter. Swiss cheeses are often mellow in flavor and have excellent melting properties. Some of the more well-known varieties of Swiss cheese include Gruyère, Emmentaler, Beaufort, and Jarlsberg.

Very Hard Cheeses

In Italy, these cheeses are known as the *granas*, or grainy cheeses, because of their granular texture (clearly visible in the cheeses shown in Figure 8-7). The most popular of these cheeses are Parmesan and Romano, which are now produced in the United States and South America but are

Figure 8-6
Hard cheeses from left to right: Cheddar, Emmentaler, Manchego.

Figure 8-7
Very hard cheeses from left to right: Romano, Parmigiano, dry Jack, aged goat cheese logs

different from their predecessors. Very hard cheeses are most often grated or shaved, but they are also traditionally eaten in chunks broken off with a special knife.

True Parmigiano–Reggiano is often referred to as the king of cheeses. It is believed that the formula for this cheese has not changed in more than seven hundred years, and its origins date back even further. This legendary cheese is made slowly and carefully following strict guidelines that require it to be aged a minimum of fourteen months, although most are aged for twenty-four months. Stravecchio, or extra aged, is ripened for as much as three years.

The flavor of Parmigiano–Reggiano is complex and unique. Steven Jenkins, author of *The Cheese Primer*, describes it as "spicy like cinnamon or nutmeg; salty like liquor accompanying an oyster; sweet like ginger cookies; and nutty like black walnuts—all at the same time."

Romano cheeses—named for the city of Rome—come in several different varieties. Pecorino Romano, which is made with sheep's milk, is probably the best known. Caprino Romano is a very sharp goat's milk version, and vacchino Romano is a mild version made from cow's milk.

Cheese Service

Selecting the Cheeses

A variety of approaches may be taken when developing a cheese board. Cheeses should be selected based on color, shape, texture, richness, and intensity. A modest selection might simply include a single cheese of the best quality from the soft, blue, and hard categories. More extensive selections continue to build their offerings by expanding selections within categories and developing a special selection to feature local or regional favorites.

Cheese plates, boards, or carts often contain a variety of cheeses, but sometimes it is interesting to compose a board that features only one type of milk, sometimes referred to as a *flight* of cheeses, in much the same way a flight of chardonnays or Pinot Noirs might be offered. A sheep's milk cheese board, for instance, gives the guests a chance to taste and compare a variety of cheeses made from the same main ingredient. This is an opportunity that many people have never had but would probably be interested in trying.

Presenting the Cheeses

Cheeses should be allowed to come to room temperature before they are served. This process, known as aromatization, brings out the fullest flavor of the cheese, so that all its nuances can be enjoyed.

Styles of Presentation

Cheeses may be served as a course in and of themselves, often preceding or in place of dessert. In à la carte service, some restaurants present their customers with a cheese cart from which they may sample a variety of cheeses. The customer chooses which cheeses he or she would like to try, and the server then prepares a plate at the tableside consisting of the desired cheeses, bread or crackers, and occasionally some fruit (see Figure 8-8).

On a buffet, cheese boards are eye-catching items that have always been very popular. The board itself can be as simple as a piece of wood, reserved strictly for cheese board service, that has been decoratively lined with clean nontoxic leaves, although serving platters and mirrors or marble are more often used (see Figure 8-9).

Partners and Accompaniments for Cheeses

Three types of foods have a natural affinity for cheese: wine or beer, bread and bread variations such as crackers, and fruit. Bread is probably the original accompaniment to cheese. The combination of the two provided portable sustenance for the traveler and a convenient meal for others.

Wine, particularly tannic wine, offers a perfect counterpoint to the richness of cheese because the acidic quality of wine cuts through the butterfat. Beer, on the other hand, works well with the salt component of cheese to make for a harmonious accompaniment.

The sweet juiciness of many fruits also pair well with the earthy richness of cheeses. Classic examples include apples and Cheddar or pears and blue cheese.

Caring for Cheeses: Storage and Handling

Because cheese is a living food with active biological attributes, it is critical to maintain the highest standards in sanitation during handling activities. Cheese may be a potentially hazardous food, if handled improperly.

When handling cheese that is not going to be cooked, it is important to either use utensils or wear food service gloves to prevent the contamination of the cheese with bacteria from your hands, and the formation of unsightly fingerprints on the cheese.

All food contact areas should be cleaned and sanitized

Figure 8-8 Cheese cart with arm for holding plate.

Figure 8-9 Cheese board on marble.

properly with hot soapy water and sanitizing solution to prevent cross-contamination. All cheese-cutting equipment should be similarly sanitized.

If cheeses become unnaturally moldy, they may be trimmed by cutting 1/2 to 1 inch past the mold. Care should be taken not to transfer the mold from the bad spot to the good portion.

Cheeses should never be allowed to sit out at room temperature for extended periods of time, beyond that required to aromatize the cheeses. Always keep cheeses and cheese preparations covered and refrigerated properly.

Making Cheese in the Kitchen

Cheese making, especially for the fresh cheeses in the accompanying recipes, is a practical and reasonable way to expand the handcrafted specialty items you can offer your guests. The raw ingredients can be obtained easily, and most of the necessary equipment is already part of a standard kitchen setup. Because cheese making involves acid, the equipment should be made of or lined with nonreactive materials, such as stainless steel, enamel, or food-grade plastic. All equipment should be thoroughly sterilized before use.

- Whole milk, heavy cream, and half-and-half are used to prepare the fresh cheeses here. You can often substitute (in whole or in part) lower-fat milk for whole milk or heavy cream for half-and-half, or substitute milk from sheep or goats, if it is available in your area. The milk should be pasteurized and homogenized to help produce consistent results.

- Fresh cheeses are most often curdled with an acid. Our recipes use cider vinegar, citric acid, tartaric acid, and lemon juice. Each acid has a particular effect on the finished cheese, and you may wish to experiment with different starters to find one that gives you the flavor you want.

- The curd for mozzarella is prepared with a rennet, or enzymatic starter. The curd can be purchased and used to prepare fresh mozzarella. For more information about preparing mozzarella curd, consult the resources found in on page 447.

- Two of the recipes in this section call for direct set cultures. These cultures start curdling the milk almost instantly, without requiring an extended incubation period. If you need a resource for direct set cultures, or to find any special cheese-making equipment, including molds, rennet starters, and mozzarella curds, consult the listing in Resource List on page 447.

Mascarpone

Yield: 1 quart

This is a delicious, rich cheese with a very high fat content. It can be used as a base for sauces by sweetening or adding fruit purées, or it can be served as is to accompany fresh or poached fruits.

2 qt	heavy cream
1/2 tsp	tartaric acid

1. Heat the cream to 180°F, stirring often to prevent scorching. Remove from the heat. Add the tartaric acid, and let the cream coagulate into a curd.
2. Drain the curd for at least 24 hours under refrigeration in a strainer lined with a coffee filter. The mascarpone is now ready to use, or transfer to a storage container and hold, covered, under refrigeration for up to 1 week.

Add tartaric acid to heated cream.

Drain the curdled cream in a lined colander.

*W*hole-Milk Ricotta Cheese

Yield: 8 ounces

Although ricotta cheese is traditionally made by recooking the whey, it can also be made by substituting milk for some or all of the whey. This version calls for whole milk. If you prefer a lower-fat cheese, use skim milk for all or part of the whole milk.

1 tsp	citric acid
1/4 cup	water
1 gal	whole milk
2 tsp	salt

1. Dissolve the citric acid in the water.
2. Heat the milk, citric acid solution, and salt to 185°F, stirring often to prevent scorching. Skim away the scum as it rises to the surface.
3. When the milk reaches 185°F, turn off the heat and allow the milk to set for 10 minutes.
4. Drain the curd for at least 1, and up to 3, hours under refrigeration in a cheesecloth-lined colander or a cheesecloth or muslin bag set over a bowl.
5. The cheese is now ready to use, or transfer to a storage container and hold, covered, under refrigeration for up to 1 week.

Chef's Notes: If desired, substitute 1 tablespoon diluted liquid citric acid for the teaspoon of citric acid. If a creamier product is desired, add 2 ounces heavy cream to the curd.

Skimming.

Curd forming.

Lemon Cheese

Yield: 3–3 1/2 pounds

This cheese has a pronounced lemon flavor. The texture is a bit dryer and coarser than mascarpone, the result of using a slightly lower-fat dairy product, as well as the additional draining and pressing this cheese undergoes.

3 qt	milk
1 qt	heavy cream
10 oz/fl	lemon juice, strained and chilled
2 tsp	salt
1 tsp	grated lemon zest

1. Heat the milk and cream over simmering water to exactly 100°F (not higher).
2. Remove from the heat and add the lemon juice. Stir very gently and briefly until the milk and cream mixture starts to curdle or thicken.
3. Rest at room temperature for 3 to 4 hours.
4. Drain the curd for 8 to 12 hours under refrigeration in a cheesecloth-lined colander or a cheesecloth or muslin bag set over a bowl.
5. Transfer the cheese to a bowl and work in the salt and lemon zest with wooden spoons. Be careful not to overwork the cheese.
6. Press into a mold, top with a weight, and allow to rest overnight under refrigeration. The cheese is now ready to unmold and serve, or wrap and hold under refrigeration for up to 4 days.

Peppered Lemon Cheese Add 2 tablespoons coarse ground black pepper with the lemon zest in step 5.
Dried Fruit and Hazelnut Cheese Replace the lemon zest with 1/2 cup each of toasted hazelnuts and dried fruit.

Making Lemon Cheese.

Add chilled lemon juice to heated milk.

Drape rinsed cheesecloth over a bowl, and add curdled milk and cream mixture.

Tie cheesecloth into a bag; suspend cheese and allow to drain.

Work in the salt.

Pack the cheese into a mold.

Let the weighted mold rest under refrigeration another 12 hours before serving.

Queso Blanco

Yield: 4 pounds

Queso blanco is a white, slightly salty, fresh cheese featured in Mexican and other Latin American cuisines. Its texture is somewhat firm and crumbly, similar to that of farmer's cheese. It is shown as a quesadilla filling on page 188.

1 gal	whole milk
1/4 cup	cider vinegar
1 tbsp	kosher salt

1. Heat the milk to 185°F, stirring often to prevent scorching.
2. Add the vinegar and salt gradually, stirring constantly. Remove from the heat when the milk has solidified into a curd.
3. Drain the curd for at least 1, and up to 3, hours under refrigeration in a cheesecloth-lined colander or a cheesecloth or muslin bag set over a bowl.
4. The cheese is now ready to use, or transfer to a storage container and hold, covered, under refrigeration for up to 1 week.

Herbed Yogurt Cheese

Yield: 1 quart

Yogurt cheese can be made from low-fat or nonfat yogurt with good results. It can be used as a dip or a spread.

2 qt	plain yogurt
3 tsp	salt
2 1/2 tsp	coarse ground black pepper
1 tbsp	chopped oregano
2 tsp	chopped thyme
2 each	small chiles, split
2 each	bay leaves
2 cups	extra-virgin olive oil

1. Mix the yogurt, salt, and pepper and drain 3 days under refrigeration in a cheesecloth-lined colander or a cheesecloth or muslin bag set over a bowl.
2. Divide the cheese into 2-ounce portions and place on parchment-lined trays. Allow to drain and dry overnight under refrigeration.
3. Combine the remaining ingredients for a marinade. Add the cheese and marinate 24 hours before serving. The cheese can be held in the marinade under refrigeration for up to 4 weeks.

Fromage Blanc

Yield: 12 cups

Fromage blanc *(French for "white cheese") has the texture of cream cheese without the calories. It can be used to make dips and spreads for sandwiches and hors d'oeuvre. Fresh herbs, spices, and dried and fresh fruits and vegetables can be added to this cheese to give it additional flavor and texture.*

1 gal	whole milk
2 packets	direct–set Fromage Blanc Starter Culture

1. Warm the milk to 72°F.
2. Stir in the starter culture.
3. Cover and allow to set (incubate) for 24 hours, or until a solid white curd forms.
4. Drain the curd for at least 3, and up to, 6 hours under refrigeration in a cheesecloth-lined colander or a cheesecloth or muslin bag set over a bowl.
5. The cheese is now ready to use, or transfer to a storage container and hold, covered, under refrigeration for up to 1 week.

Chef's Notes: A shorter draining gives a spreadable consistency; longer draining yields a cream cheese consistency.

Crème Fraîche

Yield: 3 to 4 cups

Crème fraîche is made by fermenting heavy cream that has a butterfat content as high as 60 percent with a lactic acid and the appropriate bacterial cultures. The flavor of newly prepared crème fraîche is sweet, and it has a loose, almost pourable texture. As it ages, the flavor becomes more pronounced and tart, and it thickens to the point at which it can nearly hold a spoon upright. It is important to the garde manger as a base or spread for canapés, in salad dressings, and served with fresh fruit.

1 qt	half-and-half
1 packet	direct-set Crème Fraîche Starter Culture

1. Warm the half-and-half to 72°F.
2. Stir in the starter culture.
3. Cover and allow to set (incubate) for 24 hours, until a very thick curd forms.
4. The crème fraîche is now ready to use, or transfer to a storage container and hold covered under refrigeration for up to 1 week.

Lime-Flavored Crème Fraîche Add fresh lime juice to taste.

Mozzarella Cheese

Yield: 2 pounds

Mozzarella belongs to a category of cheese known as pasta filata, *or spun curd. The procedure for turning fresh curds into mozzarella is demonstrated in the accompanying photographs.*

6 oz/wt	salt
1 gal	water
2 lb	cheese curd, cut into 1/2-inch cubes

1. Add the salt to the water and bring to 180°F. Remove the pot from the heat.
2. Lower the cheese curd in a colander into the hot water; the curds must be completely submerged.
3. Work the curd with wooden spoons, stretching it until it becomes a smooth but stringy mass. Maintain the water temperature at a constant 160°F during this process.
4. Remove the cheese from the water and continue stretching until the curd is smooth.
5. Working in ice water, shape the cheese into 4-ounce balls and store wrapped in plastic wrap or brine. They may be held, covered, under refrigeration for up to 10 days.

Chef's Note: Do not overwork or the cheese will be tough.

Submerge the curd in 160°F water.

Gently stir and stretch the curd until all the lumps are gone.

Working in ice water, shape the mozzarella into balls.

Marinated Bocconcini Prepare the mozzarella as directed through step 4. On plastic wrap, form a long tube, about 1 inch in diameter, and roll up. Tie at 1-inch intervals to form balls. Hold at least 8 hours under refrigeration. Cut into individual balls and remove the plastic wrap. Add 3 tbsp olive oil, 1 tbsp sherry vinegar, 1 tbsp basil chiffonade, and 1/2 tsp red pepper flakes. Marinate overnight. This recipe makes about 60 pieces. If desired, accompany the marinated bocconcini with roasted peppers.

Shape the mozzarella into a log.

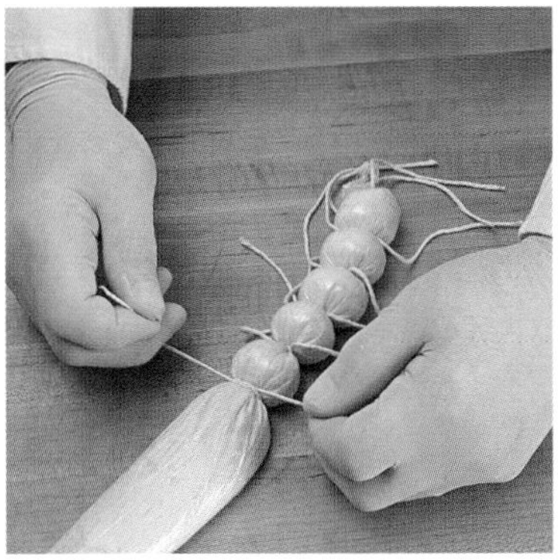

Tie off into 1-inch balls.

Marinated bocconcini served with roasted peppers and olives.

Mozzarella Roulade with Prosciutto Prepare the mozzarella through step 4. Working on a plastic tray or plastic wrap, stretch the curd into a rectangle. It should be about 1/4–inch thick and 12 inches by 14 inches. While the cheese is still warm, lay 10 paper-thin slices of prosciutto over the mozzarella in an even layer. Roll into a roulade with plastic wrap and secure the ends tightly with string. Return to the hot water for 2 to 3 minutes to lock in the garnish. Remove from the water and retie the ends to secure. Chill the roulade overnight in a water bath before slicing. The wrapped roulade can be held under refrigeration for up to 7 days. This recipe makes about thirty 1-ounce portions.

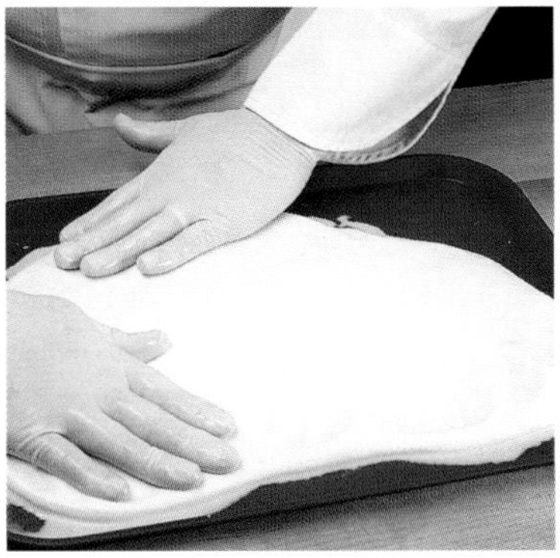

Spread the mozzarella into a sheet.

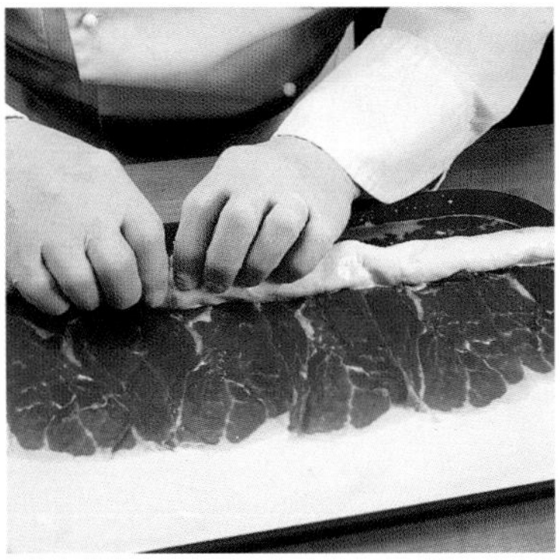

Roll the filled roulade.

Place the roulade on a platter.

Hudson Valley Camembert Crisps

Yield: 12 portions (2 ounces each)

This recipe, from Institute alumna Chef Melissa Kelly, features a special square-shaped Camembert produced at Old Chatham Sheepherding Company. You can use other semi-soft, rind-ripened cheeses in its place, of course.

6 each	sheep's milk Camembert (4 ounces each)
12 each	phyllo dough sheets
6 oz/wt	butter, melted
	(as needed for preparing phyllo and sautéing)
4 oz/fl	egg wash (2 whole eggs beaten with 1 tbsp milk)
as needed	vegetable oil for pan-frying

1. Cut the square Camembert from corner to corner, forming two equal triangles.
2. Layer three sheets of phyllo, brushing each layer with the melted butter. Repeat with remaining sheets, for a total of four stacks.
3. Cut each layered phyllo stack lengthwise into three equal strips. Wrap one strip around a triangle of cheese. Secure the seam by brushing with a bit of egg wash. Repeat procedure until all cheese is wrapped in phyllo. Cheese can be held under refrigeration for up to 24 hours before preparing further.
4. Pan-fry the wrapped Camembert over high heat in the oil until well browned on both sides and quite crisp. Drain briefly and serve hot or at room temperature.

Presentation Ideas: This can be served warm with a fruit chutney, peasant-style bread, air-dried venison, and a tossed salad as shown.

Marinated Sheep's Cheese with Herbes de Provence

Yield: 10 portions (4 ounces each)

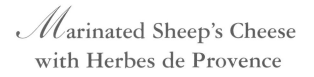

2 1/2 lb	fresh sheep's cheese
1/4 cup	Herbes de Provence (page 409)
1 1/2 tsp	salt
3/4 tsp	ground black pepper
10 each	grape leaves, rinsed
10 oz/fl	extra-virgin olive oil
20 slices	peasant-style bread

1. Divide the cheese logs into 4 equal portions.
2. Mix together the herbs, salt, and pepper and press gently into cheese, shaping the cheese portions into even disks about 3 inches in diameter.
3. Wrap the disks in grape leaves and place in a container. Pour the oil over the wrapped cheeses and marinate under refrigeration overnight. The cheese is now ready to use, or hold under refrigeration for up to 3 days.

Grilled Marinated Sheep's Cheese with Country Bread Brush slices of country-style bread with olive oil. Grill the bread and the drained wrapped cheese over hot coals until marked on both sides. The cheese should be soft and runny. Serve the cheese on a bed of greens, if desired, with the toasted bread, or arrange it on a platter for buffet-style service.

Marinated Goat Cheese Substitute buttons or logs of fresh goat cheese for the sheep's cheese.

Savory Roquefort Cheese Cake

Yield: 9-inch cake; 24 portions

This recipe makes an excellent element on any buffet or reception offering. Serve a wedge of it as an intermezzo salad on a bed of dressed greens, with a cheese course, or as an accompaniment to a wine tasting.

	Crust
1/2 cup	dry bread crumbs
1 oz/wt	butter
1/2 cup	chopped walnuts, toasted
3/4 lb	Roquefort
1 1/4 lb	cream cheese
2 tbsp	flour
3 each	shallots, minced, sautéed, and cooled
4 each	eggs
2 oz/fl	heavy cream
2 tbsp	chopped dill

1. Brown the bread crumbs in the butter; add the toasted walnuts. Cool.
2. Press into a 9-inch springform pan as for a graham cracker crust.
3. Line pan with a paper collar about 3 inches high.
4. In a food processor, blend the cheeses until smooth.
5. Add the flour, shallots, eggs, and cream.
6. Blend in the dill and pour into the prepared pan.
7. Bake in a 160°F water bath in a 300°F oven until set, 30 to 40 minutes.
8. Allow to cool overnight. Cut into 24 equal slices.

Blue Cheese Tart

Yield: Five 4-inch tarts

1 lb	Pâté Dough (page 416)
1/2 lb	cream cheese
1/2 lb	blue cheese
4 oz/wt	pasturized eggs (*or* 2 whole eggs)
3 oz/fl	sour cream
4 oz/fl	heavy cream
1 tbsp	minced chives
1 tbsp	minced flat-leaf parsley
2 tsp	minced thyme
1 tsp	minced shallots, sautéed
1/2 tsp	salt
1/4 tsp	ground white pepper

1. Roll out the dough and use it to line five 4-inch tarts; bake blind at 350°F for 15 to 20 minutes.
2. Cream the cheeses in mixer until smooth. Add the eggs gradually, scraping the sides often. Add the sour cream, heavy cream, seasonings, and herbs.
3. Pour into prepared crusts and bake at 300°F until knife comes out clean when inserted in the center of the tart, about 20 minutes.
4. Let the tarts rest at least 10 to 15 minutes before slicing. They may be served warm or at room temperature.

Chef's Notes: For canapés, pour the custard into 50 prepared barquettes and bake as directed above. Garnish with chopped toasted walnuts or pistachios.

Blue Cheese Flan Omit the crust, and prepare the custard mixture in lightly oiled 1- or 2-ounce molds. Bake in a 160°F water bath in a 300°F oven until lightly set. They may be served warm or at room temperature.

NINE

Hors d'Oeuvre

The term *hors d'oeuvre*—which translates from French as "outside the meal"—is universally recognized; we have not developed any exact equivalent in English capable of conveying as much information as this short French phrase. Typically served as a prelude to a meal, hors d'oeuvre are some of the most intriguing and demanding items produced by the garde manger. Most cuisines have a well-established form of preparing and presenting hors d'oeuvre. The zakuski table served before banquets in Russia features smoked and pickled fish, blinis with caviar, and a host of special salads.

In Spain, tapas are traditionally served as "bar food" and derive their name from the piece of bread once used to cover up a glass of sherry. "Little dishes" known as mezzes are popular throughout the Mediterranean regions and feature olives, nuts, dips, spreads, and highly seasoned items such as grilled kebabs of meat or fish. In the Scandinavian countries, a smorgasbord showcases the special dishes, hot and cold, of that region, including herring, cheeses, and pickled foods. Today, chefs have many imaginative ways to present hors d'oeuvre such as the spoon tree shown in Figure 9-1.

Hors d'oeuvre also have a place on a menu, where they may be featured as antipasti or hors d'oeuvre variées. You may be familiar with the "chef's tasting" or *amuse-gueule,* a small portion of something exotic, unusual, or otherwise special that is served when the guests are seated.

Even though hors d'oeuvre are small bite-sized items, today it is increasingly common for clients to request an entire menu made up of hors d'oeuvre to serve at a reception or cocktail party. These "standing meals" can be quite extensive, running the gamut from small portions of cold soups, meats, fish, cheeses, vegetable dishes, and pastas, to desserts and confections. In a break with the traditional notion that hors d'oeuvre should be small enough to eat in one bite and never require a knife and fork, some items at these special receptions may be plated. For these events to run smoothly, it is important to have adequate service staff on hand to continually relieve guests of used plates and cups, picks and napkins, rather than forcing the guests to resort to using ashtrays and potted palms.

The items you choose to serve as hors d'oeuvre may be very simple, requiring little if any preparation on the part of the garde manger beyond slicing and presenting. Nuts, plain or marinated olives (see Figure 9-2), and hard-cooked eggs are all traditional offerings. Dips and spreads are often served with crudité (raw or chilled lightly blanched vegetables), crackers, or chips. Sausages, pâtés, terrines, and cheeses are also served as reception or buffet items, as are thinly sliced or hand-carved smoked fish and meats. Freshly shucked clams with Salsa Verde (page 35) and Oysters with Mignonette are classics (see Figure 9-3). One "simple" but elegant food, caviar, is also featured on its own as an elegant hors d'oeuvre.

There are a few precepts to remember in general hors d'oeuvre preparation:

- When selecting hors d'oeuvre, keep in mind the nature of the event, as well as the menu to follow.
- Ice carvings and ice beds are often used to keep seafood and caviar very cold, as well as for their dramatic appeal.

Figure 9-1 Presenting hors d'oeuvre on a spoon tree.

Figure 9-2 Marinated olives.

Be certain that the ice can drain properly and that heavy or large ice carvings are very stable.

- Hors d'oeuvre served on platters or passed on trays butler style should be thoughtfully presented, so that the last person to take an hors d'oeuvre is not rummaging among jumbled garnishes.
- Use handcrafted plates such as those shown in Figure 9-4. Cut several custom-fit Plexiglass inserts to prevent items from rolling on uneven surfaces as well as to speed and simplify the refilling process.

Caviar

Caviar, a delicacy made from the roe of a sturgeon, was described by Aristotle in the fourth century B.C.E. During the Roman Empire, trumpets heralded the arrival of caviar to the table, presented with garlands of flowers.

Today caviar remains among the most expensive and exclusive of all preserved foods, partly because of overfishing and pollution and partly because caviar is labor-intensive to produce, and extremely perishable. Caviar will probably never again be given away with glasses of beer "to encourage libation" as it once was in this country. Efforts at farm-raising sturgeon and developing techniques to remove the roe without killing the fish have not yet shown signs of making caviar less expensive.

From Roe to Caviar

The roe sac must be harvested from the sturgeon while it is still alive (if the fish is dead, the membranes surrounding the individual eggs will deteriorate and rupture). The roe sacs are carefully rubbed over a sieve; the eggs (or berries) are caught in a container, washed in fresh water, drained, and then graded.

The master grader looks for consistency of grain, size, color, fragrance, flavor, gleam, firmness, and vulnerability of the roe skin. The bigger and lighter in color the eggs, the more rare and expensive the finished caviar.

Eggs of the highest quality are prepared by a method called "molossal" or "little salt," indicating that salt is added at a rate of less than 5 percent of the egg's weight. Lesser-quality caviar will be processed with greater amounts of salt. Salt both preserves the caviar and gives it its texture and flavor. However, even though caviar is a salted food, it remains quite perishable, and must be carefully refrigerated throughout processing and storage.

Figure 9-3 Clams with Salsa Verde; Oysters with Mignonette.

Figure 9-4 Using hand crafted plates with a Plexiglass insert.

Types of Caviar

In both France and the United States, only the processed roe of sturgeon can be called caviar; France still strictly enforces this rule. In the United States, however, the law has been interpreted more leniently, and as long as the type of fish is identified on the label, various kinds of fish roe may be sold as caviar (see Figure 9-5).

True Caviar

The major sturgeon species used to produce true caviar today are beluga, osetra, and sevruga. Sterlet, which is nearly extinct, was the source of the fabled "golden caviar of the Czars." One of the reasons caviar is so expensive is directly related to the age and size a sturgeon must reach before developing the valuable roe.

The individual eggs, or berries, are graded for color, with 000 indicating the lightest colored caviar and 0 the darkest. Color alone, however, does not indicate quality. The eggs are also sized. Beluga caviar has the largest eggs, graded large or coarse; osetra eggs are slightly smaller than beluga; sevruga is the smallest of all.

- Beluga caviar ranges in color from light steel gray to dark gray. The beluga sturgeon takes as long as twenty years to achieve maturity, when it may weigh up to two thousand pounds. This long growth cycle means that beluga caviar is the most expensive and least readily available. It is always sold in blue jars or tins.
- Osetra caviar is a brownish color with a golden tinge and can be distinguished from other caviar by the strong nutty flavor. This sturgeon reaches a size of ten feet and five hundred pounds and grows to maturity in twelve to fourteen years. It is always sold in yellow jars or tins.

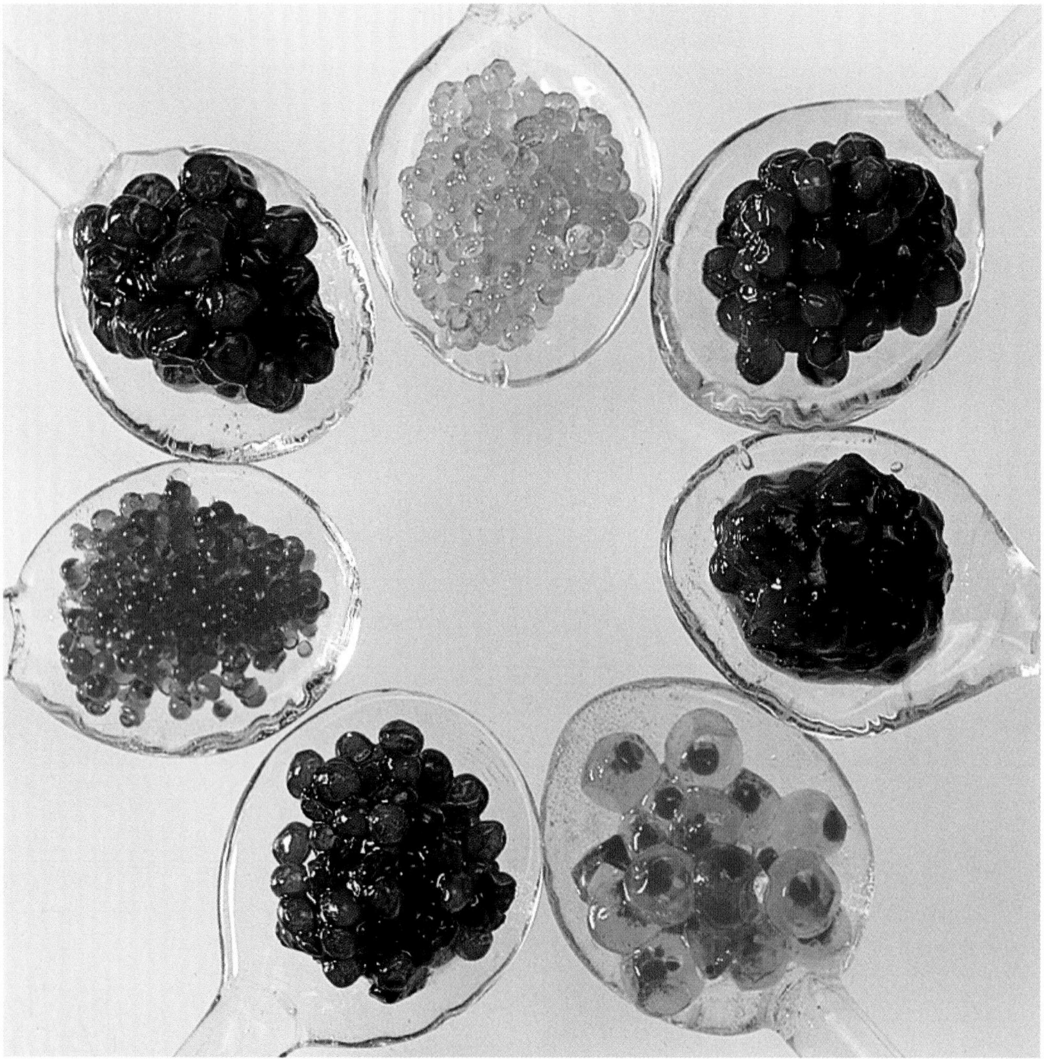

Figure 9-5 Caviars (clockwise from top): Wasabi tobikko, beluga, pressed, salmon, sevruga, orange tobikko, golden osetra.

- Sevruga caviar berries are dark brown, the smallest of the true caviars, with a strong flavor. Sevruga can grow to seven feet and about 150 pounds in eight to ten years. Sevruga caviar is less expensive than beluga and osetra. It is always sold in red jars or tins.

Pressed caviar (known in Russian as *pajusnay*) is made from mature, broken, or overripe eggs. The salted eggs are put into a linen sack and pressed (using a grape press) until all of the fatty liquid is released. The result is a marmalade-like substance, doted on by the Russians, who spread it on black bread and enjoy it with chilled vodka. The flavor of pressed caviar is more intense than other caviars, and the eating experience is quite different. Pressed caviar is also used to prepare special dishes and cold sauces.

Other Types of Caviar

Other fish roes can be processed in the same manner as sturgeon. The United States and other countries also produce caviar from the roe of salmon, paddlefish, whitefish, lumpfish, and cod. These caviars are available pasteurized or fresh. Each type is different in size, texture, and taste.

Salmon caviar is either golden or pink in color. The eggs are large, flavorful, and attractive.

Whitefish from the Great Lakes and Canada produces a roe with a natural golden color, crunchy texture, and a mild fresh taste.

The processed roe of cod and carp are quite small and are often salted, pressed, and sold as *tarama*. The gray mullet is also the source of the Mediterranean delicacy known as *poutargue* or *boutargue* in France and *botarga* in Italy. In Greece, tarama caviar is made from the roe of the gray mullet. To further confuse the issue, in the United States tarama, which is imported, is made not from mullet but from the roe of tuna.

The roe of crab, flying fish (*tobikko*), cod (*tarako*), and sea urchin (*uni*) are also processed in a similar fashion and are staples of sushi bars in Japan. They are sometimes flavored with wasabi or other ingredients to produce special flavors and colors.

Lumpfish roe, though widely available and inexpensive, is not a good substitute for true caviar. Because lumpfish roe has an unappetizing off-gray color, it is typically dyed red, gold, or black using vegetable-based dyes or cuttlefish ink.

Buying and Storing Caviar

Fresh sturgeon caviar should be plump and moist, with each individual egg shiny, smooth, separate, and intact. When you taste caviar, the eggs should release a savory flavor, faintly nutty with a hint of the sea. It should be surrounded by its own thick natural oils, but never appear to be swimming in oil.

Caviar should always be properly stored under refrigeration at 28°F to 32°F. True caviar can be held unopened under refrigeration for 4 weeks, and opened for 2 to 3 days. Pressed caviar will keep at 40°F for 10 days to 2 weeks; once opened it should be eaten within 5 days. One of the primary reasons caviar goes bad after opening is cross contamination. Be sure to use a clean spoon each time you dip some caviar from its container.

Pasteurized "caviars" and those processed with greater amounts of salt will keep in the refrigerator unopened for several weeks or even months, but once opened, they too should be consumed within 2 to 3 days.

Caviar can be purchased in jars weighing from 1 ounce (30 grams) to 2½ ounces (75 grams). Larger quantities are generally packed in tins, and are available in various weights from 4 ounces (120 grams) to 2.2 pounds (1 kilogram).

Serving Caviar

The best caviar needs no special accompaniments. It is

Figure 9-6 Caviar service.

often served in special iced containers (see Figure 9-6), with mother of pearl, bone, horn, or glass spoons to avoid any flavor change that might occur if metal spoons are used. Toast points, brioche, or blinis are often served as a base for a caviar canapé, perhaps with a few dollops of crème fraîche.

This precious item is also used as a garnish for other hors d'oeuvre and appetizers. Lesser-quality caviar may be appropriate for garnishing some items. Remember that caviar should never be added to foods as they are cooking.

Composed Hors d'Oeuvre

Composed hors d'oeuvre are built from two or more components. Many of these components can be prepared in advance, but often the final assembly and garnish has to be done at nearly the last moment. These special items—including canapés, profiteroles, tartlets, and barquettes—add greatly to the variety of offerings. Cured and smoked foods, pâtés, foie gras, salads, and vegetables are all appropriate as elements in any composed hors d'oeuvre. One special item, mousse, can be featured as a spread, piped into molds or edible containers, rolled into a roulade and sliced, or shaped into quenelles.

Cold Savory Mousses

The French word *mousse* literally means "foam" or "froth." For the garde manger, it indicates a cold item prepared by combining three basic elements: a base, a binder, and an aerator (see Figure 9-7). Mousses are often featured as an hors d'oeuvre, piped decoratively on a canapé base or into a barquette or tartlet mold; used to fill a cucumber cup or endive leaf; or shaped in a special mold as either single portion perhaps topped with a layer of crystal-clear aspic gelée, or as loaves or roulades to be sliced.

A cold mousse as the term is understood today is one that is not cooked after being assembled. It is never served hot, since subjecting the gelatin or fat binder in the mousse to heat would melt the mousse and deflate it. A "hot mousse" indicates a small portion of a mousseline forcemeat (see page 227) that has been molded in a fashion similar to a cold mousse before being cooked and served hot.

The Base

Mousse prepared by the garde manger is produced from savory items such as cooked or smoked meats and fish, cheeses, or prepared vegetables. This base is then puréed until very smooth. In some cases it may be necessary to add a liquid or moist product such as velouté, béchamel, unwhipped cream, or mayonnaise to adjust the consistency. The intent is to have the base at a consistency similar to that of pastry cream before adding the binder, if it is required, and the aerator.

Figure 9-7 Base of puréed salmon, whipped cream as aerator, and gelatin as binder.

For the best possible texture, sieve the puréed base if desired (see Figure 9-8a). This removes any last bits of sinew or fiber and gives a very delicate finished product.

The Binder

Gelatin, either powdered or in sheets, is added in a proportion similar to that called for when preparing an aspic gelée. Soften the gelatin in a cool liquid (known as "blooming"). Warm it to 90°F to 110°F to dissolve the granules or melt the sheets. Stir the dissolved gelatin into the base. It is important to blend the gelatin evenly throughout the entire base (see Figure 9-8b).

In some cases, the base product has enough body and bind to hold the mousse together without an additional binder. Cheese is a good example.

The key is to have the proper balance of binder and base so that the mousse will keep a distinct shape when chilled without melting or sagging. The amount of binder in a product should be adjusted, depending on the final use of the product. For example, if a mousse must be sliced and

Figure 9-8 Smoked Salmon Mousse.

a. The base is pushed through a sieve. b. The gelatin solution is added. c. The whipped cream is folded in.

lined up on a buffet platter that will be sitting out for any length of time, it will need more binder (gelatin) than a single serving of mousse that is taken directly from the refrigerator immediately before it is served.

The Aerator

Beaten egg whites and/or whipped cream give the mousse its frothy texture. Beat the whites or cream to soft peaks for the best results. If the aerator is overbeaten, it could begin to collapse or give the mousse a grainy appearance and texture.

Fold the aerator into the base carefully. It is a good idea to add about one-third the total amount of aerator first to make it easier to fold in the remaining two-thirds. This technique keeps the maximum volume in the finished mousse (see Figure 9-8c).

Basic Formula for a Mousse

Although each base ingredient may call for an adjustment in the amount of binder and aerator, this basic formula is a good checkpoint. It can and should be altered depending on the type of mousse being made and the intended use of the final product.

Basic Formula for a Mousse

Base	2 pounds	
Binder*	1 ounce gelatin	(*if required by recipe)
Liquid*	1 cup	(*to bloom gelatin)
Aerator	2 cups	

Once the mousse is prepared, it should be shaped in the desired way: Transfer immediately to a pastry bag and pipe out without delay into the desired "container" (see Figure 9-9) or apply it as a topping or filling for tea sandwiches and canapés. A mousse can also be rolled in the same way as a roulade (page 233), carefully secured, and chilled before slicing. Terrine molds may be used to shape a mousse into a loaf (page 229); be sure to oil the mold and line it with plastic wrap to make it easy to remove the mousse once it is properly chilled.

Figure 9-9 Piping salmon mousse into barquettes.

Barquettes and Tartlets

Pâté Dough (page 416) can be used to line a pâté en croûte as well as to create small edible containers, known as barquettes or tartlets. They may be filled with a cold mousse or other savory fillings.

The dough should be rolled out in a thin sheet using a pasta machine or by hand. Cut out the dough to fit the mold (see Figure 9-10a). Set the dough in the mold, and top with a second mold to press it into shape (see Figures 9-10b and c). Set this assembly upside down on a baking sheet (see Figure 9-10d). Bake until golden brown (see Figure 9-10e), unmold, and store in an airtight container until required.

These shells can be filled and garnished as for canapés, though it is generally not necessary to add a separate spread. Select the filling carefully. Very moist fillings can quickly make the pastry shell soggy. These hors d'oeuvre are best when assembled as close as possible to service time.

Other pastry or bread cases can be used to prepare hors d'oeuvre. Some classics from cuisines around the world include bouchées, empanadas, beurrecks and tiropettes, dim sum, and spring rolls.

Canapés

Canapés are small open-faced sandwiches (see Sandwiches, page 105). The "base" for a canapé is a small piece of bread, cut to shape and toasted. A spread of some sort—either a plain or flavored butter, spreadable cheese, or mayonnaise—is applied to the bread to act as a moisture barrier.

The filling or topping is added next. It should be cut neatly, so that nothing hangs over the edge of the canapé. A garnish gives a fresh and appealing look to the canapé, but take the time to select something appropriate and attractive. It is important to take into account the timing and size of the event.

Figure 9-10 Barquettes.

a. Cutting the dough to fit a barquette mold.

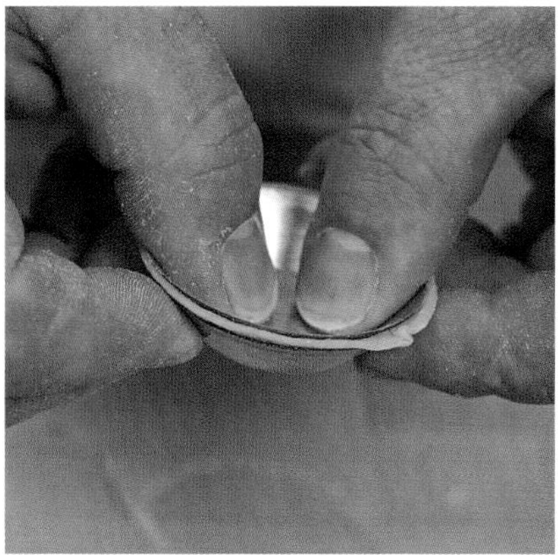

b. Pressing the dough into a tartlet mold.

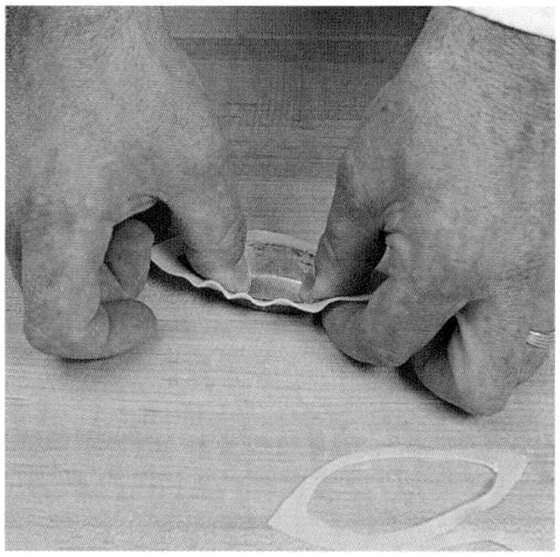

c. Pressing the dough into a barquette mold.

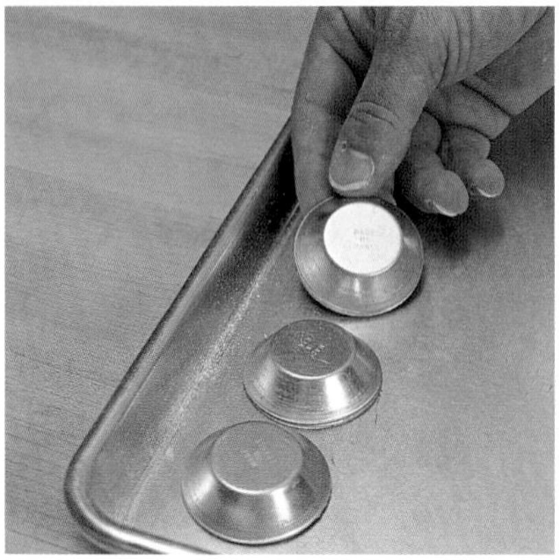

d. Baking the assembly upside down.

e. Finished barquettes and tartlets.

Profiteroles

Yield: 40 pieces

This batter can be piped into small puffs or miniature eclair shapes and filled with a wide variety of fillings.

1 cup	water
1/4 lb	butter
To taste	salt
1 cup	all-purpose flour, sifted
4 each	eggs

1. Combine the water, butter, and salt and bring to a boil.
2. Add the sifted flour all at once and stir in well; cook out until mass comes away from the pot.
3. Transfer to mixer and mix on medium speed for about 1 minute. Add the eggs one at a time, mixing well after each addition, to achieve a stiff but pliable texture.
4. Transfer the dough to a pastry bag with a plain tip and pipe out in the desired shape onto parchment-lined sheet pans. One-inch balls produced profiteroles; other shapes such as eclairs may also be prepared (see photo).
5. Bake at 400°F until golden brown, then turn down to 325°F to cook through, 12 to 15 minutes (see photo).
6. When ready to fill, slice off the tops with a sharp knife. Add filling of choice, and replace the top.

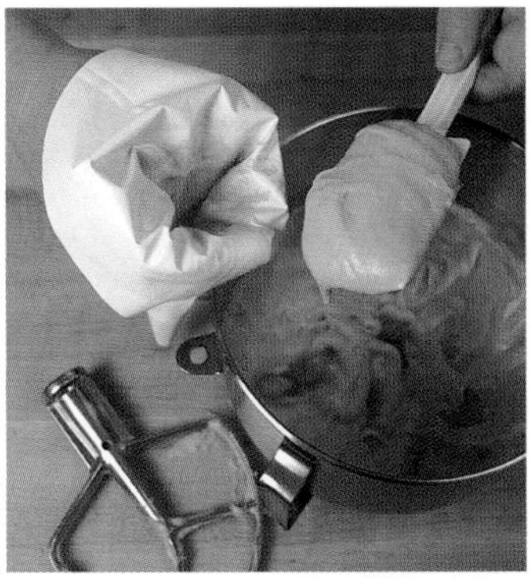

Pâte à choux dough should be stiff but still pliable.

Pâte à choux is baked at high and then low temperatures to produce a hollow middle.

Gougères (Gruyère Cheese Puffs)

Yield: 100 pieces

These puffs make a great snack item or casual reception food with cocktails. They are best when served warm from the oven, but they can be cooled, held in airtight containers, and served at room temperature if necessary.

1 cup	water
1/4 lb	butter
To taste	salt
1 cup	all-purpose flour, sifted
4 each	eggs
3/4 cup	Gruyère cheese, grated

1. Combine the water, butter, and salt and bring to a boil.
2. Add the sifted flour all at once and stir in well; cook stirring constantly, until mass comes away from the sides of the pot.
3. Transfer to mixer and mix on medium speed for about 1 minute. Add the eggs one at a time, mixing well after each addition, to achieve a stiff but pliable texture.
4. Add the grated Gruyère cheese and continue mixing for 1 minute.
5. Transfer the dough to a pastry bag with a plain tip and pipe out in the desired shape onto parchment-lined sheet pans.
6. Bake at 400°F until golden brown, then turn down to 325° to cook through, 12 to 15 minutes. Serve warm or store in airtight container, as for crackers.

Cheese Sticks (Paillettes)

Yield: 30 pieces

Cheese sticks are a quick and simple way to add a signature look and flavor to a reception table, dining table, or bar. The sticks may be twisted, curled, or shaped as desired before baking. Fanciful shapes presented in tall glasses or jars serve as eye-catching edible decorations.

1 each	Puff Pastry sheet (page 420)
1 each	egg yolk beaten with 1 tbsp milk
1/2 cup	grated Parmesan cheese
To taste	sweet Spanish paprika

1. Brush the puff pastry sheet with the egg wash.
2. Sprinkle the cheese and paprika evenly over the puff pastry sheets.
3. Cut into 1/4-inch strips, the length of the sheet.
4. Bake on parchment-lined sheet pans at 400°F until golden brown, about 10 minutes.

Chef's Note: Cajun Spice Blend (page 407), cayenne, poppy seeds, or sesame seeds may be used as alternate garnishes.

Palmiers with Prosciutto

Yield: 40 to 45 pieces

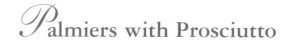

Also shown: Cheese Sticks, Gougères

This is a savory variation of the classic French pastry. The "palm leaves" are lined with prosciutto, and a dusting of Parmesan replaces the granulated sugar. The name reflects the fact that the doughs puffs into a palm-leaf shape as it bakes.

1/2 lb	Puff Pastry sheets (page 420)
2 oz/wt	tomato paste
12 each	prosciutto slices
1/4 cup	fine-grated Parmesan cheese

1. Lay out the puff pastry sheets and brush each with a small amount of tomato paste.
2. Lay thin slices of prosciutto over the puff pastry and dust with cheese. Roll long sides in toward center. Slice 1/4 inch thick and bake on parchment-lined sheet trays at 400°F until golden brown, approximately 10 minutes.

Chef's Notes: Parchment paper on top and bottom will help the pieces stay flat. The paper can be removed for the last few minutes to allow for browning.

• • •

These can be made up in batches and frozen, then bake as needed and serve warm.

Crab Meat and Avocado Profiteroles

Yield: 30 profiteroles

1/4 lb	crab meat, cleaned
1/2 each	ripe avocado, cut into small dice
1 each	lime, juiced (2 oz/fl)
1 tbsp	buttermilk
2 tsp	fine-cut chives
1 tbsp	chopped cilantro
To taste	salt
To taste	cayenne pepper
30 each	Profiteroles (page 319)

1. Combine the crab meat, avocado, lime juice, and buttermilk. Fold in the chives and cilantro and season with salt and cayenne pepper.
2. Split the puffs and fill with the crab meat mixture.

Southwest Chicken Salad in Profiteroles

Yield: 30 profiteroles

2 each	chicken legs, cooked and cut into small dice
1 each	tomato concassé
1 each	lime, segments only, cut into small dice
2 tbsp	small-dice roasted pepper
1 tsp	minced jalapeño
2 tbsp	minced shallots
1 each	garlic clove, minced (1 teaspoon)
2 tbsp	chopped cilantro
2 tsp	chopped marjoram
2 tsp	minced chives
To taste	salt
To taste	ground black pepper
30 each	Profiteroles (page 319)

1. Combine the chicken, tomato, lime, peppers, shallots, garlic, and herbs. Season with salt and pepper. Marinate for 2 hours under refrigeration.
2. Split the puffs and fill with the chicken salad.

Duck Rillettes in Profiteroles

Yield: 30 profiteroles

1/4 lb	Duck Rillettes (page 171)
1 oz/fl	heavy cream
2 tbsp	Dijon mustard
Few drops	Tabasco sauce
30 each	Profiteroles (page 319), split
2 tbsp	green peppercorns, crushed (1 per profiterole)

1. In a mixing bowl on low speed, work rillettes until softened.
2. Whip the cream to soft peaks. Fold the whipped cream, mustard, and Tabasco gently but thoroughly into the rillettes.
3. Pipe the rillette mixture into the profiteroles. Garnish each with a green peppercorn. Replace the cover.

Smoked Salmon Mousse Barquettes

Yield: 30 small barquettes

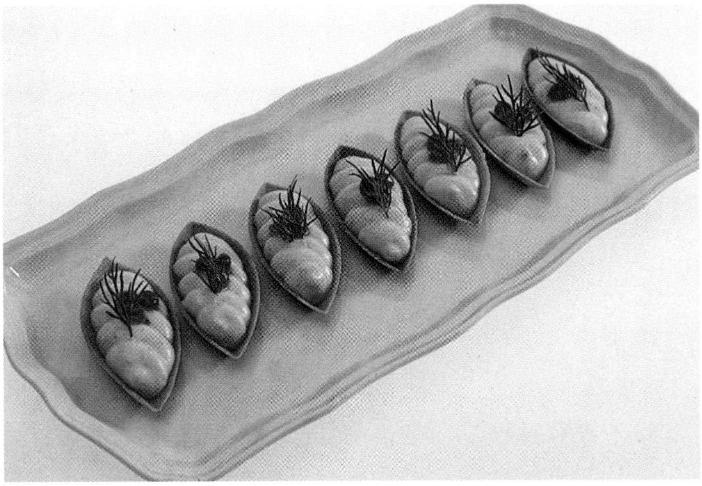

5 oz	Smoked Salmon (page 149), diced
3/4 cup	Fish Velouté (page 413)
2 tbsp	Aspic Gelée (page 45), softened
1/2 cup	heavy cream
1/4 tsp	Tabasco sauce
2 tsp	kosher salt
To taste	ground black pepper
30 each	barquettes made from Paté Dough (pages 318, 416), prebaked
2 oz/wt	salmon roe
30 each	dill sprigs

1. Make the mousse by puréeing the smoked salmon and velouté in a food processor until very smooth. Add the warm aspic gelée while the processor is running. Transfer to a bowl once fully incorporated.

2. Whip the cream to soft peaks and fold gently but thoroughly into the salmon mixture. Season with Tabasco, salt, and pepper.

3. *Barquette Assembly:* Pipe approximately 1/2 ounce salmon mousse into each barquette, garnish with a little salmon roe and a dill sprig and chill until firm. The barquettes are now ready to serve, or hold under refrigeration for up to 1 hour.

Creamed Wild Mushroom Tartlets

Yield: 30 tartlets

1 lb	assorted wild mushrooms (shiitake, porcini, oyster, etc.), cut into small dice
2 each	shallots, minced
2 oz/wt	butter
1 tbsp	brandy
1 tbsp	sherry
1/4 cup	heavy cream
30 each	tartlet shells made from Pâté Dough (page 318, 416), baked blind
	Garnish
2 oz/wt	Dry Jack cheese, grated fine
1 oz/wt	chopped flat-leaf parsley
2 tsp	ground black pepper

1. Sauté the mushrooms and shallots in the butter; add the brandy, sherry, and cream to finish the duxelles.
2. Combine the garnish ingredients and reserve.
3. *Tartlet Assembly:* Fill each tartlet with a tablespoon of duxelles and top with a sprinkle of the garnish mixture. Serve warm.

Goat Cheese Canapé with Sweet Peppers

Yield: 30 canapés

15 oz	Roasted Pepper Salad (page 77)
1/2 each	jalapeño, seeded and minced
8 oz/wt	soft fresh goat cheese *or* sour cream
1/2 cup	clabbered cream *or* sour cream
30 each	whole wheat bread canapé bases, toasted
1 cup	cilantro leaves, loosely packed (30 each)

1. Add the jalapeño to the pepper salad and allow to marinate.
2. Blend the goat cheese and clabbered cream until smooth and pipeable.
3. *Canapé Assembly:* Pipe the goat cheese mixture in a ring around the canapé base. Mound about 1 tablespoon of pepper salad in the center and top with a cilantro leaf.

Smoked Whiskey Shrimp

Yield: 30 pieces

30 pieces	shrimp (21/25 count)
3 tbsp	whiskey or bourbon
2 each	limes, juiced
1 tbsp	balsamic vinegar
1 tbsp	honey
1 each	shallot, minced
2 each	garlic cloves, minced
3 tbsp	olive oil
3 tbsp	vegetable oil
1 tbsp	minced cilantro
3/4 cup	tomato concassé
To taste	Tabasco sauce
To taste	salt
To taste	ground black pepper

1. Remove shells from shrimp and devein.
2. Combine the whiskey, lime juice, vinegar, honey, shallots, and garlic. Whisk in the oils. Add the cilantro and tomatoes, and adjust seasoning with Tabasco, salt, and pepper. Marinate the shrimp in the mixture for at least 2 hours and up to overnight.
3. Drain the shrimp and hot smoke at 185°F for 10 to 12 minutes, or until cooked through. Cool.

Presentation Ideas: Serve the shrimp on a canapé base with a chive cream cheese spread and cucumber rings. Garnish with a few curls of fine-julienne red pepper and chives.

Steak Tartare Canapé

Yield: 30 canapés

Steak tartare is traditionally made by mincing beef tenderloin very fine. It should be made as close as possible to service time for the best flavor and texture.

1 lb	beef tenderloin
2 tbsp	pasteurized egg yolks
1 oz/wt	onions, minced
2 tbsp	capers, chopped
To taste	salt
To taste	ground black pepper
To taste	Worcestershire sauce
30 each	rye bread canapé bases, toasted
5 oz/wt	Anchovy Butter (page 414), softened
2 oz/wt	hard-cooked egg, chopped, or as needed
2 oz/wt	minced onion, or as needed
2 oz/wt	minced parsley, or as needed

1. Chop the tenderloin fine. At service time, combine the beef, egg yolks, onions, and capers to prepare the tartare. Add salt, pepper, and Worcestershire to taste.
2. *Canapé Assembly:* Spread the canapé base with 1 teaspoon anchovy butter and 1 tablespoon tartare mixture, and top with chopped eggs, onions, and parsley.

Smoked Trout Canapé

Yield: 30 canapés

15 oz/wt	Hot Smoked Trout (page 148)
30 each	rye bread canapé bases, toasted
5 oz/wt	Horseradish Butter (page 415), softened
10 each	pimiento-stuffed olives, sliced

1. Flake the trout following natural seams into $3/4$- to 1-inch-wide pieces.
2. *Canapé Assembly:* Spread each canapé base with 1 teaspoon horseradish butter; top with a piece of trout. Garnish with a slice of olive.

Smoked Shrimp Canapé

Yield: 30 canapés

15 each	Smoked Shrimp (21/25 count), (page 147)
30 each	whole wheat bread canapé bases, toasted
5 oz/wt	Pimiento Butter (page 414), softened
As needed	small watercress pluches

1. Split the shrimp in half lengthwise and devein.
2. *Canapé Assembly:* Spread the canapé base with 1 teaspoon pimiento butter and top with 1 piece smoked shrimp and a small sprig of watercress.

Smoked Duck Mousse Canapé with Raspberry

Yield: 30 canapés

4 oz/wt	Smoked Duck (page 154), diced
2 tsp	powdered gelatin
2 tbsp	water
2 oz/fl	heavy cream, whipped
30 each	whole wheat canapé bases, toasted
1 oz/fl	strained puréed raspberry (see Chef's Notes)
4 oz/wt	butter, softened
30 each	thin slices Smoked Duck breast (cut to dimension of canapé base) (page 154)
30 each	fresh raspberries

1. Purée the diced duck until smooth.
2. Soften the gelatin in the water. Warm gently until dissolved. Add the gelatin to the duck and fold in the cream.
3. Blend the raspberry purée and butter until smooth.
4. *Canapé Assembly:* Spread the raspberry butter on each base. Pipe the mousse onto the canapé base; garnish with a slice of duck and a raspberry.

Chef's Notes: To prepare a raspberry purée, purée berries in a blender or food processor. Strain through a fine sieve. Taste and adjust seasoning as required with sugar and a few drops of balsamic vinegar.

• • •

The mousse is best if prepared as close as possible to service time. When preparing these canapés, prepare the raspberry purée first, and have all other mise en place ready before beginning the mousse.

Prosciutto and Melon Canapé

Yield: 30 canapés

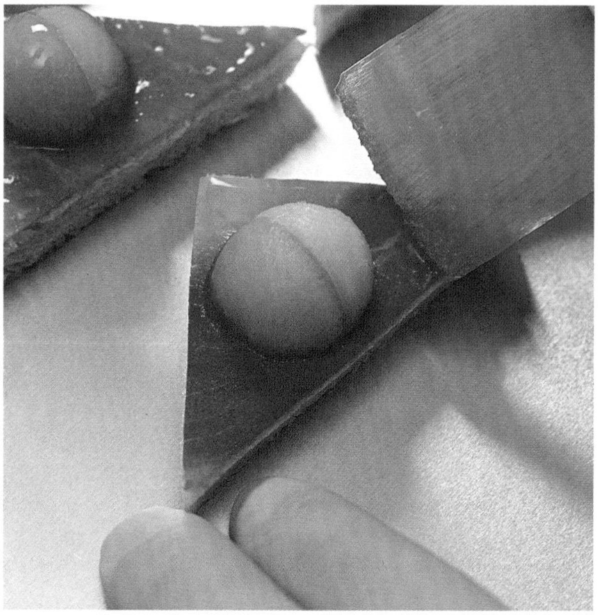

8 slices	prosciutto ham, sliced very thin (about 5 oz/wt)
30 each	white bread canapé bases, toasted
5 oz/wt	Mascarpone Cheese Spread (see Chef's Notes)
30 pieces	honeydew melon, scooped into small balls
30 pieces	cantaloupe, cut into small dice or petite pois shape
30 each	mint leaves, cut into fine chiffonade
4 oz/fl	Aspic Gelée, softened (*optional,* page 45)

1. Cut prosciutto to fit canapé bases.
2. *Canapé Assembly:* Spread the canapé bases with some of the mascarpone spread and top with a piece of prosciutto. Pipe a small mound of mascarpone in the center of each canapé, top with melon balls. Brush with aspic if desired and top with a mint leaf.

Chef's Notes: To prepare Mascarpone Cheese Spread, add Tabasco, Dijon mustard, salt, and pepper to taste to 5 ounces of Mascarpone (page 298). Mix well.

This canapé can be prepared four or more at a time, making it an excellent choice for volume production needs. Slice a Pullman loaf lengthwise, brush lightly with olive oil, and toast lightly. Spread with mascarpone cheese. Lay prosciutto in an even layer.

Deviled Quail Egg Canapé

Yield: 30 canapés

15 each	quail eggs (see Chef's Notes)
As needed	Dijon mustard
As needed	Basic Mayonnaise (page 28)
As needed	Worcestershire sauce
To taste	salt
To taste	ground white pepper
30 each	pumpernickel bread canapé bases, toasted and lightly buttered
1 oz/wt	caviar
1/4 bunch	fresh dill

1. Simmer the quail eggs for 6 1/2 minutes; shock and peel as quickly as possible under cold water.
2. Cut the eggs in half lengthwise, take out the yolks, and reserve the whites.
3. Push the yolks through a sieve into a mixing bowl. Add just enough mustard and mayonnaise to make the mixture easy to pipe out. Season with Worcestershire, salt, and pepper.
4. *Canapé Assembly:* Pipe a small rosette of the deviled yolk mixture onto the pumpernickel bread. Place the egg white on top at a slight angle tilting upward. Pipe enough yolk mixture into the cavity of the egg white just to fill it. Garnish with a small dollop of caviar and very small sprig of dill.

Chef's Notes: You may wish to add 1 or 2 hard-cooked yolks (from chicken eggs) to supplement the quail egg yolks in this recipe.

Red Pepper Mousse in Endive

Yield: 30 pieces

3 oz/wt	minced onions (3/4 cup)
1 each	garlic clove, minced fine
2 tbsp	vegetable oil
3 each	red peppers, cut into small dice (20 oz)
1 cup	Chicken Stock (page 410)
Pinch	saffron threads, crushed
2 tbsp	tomato paste
To taste	salt
To taste	ground white pepper
1 tbsp	powdered gelatin
1/4 cup	white wine
6 oz/fl	heavy cream, whipped
30 each	endive spears
	Garnish
As needed	red pepper, slivered

1. Sauté the onions and garlic in the oil until golden. Add the diced peppers, stock, saffron, tomato paste, salt, and pepper. Simmer until all ingredients are tender and liquid is reduced by half.
2. Bloom the gelatin in the wine.
3. Purée the red pepper mixture in a blender. Add the bloomed gelatin while the red pepper mixture is still hot and blend to combine all ingredients well.
4. Cool the mixture over an ice bath until it mounds when dropped from a spoon. Fold the whipped cream into the mixture.
5. *Hors d'oeuvre Assembly:* Pipe the mousse into the endive spears and garnish with a sliver of red pepper.

Blue Cheese Mousse

Yield: 3 pounds

Mise en place for blue cheese mousse.

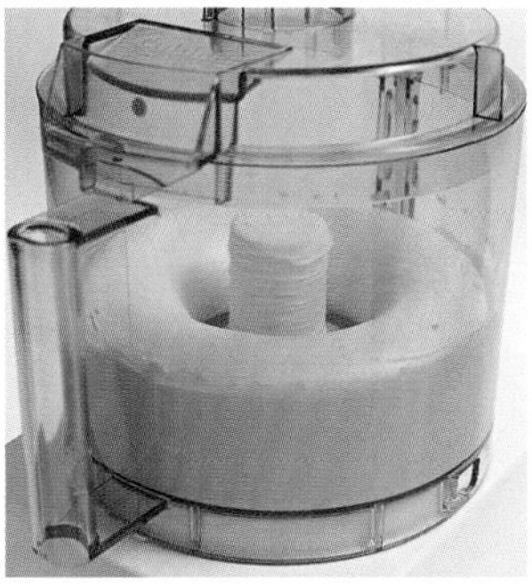

Puréed base.

Adding whipped cream to the base.

$1\frac{1}{4}$ lb	blue cheese
$\frac{3}{4}$ lb	cream cheese
1 tbsp	kosher salt
$\frac{1}{2}$ tsp	ground black pepper
4 oz/fl	heavy cream, whipped to soft peaks

1. Purée the blue and cream cheeses until very smooth (see photo). Season with salt and pepper.
2. Fold the whipped cream into the mousse until well blended (see photo). There should be no lumps.
3. The mousse is now ready to use to prepare canapés or as a filling or dip (see photo).

Goat Cheese Mousse Substitute fresh goat cheese for the blue cheese.

Smoked Trout Mousse

Yield: 3 cups

1 lb	boneless Hot Smoked Trout fillets (page 148)
1 cup	Aspic Gelée (page 45) made from Fish Stock, warmed
1/2 cup	Basic Mayonnaise (page 28)
1 tsp	Worcestershire sauce
1/4 tsp	Tabasco sauce
1 tbsp	dry white wine
1 tbsp	horseradish (prepared)
1 tsp	lemon juice
3/4 cup	heavy cream, whipped to soft peaks

1. Place all ingredients except cream into a food processor and process until very fine.
2. Fold the whipped cream into the trout mixture.
3. The mousse is now ready to use to prepare canapés, for profiteroles, or for other applications.

Barbecued Shrimp and Bacon

Yield: 30 pieces

15 strips	Basic Bacon (page 163), partially cooked and cut in half
30 each	shrimp (16/20 count), peeled and deveined
1 cup	Barbecue Sauce (page 113)

1. Preheat the broiler.
2. Wrap each shrimp with a bacon strip. Thread each shrimp on a small bamboo skewer.
3. Place the skewers on a wire rack set into a foil-lined metal tray.
4. Broil the shrimp 1 to 2 minutes on the first side. Turn and broil on the second side another 1 to 2 minutes, or until the bacon gets crispy and the shrimp are just cooked through. Remove from the broiler and baste with the barbecue sauce.

Chef's Notes: Soak the skewers in water before using to prevent them from catching fire when the shrimp are cooking.

> ***Serrano-Wrapped Shrimp*** Replace the bacon with thin slices of Serrano ham. Baste lightly with oil before grilling or broiling as directed above.

Crab Cakes with Creole-Honey Mustard Sauce

Yield: 30 pieces

1 lb	lump crab meat, picked clean
2 strips	bacon, cooked crisp and crumbled
1 pint	fresh white bread crumbs
1/4 cup	small-dice celery
2 each	scallions, minced
2 each	garlic cloves, minced
2 tsp	Dijon mustard
2 tsp	dry mustard
To taste	salt
To taste	cayenne pepper
As needed	Basic Mayonnaise (page 28), to bind
1/2 each	lemon, juiced
2 cups	Asian-style bread crumbs
1 cup	vegetable oil
1 cup	Creole Honey Mustard Sauce (page 31)

1. Combine all ingredients except the Asian-style bread crumbs, vegetable oil, and honey mustard sauce. Use just enough mayonnaise to hold the mixture together. Adjust seasoning.
2. Portion the crab cakes into 1/2-ounce balls, flatten slightly, and bread with the bread crumbs. At this point the cakes may be refrigerated or frozen for later use.
3. Heat the oil to 350°F. Pan fry the crab cakes in oil until golden. Drain briefly on paper towels. Serve immediately with the honey mustard sauce.

Petite Cod Cakes with Black Olive Butter Sauce

Yield: 30 pieces

	Cod Cakes
1 lb	potatoes, steamed or boiled and puréed
1 lb	cod fillet, poached
2 tbsp	olive oil
1 tsp	minced garlic
Pinch	cayenne pepper
1/2 tsp	salt
As needed	olive oil for sautéing
1 recipe	Black Olive Butter Sauce (recipe follows)
	Garnish
5 oz/wt	tomato, peeled, seeded, and cut into allumette
1/4 cup	Niçoise olive slivers
1/4 cup	basil chiffonade

1. Combine the cod cake ingredients, making sure to dry both the cod and the potatoes thoroughly before they are combined. Shape into 30 cylinders, each 1 inch in diameter by 2 inches long.
2. *Hors d'oeuvre Assembly:* For each portion, heat the olive oil and sauté 3 cakes, browning only on the top and bottom. Finish in a 400°F oven for about 5 minutes.
3. Spoon 1/2 ounce of the butter sauce on a warm plate and place three cakes on top. Toss 1 tablespoon tomatoes, a generous teaspoon of olives, and a pinch of basil quickly in a hot sauté pan and mound next to cod cakes.

Black Olive Butter Sauce

Yield: 5 ounces

1/4 cup	red wine
1 tbsp	minced shallots
1 sprig	thyme
1/2 each	bay leaf
2 tbsp	chopped Niçoise olives
2 tbsp	heavy cream
5 oz/wt	butter
2 tsp	soy sauce
To taste	salt
To taste	ground black pepper

1. Simmer the wine, shallots, thyme, bay leaf, and olives until reduced to a syrupy consistency.
2. Add the cream and reduce to coating consistency. Finish by whisking or swirling in butter.
3. Season with soy sauce, salt, and pepper; strain through a sieve.

Chicken Croustade

Yield: 30 pieces

1 loaf	soft white bread, sliced
3/4 cup	heavy cream
1/2 lb	raw chicken breast meat, cut into small dice
1 tbsp	olive oil
1/4 lb	prosciutto ham, cut into small dice
To taste	ground black pepper
1 each	egg yolk
1/4 cup	grated Parmesan cheese, plus as needed for topping
1 tbsp	chopped basil
1 tbsp	chopped flat-leaf parsley

1. With a rolling pin, roll out each bread slice until thin. Cut out bread with plain round cutter 1 1/2 inches in diameter and flatten again with a rolling pin.
2. Oil small muffin tins and place the bread rounds inside.
3. Bake in a 325°F oven until golden.
4. Store the croustade shells covered in a dry area.
5. Reduce the cream by half and reserve until needed.
6. Sauté the chicken in the oil until half done. Add the prosciutto and continue to cook until the prosciutto is thoroughly heated and chicken is thoroughly cooked.
7. Add the cream and black pepper; bring to a simmer. Temper the egg yolks and add to the mixture, being careful not to boil.
8. Add the cheese, basil, and parsley. Adjust seasoning.
9. Fill the croustade shells; sprinkle with a little additional grated Parmesan cheese and brown lightly under a broiler or salamander. Serve warm.

Risotto Croquettes with Fontina

Yield: 30 pieces

2 tbsp	fine-dice onions
2 oz/wt	butter
1 lb	Arborio rice
1 cup	white wine
1 1/2 qt	Chicken Stock (page 410), hot
1/4 lb	Parmesan cheese
To taste	salt
15 oz/wt	Fontina cheese, cut into 30 cubes (1/4-inch square)
1 cup	flour
2 each	eggs, beaten with 2 tbsp water or milk
1 cup	bread crumbs
30 slices	plum tomatoes (about 1/2 pound), sliced and roasted
As needed	olive oil
As needed	herbs (thyme, basil, marjoram)

1. Sauté the onions in the butter. Add the rice and coat with butter; cook until parched.
2. Add the white wine; simmer until absorbed, then add the stock in 3 parts.
3. Cook over low heat, stirring frequently, until rice is done, about 18 minutes. Add Parmesan cheese.
4. Transfer the risotto to a sheet pan and spread in an even layer. Allow rice to cool completely. Season with salt if necessary.
5. Form the chilled risotto into small balls wrapped around a cube of Fontina cheese.
6. Coat the balls using standard breading procedure (page 428).
7. Deep fry croquettes at 350°F until golden brown.
8. Garnish with oven-roasted tomato slice, olive oil, and fresh herbs.

Chef's Notes: This recipe works best when the risotto is prepared a day in advance. Other fillings can be used in place of Fontina, such as cooked sausage, seafood, vegetables, or Toasted Almonds (page 348).

New Potatoes with Snails and Brie

Yield: 30 pieces

1 bunch	basil
2 each	garlic cloves, minced
1/2 oz/wt	pine nuts, toasted
1 oz/wt	grated Parmesan cheese
6 tbsp	olive oil
3 cups	water
1 cup	white wine
1/2 lb	Mirepoix (page 404)
2 each	bay leaves
2 tsp	dried thyme
As needed	salt
As needed	cracked black pepper
30 each	fresh snails, cleaned and rinsed
4 lb	new red potatoes (30 "B" size; see Chef's Notes)
To taste	salt
To taste	ground black pepper
15 oz/wt	Brie, cut into 1/2-ounce pieces

1. Purée the basil, garlic, pine nuts, and Parmesan cheese. Slowly add 4 tablespoons of the olive oil. Reserve.
2. Combine the water, wine, mirepoix, bay leaves, thyme, 2 teaspoons salt, and 1 tablespoon pepper; simmer 5 minutes. Add the snails, simmer 5 to 7 minutes.
3. Remove the snails from their shells. Cool the snails in the liquid.
4. Scoop out a hole in the center of the potatoes and square off the bottoms.
5. Blanch the potatoes in salted boiling water until they are almost cooked through but still firm. Remove and dry.
6. Deep fry the potatoes until golden, drain on paper towels, and keep warm.
7. Remove the snails from the cooking liquid and sauté them in the remaining olive oil. Remove from the heat and add the basil sauce to the pan.
8. Mix well and adjust seasoning if necessary.
9. Place a snail in each of the potatoes with a little of the basil sauce.
10. Top with a slice of Brie and melt in a hot oven and serve very warm.

Chef's Notes: If small new potatoes are not available, use 15 larger ones. Cut the potatoes in half lengthwise and square off the bottom. Scoop out a hole in the center of each half.

Potato Crêpes with Crème Fraîche and Caviar

Yield: 30 pieces

$1\frac{1}{2}$ cups	puréed cooked potatoes
$\frac{1}{4}$ cup	flour
2 each	eggs
3 each	egg whites
$\frac{1}{4}$ cup	heavy cream, or as needed
To taste	salt
To taste	ground white pepper
Pinch	grated nutmeg
As needed	vegetable oil
$\frac{1}{2}$ cup	Crème Fraîche (page 303)
1 oz/wt	caviar
As needed	dill sprigs
6 oz/wt	smoked salmon slices (*optional*)

1. Combine the potatoes and flour in a mixer. Add the eggs one at a time, then the whites. Adjust consistency with cream to that of a pancake batter; season with salt, pepper, and nutmeg.
2. *Hors d'oeuvre Assembly:* Coat a nonstick griddle or sauté pan lightly with oil. Pour batter as for pancakes into silver dollar-size portions. Cook until golden brown; turn and finish on the second side, about 2 minutes total cooking time.
3. Serve the crêpes warm with small dollops of crème fraîche and caviar, a small dill sprig, and a smoked salmon slice, if desired.

Chef's Notes: For dill crêpes, chop some of the dill and add it to the heavy cream, which has been lightly heated. Cool before preparing the crêpe batter.

Bluepoint Oyster Martini with Beluga Caviar

Yield: 30 pieces

	Mignonette Sauce
1/4 cup	minced shallots
4 tbsp	chopped chives
1/3 cup	champagne vinegar
3 tbsp	cracked black pepper
30 each	oysters
1 oz/wt	beluga caviar

1. Combine the sauce ingredients and reserve.
2. Shuck the oysters, loosen muscle from bottom shell, then remove with top shell.
3. *Hors d'oeuvre Assembly:* Place the shells on a bed of crushed ice. Place an oyster inside each shell. Top each with mignonette sauce and a dollop of caviar.

Carpaccio-Wrapped Watercress with Blue Cheese Dip

Yield: 30 pieces

10 oz/wt	beef tenderloin
3 bunches	watercress, washed and dried
3/4 cup	Roquefort Dressing (page 32)

1. Slice the tenderloin paper thin (see Beef Carpaccio, page 354, for more detailed instructions).
2. Trim the watercress to approximately 2 1/2 inches long and make into 30 small bundles.
3. Wrap each small bundle with a thin slice of carpaccio.
4. Serve with dressing on the side.

Prosciutto Roll Filled with Arugula Sauté blanched arugula in a little olive oil and garlic. Season with salt and pepper. Chill thoroughly. Roll in thinly sliced prosciutto as for carpaccio above.

Dates Stuffed with Boursin Cheese

Yield: 30 pieces

3 oz/wt	Boursin au Poivre cheese
3 oz/wt	cream cheese
30 each	pistachios, shelled
15 each	fresh dates, pitted and split

1. Combine cheeses; mix until well blended and soft.
2. Split pistachios in half following the natural seam of the nut.
3. Pipe the cheese mixture into the cavity of the date using a plain tip.
4. Garnish with the pistachio (two halves per date).

Grapes Rolled in Blue de Bresse

Yield: 50 pieces

1/4 lb	Blue de Bresse (or other blue cheese)
1/4 lb	cream cheese
50 each	seedless green grapes
1/4 lb	pistachios, shelled

1. Combine the blue cheese and the cream cheese in a mixer with a paddle and mix well; there should be very few lumps. Refrigerate for 1 hour.
2. Wrap a small amount of cheese around each grape by rolling in the palms of your hands. Store on a sheet pan lined with parchment paper. Chill under refrigeration at least 1 hour and up to overnight.
3. Pulse the pistachios in a food processor; force through a drum sieve.
4. Roll the grapes in the nut powder and shape with the palms of your hands. This can be done up to 1 hour before service. Do not refrigerate the grapes once they have been rolled in the nut powder.

Presentation Ideas: The grapes can be arranged on a platter in the shape of a natural bunch of grapes as shown.

Scallop Seviche in Cucumber Cups

Yield: 30 pieces

6 oz/wt	sea scallops, cut into brunoise
1 each	tomato, peeled and seeded, cut into brunoise
1 tsp	minced chives
1 tbsp	chopped cilantro
1/2 each	jalapeño, minced
1/4 each	green pepper, cut into brunoise
1 tbsp	olive oil
5 drops	Tabasco sauce
1 to 2 each	limes, juiced
1 tsp	kosher salt
To taste	ground black pepper
3 each	cucumbers, sliced 1/2-inch thick (30 slices total)
As needed	sour cream (*optional*)
2 tsp	cilantro leaves (*optional*)

1. To make the seviche, combine the scallops, tomatoes, herbs, peppers, olive oil, and Tabasco. Add enough lime juice to cover the scallops. Season with salt and pepper.

2. Marinate at least 8 hours, stirring occasionally.

3. Trim the cucumber slices with a round cutter to remove the rind. Scoop a pocket out of the middle of the cucumber slices. Do not cut all the way through the slice.

4. Fill the cucumber cups with the seviche. Garnish each seviche cup with a small dot of sour cream and a cilantro leaf if desired.

Pickled Shrimp

Yield: 60 pieces (approximately 2 pounds)

1 cup	white vinegar
2 cups	water
1 tbsp	salt
2 each	garlic cloves, crushed
1 tbsp	mustard seed
1 tbsp	celery seed
1 tsp	ground cumin
2 each	whole cloves
12 each	allspice berries
2 tbsp	light brown sugar
3 each	jalapeños, minced
4 each	bay leaves
60 each	shrimp (21/25 count), cooked and deveined

1. Combine all ingredients except the shrimp and bring to a boil. Cool.

2. Pour the cold pickling mixture over the shrimp and marinate overnight.

Presentation Ideas: Roll out and cut Pâté Dough to make netting to create an attractive buffet presentation (page 418).

Spiced Mixed Nuts

Yield: 1 pound

3 tbsp	butter
1 tbsp	Worcestershire sauce
3 1/2 cups	unsalted raw whole mixed nuts (1 lb)
1/2 tsp	celery seed
1/2 tsp	garlic powder
1/2 tsp	chili powder
1/4 tsp	ground cumin
1/8 tsp	cayenne pepper
1/2 tsp	salt

1. Melt the butter over medium heat. Add the Worcestershire and bring to a simmer. Add the nuts and toss well to coat evenly.
2. Sprinkle the combined spices and salt over the nuts and toss well to coat evenly.
3. Place the nuts on a nonstick or well-greased baking sheet and bake in a 375°F oven, stirring occasionally, for 10 to 12 minutes, or until evenly browned. Let cool completely before serving.
4. Store in an airtight container for up to 2 weeks.

Chef's Notes: If saltier nuts are desired, sprinkle with kosher salt while still warm.

Chili-Roasted Peanuts with Dried Cherries

Yield: 1 pound

1 oz	unsalted butter
1 lb	raw peanuts
1 tbsp	mild chili powder
2 tsp	ground cumin
2 tsp	ground white pepper
1 tbsp	salt
1/2 tsp	dried oregano
1/2 tsp	cayenne pepper
1/2 lb	dried cherries (or raisins)

1. Melt the butter in a small sauce pan.
2. Coat the raw peanuts with the melted butter.
3. Mix together the remaining ingredients except the cherries; reserve.
4. Place peanuts on a large sheet pan and lightly toast in a 300–325°F oven for about 10 minutes, shaking pan occasionally.
5. Transfer the peanuts into a large bowl and coat with the dry ingredients. Mix in cherries until uniformly blended.
6. Cover and store at room temperature.

Candied Pecans

Yield: 1 pound

4 3/4 cups	whole pecans (1 pound)
2 each	egg whites beaten with 2 tbsp water
1 cup	superfine sugar
2 tsp	salt
1 tbsp	ground cinnamon
2 tsp	ground ginger
2 tsp	ground cardamom
1 1/2 tsp	ground allspice
1 tsp	ground coriander
1/8 tsp	cayenne pepper

1. Preheat the oven to 250°F.
2. Stir the nuts into the beaten egg white mixture until completely coated. Drain well in a colander.
3. Combine the sugar, salt, and spices and toss the nuts in this mixture until evenly coated.
4. Turn onto a baking sheet and spread in a single layer. Bake for about 10 minutes, then lower the oven temperature to 225°F and bake, stirring occasionally, for another 10 minutes, or until the nuts are dark golden brown.
5. Let cool completely before serving.
6. Store in an airtight container for up to 2 weeks.

Chef's Notes: These nuts are used to garnish the Smoked Duck Tart (page 373).

Toasted Almonds

Yield: 1 pound

1 lb	whole almonds
2 tbsp	pure olive oil
To taste	kosher salt

1. Put the almonds on a sheet pan and roast in a 400°F oven. Check for doneness after 10 minutes. Cut an almond open. It should be the color of a wooden cutting board.
2. When the almonds are done, put them in a bowl and toss with the olive oil and salt. Let cool before serving.

Smoked Toasted Almonds Cold smoke almonds on a cooling rack before roasting.

Spicy Curried Cashews

Yield: 1 pound

1 lb	whole, raw cashews
1 oz/wt	unsalted butter, melted
1/2 tsp	salt
1 tbsp	curry powder
1/4 tsp	garlic powder
1/4 tsp	onion powder
1/8 tsp	cayenne pepper

1. Preheat the oven to 350°F.
2. Toss the cashews and melted butter together until evenly coated.
3. Place on a sheet pan and bake until golden brown.
4. Combine the salt and spices; reserve.
5. Remove the cashews from the oven and toss with the combined spices while still warm. Allow to cool before serving.
6. Store in an airtight container for up to 10 days.

TEN

Appetizers

The distinctions between appetizers and hors d'oeuvre have more to do with how and when they are served than the actual foods being served. Appetizers are served as the first course of a meal. The usual admonition to "build" a menu from one course to the next calls for some logical connection between the appetizer and all the courses that follow. For every rule you read about what types of foods should or shouldn't constitute an appetizer, you will find at least one good exception. What holds most appetizers in common is the careful attention to portioning and proper technical execution and plating. Typically, appetizers are small portions of very flavorful items, meant just to take enough edge off the appetite to permit thorough enjoyment of an entrée.

Figure 10-1 Foie Gras Roulade with Roasted Beet Salad (page 371).

When you choose a rich food, such as foie gras (as shown in Figure 10-1) to feature in an appetizer, a small bite or two, paired with a bitter green salad is fine.

Appetizers on the à la Carte Menu

It is important to provide enough appropriate options that work with the main course offerings. In an à la carte situation, the garde manger may have relatively little control over what a guest might choose. Furthermore, there is no guarantee that the guests will order an appetizer just as a first course. This has led to some interesting and challenging new approaches to featuring appetizers on the menu. Grazing menus or *degustation* menus are produced by selecting a series of appetizer-size portioned items served in a logical sequence.

Guests today may look for appetizers that can be shared, or that can be ordered in a larger size to enjoy as a main course. In some restaurants, waitstaff may suggest an appetizer for the table to share and enjoy while their entrées are being prepared, both as a way to expose guests to something new or unusual as well as to "sell up the menu."

Appetizers for a Banquet

Banquet menus frequently call for one or more appetizers. In this case, the chef does have the ability to "build" a menu, progressing from one flavor and texture experience to the next, so in this instance, thoughtful consideration of how each element of the menu will relate to what precedes and follows is the key to success. Taking a cue from the principles used by sommeliers to build from one wine to another, going from the more understated to the more robust, it is a common practice for the meal to progress from subtle to more assertive flavors.

It is important to consider the entire experience when designing appetizers in a banquet menu. They should be served in sensible portions, perhaps smaller than you might offer on an à la carte menu, so that guests can sample a few appetizers and still enjoy their main course and dessert.

Selecting and Preparing Appetizers

Classic hors d'oeuvre can be served as appetizers if you increase the portion size slightly. Perfectly fresh clams and oysters, for example, shucked as close to service time as possible and served with sauces designed to enhance their naturally briny savor, or a classic shrimp "cocktail," served with a cocktail sauce, salsa, or other pungent sauce, are perennial favorites in any appetizer category. These items are included in the hors d'oeuvre chapter (see pages 309-347), but they can be served in larger portions as appetizers.

Smoked fish, meats, or poultry; sausages, pâtés, terrines, and galantines; air-dried hams and beef sliced paper thin—all of these items can be used to create appetizer plates, on their own with a few accompaniments or garnishes or as a sampler plate (see Figure 10-2). Refer to Chapters Six, Seven, and Eight for specific recipes and presentation ideas.

Salads are also served as appetizers. Several salads in Chapter Three can fit this category quite well. You may prefer to change the portion size, substitute a different sauce or garnish to give your menu items a special look, vary it from season to season, or showcase a range of flavors and textures from other cuisines.

Warm and hot appetizers may include small portions of pastas, such as ravioli or tortellini, served on their own or in a sauce or broth. Puff pastry shells can be cut into *vols au vent* or made into turnovers, filled with savory ragouts or foie gras. Broiled or grilled fish, shellfish, or poultry may be featured. Crêpes, blinis, and other similar dishes

Figure 10-2 Smoked trout and a cucumber salad.

have been popular in many different cuisines. Meatballs and other highly seasoned ground meat appetizers are also found on today's menu. Swedish meatballs share space in the garde manger's repertoire with kefta (spicy kebabs made from ground lamb).

Vegetables are more important than ever as an appetizer. Sometimes they are presented very simply; for example, steamed artichokes may be served with a dipping sauce such as a flavored mayonnaise or vinaigrette, chilled asparagus may be served drizzled with a flavored oil, or a plate of grilled vegetables may be accompanied by a vinaigrette sauce.

Principles for Presenting Appetizers

The recipes in this chapter include such traditional favorites as carpaccio, melon and prosciutto, foie gras in brioche, and vitello tonnato. Keep in mind some of the following basic principles as you select, prepare, and plate appetizers: (See Figure 10-3.)

- Serve all appetizers at the proper temperature. Remember to chill or warm plates.
- Season all appetizer items with meticulous care. Appetizers are meant to stimulate the appetite, so seasoning is of the utmost importance.
- Slice, shape, and portion appetizers properly. There should be just enough of any given item to make the appetizer interesting and appealing from start to finish, but not so much on the plate that the guest is overwhelmed.
- Neatness always counts, but especially with appetizers. Your guests will most likely judge their entire meal based on the impression the appetizer gives.
- When offering shared appetizers, consider how they will look when they come to the table. It may be more effective to split a shared plate in the kitchen, rather than expecting the guests to divide it up themselves.
- Color, shape, and "white space" play a role in the overall composition of your plate. Take the time to choose the right size and shape serving pieces and to provide the guest with all the items necessary for the appetizer, including cups for dipping sauces, special utensils, and if necessary, finger bowls.

Figure 10-3 Plated Appetizer Composition Balance Wheel.

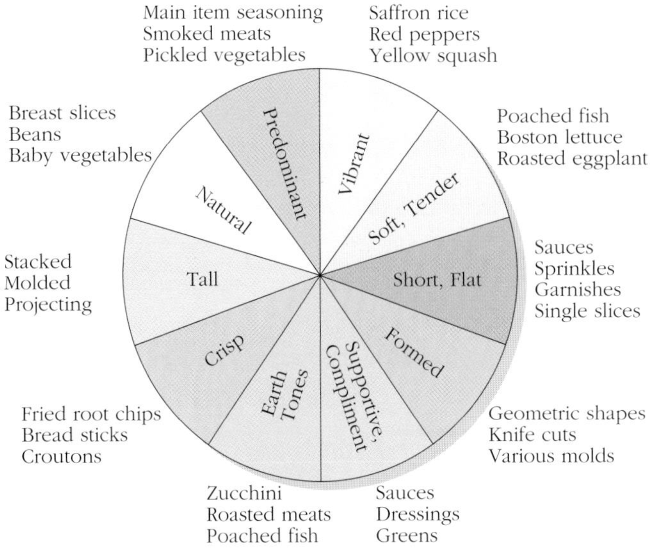

Beef Carpaccio

Yield: 10 servings

Carpaccio was first served at Harry's Bar in Venice, Italy. Mr. Cipriani was inspired by an exhibition of art by the famed Italian artist Carpaccio, since the deep red color of the beef is typical of Carpaccio's color palette. In this presentation, the greens are nestled in a cucumber ring.

$1\frac{1}{2}$ lb	beef sirloin or tenderloin, trimmed of all fat
2 tbsp	pure olive oil
1 tbsp	chopped rosemary
1 tbsp	chopped sage
1 tbsp	chopped thyme
1 tbsp	balsamic vinegar
2 tsp	kosher salt
1 tbsp	mignonette pepper
	Garnish
5 oz/wt	mixed greens, washed and dried
5 oz/fl	Lemon Vinaigrette (page 23)
$\frac{1}{4}$ cup	extra-virgin olive oil
3 oz/wt	Parmesan cheese
2 tbsp	chopped flat-leaf parsley
4 tbsp	capers, rinsed, dried, and fried in hot oil (*optional*)

1. *Optional:* Tie the beef to give it a uniform shape. Heat the oil over high heat and sear the beef on all sides. Remove it from the heat and cool.
2. Combine the herbs, vinegar, salt, and pepper and coat the beef evenly with this mixture. Wrap tightly in plastic wrap and refrigerate at least 8 hours before slicing.
3. *Appetizer Assembly:* For each portion, cut 6 or 7 very thin slices of beef by hand or with an electric slicer. Arrange on a chilled plate. Toss 1 ounce (about $\frac{1}{4}$ cup) of greens with 1 tablespoon of the vinaigrette and arrange on the plate. Drizzle the meat with a few drops of extra-virgin olive oil and add a few Parmesan curls, parsley, and capers.

Tuna Carpaccio with Shiitake Salad

Yield: 10 servings

Tuna makes a beautiful carpaccio, without the fat and cholesterol of beef. This recipe was developed by Chef Tim Rodgers for St. Andrew's Cafe, the Institute's healthful-cuisine restaurant. The tuna for this dish must be of the highest quality and impeccably fresh.

25 oz/wt	trimmed tuna fillet
	Salad
8 oz/wt	shiitake mushrooms, stemmed and cut into julienne
3 oz/wt	carrot, cut into julienne
3 oz/wt	red onion, cut into julienne
2 oz/wt	bok choy, cut into chiffonade
1/2 cup	rice wine vinegar
1/4 cup	sake
2 tbsp	reduced-sodium soy sauce
	Wasabi Sauce
3/4 cup	yogurt
To taste	wasabi powder
To taste	reduced-sodium soy sauce

1. Slice the tuna very thin and flatten it between plastic wrap to the dimensions of the plating area of your appetizer plate.
2. Combine the salad ingredients and reserve. (The salad may be prepared up to 3 hours in advance)
3. Combine the wasabi sauce ingredients; keep refrigerated until ready to assemble the appetizer.
4. *Appetizer Assembly:* For each portion, lay 2 1/2 ounces of the sliced tuna on a chilled plate and mound a 1-ounce portion of the shiitake salad in the center of the tuna. Pipe or drizzle the wasabi sauce over the plate.

Chef's Notes: The tuna can be flattened ahead of time and held between sheets of plastic wrap for up to 3 hours.

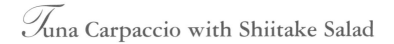

Escabèche of Tuna

Yield: 10 servings

Escabèche, *originally an Arabic form of preserving cooked fish in an acid, gets its name from the Spanish word meaning "headless," since the fish were beheaded before preparing them as an escabèche. Today, many foods are prepared throughout South America in this fashion, including cooked poultry, game, vegetables, and even eggs.*

30 oz/wt	tuna steak
To taste	salt
To taste	ground black pepper
4 tbsp	olive oil
3 tbsp	lime juice
3 oz/wt	small-dice tomato concassé
1/2 oz/wt	small-dice red onion
1/2 each	serrano chile, minced
1 each	scallion, sliced thin on bias
1/2 tsp	minced garlic
1 tsp	chopped cilantro

1. Cut the tuna into 1-inch cubes or 3-ounce steaks. Season with salt and pepper, rub with 2 tablespoons of the oil, and sear in a hot, well-seasoned pan. (It should be cooked "black and blue"—colored on the exterior but still extremely rare.)

2. Remove the tuna and chill thoroughly.

3. To make a marinade, mix the remaining olive oil with the lime juice, tomato, onion, chile, scallion, garlic, and cilantro.

4. Pour the marinade over the tuna and turn or gently toss the coat evenly. Marinate at least 12 hours or overnight before serving.

Presentation Ideas: This dish can be served with a small salad as an appetizer, used to fill cucumber cups as an hors d'oeuvre, or served as part of an antipasti offering.

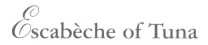

Vitello Tonnato (Cold Veal with Tuna Sauce)

Yield: 10 servings

The traditional recipe for this northern Italian dish calls for the veal to be gently stewed or braised in a mixture of water, wine, and seasonings. Here, however, we have opted to roast the veal for a deep, intense flavor. Remember to deglaze the roasting pan and add the drippings to the tuna sauce. The veal will need to chill at least 12 hours before slicing and serving.

1 1/2 lb	veal bottom round, tied and seasoned
	Tonnato Sauce
2 oz/wt	small-dice onion
1 oz/wt	small-dice carrot
1 oz/wt	small-dice celeriac
2 tbsp	olive oil
1 tbsp	tomato paste
1/2 tsp	minced garlic
3 tsp	drained capers
4 each	anchovy fillets
1/4 cup	lemon juice
1/2 cup	white wine
1 cup	Brown Veal Stock (page 410)
1 each	sachet d'épices made of bay leaf, cracked pepper, thyme sprig, rosemary sprig
2 oz/wt	canned imported tuna *or* Tuna Confit (page 172)
1/2 cup	Basic Mayonnaise (page 28)
To taste	salt
To taste	ground white pepper
	Garnish
1 each	red onion, sliced paper thin
10 tsp	capers, drained and rinsed
10 each	anchovy fillets

1. Roast the veal to an internal temperature of 145°F. Chill for 12 hours and up to 3 days.
2. Sauté the onion, carrot, and celeriac in the olive oil until browned; add the tomato paste and garlic and sauté another minute. Add the capers, anchovies, lemon juice, wine, stock (as well as the fond from the roasting pan, if available), and sachet; simmer for 30 minutes and strain.
3. Return the strained sauce to the heat and reduce to 6 fluid ounces (3/4 cup). Let cool.
4. Purée the tuna fish with the reduced sauce until smooth.
5. Finish the sauce with the mayonnaise and adjust seasoning.
6. *Appetizer Assembly:* For each portion, slice the cold veal about 1/8-inch thick and arrange 2 to 3 slices (about 2 ounces) on a pool of 1 1/2 ounces tonnato sauce. Garnish each portion with red onion, a teaspoon of capers, and an anchovy fillet.

Grilled Vegetable Appetizer with Balsamic Vinaigrette

Yield: 10 servings

1 lb	eggplant, sliced into 1/2-inch-thick rounds
1 lb	zucchini, sliced on bias 1/2-inch-thick
1 lb	yellow squash, sliced on bias 1/2-inch-thick
1 1/2 lb	red peppers (about 3 each), cut into eighths
3/4 lb	yellow peppers (about 2 each), cut into eighths
1 lb	portobello mushrooms, stem removed
5 each	plum tomatoes, cored and halved
10 each	scallions, trimmed
1/2 cup	olive oil
1/2 bunch	thyme, leaves only
To taste	salt
To taste	ground black pepper
15 oz/fl	Balsamic Vinaigrette (page 22)

1. Combine the olive oil with the thyme, salt, and pepper. Brush the vegetables with this mixture. Grill the eggplant until very soft and cooked through. Grill or broil the remaining vegetables to mark on all sides; they should be tender and very hot. Slice the portobellos as necessary to make 10 servings.
2. *Appetizer Assembly:* For each serving, arrange 2 to 3 slices each of eggplant, zucchini, and yellow squash on each plate. Add 2 strips of red pepper and 1 of the yellow pepper, a grilled tomato half, and a scallion. Drizzle with vinaigrette and serve warm or at room temperature.

Chef's Notes: Use a variety of tomatoes if available for extra color in this dish. If preferred, the tomatoes may be lightly broiled just until hot. They should still retain their shape.

Roasted Vegetables Provençale Style

Yield: 30 servings (3 ounces each)

This dish can be baked and served in a decorative shallow baking dish or casserole, if desired. It may be served warm, at room temperature, or chilled.

1/2 cup	olive oil
1 tbsp	chopped thyme
1 tbsp	chopped savory
1 oz/wt	roasted garlic purée
1 oz/wt	salt
2 tsp	ground black pepper
2 tbsp	basil chiffonade
2 lb	eggplant, sliced into 1/4-inch-thick rounds
1 lb	yellow squash, sliced on bias 1/4-inch thick
1 lb	zucchini, sliced on bias 1/4-inch thick
1 lb	Spanish onion, sliced 1/8-inch thick
1 lb	ripe red tomatoes, sliced 1/4-inch thick

1. Combine the olive oil with the thyme, savory, roasted garlic, salt, and pepper. Brush some of this mixture on a sheet pan, and layer the sliced vegetables on the pan. (*Optional:* Prepare as individual servings or larger batches in a ceramic or earthenware casserole, and shingle the vegetables, alternating colors.) Drizzle the vegetables with a little of the olive oil mixture.

2. Bake uncovered in a 200°F oven for 4 to 5 hours or until vegetables are tender and wilted. Drizzle them with a little more of the olive oil mixture every hour as they roast.

3. Arrange the vegetables on a serving platter (or leave them in the baking dish if prepared that way) and garnish with the basil chiffonade. Vegetables can be served warm, cold, or at room temperature.

Marinated Tomatoes with Mozzarella

Yield: 10 servings

Select a variety of tomatoes—red and yellow slicing tomatoes; cherry, pear, or currant tomatoes—whenever they are in season. Rub a slice of sturdy peasant-style bread with garlic and olive oil and grill it lightly to accompany this simple, seasonal favorite.

2 1/2 lb	Marinated Tomatoes (page 76)
2 lb	Fresh Mozzarella (page 304)
1 each	red slicing tomato
1 each	yellow slicing tomato
3 tbsp	basil chiffonade

1. Prepare the tomato salad and reserve until ready to assemble appetizer.
2. Slice the mozzarella 1/4-inch thick and reserve.
3. Slice the tomatoes 1/4-inch thick, and halve or quarter the slices. Reserve.
4. *Appetizer Assembly:* For each serving, mound 4 ounces of tomato salad on a chilled plate. Arrange 3 ounces of the sliced mozzarella and several slices of red and yellow tomatoes around the tomato salad. Scatter a little basil chiffonade over the appetizer. Serve chilled or at room temperature.

Chef's Notes: For buffet presentation, mound the tomato salad on a chilled platter, and arrange sliced tomatoes and mozzarella around the salad. You may wish to add a small bed of a mixed green salad, lightly dressed with a Basic Red Wine or Balsamic Vinaigrette (page 22), for individual servings.

Prosciutto and Summer Melon Salad

Yield: 10 servings

This classic presentation for prosciutto pairs the silky smooth texture of the best prosciutto ham with sweet cool melon, drizzled with authentic balsamic vinegar. The combination of aromas and textures is exquisite. Prepare this dish with fresh figs when they are in season.

20 oz/wt	prosciutto di Parma
30 oz/wt	sliced or diced mixed melons (cantaloupe, honeydew, casaba, etc.)
To taste	cracked black pepper
20 each	Grissini (page 423)
5 tsp	aged balsamic vinegar (*optional*)

1. Slice prosciutto as thin as possible, laying it out on butcher's paper for easy handling. This should be done as close to service time as possible.
2. *Appetizer Assembly:* For each serving, arrange the melon on the plate, and add the prosciutto (drape it over melon slices or arrange it next to diced melon).
3. If desired, drizzle a few drops of excellent aged balsamic vinegar on the melon just before serving. Scatter a little pepper on the plate and serve with a grissini.

Chef's Notes: This simple appetizer can be prepared as a plattered item for buffet service. Or individual cubes or spears of melon may be wrapped with a bit of prosciutto and skewered for service as an hors d'oeuvre.

• • •

If you have a prosciutto slicing stand in the dining room, this appetizer can be prepared in the dining room, with the prosciutto sliced to order in front of the guest, as long as the melon mise en place has been properly assembled by the kitchen staff.

Smoked Salmon with Potato Galette

Yield: 10 servings

	Galette
$2^1/_2$ lb	Yukon gold potatoes
4 oz/wt	butter
To taste	salt
To taste	ground white pepper
2 cups	Crème Fraîche (page 303)
1/2 cup	minced shallots
1/4 cup	chopped Fines Herbes (page 408)
25 oz/wt	Smoked Salmon, sliced thin (page 149)
5 bunch	mâche
5 oz/fl	Chive Oil (page 397)
1 bunch	minced chives
1 oz/wt	sevruga caviar

1. Grate the potatoes on a mandolin or box grater into fine julienne. Season with salt and pepper.
2. Heat the butter in a griswold or rondeau. Drop spoonfuls of the potatoes into the butter to make galettes (they should be about 4 inches in diameter and 1/4-inch thick). Sauté until golden brown on both sides; remove from the pan and keep warm until ready to assemble the appetizer.
3. Fold the crème fraîche together with the shallots and fines herbes and season with salt and pepper.
4. *Appetizer Assembly:* For each serving, place a small dollop of seasoned crème fraîche on a plate. Top with 1 galette and about 1 1/2 ounces of sliced smoked salmon. Drizzle the salmon with a little more crème fraîche; top with a second galette. Roll another slice of smoked salmon into a rosette and place on top of the galette. Garnish the salmon with 1/2 bunch of mâche. Drizzle chive oil on the plate and garnish with the chives and caviar. Top with another galette and then more salmon. Place dressed mâche sprigs inside of salmon so that they appear to flower up.

Air-Dried Ham with Lentil Salad

Yield: 10 servings

1/2 lb	air-dried ham (Serrano or prosciutto)
20 each	cherry tomatoes, halved
8 oz/fl	Vinaigrette (page 22), made with sherry wine vinegar
1 1/4 lb	Lentil Salad (page 89)
10 oz/wt	mixed baby greens
10 each	Parmesan Crisp (page 428)
2 tbsp	chopped flat-leaf parsley

1. Slice ham as thin as possible and lay it out on food service paper. Cover and hold under refrigeration.

2. Toss the cherry tomatoes in 2 tablespoons of the vinaigrette and roast in a 275°F oven until dry, about 2 hours. Reserve.

3. *Appetizer Assembly:* For each portion, place a 2-ounce (1/3 cup) serving of lentil salad on the plate and drape with 2 to 3 slices of ham (about 3/4 ounce for each serving). Toss 1 ounce (about 1/4 cup) of greens with 1 tablespoon of the vinaigrette and arrange on the plate. Add a Parmesan crisp and 4 pieces roasted cherry tomato halves. Garnish with parsley.

Grilled Honey-Smoked Quail with Mango Sauce

Yield: 10 servings

10 each	Honey-Smoked Quail (page 156)
25 oz/wt	Mixed Bean and Grain Salad (page 90)
20 oz/fl	Mango Sauce (page 369)
3 oz/wt	mixed baby greens
3 tbsp	Basic Red Wine Vinaigrette (page 22)

1. *Appetizer Assembly:* For each serving, grill a quail until heated through and marked. Arrange 2 1/2 ounces of grain salad on the plate. Pool 2 ounces of sauce and top with the grilled quail. Arrange dressed baby greens on the plate.

Smoked Breast of Duck Niçoise Style

Yield: 10 servings

25 oz/wt	Mediterranean Potato Salad (page 88)
20 oz/wt	Smoked Duck Breast (page 154)
1/2 lb	haricots verts
5 each	tomatoes, blanched, peeled, seeded, and cut into strips
1/4 cup	Basic Red Wine Vinaigrette (page 22)
5 tbsp	Tapenade (page 41)

1. Prepare the potato salad.
2. Slice the duck breast thin and reserve until ready to assemble the appetizer.
3. Blanch the haricots verts and refresh.
4. *Appetizer Assembly:* For each serving, arrange 2 1/2 ounces of potato salad on the plate. Fan 2 ounces of sliced duck on the plate. Toss 3/4 ounce haricots verts and several strips of tomato in the vinaigrette and arrange on the plate. Garnish with 1 1/2 teaspoons of tapenade.

Duck Confit with Frisée and Roasted Shallot Vinaigrette

Yield: 10 servings

10 pieces	Duck Confit, legs only (page 170)
5 each	Idaho potatoes, peeled and sliced into $1^{1}/_{2} \times {}^{1}/_{8}$-inch disks
1 qt	duck fat, for frying
To taste	salt
To taste	coarse ground black pepper
25 oz/wt	frisée lettuce, washed and dried
15 oz/fl	Roasted Shallot Vinaigrette (page 26)

1. Scrape off excess fat from duck legs, reserving fat for frying potatoes. Roast duck legs at 450°F until warm and crisp, approximately 15 minutes. Keep warm.
2. Fry the potatoes in duck fat heated to 350°F until browned and crisp, about 8 minutes. Drain on absorbent paper, season with salt and pepper, and keep warm.
3. *Appetizer Assembly:* For each serving, toss 3 ounces frisée in 1 ounce of vinaigrette and mound on a chilled plate. Top with a duck leg, 2 ounces fried potatoes, and a few roasted shallots from the dressing. Serve at once.

Chef's Notes: Serve this as an appetizer, composed salad, or light meal.

Crab Meat Rolls with Infused Pepper Oils, Fried Ginger, and Tamari-Glazed Mushrooms

Yield: 10 servings

Traditional Asian ingredients are combined in a modern presentation for this exciting appetizer. This dish can easily be adapted for hors d'oeuvre by cutting the colorful rolls into bite-sized pieces and standing them on end.

1 1/2 lb	lump crab meat
4 oz/wt	carrots, cut into fine julienne
1 oz/wt	red peppers, cut into brunoise
1 oz/wt	yellow peppers, cut into brunoise
1 oz/wt	green peppers, cut into brunoise
1/2 oz/wt	minced chives
1 tbsp	black sesame seeds
3 tbsp	rice wine vinegar
To taste	salt
To taste	ground white pepper
10 each	rice paper wrappers (8-inch diameter)
10 oz/wt	Tamari-Glazed Mushrooms (see Chef's Notes)
10 tsp	Red Pepper Oil (page 399)
10 tsp	Green Pepper Oil (page 399)
10 tsp	Yellow Pepper Oil (page 399)
2 each	ginger root pieces (2 inches long), peeled, sliced thin, and fried for garnish

1. Clean the crab meat, removing any shell or cartilage. Combine with the carrots, peppers, chives, sesame seeds, and rice wine vinegar. Season with salt and pepper.

2. Moisten the rice paper wrappers and fill each one with about 3 ounces (1/3 cup) of the crab meat mixture. Roll the wrapper to completely encase the filling; it should be about 1 inch in diameter. Keep covered with a lightly dampened cloth under refrigeration until ready to serve.

3. *Appetizer Assembly:* For each serving, cut 1 crab roll on the bias and arrange on a chilled plate. Add 1 ounce of tamari-glazed mushrooms, 1 teaspoon each of the pepper-flavored oils, and a few pieces of fried ginger.

Chef's Notes: To make tamari-glazed mushrooms, sauté 1 pound of diced shiitake mushrooms in 2 tablespoon of olive oil until very hot. Add 1 ounce of tamari sauce to deglaze the pan, and season to taste with sugar, dark sesame oil, salt, and pepper.

Shrimp and Avocado Quesadillas

Yield: 10 servings

2 lb	Smoked Shrimp (21/25 count) (page 147)
1/2 lb	tomatillos, charred, husks removed (about 9)
2 each	avocados, pitted, peeled, and diced
1 each	onion, diced and sautéed until golden
1/4 bunch	cilantro, chopped
1 tbsp	toasted cumin seeds
To taste	salt
To taste	ground black pepper
20 each	flour tortillas (4-inch diameter)
1/2 lb	Monterey Jack cheese, shredded
2 tbsp	olive oil
2 bunches	watercress, washed and dried
10 oz/fl	Orange Vinaigrette (page 23)

1. Peel and devein the shrimp; reserve.

2. Chop the tomatillos fine. Combine with the diced avocado and onion and work with a wooden spoon or a fork to form a coarse paste. Stir in the cilantro and cumin and season with salt and pepper. Spread this mixture on a tortilla, top with 3/4 ounce cheese, and close with a second tortilla. Continue until 10 quesadillas are filled. This may be done up to 1 hour in advance.

3. *Appetizer Assembly:* When ready to serve, lightly oil both sides of the quesadillas, and cook over low heat in a well-seasoned or nonstick pan until golden brown on both sides. Place the quesadilla on a plate; top with 4 shrimp. Dress 3/4 ounce of the watercress with 2 teaspoons of vinaigrette and arrange on the plate. Drizzle the perimeter of the plate with another 2 teaspoons of vinaigrette.

Lobster and Truffle Salad

Yield: 10 servings

Although it is called a salad, this elegant dish works well as an appetizer or even a light luncheon main dish.

5 each	whole lobsters (1 pound each)
1/2 lb	haricots verts
5 bunches	mâche
	Vinaigrette
3 each	oranges, juiced
1/4 cup	champagne vinegar
1 1/2 oz	Fines Herbes (page 408)
To taste	salt
To taste	ground white pepper
1/2 cup	extra-virgin olive oil
	Garnish
1 each	tomato, peeled, seeded, and cut into diamond shapes
1/2 oz	chervil pluches
1 oz	truffles

1. Cook the lobsters in simmering salted water until fully cooked, about 9–10 minutes. Remove and cool under refrigeration. When cold, remove the tail and claw meat. Slice each tail in half to make 10 equal servings; hold lobster under refrigeration until ready to assemble the appetizer.
2. Blanch the haricots verts in boiling salted water until bright green; refresh, drain, and hold under refrigeration until ready to assemble the appetizer.
3. Rinse the mâche carefully and divide each bunch in half. Dry thoroughly and hold under refrigeration until ready to assembly the appetizer.
4. To prepare the vinaigrette, combine the orange juice, vinegar, fines herbes, salt, and pepper. Gradually add the oil, whisking constantly. Adjust seasoning and reserve.
5. *Appetizer Assembly:* For each serving, slice one portion of lobster tail meat into medallions. Dress 3/4 ounce haricots verts and 1/2 bunch mâche with the vinaigrette and arrange on chilled plates. Add the lobster tail medallions and a claw portion. Garnish with tomato diamonds and a chervil pluche. Shave a few pieces of truffle over the salad and serve at once.

Lobster Tabbouleh with Mango Sauce

Yield: 10 servings

5 each	whole lobsters
20 oz/wt	Tabbouleh Salad (page 89)
	Mango Sauce
2 each	mangoes, flesh only
1/4 cup	extra-virgin olive oil
1/4 cup	orange juice
1 tbsp	lemon juice
To taste	salt
To taste	ground white pepper
To taste	cayenne pepper
	Garnish
10 each	basil leaves, cut into fine chiffonade
2 1/2 cups	mixed baby greens
10 oz/fl	Lemon Vinaigrette (page 23)

1. Cook the lobster in simmering salted water until fully cooked, about 9–10 minutes. Remove and cool under refrigeration. When cold, remove the tail and claw meat. Slice each tail in half to make 10 equal servings; hold lobster under refrigeration until ready to assemble the appetizer. *Optional:* Reserve the roe and roast in a 200°F oven until dry and a brilliant red color. Cool, then push through a fine mesh sieve. Reserve for garnish.
2. Using a small melon baller (petit pois size), scoop 10 tablespoons of mango balls and reserve for garnish. To prepare the mango sauce, purée the remaining mango with the olive oil and orange and lemon juices in a blender until very smooth. Add the salt, pepper, and cayenne. Hold under refrigeration until ready to assemble the appetizer.
3. *Appetizer Assembly:* For each serving, mold 2 ounces (1/3 cup) tabbouleh in a 2 1/2-inch ring mold in the center of a chilled plate. Slice 1/2 lobster tail into medallions and lay over the salad. Add 1 claw portion. Dress 1/4 cup of the mixed greens with 1 tablespoon of vinaigrette and arrange on the plate. Finish with a generous tablespoon of mango sauce. Garnish with mango balls, sieved lobster roe (if desired), and basil.

Foie Gras in Brioche

Yield: 10 servings (about 5 ounces each)

This traditional presentation for foie gras is one of the great legacies of Fernand Point, chef of La Pyramide, Vienne, France.

1/2 recipe	Foie Gras Roulade (page 281), well chilled
	Brioche Dough
1/2 oz/wt	yeast
12 oz/fl	milk, boiled and cooled to 90°F
4 1/2 to 5 cups	all-purpose flour
1 each	whole egg
1/2 tsp	salt
1/4 tsp	grated nutmeg
1 oz/wt	butter, melted
20 oz/fl	Port Wine Gelée (page 45)
20 each	red grapes, sliced very thin

1. To prepare the brioche dough, dissolve the yeast in the warm milk. Add half the flour and mix well. Let the dough rest for 15 minutes. Add the egg, salt, nutmeg, and butter and mix well. Work in the remaining flour to make a smooth dough. Knead until very elastic. Let the dough rest for 20 minutes. Roll or press it into a rectangle as long as a Pullman loaf pan and twice its width.
2. Unwrap the foie gras roulade and center it on the dough. Roll the dough around the roulade, pressing the dough to seal the seams. Set in a well-greased Pullman loaf pan, seam side down. Place the lid on the Pullman pan. Allow the brioche dough to rise for 30 minutes. Bake at 350°F for about 40 minutes, or until the brioche is thoroughly baked. Let cool before unmolding and cutting into 10 equal slices.
3. *Appetizer Assembly:* Pool 2 ounces of aspic on each plate, decorate with sliced grapes, and allow to firm under refrigeration. At service, top with a slice of foie gras in brioche.

Foie Gras Roulade with Roasted Beet Salad and Smoked Duck Breast

Yield: 10 servings

This dish was created by the Culinary Institute's Chef Tim Rodgers and was one of the highlights of the dinner served to President Clinton and Russia's president Boris Yeltsin at a summit meeting held during the fall of 1996 at Franklin D. Roosevelt's home in Hyde Park, New York. It features one of the Hudson Valley's specialties—fresh foie gras.

1 lb	Foie Gras Roulade or Terrine (pages 280, 281)
15 oz/wt	Smoked Duck Breast (page 154)
20 oz/wt	Roasted Beet Salad (page 76), made with gold and red beets
20 pieces	Parsnip Chips (page 393)
2 1/2 cups	baby beet greens
5 oz/fl	Beet Vinaigrette (page 27)

1. Slice the foie gras roulade into 10 servings, each weighing about 1 1/2 ounces. If done in advance, hold the slices, covered, under refrigeration until ready to assemble the appetizer.

2. Slice the duck breasts thin and portion at 4 slices per appetizer.

3. *Appetizer Assembly:* For each serving, place 1 slice of foie gras on the plate and serve with 2 ounces beet salad, 4 slices of duck breast, 2 parsnip chips, and 1/4 cup of baby beet greens dressed with 1 tablespoon of vinaigrette.

Chef's Notes: This photo shows both red and golden beet salads made using the same recipe. Fresh figs can also be used to garnish this dish.

Shrimp Mousse with Dill Gelée

Yield: 10 servings

1 qt	Court Bouillon (page 412)
1/2 bunch	dill, separated into leaves and stems
12 oz/wt	shrimp (still in shell)
1/4 oz/wt	powdered or sheet gelatin
1 oz/fl	cool water
3 oz/fl	Basic Mayonnaise (page 28)
4 each	egg whites (6 oz/fl), whipped to soft peaks
6 oz/fl	heavy cream, whipped to soft peaks
To taste	salt
To taste	ground white pepper
To taste	lemon juice
Pinch	cayenne pepper
	Garnish
1/2 oz/wt	caviar
2 each	seedless cucumber, sliced thin
1/4 cup	Lemon Vinaigrette (page 23)

1. To cook the shrimp and prepare the aspic: Bring the court bouillon and dill stems to a simmer. Add the shrimp and poach just until cooked through, about 5 minutes. Remove the shrimp. Strain the court bouillon and reserve 1 cup; keep warm (90°F). Bloom the gelatin in the water and add to the warm court bouillon. Stir until the gelatin is completely dissolved. Reserve.
2. To prepare the mousse: Shell and devein the shrimp. Split 5 shrimp in half lengthwise. Dice the remaining shrimp and purée with the mayonnaise to form a smooth paste. Transfer to a mixing bowl and fold in the egg whites and cream. Season with salt, pepper, lemon juice, and cayenne.
3. Pipe the mousse into 2-inch PVC pipe molds (or other molds as desired). Top each mousse with a shrimp half and 1 ounce of aspic. Chill for at least 3 hours before unmolding. Garnish as shown with caviar, dill, and cucumbers dressed in vinaigrette.

Smoked Duck Tart

Yield: 10-inch tart; 12 servings (about 3 ounces each)

1/2 lb	Pâté Dough (page 416)
1 each	Smoked Duck (page 154)
1/2 cup	heavy cream, whipped
1/4 oz/wt	powdered or sheet gelatin
2 tbsp	brandy
36 each	Candied Pecan halves (page 348)
10 oz/fl	Cumberland Sauce (page 37)

1. Roll out the dough to a thickness of about 3/16 inch. Line a tart pan with a removable bottom with the dough, trimming the edges. Bake blind at 350°F for 8 minutes, until golden brown and fully baked. Reserve until the mousse is prepared.
2. Remove the bones and skin from the duck. Trim the breast portions and slice very thin for garnish; reserve. Dice the leg and thigh meat, removing all sinew and gristle.
3. Make a mousse as described on page 316: Grind leg, thigh, and any additional useable trim through the medium plate (1/4 inch) of a meat grinder. Purée the ground duck to a fine paste. Fold in the cream. Bloom the gelatin in the brandy, warm to dissolve the gelatin, and fold into the duck mixture.
4. Fill the prepared tart shell with mousse and top with thin-sliced duck breast arranged symmetrically in a spiral pattern covering the surface of the tart. Garnish the rim of the tart with candied pecans. Chill at least 4 hours before slicing and serving.
5. *Appetizer Assembly:* Slice the tart into 12 servings; serve on chilled plates with 1 ounce Cumberland sauce per serving.

ELEVEN

Condiments, Crackers, and Pickles

Condiments, crackers, and pickles are those little extras that can elevate a dish from the ordinary to the sublime. Although most of these foods are available commercially, they are not difficult to produce, and are always more interesting when made by hand.

Condiments

Condiments are assertive, saucelike creations, typically served on the side and added at the diner's discretion. However, condiments can also be found as spreads or dips, adding a little extra to sandwiches, dressings, and salads.

Mustard

Plain and flavored mustards have a wonderful aroma and a complex flavor that pairs beautifully with meats, cheeses, and poultry; mustard can even be served as a dip. It is frequently added to vinaigrettes and other dressings and used to glaze meats as they roast. Special mustards from around the world have their own unique qualities. Some are very hot, others are mild; some are very smooth, others are grainy.

Ketchup

Lancelot Sturgeon, a British author, wrote that ketchup was invented by the French in the seventeenth century. However, early French cookbooks claim that the British formulated the condiment. Still others trace its origins to East Asia. Early English recipes for ketchup called for such ingredients as kidney beans, mushrooms, anchovies, liver, and walnuts. Now predominantly tomato-based, the product is also spelled "catsup" or even "catchup."

Chutney

Chutneys are sweet-and-sour condiments, often fruit-based (though vegetable-based versions exist as well) and generally highly spiced, favored in Indian cuisines. Chutneys may be cooked, similar to a pickle or relish, or they may be raw, making them similar to other cold raw sauces such as salsa.

Mango chutney is probably most familiar worldwide, but tomatoes, eggplant, melons, apples, and pineapples are also commonly used to prepare chutneys.

Relish

A relish may be as simple as a mound of sliced cucumbers or radishes, or as complex as a curried onion relish, cooked in a pickle or brine, highly seasoned and garnished with dried fruits. Relishes are served cold to act as a foil to hot or spicy foods, or to liven up dishes that need some extra kick.

Compote

Compotes are often made by cooking fruits in a syrup. For the garde manger, savory compotes can be used to accompany galantines or pâtés in much the same way that a Cumberland sauce is used.

Flavored Oils and Vinegars

Good-quality oils and vinegars can be infused with spices, aromatics, herbs, and fruits or vegetables to produce products with many applications. They work well as condiments, added in a drizzle or as droplets to lend a bit of intense flavor and color to a plated dish. They also are excellent to use as a dressing for vegetables, pastas, grains, or fruits. And, of course, they are well suited to use in vinaigrettes and other dressings for a special effect. (Figure 11-1 shows various flavored oils.)

To infuse oils and vinegars, use one of the following methods:

Method 1: *A Warm Infusion*

Heat the oil or vinegar very gently over low heat with flavoring ingredients such as citrus zest, just until the aroma is apparent. Let the oil or vinegar steep off the heat with the flavoring ingredients until

Figure 11-1 Flavored oils, left to right: yellow pepper, basil, curry, rosemary-garlic, red pepper.

cool, then pour into storage bottles or containers. You may opt to strain the vinegar or oil for a clearer final product, or leave the flavoring ingredients in for a more intense flavor.

Method 2: *Steeping*

Place the herbs or other aromatics in a glass or plastic bottle. Heat the oil or vinegar briefly, just until warm. Pour the warm oil or vinegar over the aromatics, and let the vinegar rest until the desired flavor is achieved. You may wish to add fresh aromatics after the oil or vinegar has steeped for several days to give an even more intense flavor (see Figure 11-2).

Method 3: *Purées*

Purée raw, blanched, or fully cooked vegetables, herbs, or fruits and bring the purée to a simmer, reducing if necessary to concentrate the flavors. Add the oil or vinegar and transfer to a storage container. You may leave the oil or vinegar as is, and use it as you would a purée. Or you may strain it to remove the fiber and pulp (see Figure 11-3).

Figure 11-2 Making flavored vinegar with garlic, rosemary, basil, and peppercorns.

Figure 11-3 Wringing yellow pepper oil through cheesecloth.

Figure 11-4 Decanting curry oil.

Method 4: *Cold Infusion*

Combine room-temperature oils or vinegars with ground spices and transfer to a storage container. Let the mixture settle until the vinegar or oil is clear and the spices have settled in the bottom of the container. Carefully decant the vinegar or oil once the desired flavor is reached (see Figure 11-4).

Note: **When you introduce fresh or raw ingredients to an oil or vinegar, you run the risk of foodborne illness if the finished products are not carefully stored. Although commercially prepared versions of flavored oils and vinegars are shelf-stable, you should keep yours stored under refrigeration, especially if you have included raw garlic or shallots. Use them within a few days to be sure that they will have the best flavor and color.**

Pickles

Pickles encompass any food that has been brined. They can be made from vegetables, fruit, or eggs. The brine often contains vinegar, though a salt brine can also be used to make special pickles. Pickles may be extremely tart, such as cornichons, or sweet, like the Sweet Pickle Chips on page 390.

Chips and Crisps

Crackers and other breads may be eaten alone or as a support item that adds flavor and a textural counterpoint. They are served to accompany dips and spreads, or with a salad or appetizer to add a bit of crunch to the plate.

Fried and Baked Chips

We are all familiar with potato chips, made by slicing potatoes very thin and frying them in oil until crisp. Other vegetables can also be made into chips: sweet potatoes, beets, and artichokes are all excellent choices (see Figure 11-5).

Baked chips are also wonderful additions to salads and composed appetizers, or on their own as "snack food." Pears, apples, bananas, and other fruits can be sliced thin

Figure 11-5 Artichoke Chips.

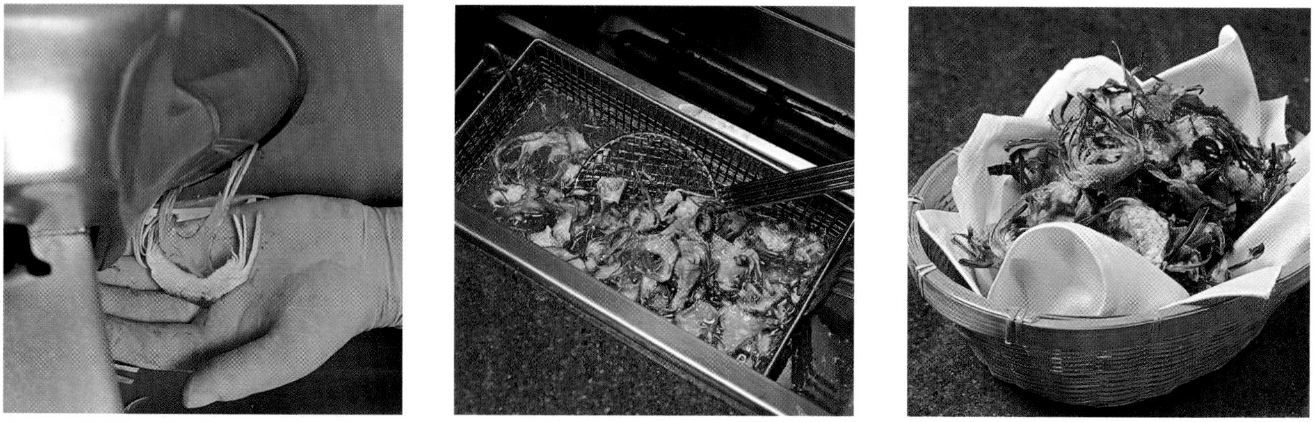

a. Slicing artichokes on an electric slicer. b. Deep-frying artichoke slices. c. Basket of fried artichoke chips.

and then baked until they are dry and crisp. If they are sliced a little thicker and baked at a lower temperature, they take on an appealing chewy texture (see Figure 11-6).

Crackers

Crackers can be produced in a number of ways. Icebox-style crackers are made in much the same way as cookies. A savory dough is prepared, rolled into a log, chilled, and then sliced and baked. Cheese and nuts are often used to season and flavor these crackers.

Still other crackers are made from a batter that is baked. These delicate crackers can be shaped before baking by spreading them on a greased sheet pan or silicone baking pad. They can be shaped when they are still warm from the oven by draping them over rolling pins or pressing them into cups or other molds (Figure 11-7 shows a variety of crackers).

Figure 11-6 Fruit Chips.

a. Oven-dried pear chips.

b. Pear chips as a garnish on a salad of buttercrunch, red leaf lettuce, gorgonzola, and toasted walnuts.

Figure 11-7 Packing potato, polenta, parsnip, and risotto crackers for storage.

Harissa

Yield: 2 cups

This intense sauce can be used as a condiment or to flavor dips and spreads.

10 each	jalapeños, roasted, peeled, and seeded
3–4 each	red peppers, roasted, peeled, and seeded
1 tbsp	whole cumin seeds, toasted and ground
1 tbsp	garlic paste
3 tbsp	hot Hungarian paprika
1 1/2 tsp	cayenne pepper
3/4 cup	olive oil
3 tbsp	lemon juice
To taste	salt

1. Combine the jalapeños, peppers, cumin, garlic paste, paprika, and cayenne in a blender. Grind to a paste-like consistency.
2. Remove the paste to a bowl. Slowly whisk in the oil to create a smooth sauce. Add the lemon juice and salt to taste.
3. Transfer to a clean storage container. Hold, covered, under refrigeration for up to 2 weeks.

Heywood's Mustard

Yield: 1 quart

1 1/4 cups	dry mustard
2 tbsp	sugar
2 tsp	salt
12 oz/wt	pasteurized eggs
2 cups	malt vinegar
1/4 tsp	Tabasco sauce
1/4 cup	honey

1. Combine the mustard, sugar, and salt.
2. Add the eggs and mix until smooth.
3. Whip in the vinegar, Tabasco, and honey. Let rest under refrigeration for 1 to 2 hours.
4. Beat over a double boiler until thick and creamy.
5. Chill.
6. Transfer to a clean storage container. Hold, covered, under refrigeration for up to 2 weeks.

Southwestern Spicy Green Chili Mustard

Yield: 1 quart

1 cup	dry mustard
3/4 cup	dark Mexican beer
3/4 cup	sherry wine vinegar
12 each	egg yolks
1 tbsp	soy sauce
1 cup	green chiles, diced
1 each	jalapeño, minced
1/4 cup	cumin seeds, toasted whole
2 tbsp	dry Mexican oregano
1/4 cup	honey
1/2 tbsp	salt

1. Combine the mustard, beer, vinegar, egg yolks, and soy sauce in a stainless-steel bowl.
2. Let rest under refrigeration for 1 hour.
3. Beat over a double boiler until thick and creamy.
4. Add the green chiles, jalapeño, cumin, oregano, honey, and salt. Mix well.
5. Transfer to a clean storage container. Hold, covered, under refrigeration for up to 2 weeks.

Dried Cranberry Mustard

Yield: 1 quart

1 cup	dry mustard
6 each	eggs
8 oz/fl	cranberry juice
3 oz/fl	white vinegar
1/2 tsp	salt
1 tbsp	Worcestershire sauce
1/4 cup	packed brown sugar
1/2 cup	chopped dried cranberries

1. Combine all ingredients except cranberries in a stainless-steel bowl.
2. Cook over a boiling water bath, stirring constantly until thick and smooth.
3. Add cranberries and mix well.
4. Store, covered, under refrigeration for 48 hours before using. Hold, covered, under refrigeration for up to 2 weeks.

Beer Mustard with Caraway Seeds

Yield: 1 quart

$1\frac{1}{2}$ cups	dark beer
6 each	eggs
$1\frac{1}{2}$ cups	dry mustard
2 tsp	salt
1 tsp	Worcestershire sauce
$\frac{1}{4}$ cup	packed brown sugar
$\frac{1}{4}$ cup	white vinegar
2 tbsp	caraway seeds, toasted

1. Combine all ingredients except caraway seeds and mix well.
2. Let mixture rest for 1 hour.
3. Cook over a double boiler until thick and smooth.
4. Add the caraway seeds and mix well.
5. Transfer to a clean storage container. Hold, covered, under refrigeration for up to 2 weeks.

Swedish Mustard Sauce

Yield: 1 quart

2/3 cup	prepared mustard
1/4 cup	finely grated horseradish
2 cups	Basic Mayonnaise (page 28)
1 tsp	salt
2 tsp	Worcestershire sauce
1 cup	heavy cream, whipped

1. Purée all ingredients except cream.
2. Fold in the cream; chill.
3. Transfer to a clean storage container. Hold, covered, under refrigeration for up to 12 hours.

Tomato Ketchup

Yield: 1 quart

1/2 cup	sugar
3/4 cup	minced onion
1 tbsp	minced garlic
3 qts	crushed tomatoes
2 each	roasted red peppers, chopped
1 cup	red wine vinegar
1/2 cup	balsamic vinegar
To taste	cayenne pepper

1. Cook the sugar over moderate heat until it turns an amber color.
2. Add the onion and garlic.
3. Add the tomatoes and roasted peppers; cook 5 to 10 minutes over moderate heat.
4. Add the vinegars and reduce until thickened, about 20 minutes.
5. Season with cayenne pepper to taste (mild).
6. Strain through a fine china cap.
7. Transfer to a clean storage container. Hold, covered, under refrigeration for up to 2 weeks.

Yellow Pepper Ketchup

Yield: 1 quart

2 lb	yellow peppers, seeded and coarsely chopped (8 each)
3 oz	jalapeños, seeded and chopped (about 4 each)
12 oz/wt	onions, coarsely chopped (2 each)
2 tbsp	chopped garlic
As needed	vegetable oil
3/4 cup	red wine vinegar
3/4 cup	sugar
To taste	salt
To taste	ground white pepper

1. Sauté the peppers, onions, and garlic in oil until tender but not browned, about 12 minutes.
2. Add the vinegar and sugar; simmer 30 to 45 minutes.
3. Purée until smooth.
4. Adjust seasoning.
5. Cool and transfer to a clean storage container. Hold, covered, under refrigeration for up to 2 weeks.

Spicy Mango Chutney

Yield: 1 quart

3 each	mangoes, peeled and chopped
2/3 cup	raisins
1 each	jalapeño, minced
4 each	garlic cloves, minced
1 tbsp	minced ginger
1 cup	packed dark brown sugar
1 cup	white wine vinegar
1/2 tsp	salt
1 tsp	turmeric

1. Combine the mangoes, raisins, pepper, garlic, ginger, and sugar. Rest under refrigeration for 24 hours.
2. Add the vinegar; bring to a boil and simmer 15 minutes.
3. Add the salt; simmer 10 minutes.
4. Add the turmeric; simmer 5 minutes.
5. Cool and transfer to a clean storage container. Hold, covered, under refrigeration for up to 2 weeks.

Apricot-Cherry Chutney

Yield: 1 quart

1 tbsp	peanut oil
4 oz/wt	onion, sliced thin
2 tbsp	minced ginger
1/2 cup	cider vinegar
1/4 cup	honey
1 cup	orange juice
2 cups	water
1 each	lemon, juiced
1/2 tsp	ground coriander
1/4 tsp	ground cardamom
1/2 tsp	curry powder
1/4 tsp	red pepper flakes
1/2 lb	dried apricots, halved
1/2 lb	dried cherries

1. Sauté the onion and ginger in the peanut oil until limp, but not browned.
2. Add the remaining ingredients and simmer for 20 minutes. Add more water if the chutney is too thick.
3. Cool and transfer to a clean storage container. Hold, covered, under refrigeration for up to 2 weeks.

Beet Chutney

Yield: 1 quart

6 each	beets
As needed	water
1 tsp	kosher salt
1 tbsp	finely chopped ginger
1/4 cup	vegetable oil
2 tsp	salt
1 oz/fl	red wine vinegar
1 tbsp	lime juice
1/4 tsp	cayenne pepper
1 tsp	finely chopped jalapeño
1 tbsp	finely chopped cilantro

1. Preheat the oven to 375°F.
2. Wash the beets well. Leave one inch of stem attached to the beets. Put the beets in a 2-inch hotel pan, in a single layer, and add water just to cover the bottom of the pan. Season with kosher salt. Cover the pan with aluminum foil and roast the beets until fork tender, about 1 hour depending on size. Shake the pan every 20 minutes so the beets do not stick or burn.
3. When the beets are done but still warm, remove the skin. Cut the beets into a small dice and combine with remaining ingredients. (Note: If preferred, add the peppers and cilantro on the day of service.) This chutney should be very spicy.
4. Cool and transfer to a clean storage container. Hold, covered, under refrigeration for up to 2 weeks.

Cranberry Relish

Yield: 1 quart

12 oz/wt	cranberries
3 oz/fl	orange juice
3 oz/fl	triple sec (*optional*)
3 oz/wt	sugar
2 each	oranges, zest and segments with membranes removed

1. Combine all ingredients except the orange segments in a sauce pot and stir to combine.
2. Cover and let simmer 15 to 20 minutes, stirring occasionally.
3. When berries burst and liquid starts to thicken, remove from heat and add the orange segments. Adjust sweetness with sugar.
4. Transfer to a clean storage container. Hold, covered, under refrigeration for up to 2 weeks.

Curried Onion Relish

Yield: 1 quart

1 lb	onions, cut into 1/4-inch dice
1 each	garlic clove, minced
1 cup	white vinegar
1 cup	sugar
1/2 tsp	salt
2 tbsp	pickling spice, tied into a sachet
1 tbsp	curry powder

1. Combine all ingredients; mix well.
2. Simmer, covered, in a small nonreactive saucepan for 1/2 hour. Stir often, being careful not to scorch. Chill.
3. Transfer to a clean storage container. Hold, covered, under refrigeration for up to 2 weeks.

Red Onion Confiture

Yield: 1 quart

2 tbsp	vegetable oil
8 cups	red onion, julienned
1/2 cup	honey (see Chef's Notes)
1/2 cup	red wine vinegar
3/4 cup	red wine
To taste	salt
To taste	ground white pepper

1. Heat the oil in a sauteuse over high heat. Sweat the onions.
2. Stir in the honey; cook the mixture until the onions are lightly caramelized.
3. Add the vinegar and wine; reduce until the liquid is cooked away.
4. Adjust seasoning.
5. Cool and transfer to a clean storage container. Hold, covered, under refrigeration for up to 2 weeks.

Chef's Notes: Grenadine can be substituted for the honey for sweetness and will enhance the color as well.

Dried Apricot Relish

Yield: 1 quart

1 lb	medium-dice dried apricots
1/2 tsp	minced garlic
2 drops	Tabasco sauce
1 each	lemon, juice and zest
1/2 cup	honey
2 tbsp	soy sauce
2 cups	ginger ale
4 oz/wt	sliced almonds, toasted

1. Combine all ingredients except almonds; simmer for 20 minutes. Cool.
2. Stir in the almonds.
3. Cool and transfer to a clean storage container. Hold, covered, under refrigeration for up to 2 weeks.

Sweet Pickle Chips

Yield: 2 quarts

4 lb	cucumbers
1 lb	onions
3 cups	cider vinegar
1 tbsp	salt
1 tsp	mustard seeds
4 cups	sugar
2 qts	water
$2\frac{1}{2}$ cups	white vinegar
2 tbsp	celery seed
1 tbsp	whole allspice, crushed
2 tsp	turmeric

1. Wash the cucumbers and slice $\frac{1}{4}$-inch thick. Slice the onions $\frac{1}{4}$-inch thick.
2. Combine the cucumber and onions with cider vinegar, salt, mustard seeds, 2 tablespoons of the sugar, and the water.
3. Simmer for 10 minutes and drain. Discard liquid.
4. Bring the white vinegar, celery seed, allspice, turmeric, and remaining sugar to a boil.
5. Pour the pickle mixture over the cucumbers and onions and let rest under refrigeration for 3 to 4 days before serving. Hold under refrigeration for up to 4 weeks.

Dill Pickles

Yield: 10 pounds

10 lb	pickling cucumbers
$6^1/_2$ gal	water
$2^1/_4$ lb	salt
2 qts	white *or* cider vinegar
$1^1/_2$ tbsp	dill seed
$^1/_4$ cup	pickling spice
1 tbsp	ground turmeric
$^1/_4$ lb	sugar
4 each	dried hot chiles
1 bunch	dill sprigs
5 each	garlic cloves, smashed

1. Soak the cucumbers overnight or up to 48 hours in 6 gallons of water combined with 2 pounds of salt. Drain.
2. Combine the vinegar, remaining water, dill seed, pickling spice, turmeric, sugar, and remaining salt and bring to a boil; simmer for 10 minutes.
3. Pack the cucumbers in a large plastic bucket with the hot chiles, dill sprigs, and garlic.
4. Pour the pickling liquid over the pickles; weigh down with some plates and cover with cheesecloth. Let cool for $^1/_2$ to 1 hour, put in refrigerator and chill. May be used after $1^1/_2$ weeks. Hold under refrigeration for up to 4 weeks.

Half-Sour Pickles

Yield: 3 pounds

4 lb	pickling cucumbers, cut into spears
	Brine
$^1/_2$ oz/wt	dill sprigs
3 each	garlic cloves, smashed
2 each	bay leaves
2 qts	water
4.5 oz/wt	salt
1 oz/wt	sugar
1 cup	white vinegar

1. Place the dill, garlic, and bay leaves in a noncorrosive container. Pack the spears on top.
2. Bring the water, salt, sugar, and vinegar to a boil, pour over pickles, and allow to cool.
3. Hold under refrigeration at least 3 days and up to 4 weeks.

Chef's Notes: The pickles will change in texture from half raw/half cured to a fully-cured pickle the longer they sit in the refrigerator.

Pickled Vegetables

Yield: 3 quarts

1 qt	water
1 cup	malt vinegar
1/2 cup	salt
1 cup	sugar
1/2 cup	pickling spices
6 lb	assorted vegetables: baby golden, red, or Chioggia beets; pearl onions; okra; baby carrots; broccoli, trimmed and cut into small pieces
2 tbsp	minced garlic
2 sprigs	dill

1. Bring the water, vinegar, salt, sugar, and pickling spices to a boil to make a brine.
2. Pack vegetables, garlic, and dill in a plastic bucket. Pour the brine over the vegetables. Let cool and then cover.
3. Allow to marinate for at least 24 hours before serving. Hold under refrigeration for up to a week.

Pickled Grapes or Cherries

Yield: 2 quarts

8 cups	sugar
5 1/2 cups	white wine vinegar
3 each	cinnamon sticks
1 tsp	salt
5 lb	seedless grapes or sweet cherries (grapes removed from stems; cherries pitted)

1. Combine the sugar, vinegar, cinnamon sticks, and salt. Simmer for 5 minutes.
2. Pour over the grapes or cherries, allow to cool, and refrigerate.
3. The grapes or cherries are ready to serve now, or hold, covered, under refrigeration, in a glass or stainless-steel container for up to 3 weeks.

Assorted Vegetable Chips

Yield: 30 servings

1/2 lb	taro root
1/2 lb	sweet potatoes
1/2 lb	parsnips
1/2 lb	carrots
1/2 lb	baking potatoes (such as Idaho or russet)
1/2 lb	beets
1/2 lb	plantains
As needed	vegetable oil for frying
As needed	salt

1. Peel all vegetables. Slice all very thin (1/16 inch). Hold taro and potato slices separately in cold water; all other vegetables may be held dry. Keep them separate since they all require different cooking times.

2. Heat a fryer with clean oil to 325°F. Fry each vegetable separately until crisp, drain on paper towel, and season with salt.

3. Serve immediately or hold in an airtight container, as you would crackers, for later service. Serve within 24 hours for best quality.

Artichoke Chips Remove choke and some of the stem. Slice trimmed artichokes very thin on a slicer and fry in 350°F oil until crisp. Drain and salt to taste.
Fennel Chips Remove stem ends from fennel, trim root end and halve or quarter (depending upon the size of the fennel bulb). Slice very thin using a knife, electric slicer, or mandolin. Fry in 350°F vegetable oil in a deep fryer or over medium heat until crisp. Drain and salt to taste.
Garlic Chips Use large garlic (elephant garlic) and slice peeled cloves very thin using a knife or a garlic slicer. Fry in olive oil over moderate heat until lightly browned. Reserve the flavored oil for other use, if desired.
Apple or Pear Chips Remove the core from rinsed apples or pears, slice thin, and bake on a silicone baking pad or a lightly oiled sheet pan in a 375° oven for 20 to 30 minutes or until crisp.

Pepper Jack and Oregano Crackers

Yield: 100 crackers

2 cups	all-purpose flour
8 oz/wt	shredded pepper Jack cheese
2 tsp	dried oregano, *or* 1 tablespoon fresh oregano
1/2 tsp	salt
1/2 tsp	ground black pepper
1/2 cup	vegetable oil
1/2 to 2/3 cup	water
	Spice Mixture
1/4 tsp	cayenne pepper
1 tsp	sugar
1 tsp	kosher salt

1. Combine the flour, cheese, oregano, salt, and pepper in a food processor or by hand. Add the oil and mix just until a coarse meal consistency is achieved. Add the water gradually until the dough forms a cohesive ball that pulls away from the sides of the bowl.
2. Divide the dough into equal portions, wrap, and refrigerate. Combine the spice mixture ingredients; reserve.
3. Roll the dough through a pasta machine to 1/8-inch thickness.
4. Cut the dough using a pizza cutter, knife, or shaped cutters into the desired cracker shapes and place on a doubled sheet pan. Sprinkle with the spice mixture.
5. Bake at 325°F until lightly golden; turn and bake until medium golden brown, 15 to 20 minutes.

Chef's Notes: Chill the dough if it becomes soft during rolling or cutting.

Cheddar and Walnut Icebox Crackers

Yield: About 100 small crackers

1/2 cup	butter
8 oz/wt	aged Cheddar cheese, grated
1 1/2 cups	flour
1 tsp	salt
1/2 cup	finely chopped walnuts

1. Cream the butter; add cheese and mix well.
2. Add the flour and salt, and mix well. Blend in the nuts.
3. Roll out into 3 logs, about 1 1/2 inches in diameter. Chill at least one hour.
4. Cut into 1/4-inch slices and place on parchment-lined sheet pan. Bake at 350°F until crisp (see photo). Cool on a wire rack. Store in an airtight container. Serve within 3 days.

Blue Cheese and Pecan Crackers Substitute an equal amount of blue cheese for the Cheddar and pecans for the walnuts.

Potato Crisps

Yield: 50 crisps

1 lb	russet potatoes
1/4 cup	egg whites
As needed	milk

1. Bake the potatoes until done, about 1 hour.
2. Scoop out the pulp and pass through a food mill. Cool.
3. Mix in the egg whites; add milk and mix to consistency of crêpe batter.
4. Lay out a thin layer of the mixture on a silicone baking pad or nonstick baking sheet and bake in a convection oven at 300°F for 3 to 4 minutes. Score into crackers of the size and shape desired; finish baking until golden, about 2 to 3 minutes. Cool on a wire rack and store in an airtight container. Serve within 3 days.

Parsnip Crisps Replace potatoes with parsnips.
Celeriac Chips Replace potatoes with peeled celeriac (celery root).

Basil Oil (Basic Herb Oil)

Yield: 2 cups

Blanching the basil leaves before puréeing with the oil helps maintain a bright color.

3 oz/wt	basil leaves
1 oz/wt	flat-leaf parsley leaves
2 cups	pure olive oil

1. Blanch the basil and parsley leaves in salted water for 20 seconds. Shock and drain on paper towels.
2. Combine the blanched herbs with half the oil in a blender and purée very fine. Add this purée to the remaining oil. Strain the oil through cheesecloth, if desired.
3. Transfer to a storage container or squirt bottle. Keep chilled. Use within 3 to 4 days.

Chef's Notes: This recipe will work well for most green herbs, such as chives, tarragon, chervil, or parsley.

Chive Oil Replace the basil leaves with chives. Blanching is not necessary.

Adding the purée to the remaining oil.

Cinnamon Oil (Basic Spice Oil)

Yield: 2 cups

19 oz/fl	sunflower oil
12 each	cinnamon sticks, crushed
1 each	nutmeg, quartered

1. Heat the oil in a small sauce pot with the cinnamon and nutmeg until approximately 150°F. Remove from heat and allow to cool.
2. Strain the oil into a bottle or other clean container. Allow to cool and recap.
3. Store in a cool, dark area. Use within 3 to 4 days.

Curry Oil Replace the cinnamon and nutmeg with 2 ounces (about 1/2 cup) Curry Powder (page 407).

Orange Oil (Basic Citrus Oil)

Yield: 2 cups

1 1/2 cups	pure olive oil
1 1/2 cups	extra-virgin olive oil
3 each	oranges, zest only, cut into 1 × 3-inch strips

1. Combine both oils and heat to 140°F. Do not leave oil unattended—it warms very quickly.
2. Add the orange zest. Transfer to a storage container and infuse overnight under refrigeration.
3. The next day, taste and strain out the zest if the flavor is good, or allow to infuse longer.
4. Keep chilled. Use within 3 to 4 days.

Red Pepper Oil

Yield: 2 cups

8 each	red peppers
2 oz/wt	prepared mustard
$2^{1/2}$ cups	extra-virgin olive oil
To taste	salt

1. Wash the peppers, remove the stems and seeds, and rough cut into small dice.
2. Purée the peppers very fine in a blender. Place this purée juice in a stainless-steel sauce pan and reduce to one fourth original volume. Strain through a chinois and cool.
3. When the pepper purée is cool, add the mustard. Add the olive oil. Season with salt.
4. Transfer to a storage container or squirt bottle. Keep chilled. Use within 2 to 3 days.

Chef's Notes: Yellow or green peppers can be substituted with excellent results. For a spicy variation, use chiles and omit the mustard.

Raspberry and Thyme Vinegar (Basic Flavored Vinegar)

Yield: 2 cups

2 cups	red wine vinegar
8–10 sprigs	thyme
1/2 cup	raspberries (25 each)

1. Heat the vinigar until slightly warm, about 120°F.
2. Place the thyme sprigs and raspberries in glass jar or other storage container.
3. Pour the vinegar back into the bottle.
4. Allow to cool and recap.
5. Keep chilled. Use within 5 to 6 days.

Chef's Notes: Champagne wine vinegar can be substituted for the red wine vinegar.

Rosemary-Garlic Vinegar

Yield: 2 cups

2 cups	white wine vinegar
4 each	garlic cloves
6–8 each	rosemary sprigs
1 each	opal basil sprig (*optional*)
1 tbsp	whole black peppercorns

1. Heat the vinegar until slightly warm, about 120°F.
2. Thread the garlic on a skewer. Place it in a glass or plastic bottle with the rosemary, basil (if desired), and peppercorns.
3. Pour the vinegar over the herbs and garlic.
4. Allow to cool and recap.
5. Keep chilled. Use within 5 to 6 days.

TWELVE

Basic Recipes

Mirepoix

Yield: 1 pound

8 oz/wt	onions, peeled and chopped
4 oz/wt	carrots, trimmed and chopped
4 oz/wt	celery, trimmed and chopped

1. Cut the vegetables into an appropriate size based on the cooking time of the dish.

White Mirepoix For 1 pound: Reduce the onions to 4 ounces. Replace the carrots with 4 ounces each of chopped leeks (white parts only) and parsnips. If desired, add 2 to 3 ounces of mushroom trimmings.

Standard Bouquet Garni

Yield: 1 bouquet, enough to flavor 1 gallon of stock

4 oz/wt	whole celery stalk, trimmed
3 or 4 each	fresh parsley stems
1 each	fresh thyme sprig
1 each	bay leaf
2 or 3 each	leek leaves

1. Halve the celery stalk crosswise. Sandwich the herbs between the celery pieces and fold the leek leaves around the herbs and celery.
2. Tie the bundle securely with butcher's twine, leaving a long tail of string to tie the bouquet to the stockpot handle.

Chef's Notes: Savory, sage, rosemary, or other fresh herbs may be used in addition to or in place of the ingredients called for above, depending on the recipe or desired result.

Standard Sachet d'Epices

Yield: 1 sachet, enough to flavor 1 gallon of stock

3 or 4 each	fresh parsley stems
1/2 tsp	fresh thyme leaves
1 each	bay leaf
1/2 tsp	peppercorns, cracked
1 each	garlic clove, crushed (*optional*)

1. Place all ingredients on a piece of cheesecloth approximately 4 inches square. Gather up the edges and tie with butcher's twine, leaving a long tail of string to tie to the stockpot handle.

Chef's Notes: Cloves, dill, tarragon stems, juniper berries, star anise, allspice, and other herbs and spices may be included, depending on the recipe or desired result.

Chinese Five-Spice Powder

Yield: about 1 cup

4 tbsp	star anise
3 tbsp	cloves
3 tbsp	Szechwan pepper
3 tbsp	fennel seeds
3 tbsp	cinnamon (or cassia)

1. Grind the spices in a spice mill or with a mortar and pestle. Store any unused spice powder in an airtight container in a cool, dry place. Keeps well for several weeks.

Barbecue Spice Mix

Yield: about 1 cup

4 tbsp	hot Hungarian paprika
2 tbsp	chili powder
2 tbsp	salt
4 tsp	ground cumin
4 tsp	sugar
1 tbsp	dried thyme
2 tsp	dry mustard
2 tsp	ground black pepper
2 tsp	dried oregano
2 tsp	curry powder
1 tsp	cayenne pepper

1. Combine all ingredients thoroughly. Store any unused spice blend in an airtight container in a cool, dry place.

Quatre Epices

Yield: about 1 cup

8 tbsp	black peppercorns
3 tbsp	ground nutmeg
2 tbsp	ground cinnamon
2 tbsp	whole cloves
2 tbsp	ground ginger (*optional*)

1. Grind together the spices in a spice mill or with a mortar and pestle. Store any unused spice blend in an airtight container in a cool, dry place.

Cajun Spice Blend

Yield: about 1 cup

6 tbsp	hot Hungarian paprika
1 tbsp	kosher salt
2 tbsp	onion powder
2 tbsp	garlic powder
2 tbsp	cayenne pepper
1 tbsp	ground white pepper
1 tbsp	ground black pepper
1 tbsp	dried thyme
1 tbsp	dried oregano

1. Combine all ingredients thoroughly. Store any unused spice blend in an airtight container in a cool, dry place.

Curry Powder

Yield: about 1 cup

3 tbsp	cumin seeds
3 tbsp	coriander seeds
2 tsp	whole mustard seeds
8 each	dried red chiles, to taste
2 tbsp	ground cinnamon
2 tbsp	ground turmeric
2 tbsp	ground ginger

1. Combine all the seeds and chiles. Roast them in a 350°F oven for 5 minutes. Remove and cool slightly. Split the chiles and remove and discard the seeds.
2. Grind the whole seeds, ground spices, and chiles in a spice mill or with a mortar and pestle until evenly blended. Store any unused powder in an airtight container in a cool, dry place.

Chef's Notes: Add hot Hungarian paprika, cloves, or fresh curry leaves to the blend.

Fines Herbes

Yield: 2 ounces

1/2 oz/wt	chervil leaves
1/2 oz/wt	chives
1/2 oz/wt	parsley leaves
1/2 oz/wt	tarragon leaves

1. Rinse and dry all herbs. Combine all the herbs and chop or mince to the desired finess. Use at once.

Pâté Spice

Yield: 1 pound

1 1/2 oz/wt	white peppercorns
3 oz/wt	coriander seeds
1 3/4 oz/wt	dried thyme
1 3/4 oz/wt	dried basil
3 oz/wt	whole cloves
1 1/2 oz/wt	grated nutmeg
1/2 oz/wt	bay leaf
3/4 oz/wt	mace
1 oz/wt	dry cèpes (*optional*)

1. Combine all ingredients and grind them using a mortar and pestle or a blender. Store any unused spice blend in an airtight container in a cool, dry place.

Hot Italian Sausage Blend

Yield: about 1 cup

3 tbsp	fennel seeds
2 tbsp	ground coriander
1 tbsp	sugar
2 tbsp	sweet Spanish paprika
2 tbsp	hot Hungarian paprika
1 1/2 tsp	cayenne pepper
4 tbsp	crushed red pepper
1 tbsp	coarse ground black pepper

1. Combine all ingredients. Store any unused spice blend in an airtight container in a cool, dry place.

Herbes de Provence

Yield: about 1 cup

5 tbsp	dried thyme
5 tbsp	dried marjoram
3 tbsp	dried savory
1 tbsp	dried rosemary
1 tsp	dried sage
1 tsp	dried mint
1 tsp	dried fennel seeds
1 tsp	dried lavender flowers

1. Combine all ingredients. Store any unused spice blend in an airtight container in a cool, dry place. The herbs may be crushed fine with a mortar and pestle before use if desired.

Chef's Notes: Crushed bay leaves are sometimes included in this blend. As with other spice blends in this chapter, amounts of herbs may be adjusted according to personal taste.

Brown Veal Stock

Yield: 1 gallon

8 lb	veal bones, including knuckles and trim
6 qts	cold water
1 lb	Mirepoix (page 404)
6 oz/wt	tomato paste
1 each	Standard Sachet d'Epices (page 405)

1. Rinse the bones and dry them well. Preheat an oiled roasting pan in a 450°F oven. Brown the bones in a roasting pan in the oven.
2. Combine the bones and water in a stockpot. Bring the stock to a boil over low heat. Simmer for about 6 hours, skimming the surface as necessary.
3. Brown the mirepoix and tomato paste; add to the stock in the last hour of simmering. Deglaze the drippings in the roasting pan with water and add to the stock. Add the sachet d'épices.
4. Simmer an additional hour. Strain the stock. Cool and store under refrigeration.

Venison Stock Replace the veal bones with an equal weight of venison bones and lean trim. Include fennel seeds and/or juniper berries in standard sachet d'épices, if desired.

Chicken Stock

Yield: 1 gallon

8 lb	chicken bones, cut into 3-inch lengths
6 qts	cold water
1 lb	Mirepoix (page 404)
1 each	Standard Sachet d'Epices (page 405)

1. Rinse the bones in cool water. Combine the bones and water in a stockpot.
2. Bring the stock to a boil over low heat. Skim the surface, as necessary. Simmer 4 to 5 hours.
3. Add the mirepoix and sachet d'épices in the last hour of simmering. Strain the stock. Cool and store under refrigeration.

White Duck Stock Substitute equal amounts of duck bones for the chicken bones.
Turkey Stock Substitute equal amounts of turkey bones for the chicken bones.
White Beef Stock Substitute equal amounts of beef bones for the chicken bones. Increase the simmering time in step 2 to 6 to 7 hours.

Shellfish Stock

Yield: 1 gallon

10 lb	shellfish shells (lobster, shrimp, or crab)
2 oz/fl	vegetable oil
1 lb	Mirepoix (page 404)
3 to 4 oz/wt	tomato paste
5 qts	cold water
1 each	Standard Sachet d'Epices (page 405)
1 cup	white wine

1. Sauté the shellfish shells in the oil until deep red. Add the mirepoix and continue to sauté another 10 to 15 minutes. Add the tomato paste and sauté briefly.
2. Add the water, seasonings, and wine and simmer 30 minutes. Strain the stock. Cool and store under refrigeration.

Fish Stock Substitute an equal amount of bones and trim from lean white-fleshed fish for the shellfish shells. In step 1, sauté in oil over low heat until the bones become white. Use White Mirepoix. Omit the tomato paste.

Vegetable Stock

Yield: 1 gallon

2 oz/wt	vegetable oil
4 oz/wt	onions, sliced
4 oz/wt	leeks, green and white parts, chopped
2 oz/wt	celery, chopped
2 oz/wt	green cabbage, chopped
2 oz/wt	carrots, chopped
2 oz/wt	turnips, chopped
2 oz/wt	tomatoes, chopped
3 each	garlic cloves, crushed
$4\frac{1}{2}$ qt	cold water
1 each	Standard Sachet d'Epices (page 405), with:
1 tsp	fennel seeds (place in sachet)
3 each	whole cloves (place in sachet)

1. Heat the oil. Add the vegetables and garlic and sweat for about 5 minutes.
2. Add the water and sachet d'épices and simmer for 30 to 40 minutes. Strain the stock. Cool and store under refrigeration.

Glace de Viande

Yield: 4 to 8 ounces (see Chef's Notes)

1 qt	Brown Veal Stock (page 410)

1. Place the stock in a heavy-gauge pot over moderate heat. Bring to a simmer and reduce until volume is halved, then transfer to a smaller pot.
2. Continue to reduce, transferring to successively smaller pots, until very thick and syrupy.

Chef's Notes: The yield will vary depending on cooking time and desired consistency.

Glace de Volaille Substitute Chicken Stock (page 410) for the brown veal stock.

Court Bouillon

Yield: 1 gallon

2 1/2 qts	cold water
2 1/2 qts	white wine
2 tsp	salt (*optional*)
12 oz/wt	carrots, sliced
1 lb	onions, sliced
Pinch	dried thyme leaves
3 each	bay leaves
1 bunch	fresh parsley stems
1/2 oz/wt	black peppercorns

1. Combine all ingredients except the peppercorns.
2. Simmer for 50 minutes.
3. Add the peppercorns and simmer for an additional 10 minutes. Strain the court bouillon before using.

Vinegar Court Bouillon Double the amount of water. Replace all the white wine with 1 cup of vinegar.

Chicken Consommé

Yield: 1 gallon

	Clarification
1 lb	Mirepoix (page 404)
3 lb	lean chicken, ground
10 each	egg whites, beaten
12 oz/wt	tomato concassé
5 qts	Chicken Stock (page 410), cold
1 each	Standard Sachet d'Epices (page 405), plus:
1 each	whole clove (place in sachet)
2 each	allspice berries (place in sachet)
1 tsp	kosher salt
1/2 tsp	ground white pepper

1. Mix the ingredients for the clarification and blend with the stock. Mix well.
2. Bring the mixture to a slow simmer, stirring frequently until raft forms.
3. Add the sachet d'épices and simmer for 45 minutes, or until the appropriate flavor and clarity are achieved. Baste raft occasionally.
4. Strain the consommé; adjust seasoning with salt and white pepper.

Velouté

Yield: 2 quarts

2 1/2 qts	Chicken Stock (page 410)
4 to 8 oz/wt	white blonde roux, as needed
1/2 tsp	salt
1/4 tsp	ground black pepper

1. Bring the stock to a boil.
2. Whip the roux into the stock; work out all the lumps.
3. Simmer for 30 to 40 minutes, skimming the surface as necessary.
4. Season with salt and pepper to taste and then strain the sauce.

Fish Velouté Use Fish Stock (page 411) instead of chicken stock.
Shellfish Velouté Use Shellfish Stock (page 411) instead of chicken stock.
Vegetable Velouté Use Vegetable Stock (page 411) instead of chicken stock.

Pimiento Butter

Yield: 1 pound

12 oz/wt	butter, softened
$3^{1}/_{2}$ oz/wt	pimientos, minced
$^{1}/_{4}$ tsp	garlic, minced
1 tbsp	lemon juice
To taste	salt
To taste	pepper

1. Purée all ingredients and mix well.
2. Wrap tightly and refrigerate until needed.
3. Soften if needed for spreading.

Anchovy Butter

Yield: 1 pound

1 lb	butter, softened
2 to 3 tbsp	lemon juice
1 to 2 oz/wt	anchovy paste
To taste	salt
To taste	ground black pepper
1 tbsp	chopped drained capers

1. Combine all ingredients and mix well.
2. Wrap tightly and refrigerate until needed.
3. Soften if needed for spreading.

Horseradish Butter

Yield: 1 1/4 pounds

1/3 cup	prepared horseradish
1 lb	butter, softened
1 tbsp	prepared mustard
2 tsp	Worcestershire sauce
1 tbsp	sugar
1 tsp	lemon juice

1. Squeeze excess liquid out of the horseradish.
2. Combine all ingredients and mix well.
3. Wrap tightly and refrigerate until needed.
4. Soften if needed for spreading.

Mayonnaise Collée

Yield: 24 fluid ounces

2 cups	Basic Mayonnaise (page 28)
8 oz/fl	Aspic Gelée (page 45), firm gel strength, warmed to 110°
2 tsp	kosher salt
1/4 cup	ground white pepper
to taste	Tabasco sauce

1. Combine mayonnaise with aspic, strain, add seasonings.

Pâté Dough

Yield: 2 pounds

20 oz/wt	bread flour, sifted
1 1/2 oz/wt	powdered milk
1/4 oz/wt	baking powder
1/2 oz/wt	salt
3 1/2 oz/wt	shortening
2 1/2 oz/wt	butter
2 each	eggs
1/2 oz/fl	vinegar
8 to 10 oz/fl	milk, as needed

1. Place all ingredients except the eggs, vinegar, and milk into a food processor and pulse until dough is a fine meal, or mix in a mixer fitted with a dough hook.
2. Add the eggs and vinegar. Pulse for five seconds.
3. Place the dough into a mixer, add 4 to 5 ounces of milk, and knead for 3 to 4 minutes on medium speed, until the dough forms a ball. Check consistency and add more milk if necessary.
4. Remove the dough from the mixer and knead by hand until smooth; square it off. Wrap in plastic wrap and rest for 30 minutes before rolling and cutting to line pâté or barquette molds (pages 231-233 and 318, respectively).

Chef's Notes: The flavor of this dough can be varied by adding ground spices and herbs, lemon zest, or grated cheese. For a different flavor, texture, and appearance, rye or whole wheat flour, or cornmeal, may be used to replace up to one third of the bread flour.

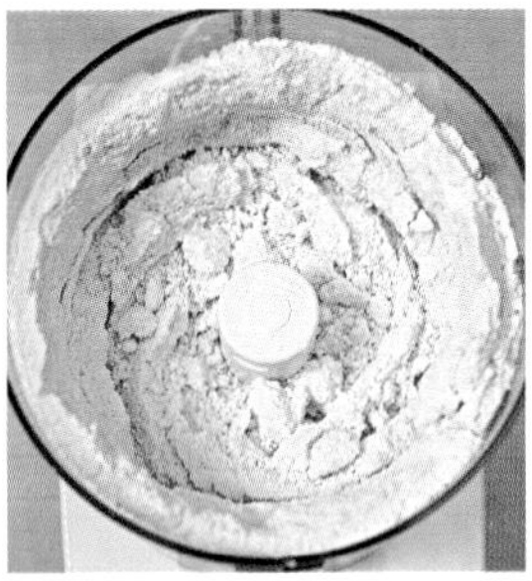

Flour and butter are cut together in a food processor...

or mix in a mixer fitted with a dough hook.

Final kneading done by hand on lightly floured board.

The dough is blocked.

Tomato Cilantro Pâté Dough

1 recipe	Pâté Dough (page 416)
2 tsp	ground coriander
2 tsp	ground cumin
$1\frac{1}{2}$ oz/wt	tomato paste
2 tbsp	chopped cilantro

1. Prepare the pâté dough according to the basic recipe, adding the coriander and cumin in step 1, and the tomato paste and cilantro in step 2.

Saffron Pâté Dough

Large pinch	saffron
5 oz/fl	warm water
1 recipe	Pâté Dough (page 416)
2 tbsp	chopped dill (*optional*)
2 tbsp	chopped chives (*optional*)

1. Infuse the saffron in the water. Replace 5 ounces of the milk with the saffron water in the basic pâté dough recipe. Add the chopped herbs in step 2.

Sweet Potato Pâté Dough

1 recipe	Pâté Dough (page 416)
$\frac{1}{2}$ tsp	ground cinnamon
$\frac{1}{2}$ tsp	ground cardamom
$\frac{1}{2}$ tsp	ground mace
5 oz/wt	sweet potato, baked, boiled, or steamed, and puréed

1. Prepare the pâté dough according to the basic recipe, adding the ground spices in step 1 and the sweet potato in step 2. You may need to reduce the amount of milk called for in the recipe.

Chef's Notes: To make decorative display pieces with the pâté dough, roll the dough into thin sheets using a pasta machine. Here, pâté dough is cut to give the effect of fish netting. Score the dough with a lattice cutter. Gently pull apart the dough, lay it on crumbled foil, and paint with egg wash. The crumbled foil gives additional height and texture to the pâté dough netting. Bake at 325°F for 8 to 10 minutes, until dried and cooked through.

Pâté Dough.

Rolling pasta machine.

Cutting netting.

Baking netting.

Making Decorations for Pâte en Croûte.

Cutting out leaf shapes.

Making veins.

Grape clusters with leaves and tendrils.

Combine ingredients for the dough.

A loose shaggy mass is formed.

Roll dough into rectangle.

Blitz Puff Pastry

Yield: 2 1/2 pounds

1/2 lb	bread flour
1/2 lb	pastry flour
1 lb	cold butter, cut into 1/2-inch cubes
1/4 oz/wt	salt
1 cup	ice water

1. Sift the flours into a bowl or onto a table surface. Coat the butter with flour and make a well in the flour.
2. Dissolve the salt in the water and pour into the well.
3. Combine all ingredients to form a loose, shaggy mass.
4. On a floured surface, roll the dough into a 1/2-inch-thick rectangle. Make a bookfold.
5. Repeat this step 2 or 3 times.
6. Wrap and hold under refrigeration for up to 3 days.
7. Roll out the dough and use as recipe directs.

Chef's Notes: More folds will yield finer and more even layers with less height. Fewer folds yield a lighter product, with irregular layers and more height.

First stage of a bookfold.

Completed bookfold.

Pasta Dough

Yield: 1 1/2 pounds

1 lb	all-purpose *or* bread flour
6 each	eggs
2 tsp	salt
2 oz/fl	water, as needed

1. Combine all ingredients in a large bowl and knead the mixture until it is smooth and elastic.
2. Cover the dough and allow to rest for 1 hour before rolling and shaping.

Spinach Pasta Add 6 ounces of puréed raw spinach. Add additional flour if necessary.
Malfatti Pasta Run the basic pasta dough through a pasta machine to create thin sheets. Cut the pasta into rectangles 1 1/2 by 2 1/2 inches.

Simple Syrup

Yield: 1 quart

1 qt	water
8 oz/wt	sugar
3 each	lemons, juice only
3 each	oranges, juice only

1. Bring the water and sugar to a boil; stir until sugar dissolves; cool.
2. Flavor with lemon and orange juice and refrigerate until needed.

Olive Bread

Yield: 2 loaves (1 pound each)

1 oz/wt	fresh yeast *or* 1 tablespoon dried yeast
1 tsp	sugar
7 oz/fl	tepid water
1 lb	bread flour
1/2 tsp	salt
4 tbsp	virgin olive oil
5 oz/wt	dry-cured olives, pitted and chopped

1. Mix the yeast and sugar with 2 1/2 ounces of the water. Let the yeast develop for 15 minutes in a warm but not hot place.
2. Add the yeast mixture to the flour, salt, 3 tablespoons of the olive oil and the remaining water. Knead 8 to 10 minutes until elastic. Add the olives and mix well.
3. Rub the remaining tablespoon of oil on the dough to prevent a skin from forming. Place in a stainless-steel bowl and cover with a wet towel. Let rise in a warm place until the dough has doubled in volume.
4. When the dough has doubled, divide in half and knead into small loaf shapes. Cover with a wet towel and let the loaves rise for about an hour. Preheat the oven to 475°F.
5. Bake for about 30 minutes or until the loaves sound hollow when tapped on the bottom. Cool on a wire rack. This bread is best eaten the day it is made.

Foccacia

Yield: 3 pounds

Foccacia may be lightly brushed with garlic and olive oil and served on its own, used as the base of an hors d'oeuvre or sandwich (see page 118), or dressed with various additions (see photo).

As needed	cornmeal
2 1/4 cups	water
1/2 oz/wt	compressed yeast
1/4 cup	extra-virgin olive oil
1 3/4 lb	hard wheat flour
1/2 oz/wt	salt
	Garnish Options
As needed	crumbled goat cheese
As needed	olives, pitted and sliced
As needed	pine nuts
As needed	sun-dried tomatoes
As needed	chopped herbs such as basil and oregano

1. Line baking sheets with parchment. Scatter with cornmeal.
2. Combine the water, yeast, and oil until yeast is dissolved. Add the flour and salt. Mix the dough until smooth and elastic. Cover the bowl and allow the dough to ferment for 75 minutes. Punch down and scale the dough at 10 ounces per foccacia. Round off dough. Set dough on prepared sheet pan and proof for 1 hour.
3. Press the balls of dough flat and stretch slightly. Brush with olive oil and add any optional garnish items desired. Pan-proof an additional 30 minutes.
4. Bake in a 425°F oven for approximately 30 minutes.

Grissini Prepare the dough through step 4. Punch down and scale at 1 1/2 ounces. Round off the dough. Set on a sheet pan and proof for 1 hour. Roll the balls into long, thin sticks. Brush with olive oil or egg wash and top with desired seasoning: kosher salt, sesame seeds, or fresh herbs. Pan-proof an additional 15 minutes. Bake in 425°F oven for 10 to 12 minutes.

Roasting Garlic

The flavor of garlic and shallots becomes rich, sweet, and smoky after roasting. Roasted garlic can be found as a component of marinades, glazes, and vinaigrettes, as well as a spread for grilled breads and foccacia.

1. Place the unpeeled head of garlic (or shallot bulbs) in a small pan. Some chefs like to place it on a bed of salt, which holds the heat, roasting the garlic quickly and producing a drier texture in the finished product.
2. Roast at a moderate temperature until the garlic or shallots are quite soft. Any juices that run from the garlic or shallots should be browned. The aroma should be sweet and pleasing, with no hints of harshness or sulfur.

Tomato Concassé

Make only enough tomato concassé to last through a single service period. Once peeled and chopped, tomatoes begin to lose some of their flavor and texture.

1. Cut away the core ends and score skin away using a paring knife.
2. Bring a pot of water to a rolling boil. Drop the tomatoes into the water. After 10 to 35 seconds (depending upon the tomatoes' age and ripeness), remove them with a slotted spoon, skimmer, or spider. Immediately plunge them into very cold or ice water. Pull away the skin.
3. Halve each tomato crosswise at its widest point and gently squeeze out the seeds. (Plum tomatoes are more easily seeded by cutting lengthwise.)
4. Cut the flesh into dice or julienne, as desired.

Roasting Tomatoes

Roasted tomatoes can be made by either halving or slicing ripe tomatoes. While the flavor of roasted tomatoes is deeper and more intense than that of fresh or canned unroasted peppers, it is not so intense as that of sun-dried tomatoes.

1. Core the tomato and cut it into halves or slices.
2. Coat lightly with oil, and add seasonings and aromatics as desired. Salt, pepper, fresh or dried herbs, plain or infused oils, chopped garlic, or shallots are all good choices.
3. Roast the tomatoes until they are browned and have a rich "roasted" aroma.

Roasting Peppers

To roast and peel small quantities, roast the peppers over a flame:

1. Hold the pepper over the flame of a gas burner with tongs or a kitchen fork, or place the pepper on a grill. Turn the pepper and roast it until the surface is evenly charred.
2. Place in a plastic or paper bag or under an inverted bowl to steam the skin loose.
3. When the pepper is cool enough to handle, remove the charred skin, using a paring knife if necessary.

For larger quantities, oven roast the peppers:

1. Halve the peppers and remove stems and seeds. Place cut side down on an oiled sheet pan.
2. Place in a 475°F oven or under a broiler. Roast or broil until evenly charred.
3. Remove from the oven or broiler and cover immediately, using an inverted sheet pan. This will steam the peppers, making the skin easier to remove.
4. Peel, using a paring knife if necessary.

Roasting Corn

To roast corn, dampen the husk and place in a hot (475 to 500°F) oven or over hot coals. Roast or grill for approximately 15 to 20 minutes. The husks should become a deep brown. The corn should be tender (to check for doneness, pull back some of the husk and pierce a kernel). When the corn is cool enough to handle, pull away the corn and the silk. Cut the corn away from the cob with a sharp knife paring knife.

Plumping Dried Fruits and Vegetables

1. Check the dried ingredient and remove any obvious debris or seriously blemished or moldy specimens.
2. Place the ingredient in a bowl or other container and add enough boiling or very hot liquid (water, wine, fruit juices, or broth can all be used) to cover.
3. Let the dried ingredient steep in the hot water for several minutes, until softened and plumped.
4. Pour off the liquid, reserving it if desired for use in another preparation. If necessary, the liquid can be strained through a coffee filter or cheesecloth to remove any debris.

Toasting Nuts, Seeds, and Spices

Toasting nuts, seeds, and spices improves their flavor, as long as they are not allowed to scorch.

To toast small quantities, use a dry skillet (cast iron is an excellent choice, but other materials will also work well).

1. Heat the skillet over direct heat and add the nuts, seeds, or spices.
2. Toss or stir frequently, stopping just as a good color and aroma are achieved.
3. Pour the nuts, seeds, or spices out into a cool container and spread into a thin layer to stop any further browning.

Large quantities can be toasted in a moderate oven.

1. Spread out the nuts, seeds, or spices on a dry sheet pan and toast just until a pleasant aroma is apparent. The oils in nuts, seeds, and spices can scorch quickly so be sure to check frequently.

2. Stir them often to encourage even browning.

3. Be sure to transfer nuts and spices toasted in the oven to a cool container also, so that they don't become scorched from residual heat in the pan.

Dried chiles may be toasted in the same manner, in a dry skillet or in the oven. They may also be passed repeatedly through a flame until toasted and softened. The pulp and seeds are then scraped from the skin, or the whole chile may be used, according to individual recipes.

Rendering Fats

Occasionally the fat from ducks, geese, or pork may be required for such dishes as confit or rillettes.

1. Cube the fat, if necessary.

2. Place the fat in a sauteuse. Add about 1/2 inch of water to the uncooked fats if there are no drippings present.

3. Cook over low heat until the water evaporates and the fat is released. (This is the actual clarifying process.)

4. Remove the cracklings, if any, with a slotted spoon (they may be reserved for garnish).

5. Store the rendered fat under refrigeration for up to several weeks.

Cooked Lobster

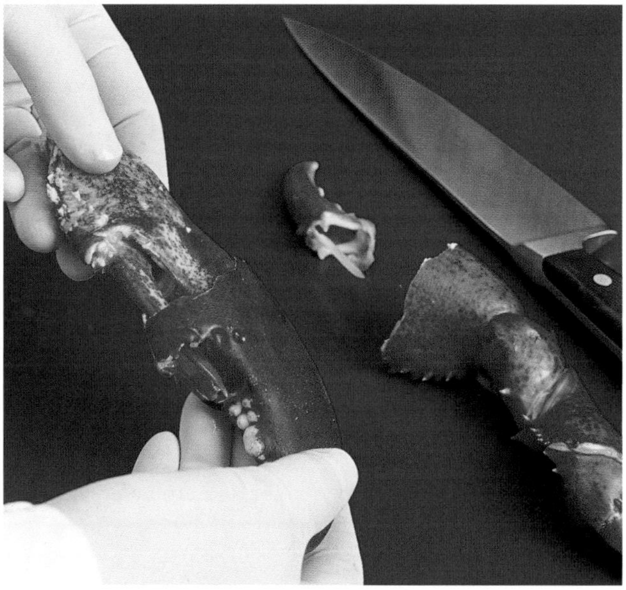

To remove the meat from the shell, pull away the tail. Split the shell on the underside with kitchen shears and pull out the tail meat in one piece. To remove the meat from the claw, crack the claw in half with the spine of a knife. Pull out the meat carefully, in order to keep the meat intact. Cut the knuckles from end to end and remove nuggets of meat.

Parmesan Crisp

To prepare a parmesan crisp, shred Parmesan cheese. Preheat an oven to 350°F and line a sheet pan with parchment paper. If desired, trace a circle or other shape on the paper. Allow room between the tracing to permit some spread (about 1/2 inch). Scatter the cheese in an even layer (enough to fill cover the paper, but not too thick). Bake the cheese for 10 minutes, or until cheese is melted and bubbly and looks like lace. Remove the sheet pan from the oven and allow the cheese to cool for a few minutes. The cheese crisp can be rolled or draped inside bowls or over dowels or cups to create containers or fans, as desired. This must be done while the cheese is very warm. Cheese crisps will keep for several days, stored in a parchment lined air-tight container.

Bread Crumbs

Bread crumbs may be "dry" or "fresh." Fresh bread crumbs (*mie de pain*) are prepared by grating or processing a finely textured bread, such as 1- or 2-day-old hard rolls. Dry bread crumbs can be prepared from slightly stale bread that has been additionally dried or toasted in a warm oven.

Standard Breading Procedure

For the best possible results, breading needs a little time to firm up before it is pan fried. If you bread an item and then immediately put it into hot oil, there is a good chance that the breading will fall away. Not only will this have a negative impact on the dish's finished texture, it will also make the cooking oil break down quickly, and subsequent batches cooked in the same oil will blacken without cooking properly.

1. Dry the main item well, then hold it in one hand (left hand if you are right-handed, and right hand if you are left-handed) and dip it in the flour. Shake off any excess flour, and transfer the food to the container of egg wash.

2. Switch hands, pick up the food, and turn it if necessary to coat it on all sides. Transfer it to the container of bread crumbs. Use your dry hand to pack bread crumbs evenly around the food. Shake off any excess, then transfer the food to a holding tray.

3. Let the food rest under refrigeration for about 1 hour or longer before continuing with pan frying.

4. Discard any unused flour, egg wash, and bread crumbs.

Croutons

Yield: 1 pound (450 grams)

1 lb	white bread
4 ounces	butter, melted or olive oil, as needed
1 tsp	salt, to taste
1/2 tsp	pepper (optional), to taste

1. Remove the crust from the bread if desired. Slice and cube the bread into desired size (from small cubes to garnish soups served in cups to large slices to garnish salads). If the bread is very fresh, let the bread cubes dry out in the oven for 5 minutes before continuing.
2. Toss the bread, butter or oil, and seasonings together on a baking sheet or in a hotel pan.
3. Bake for 8 to 10 minutes until lightly golden.

Chef's Notes: Croutons can be prepared in advance and stored in an airtight container for several days. For smaller batches, the croutons can be cooked on top of the stove in a skillet or sute pan. Although quicker, deep fat frying is not recomended for croutons. They absorb too much oil and become greasy.

Garlic-Flavored Croutons Add 2 teaspoons very finely minced garlic (garlic paste) to the oil or butter before tossing with the bread cubes.
Cheese Croutons After the bread cubes have been tossed with the butter, toss generously with grated Parmasan, Romano, or other hard grating cheese to taste.
Herb-Flavored Croutons Add chopped fresh or dried herbs (such as oregano or rosemary) to the bread cubes along with the butter.

Cleaning a Soft-Shelled Crab

1. Peel back the pointed shell and scrape away the gill filament on each side.
2. Cut off the head and carefully squeeze out the green bubble behind the eyes.
3. Bend back the apron and twist to remove it and the intestinal vein at the same time.

Glossary

A

Acid: A substance having a sour or sharp flavor. A substance's degree of acidity is measured on the pH scale; acids have a pH of less than 7. Most foods are somewhat acidic. Foods generally referred to as "acids" include citrus juice, vinegar, and wine. *See also* Alkali.

Aerobic bacteria: Bacteria that require the presence of oxygen to function.

Aioli (Fr.): Garlic mayonnaise, often based on olive oils (Italian, *allioli,* Spanish, *aliolio*).

Air drying: Exposing meats and sausages to proper temperature and humidity conditions to change both flavor and texture for consumption or further processing. Times and temperatures will vary depending upon the type of meat or sausage.

Albumen: The white of an egg; also the major protein in egg whites (also spelled *albumin*); used in dry form in some cold food preparations.

Alkali: A substance that tests at higher than 7 on the pH scale. Alkalis are sometimes described as having a slightly soapy flavor. Olives and baking soda are some of the few alkaline foods. *See also* Acid.

Allumette: Vegetables, potatoes, or other items cut into pieces the size and shape of matchsticks; $1/8$ inch × $1/8$ inch × 1 to 2 inches is the standard.

Anaerobic bacteria: Bacteria that do not require oxygen to function.

Andouille: A spicy pork sausage that is French in origin, but now more often associated with Cajun cooking. There are hundreds of variations of this regional specialty.

Antipasto: Italian for "before the pasta." Typically a platter of cold hors d'oeuvre that includes meats, olives, cheese, and vegetables.

AP/as purchased weight: The weight of an item before trimming or other preparation (as opposed to edible portion weight, or EP).

Appareil: A prepared mixture of ingredients used alone or as an ingredient in another base preparation, such as duchesse potatoes or duxelle.

Appetizer: One or more of the initial courses in a meal. These may be hot or cold, plated or served as finger food. They should stimulate the appetite and should go well with the remaining meal.

Aromatics: Plant ingredients, such as herbs and spices, used to enhance the flavor and fragrance of food.

Arrowroot: A powdered starch made from cassava, a tropical root. Used primarily as a thickener. Remains clear when cooked.

Aspic: A clear jelly made from clarified stock (or occasionally from fruit or vegetable juices) thickened with gelatin. Used to coat foods, or cubed and used as a garnish.

B

Bacteria: Microscopic organisms. Some have beneficial properties, others can cause food-borne illnesses when contaminated foods are ingested.

Bain-marie: A water bath used to cook foods gently by surrounding the cooking vessel with simmering water. Also, a set of nesting pots with single, long handles used as a double boiler. Also, round steam table inserts.

Barbecue: A variation of a roasting method involving grilling or slow smoke-roasting food over a wood or charcoal fire. Usually some sort of rub, marinade, or sauce is brushed on the item during cooking.

Bard: To cover an item with thin slices or sheets or strips of fat, such as bacon or fatback, to baste it during roasting. The fat is usually tied on with butcher's twine.

Barquette: A boat-shaped tart or tartlet, which may have a sweet or savory filling.

Baste: To moisten food during cooking with pan drippings, sauce, or other liquid. Basting prevents food from drying out, improves color, and adds flavor.

Baton/Batonnet (Fr.): Literally, "stick" or "small stick." Items cut into pieces somewhat larger than allumette or julienne; 1/4 inch × 1/4 inch × 2 to 2 1/2 inches is the standard.

Béchamel: A white sauce made of milk thickened with white or pale roux and flavored with onion. It is one of the grand sauces.

Binder: An ingredient or appareil used to thicken a sauce or hold together a mixture of ingredients.

Blanch: To cook an item briefly in boiling water or hot fat before finishing or storing it. This will set the color and can make the skin easier to remove.

Blood sausage: Also called black pudding or blood pudding, a sausage where the main ingredient is liquid blood.

Bloom: To soften gelatin in lukewarm liquid before use. Also to allow casing on smoked sausage to darken at room temperature after smoking.

Boil: A cooking method in which items are immersed in liquid at or above the boiling point of water (212°F/100°C).

Botulism: A food-borne illness caused by toxins produced by the anaerobic bacterium *Clostridium botulinum.*

Bouchée: A small puff pastry shell that may be filled with meats, cheese, seafood, or even fruit. Served as an hors d'oeuvre or as a garnish on a larger entrée.

Boucher (Fr.): Butcher.

Bouillon (Fr.): Broth.

Bouquet garni: A small bundle of herbs tied with string, used to flavor stocks, braises, and other preparations. Usually contains bay leaf, parsley, thyme, and possibly other aromatics, such as leek and celery stalk.

Braise: A cooking method in which the main item, usually a tough cut of meat, is seared in fat, then simmered in stock or another liquid in a covered vessel, slowly tenderizing it by breaking down collagen.

Brine: A solution of salt, water, and seasonings used to flavor and preserve foods.

Brisket: A cut of beef from the lower forequarter, best suited for long-cooking preparations like braising. Corned beef is cured beef brisket.

Broil: A cooking method in which items are cooked by a radiant heat source placed above the food.

Brunoise (Fr.): Small dice; 1/8 inch square is the standard. For a brunoise cut, items are first cut in julienne, then cut crosswise. For a fine brunoise, 1/16 inch square, cut items first into fine julienne.

Bubble knot: Also called a triple knot, used to tie beef round, middle, and bung casings. A piece of casing is caught between the two first knots, and a third knot is used to lock the previous knots in place. A length of string is often left at the end for hanging.

Buffet: Historically a traditional Swedish mode of dining where people serve themselves from a table or sideboard. Buffet foods commonly include cold meat and cheese platters, pickled fish, salads, sandwiches, and desserts.

Bulk sausage: Sausage that is not contained in a casing. Sausages commonly found in bulk include breakfast sausage and Italian sausages meant to be used in pizzas or other dishes. Generally only fresh sausage is packaged bulk.

(Beef) Bung cap: Beef appendix, typically used for larger sausages such as bologna and mortadella. Generally 2 to $2^{1}/_{2}$ feet long with a diameter of about 4-6 inches, a beef bung can hold from 10 to 20 pounds of sausage.

Butcher: A chef or purveyor responsible for butchering meats, poultry, and occasionally fish. In the brigade system, the butcher may also be responsible for breading meat and fish items and other mise en place operations involving meat.

Butterfly: To cut an item (usually meat or seafood) and open out the edges like a book or the wings of a butterfly, to promote attractive appearance and even cooking.

C

Canapé: An hors d'oeuvre consisting of a small piece of bread or toast, often cut in a decorative shape, garnished with a savory spread or topping.

Caramelization: The process of browning sugar in the presence of heat. The temperature range in which sugar begins to caramelizes is approximately 320°F to 360°F (160° to 182°C).

Carry-over cooking: Heat retained in cooked foods that allows them to continue cooking even after removal from the cooking medium; especially important to roasted foods. The internal temperature rises, a function of cooling as the meat or item seeks equilibrium of temperature.

Casing: A synthetic or natural membrane (usually pig, beef, or sheep intestines) used to enclose sausage forcemeat.

Cassoulet: A stew of beans baked with pork or other meats, duck or goose confit, and seasonings.

Caul fat: A fatty membrane from a pig or sheep that lines the stomach and resembles fine netting; used to bard roasts and pâtés and to encase sausage forcemeat.

Cellulose: A complex carbohydrate; the main structural component of plant cells.

Charcuterie (Fr.): The preparation of pork and other meat items, such as hams, terrines, sausages, pâtés, and other forcemeats that are usually preserved in some manner, such as smoking, brining, and curing.

Chaud-froid (Fr.): Literally, "hot-cold." A sauce that is prepared hot but served cold as part of a buffet display, usually as a decorative coating for meats, poultry, or seafood; classically made from béchamel, cream, or aspic.

Cheesecloth: A light, fine mesh gauze cloth used for straining liquids and making sachets and many other kitchen operations including cheese making.

Chiffonade: Leafy vegetables or herbs cut into fine shreds; often used as a garnish.

Chile: The fruit of certain types of capsicum peppers (not related to black pepper), used fresh or dry as a seasoning. Chiles come in many types (for example, jalapeño, serrano, poblano) and varying degrees of spiciness and heat, measured in Scoville units.

Chili powder: Dried, ground, or crushed chiles, often including other ground spices and herbs.

Chinoise: A conical sieve made from fine metal mesh screen, used for straining and puréeing foods.

Chipolata: A small, spicy sausage usually made from pork or veal and stuffed into a sheep casing.

Chitterlings: Hog middle intestines.

Chop: To cut into pieces of roughly the same size. Also, a small cut of meat including part of the rib.

Choucroute (Fr.): Sauerkraut; preserved cabbage with a sour flavor. Choucroute garni is sauerkraut garnished with various meats such as cured meats and sausages.

Clarification: The process of removing solid impurities from a liquid (such as butter or stock). Also, a mixture of ground meat, egg whites, mirepoix, tomato purée, herbs, and spices used to clarify stock for consommé.

Clarified butter: Butter from which the milk solids and water have been removed, leaving pure butterfat. Has a higher smoking point than whole butter but less butter flavor. Also known as *ghee*.

Coagulation: The curdling or clumping of protein usually due to the application of heat or acid.

Coarse chop: To cut into pieces of roughly the same size; used for items such as mirepoix, where appearance is not important.

Cold smoking: Used to give smoked flavor to products without cooking them.

Collagen: A fibrous protein found in the connective tissue of animals, used to make sausage casings as well as glue and gelatin. Breaks down into gelatin when cooked in a moist environment for an extended period or time.

Collagen casing: Casings made from collagen that is usually obtained from animal hides. Collagen casings are easy to use and store and have the advantage of being uniform and consistent.

Compote: A dish of fruit—fresh or dried—cooked in syrup flavored with spices or liqueur.

Compound butter: Whole butter combined with herbs or other seasonings and usually used to sauce grilled or broiled items, vegetables, pastas, or used as a spread for sandwiches and canapés.

Concassé/concasser (Fr.): To pound or chop coarsely. Usually refers to tomatoes that have been peeled, seeded, and chopped.

Condiment: An aromatic mixture, such as pickles, chutney, and some sauces and relishes, that accompanies food (usually kept on the table throughout service).

Confit (Fr.): Preserved meat (usually goose, duck, or pork) cooked and preserved in its own fat.

Confiture (Fr.): Referring to jam or preserves.

Corned beef: Beef brisket preserved with salt and spices. The term "corned" refers to the chunks of salt spread over the brisket during the corning process.

Cornichon (Fr.): A small, sour, pickled cucumber.

Cornstarch: A fine, white powder milled from dried corn; used primarily as a thickener for sauce and occasionally as an ingredient in batters. Viscous when hot, gelatinizes when cold.

Coulis: A thick purée, usually of vegetables or fruit. (Traditionally meat, fish, or shellfish purée; meat jus; or certain thick soups.)

Country-style: A forcemeat that is coarse in texture, usually made from pork, pork fat, liver, and various garnishes.

Court bouillon (Fr.): Literally, "short broth." An aromatic vegetable broth that usually includes an acidic ingredient, such as wine or vinegar; most commonly used for poaching fish.

Crème fraîche (Fr.): Heavy cream cultured to give it a thick consistency and a slightly tangy flavor; used in hot preparations since it is less likely to curdle when heated than sour cream or yogurt.

Cross-contamination: The transference of disease-causing elements from one source to another through physical contact.

Crouton (Fr.): A bread or pastry garnish, usually toasted or sautéed until crisp.

Croustade: A small baked or fried edible container for meat, chicken, or other mixtures, usually pastry but may be made from potatoes or pasta.

Crudité: Usually raw vegetables but sometimes fruit, served as an appetizer or hors d'oeuvre. Some vegetables may be blanched to improve taste and appearance.

Cuisson (Fr.): Poaching liquid, including stock, fumet, court bouillon, or other liquid, which may be reduced and used as a base for the poached item's sauce.

Cure: To preserve a food by salting. Also, the ingredients used to cure an item.

Curing salt: A mixture of 94 percent table salt (sodium chloride) and 6 percent sodium nitrite used to preserve meats. Also known as tinted curing mixture, or TCM. Curing salt is distinguished by its pink color.

Curry: A mixture of spices used primarily in Indian cuisine; may include turmeric, coriander, cumin, cayenne or other chiles, cardamom, cinnamon, clove, fennel, fenugreek, ginger, and garlic. Also, a dish seasoned with curry.

D

Deglaze/Déglacer: To use a liquid, such as wine, water, or stock, to dissolve food particles and/or caramelized drippings left in a pan after roasting or sautéing.

Degrease/Dégraisser: To skim the fat off the surface of a liquid, such as a stock or sauce, or to pour off excess fat from a sauté pan before deglazing.

Demi-glace (Fr.): Literally, "half-glaze." A mixture of equal proportions of brown stock and brown sauce that has been reduced by half. One of the grand sauces.

Dice: To cut ingredients into small cubes (1/8 inch for small or fine, 1/4 inch for medium, 3/4 inch for large is standard).

Drawn: A whole fish that has been scaled and gutted but still has its head, fins, and tail.

Dressed: Prepared for cooking or service; a dressed fish is gutted and scaled, and its head, tail, and fins are removed (same as pan-dressed). Dressed poultry is plucked, drawn, singed, trimmed, and trussed. Also, coated with dressing, as in a salad.

Drum sieve: A sieve consisting of a screen stretched across a shallow cylinder of wood or aluminum. Also known as a *tamis*.

Dry cure: A combination of salts and spices used usually before smoking to process meats and forcemeats.

Dumpling: Any of a number of small soft dough or batter items that are steamed, poached, or simmered (possibly on top of a stew); may be filled or plain.

Duxelles: An appareil of finely chopped mushrooms and shallots sautéed gently in butter.

E

Egg wash: A mixture of beaten eggs (whole eggs, yolks, or whites) and a liquid, usually milk or water, used to coat baked goods before or during baking to give them a sheen or to enhance browning.

Emincer (Fr.): To cut an item, usually meat, into very thin slices.

Emulsion: A mixture of two or more liquids, one of which is a fat or oil and the other of which is water-based, so that tiny globules of one are suspended in the other. This may involve the use of stabilizers, such as egg or mustard. Emulsions may be temporary, permanent, or semi-permanent.

En croûte (Fr.): Encased in a bread or pastry crust.

EP/Edible portion: The weight of an item after trimming and preparation (as opposed to the purchased weight, or AP).

F

Facultative bacteria: Bacteria that can survive both with and without oxygen.

Farce (Fr.): Forcemeat or stuffing (*farci* means "stuffed").

Fatback: Pork fat from the back of the pig, used primarily for barding.

Fat: One of the basic nutrients used by the body to provide energy. Fats also provide flavor in food and give a feeling of fullness.

Fermentation: The breakdown of carbohydrates into carbon dioxide gas and alcohol, usually through the action of yeast on sugar.

Fermento: A commonly used brand of dairy-based fermentation product for semi-dry fermented sausages, used to lower pH and give a tangy flavor.

Fillet/Filet: A boneless cut of meat, fish, or poultry.

Fines herbes: A mixture of fresh herbs, usually parsley, chervil, tarragon, and chives.

Foie gras: The fattened liver of a force-fed duck or goose.

Food-borne illness: An illness in humans caused by the consumption of an adulterated food product. In order for a food-borne illness outbreak to be considered official, it must involve two or more people who have eaten the same food and it must be confirmed by health officials.

Food mill: A type of strainer with a crank-operated, curved blade; used to purée soft foods.

Food processor: A machine with interchangeable blades and disks and a removable bowl and lid separate from the motor housing. It can be used for a variety of tasks, including chopping, grinding, puréeing, emulsifying, kneading, slicing, shredding, and cutting julienne.

Forcemeat: A mixture of chopped or ground meat or seafood and other ingredients used for pâté, sausages, and other preparations.

Fumet (Fr.): A type of stock in which the main flavoring ingredient is smothered with wine and aromatics; fish fumet is the most common type.

G

Galantine: Boned meat (usually poultry) that is stuffed into its own skin, rolled, poached, and served cold, usually in aspic.

Garde manger (Fr.): Cold kitchen chef or station; the position responsible for cold food preparations, including salads, cold appetizers, pâtés, and more.

Garnish: An edible decoration or accompaniment to a dish.

Gelatin: A protein-based substance found in animal bones and connective tissue. When dissolved in hot liquid and then cooled, it can be used as a thickener and stabilizer.

Gelatinization: A phase in the process of thickening a liquid with starch in which starch molecules swell to form a network that traps water molecules.

Gherkin: A small pickled cucumber.

Giblets: Organs and other trim from poultry, including the liver, heart, gizzard, and neck.

Glace (Fr.): Reduced stock; ice cream; icing.

Glaze: To give an item a shiny surface by brushing it with sauce, aspic, icing, or another appareil. For meat, to coat with sauce and then brown in an oven or salamander.

Gratiné (Fr.): Browned in an oven or under a salamander (*au gratin, gratin de*). Gratin can also refer to a forcemeat in which some portion of the dominant meat is seared and cooled before grinding.

Gravlax: Raw salmon cured with salt, sugar, and fresh dill. A regional dish of Scandinavian origin.

Grill: A technique in which foods are cooked by a radiant heat source placed below the food. Also, the piece of equipment on which grilling is done. Grills may be fueled by gas, electricity, charcoal, or wood.

Grill pan: An iron skillet with ridges that is used on the stove top to simulate grilling.

Grinder: A machine used to grind meat, ranging from small hand-operated models to large capacity motor driven models. Meat or other foods are fed through a hopper into the grinder where the worm or auger pushes them into a blade. The blade cuts and forces the item through different-size grinder plates. Care should be taken to keep the machine as clean as possible to lessen the chances of cross contamination when using.

Grinder plates: Used to determine the texture of the ground meat, plates come in varying sizes, from as small as 1/8 inch for fine-textured ground meat, to as large as 3/4 inch, used mostly to create garnishes for emulsion sausages.

Griswold: Brand name for a pot, similar to a rondeau, made of cast iron; may have a single short handle rather than the usual loop handles.

Grosse pièce (Fr.): Literally, "large piece." The main part of a pâté or terrine that is left unsliced and serves as a focal point for a platter or other display.

Gumbo: A Creole soup-stew thickened with filé or okra.

H

Haricot (Fr.): Bean. *Haricots verts* are thin green beans.

Head cheese: A jellied meat product typically made from diced boiled pork head meat held together by the natural gelatin contained in the reduced stock left over from boiling the head. Garnished with pickles, pimientos, and parsley and flavored with vinegar.

Hock: The lowest part of an animal's leg, could be considered the ankle, usually for pork (i.e., ham hock).

Hog casing: Casings are made from the small and middle hog intestine (as well as the beef bung). Used for countless different sausages, hog casings range in diameter size from 32 to 35 mm (used for bratwurst and Italian sausage) to slightly larger (38 to 42 mm; used for Polish sausage and pepperoni). The type of hog casing used will depend on the intended application.

Hors d'oeuvre (Fr.): Literally, "outside the work." An appetizer.

Hot smoking: Used when a fully cooked smoked item is desired. Both cured and uncured items can be hot smoked. Smoking temperature and time will depend on the product.

Hygiene: Conditions and practices followed to maintain health, including sanitation and personal cleanliness.

I

Infusion: Steeping an aromatic or other item in liquid to extract its flavor. Also, the liquid resulting from this process.

Instant-read thermometer: A thermometer used to measure the internal temperature of foods. The stem is inserted in the food, producing an instant temperature readout.

J

Julienne: Vegetables, potatoes, or other items cut into thin strips; 1/8 × 1/8 inch × 1 to 2 inches is standard. Fine julienne is 1/16 × 1/16 × 1 to 2 inches

Jus (Fr.): Juice. *Jus de viande* is meat juice. Meat served *au jus* is served with its own juice.

Jus lié (Fr.): Meat juice thickened lightly with arrowroot or cornstarch.

K

Kosher: Prepared in accordance with Jewish dietary laws.

Kosher salt: Pure, refined rock salt often preferred for pickling because it does not contain magnesium carbonate and thus it does not cloud brine solutions. Also used to kosher items. (Also known as coarse salt or pickling salt.)

L

Lard: Rendered pork fat used for pastry and frying. Also the process of inserting strips of fat or seasonings into meat before roasting or braising to add flavor and succulence.

Lardon (Fr.): A strip of pork fat, used for larding; may be seasoned.

Liaison: A mixture of egg yolks and cream used to thicken and enrich sauces. Also, loosely applied to any appareil used as a thickener.

Links: Particular segments of sausage created when a filled casing is twisted or tied off at intervals.

Liquid smoke: Distilled and bottled smoke that can be used in place of actual smoking to provide a smoked flavor.

Looped sausage: Also known as ring-tied sausages; kielbasi is an example of these longer sausages. Also refers to sausage made in beef round casings.

M

Maillard reaction: A complex browning reaction that results in the particular flavor and color of foods that do not contain much sugar, including roasted meats. The reaction, which involves carbohydrates and amino acids, is named after the French scientist who first discovered it. There are low-temperature and high-temperature Maillard reactions; high temperature starts at 310°F.

Mandoline: A slicing device of stainless steel with carbon-steel blades. The blades may be adjusted to cut items into various cuts and thickneses.

Marbling: The intramuscular fat found in meat that makes the meat tender and juicy when cooked.

Marinade: An appareil used before cooking to flavor and moisten foods; may be liquid or dry. Liquid marinades are usually based on an acidic ingredient, such as wine or vinegar; dry marinades are usually salt- or spice-based.

Mayonnaise: A cold emulsion sauce made of oil, egg yolks, vinegar, mustard, and seasonings.

Medallion (Fr.): A small, round scallop-shaped cut of meat.

Mesophilic: A term used to describe bacteria that thrive within the middle-range temperatures—between 60°F and 100°F (16°C to 43°C).

Mie de pain (Fr.): The soft part of bread (not the crust) used to make fresh white bread crumbs.

Mince: To chop into very small pieces.

Mirepoix: A combination of chopped aromatic vegetables—usually two parts onion, one part carrot, and one part celery—used to flavor stocks, soups, braises, and stews.

Mise en place (Fr.): Literally, "put in place." The preparation and assembly of ingredients, pans, utensils, and plates or serving pieces needed for a particular dish or service period.

Molasses: The dark brown, sweet syrup that is a by-product of sugar cane refining.

Mousse (Fr.): A dish made with beaten egg whites and/or whipped cream folded into a flavored base appareil; may be sweet or savory, and should be foamy or frothy consistency. Can be made with cooked items, bound with gelatin, and served cold.

Mousseline (Fr.): A very light forcemeat based on white meats or seafood lightened with cream and eggs.

N

Napper/Nappé (Fr.): To coat with sauce. Also, thickened.

New potato: A small, waxy potato that is usually prepared by boiling or steaming and is often eaten with its skin. Refers to "new" harvest; not always small but with very thin skin.

O

Offal: Variety meats, including organs (brains, heart, kidneys, lights or lungs, sweetbreads, tripe, tongue), head meat, tail, and feet.

Oignon piqué (Fr.): Literally, "pricked onion." A whole, peeled onion to which a bay leaf is attached, using a whole clove as a tack; used to flavor béchamel sauce and some soups.

Organ meat: Meat from an organ, rather than the muscle tissue of an animal.

P

Panada: An appareil based on starch (such as flour or crumbs), moistened with a liquid; used as a binder.

Parchment: Heat-resistant paper used in cooking for such preparations as lining baking pans, cooking items en papillote, constructing pastry cones, and covering items during shallow poaching.

Parcook: To partially cook an item before storing or finishing by another method; may be the same as blanching.

Pellicle: A sticky "skin" that forms on the outside of produce, salmon, sausage, or meats through air drying and helps smoke particles adhere to the food, resulting in better, more evenly smoked product.

Pâte à choux (Fr.): Cream puff paste, made by boiling a mixture of water, butter, and flour, then beating in whole eggs. (Also known as choux paste.)

Pâte brisée (Fr.): Short (rich) pastry for pie crusts.

Pâte (Fr.): Pastry or noodle dough.

Pâté (Fr.): A rich forcemeat of meat, game, poultry, seafood, and/or vegetables, baked in pastry or in a mold or dish.

Pâte en croûte: Pâté baked in a pastry crust.

Pâté de campagne: Country-style pâté, with a coarse texture.

Paysanne/fermier cut: A knife cut in which ingredients are cut into flat, square pieces; 1/2 inch by 1/2 inch by 1/8 inch is standard.

Pesto (It.): A thick, puréed mixture of an herb, traditionally basil, and oil used as a sauce for pasta and other foods and as a garnish for soup. Pesto may also contain grated cheese, nuts or seeds, and other seasonings.

pH scale: A scale with values from 0 to 14 representing degree of acidity. A measurement of 7 is neutral, 0 is most acidic, and 14 is most alkaline. Chemically, pH measures the concentration/activity of the element hydrogen.

Phyllo dough: Flour-and-water dough rolled into very thin sheets; layered with butter and/or crumbs to make pastries. (Also known as filo.)

Pickling spice: A mixture of herbs and spices used to season pickles; often includes dill seed, coriander seed, cinnamon stick, peppercorns, bay leaves, and others.

Pilaf: A technique for cooking grains in which the grain is sautéed briefly in butter, then simmered in stock or water with various seasonings. (Also known as pilau, pilaw, pullao, and pilav.)

Pincé (Fr.): To caramelize an item by sautéing; usually refers to a tomato product.

Poach: A method in which items are cooked gently in liquid at 160°F to 180°F.

Proscuitto: A dry-cured ham. True proscuitto comes from Parma, Italy, although variations can be found throughout the world.

Purée: To process food (by mashing, straining, or chopping very fine) in order to make it into a smooth paste. Also, a product produced using this technique.

Q

Quenelle (Fr.): A light, poached dumpling based on a forcemeat (usually chicken, veal, seafood, or game) bound with eggs that is typically shaped into an oval.

R

Ramekin: A small, oven-proof dish, usually ceramic. (Also, in French, *ramequin.*)

Reduce: To decrease the volume of a liquid by simmering or boiling; used to provide a thicker consistency and/or concentrated flavors and color.

Reduction: The product that results when a liquid is reduced.

Refresh: To plunge an item into, or run under, cold water after blanching to prevent further cooking. Also referred to as shocking, boiling, or par-cooking.

Render: To melt fat and clarify the drippings for use in sautéing or pan frying.

Rennet: An enzyme used in cheese making to turn milk into cheese; usually taken from the stomach lining of a calf or reproduced chemically in a laboratory.

Roast: A dry-heat cooking method in which items are cooked in an oven or on a spit over a fire.

Roe: Fish or shellfish eggs.

Roulade (Fr.): A slice of meat or fish rolled around a stuffing. Also, filled and rolled sponge cake.

S

Sachet d'épices (Fr.): Literally, "bag of spices." Aromatic ingredients, encased in cheesecloth, that are used to flavor stocks and other liquids. A standard sachet contains parsley stems, cracked peppercorns, dried thyme, and a bay leaf.

Salé (Fr.): Salted or pickled.

Salt cod: Cod fish that has been salted and dried to preserve it. Also referred to as baccalà.

Saltpeter: Potassium nitrate. Formerly used to preserve meat (a component of curing salt); it gives certain cured meats their characteristic pink color. Not used commercially since 1975 because its residual amounts are not consistent.

Sanitation: The practice of preparation and distribution of food in a clean environment by healthy food workers.

Sanitize: To kill pathogenic organisms by chemicals and/or moist heat.

Sauté: A cooking method in which naturally tender items are cooked quickly in a small amount of fat in a pan on the range top.

Sauteuse: A shallow skillet with sloping sides and a single, long handle; used for sautéing. Often referred to as a sauté pan.

Savory: Not sweet. Also, the name of a course (savory) served after dessert and before port in traditional British meals. Also, a family of herbs (including summer and winter savory).

Scald: To heat a liquid, usually milk or cream, to just below the boiling point. May also refer to blanching fruits and vegetables.

Score: To cut the surface of an item at regular intervals to allow it to cook or cure evenly.

Sear: To brown the surface of food in fat over high heat before finishing by another method (for example, braising) to add flavor and color.

Sea salt: Salt produced by evaporating sea water. Available as refined or unrefined, crystallized or ground. (Also, *sel gris,* French for "gray salt.")

Shallow poach: A method in which items are cooked gently in a shallow covered pan of simmering liquid. The liquid can then be reduced and used as the basis of a sauce.

Sieve: A container made of a perforated material, such as wire mesh, used to drain, rice, or purée foods. Also known as tamis.

Silverskin: The tough, connective tissue that surrounds certain muscles.

Simmer: To maintain the temperature of a liquid just below boiling. Also, a cooking method in which items are cooked in simmering liquid.

Slurry: Starch (flour, cornstarch, or arrowroot) dispersed in cold liquid to prevent it from forming lumps when added to hot liquid as a thickener.

Smearing: A fault in sausages; if sausage is processed at too high a temperature, fat will soften and become smeared throughout the sausage. Smeared fat has a tendency to leak out of the sausage and leave it dry.

Smoke roasting: Roasting over wood or chips in a oven to add a smoky flavor. A method for roasting foods in which items are placed on a rack in a pan containing wood chips that smolder and emit smoke when the pan is placed on the range top or in the oven.

Smoking: Any of several methods for preserving and flavoring foods by exposing them to smoke. Methods include cold smoking (in which smoked items are not fully cooked), hot smoking (in which the items are cooked), and smoke roasting.

Smoking point: The temperature at which a fat begins to smoke when heated.

Smorgasbord: A classic Swedish manner of dining, where guests serve themselves from a table laden with food; one of the earliest forms of buffets.

Sodium: An alkaline metal element necessary in small quantities for human nutrition; one of the components of most salts used in cooking.

Sodium nitrate: Used in curing meat products that are not going to be heated by either cooking, smoking, or canning.

Sodium nitrite: Used in curing meat products that are going to be heated by either cooking, smoking, or canning.

Stabilizer: An ingredient (usually a protein or plant product) that is added to an emulsion to prevent it from separating (for example, egg yolk, cream, or mustard). Also, an ingredient, such as gelatin, that is used in various desserts to prevent them from separating (for example, Bavarian creams).

Standard breading procedure: The procedure in which items are dredged in flour, dipped in beaten egg, then coated with crumbs before being pan fried (or deep fried).

Stock: A flavorful liquid prepared by simmering bones and/or vegetables in water with aromatics until their flavor is extracted. It is used as a base for soups, sauces, and other preparations.

Straight forcemeat: A forcemeat combining pork and pork fat with another meat, made by grinding the mixture together.

Sweetbreads: The thymus glands of young animals, usually calves but possibly lambs. Usually sold in pairs of lobes.

T

Table salt: Refined, granulated rock salt. May be fortified with iodine and treated with magnesium carbonate to prevent clumping.

Tart: A shallow pie without a top crust; may be sweet or savory.

Tartlet: A small, single-serving tart.

TCM/tinted curing mix: See *curing salt.*

Temper: To heat gently and gradually. May refer to the process of incorporating hot liquid into a liaison to gradually raise its temperature. May also refer to the proper method for melting chocolate.

Tenderloin: A cut of tender expensive meat, usually beef or pork, from the loin or hind quarter.

Terrine: A loaf of forcemeat, similar to a pâté but cooked in a covered mold in a bain-marie. Also, the mold used to cook such items, usually a loaf shape made of ceramic.

Thermophilic: Heat-loving; describes bacteria that thrive within the temperature range of 110°F to 171°F (43°C to 77°C).

Timbale: A small, pail-shaped mold used to shape rice, custards, mousselines, and other items. Also, a preparation made in such a mold.

Tomalley: Lobster liver, which is olive green in color and turns red when cooked or heated.

Total utilization: The principle advocating the use of as much of a product as possible in order to reduce waste and increase profits.

Trichinella spiralis: A spiral-shaped parasitic worm that invades the intestines and muscle tissue; transmitted primarily through infected pork that has not been cooked sufficiently.

Trichinosis: The disease transmitted by *Trichinella spiralis.*

Tripe: The edible stomach lining of a cow or other ruminant. Honeycomb tripe comes from the second stomach and has a honeycomb-like texture.

Truss: To tie up meat or poultry with string before cooking it in order to give it a compact shape for more even cooking and better appearance.

V

Variety meat: Meat from a part of an animal other than the muscle; for example, organs.

Velouté: A sauce of white stock (chicken, veal, or seafood) thickened with blond (or pale) roux; one of the grand sauces. Also, a cream soup made with a velouté sauce base and flavorings (usually puréed) that is usually finished with a liaison.

Venison: Originally meat from large game animals; now specifically refers to deer meat.

Vertical chopping machine (VCM): A machine, similar to a blender, that has rotating blades used to grind, whip, emulsify, or blend foods.

Vinaigrette (Fr.): A cold sauce of oil and vinegar, usually with various flavorings; it is a temporary emulsion sauce. (The standard proportion is three parts oil to one part vinegar.)

W

Whip: To beat an item, such as cream or egg whites, to incorporate air. Also, a special tool (whisk for whipping made of looped wire attached to a handle).

White mirepoix: Mirepoix that does not include carrots and may include chopped mushrooms or mushroom trimmings and parsnips; used for pale or white sauces and stocks.

White stock: A light-colored stock made with bones and/or vegetables that have not been browned.

Y

Yeast: Microscopic fungus whose metabolic processes are responsible for fermentation; used for leavening bread and in making cheese, beer, and wine.

Yogurt: Milk cultured with bacteria to give it a slightly thick consistency and sour flavor.

Z

Zest: The thin, brightly colored outer part of citrus rind. It contains volatile oils, making it ideal for use as a flavoring.

Bibliography and Recommended Reading

Amendola, Joseph. *Ice Carving Made Easy.* 1st rev. ed. Chicago: National Restaurant Association, 1969.

Aylward, Larry. "The Absolute Wurst." *Meat Marketing and Technology.* February 1996.

Batterberry, Ariane. "High Livers." *Food Arts.* July–August 1993, pp. 58–60.

Beard, James. *American Cookery.* Boston: Little Brown, 1972.

Beard, James. *Beard on Bread.* New York: Knopf, 1973.

Behr, Edward. *The Artful Eater: A Gourmet Investigates the Ingredients of Great Food.* New York: Atlantic Monthly Press, 1992.

———. "Olive Oil." *The Art of Eating.* Winter 1995, pp. 1–10.

———. "Red Wine Vinegar." Spring 1994, pp. 1–4.

Black, Maggie. *The Medieval Cookbook.* New York: Thames and Hudson, 1996.

Blomquist, Torsten, and Werner Voëli. *A Gastronomic Tour of the Scandinavian Arctic,*Stockholm: Timbro, 1987.

Braudel, Ferdinand. *The Structures of Everyday Life: The Limits of the Possible.* Berkley, Calif.: 1992.

Brown, Dale. *The Cooking of Scandinavia.* New York: Time Life Books, 1968.

Cetre, F. O. *Practical Larder Work.* London: Sir Isaac Pitman and Sons, 1954.

Cerveny, John G. "Effects of Changes in the Production and Marketing of Cured Meats on the Risk of Botulism." *Food Technology,* May 1980, pp. 240–53.

Church, Ruth Ellen. *Mary Meade's Sausage Cook Book.* Chicago: Rand McNally, 1967.

Clayton, Bernard. *The Breads of France.* Indianapolis: Bobbs-Merrill, 1978.

Costner, Susan. *Great Sandwiches.* New York: Crown Publishers, 1990.

Coxe, Antony Himmisley. *The Great Book of Sausages.* Woodstock, N.Y.: Overlook Press, 1992.

Culinary Institute of America. *The New Professional Chef* 5th and 6th ed. Linda Glick Conway, ed. New York: John Wiley & Sons, Inc., 1991.

———. *Techniques of Healthy Cooking.* New York: John Wiley & Sons, Inc., 1993.

Dahl, J. O. *Kitchen Management: Construction, Planning, Administration.* New York: Harper and Brothers, 1928.

De Gouy, Louis Pullig. *Sandwich Manual for Professionals.* Stamford, Conn: The Dahls, 1939.

Desaulniers, Marcel. *Burger Meisters.* New York: Simon and Schuster, 1993.

Diggs, Lawrence, J. *Vinegar.* San Francisco: Quiet Storm Trading Co., 1989.

Dornenburg, Andrew, and Karen Page. "Tall Food Tales." *National Culinary Review.* January 1997, pp. 12–15.

Ehlert, Friedrich W., Edouard Longue, Michael Raffael, and Frank Wesel. *Pâtés and Terrines.* New York: Hearst Books, 1984.

Escoffier, Auguste. *The Complete Guide to the Art of Modern Cookery.* London: Heinemann, 1986.

Escoffier, Auguste. *The Escoffier Cookbook: A Guide to the Fine Art of Cookery.* American ed. New York: Crown, 1976. (Translation of Le Guide Culinairé, 4ed.)

Freeland-Graves, Jeanne Himich, and Gladys C. Peckham. *Foundations of Food Preparation.* 6th ed. New York: Prentice Hall, 1996.

"Feasting and Fasting." http://www.ftech.net/~regia/feasting.htm, September, 1997.

Flower, Barbara, and Elisabeth Rosenbaum, eds. *The Roman Cookery Book* by Apicius. London: Harrap, 1961.

"The Foie Gras Story." *Wine Spectator.* November 1993, pp. 71–72.

Giascosa, Ilaria Gozzini. *A Taste of Ancient Rome.* London: University of Chicago Press, 1992.

Gingrass, David. "Hand-Crafted Salamis: An Experienced Sausagemaker Shares His Method." *Fine Cooking.* February–March 1995, pp. 56–59.

Guy, Christian. *An Illustrated History of French Cuisine.* New York: Bramhall House, 1962.

Harlow, Jay. *The Art of the Sandwich.* San Francisco: Chronicle Books, 1990.

Hazani, Giuliano, and Marcella Hazan. *The Classic Pasta Cookbook.* London, New York: Dorling Kindersley, 1993.

"History of Sushi." http://www.net-army.com/sushi/history-E.html, August 1997.

Hodgson, W. C. *The Herring and Its Fishery.* London: Routledge and Kegan Paul, 1957.

Igoe, Robert S. *Dictionary of Food Ingredients.* New York: John Wiley & Sons, Inc., 1989.

Janericco, Terrence. *The Book of Great Hors d'oeuvre.* New York: John Wiley & Sons, Inc., 1990.

Jensen, Albert C. *The Cod.* New York: Thomas Y. Crowell Company, 1972.

Jordan, Michele Anna. *The Good Cook's Book of Oil and Vinegar.* Reading, Mass: Perseus Press, 1992.

Kaufman, William. *The Hot Dog Cookbook.* Garden City, N.Y.: Doubleday, 1966.

Killeen, Johanne, and George Germon. *Cucina Simpatica: Robust Trattoria Cooking.* New York: Harper, 1991.

Klein, Maggie Blyth. *The Feast of the Olive.* San Francisco: Chronicle Books, 1994.

Lang, Jenifer Harvey, ed. *Larousse Gastronomique.* New York: Crown Publishers, 1984.

Lawrie, R. A. *Meat Science.* New York: Pergamon Press, 1991.

Leader, Daniel, Judith Blahnik, and Patricia Wells. *Bread Alone: Bold Fresh Loaves from Your Own Hands.* New York: William Morrow & Company, 1993.

Gerard, C. "Let Them Eat Foie Gras." *Art Culinaire* 26 (Fall 1992).

Leto, M. T., and W. K. H. Bode. *The Larder Chef.* London: Heinemann, 1969.

Martin, Richard. "Foie Gras: Richly Diverse." *Nation's Restaurant News.* February 8, 1993, pp. 27, 33.

Martini, Anna. *Pasta and Pizza.* New York: St. Martin's Press, 1977.

McGee, Harold. *The Curious Cook: More Kitchen Science and Lore.* San Francisco: North Point Press, 1990.

———. *On Food and Cooking.* New York: Collier Books, 1988.

McHenry, ed. *The New Encyclopedia Britanica.* Chicago: Encyclopedia Britannica, 1992.

McNeill, F. Marian. *The Scots Kitchen: Its Traditions and Lore with Old-Time Recipes.* London: Blackie and Son, 1971.

Mengelatte, Pierre, Walter Bickel, and Albin Abelanet. *Buffets and Receptions.* English language ed. Surrey, England: Couldson, Virtue 1988.

Metz, Ferdinand E., and the United States Culinary Olympic Team. *The 1984 Culinary Olympics Cookbook: U.S. Team Recipes from the Sixteenth International Culinary Competition (International Kochkunst Ausstellung), Frankfurt, West Germany.* Des Plaines, Ill.: Restaurants & Institutions Magazine, Cahners Pub., 1985.

Metz, Ferdinand E., L. Timothy Ryan. *Taste of Gold, the 1988 U.S. Culinary Team Cookbook: The Road to the World Championship.* Des Plaines, Ill.: Restaurants & Institutions Magazine, Cahners Pub., 1989.

Meyer, Danny, and Michael Romano. *The Union Square Cafe Cookbook.* New York: Harper, 1994.

Midgley John. *The Goodness of Vinegars.* New York: Random House, 1994.

Murray, Joan. "Is Free-Range Better?" *Washingtonian,* October 1994.

Nicoloas, Jean F. *Elegant and Easy: Decorative Ideas for Food Presentations.* Boston: CBI Publishing Company, 1983.

Nish, Wayne. "Understanding Foie Gras." December 1994–January 1995.

"Nitrate, Nitrite, and Nitroso Compounds in Foods." *Food Technology.* April 1997, pp. 127–36.

"Non Meat Ingredients." *Meat Industry,* 1986.

O'Neill, Molly. "Can Foie Gras Help the Heart?" *New York Times,* November 17, 1991.

Pearson, A. M., and F. W. Tauber. *Processed Meats.* New York: John Wiley & Sons, Inc., 1984.

Pellaprat, Henri-Paul, and John Fuller, eds. *Modern French Culinary Art: The Pellaprat of the 20th Century.* London: Virtue, 1978.

Perdue, Charles L., ed. *Pig's Foot Jelly and Persimmon Beer: Foodways from the Virginia Writers' Project.* Santa Fe: Ancient City Press, 1992.

Peterson, Sarah T. *Acquired Taste: The French Origins of Modern Cooking.* Ithaca, N.Y.: Cornell University Press, 1994.

Phalon, Richard. "Diversifying into Pâté de Foie Gras." *Forbes,* November 21, 1994.

Price, James F., and Bernard S. Schweigert, eds. *The Science of Meat and Meat Products.* Westport, Conn.: Food & Nutrition Press, 1987.

Regenstein, Joe M., and Carrie E. Regenstein. *Introduction to Fish Technology.* New York: John Wiley & Sons, Inc., 1991.

Revel, Jean François. *Culture and Cuisine.* New York: Double Day, 1982.

Rey, Alain. *Dictionnairie historique de la langue fançaise.* Paris: Dictionnaires le Robert, 1995.

Romans, John. *The Meat We Eat.* Danville, Ill.: Insterstate Printers & Publishers, 1985.

Root, Waverly, and Richard de Rochemont. *Eating in America: A History.* New York: Ecco Press, 1981.

Rosengarten, David. "Bringing Home the Game." *Wine Spectator,* November 30, 1993, pp. 67–70.

Schmidt, Arno. *Chefs' Book of Formulas, Yields, and Sizes.* New York: John Wiley & Sons, Inc., 1990.

Shaw, Timothy. *The World of Escoffier.* New York: St. Martin's Press, 1995.

Sonnenschmidt, Frederic H., and Jean Nicolas. *The Professional Chef's Art of Garde Manger,* Boston: Institutions/Volume Feeding Magazine, 1973.

———. *The Professional Chef's Art of Garde Manger.* 4th ed. New York: John Wiley & Sons, Inc., 1988.

Soyer, Alexis. *The Pantropheon: or a History of Food and Its Preparation in Ancient Times.* New York: Paddington Press, 1977.

Strayer, Joseph R., ed. *Dictionary of the Middle Ages,* vol. 13. New York: Charles Scribner's Son, 1983.

Time-Life Books, eds. "Terrines, Pâtés & Galantines." *The Good Cook: Techniques and Recipes.* Alexandria, VA.: Time-Life Books, 1982.

Tobias, Doris. "Gascon Commissary: Game and Foie Gras from the Wilds of Jersey City." *Wine and Spirits.* October 1993, pp. 43–45.

Toussaint-Samat, Maguelonne. *A History of Food.* Cambridge, MA.: Blackwell Reference, 1992.

Verroust, Jacques Winker, Michel Pastoureau, and Raymond Buren. *Le Cochon.* Paris: Sang de la Terre, 1987.

Veale, Wency. *Step by Step Garnishing.* London: Quintet Publishing, 1989.

Vongerichten, Jean George. *Simple Cooking.* New York: Prentice Hall Press, 1990.

Wheaton, Barbara Ketcham. *Savoring the Past: The French Kitchen and Table from 1300 to 1789.* New York: Touchstone Books, 1996.

Whelan, Jack. *Smoking Salmon and Trout: Plus Pickling, Salting, Sausaging, and Care.* Bowser, B.C.: Aerie Publishing, 1982.

Wilson, C. Anne. *Food and Drink in Britain: From Stone Age to Recent Times.* London: Constable and Company, 1973.

Winker, Mac, and Claire Winkler. *Ice Sculpture: The Art of Ice Carving in Twelve Systematic Steps.* Memphis, Tenn.: Duende Publications, 1989.

Resource List

Architectural Plastics
1299 North McDowell Boulevard
Petaluma, CA 94954
Phone: 707-765-9898
Fax: 707-765-9901

Broken Arrow Ranch
104 Junction Highway
Ingram, TX 78025
Phone: 800-962-4263

Carolyn Collins Caviar Company
925 W. Jackson Boulevard
Third Floor
Chicago, IL 60607
Phone: 800-226-0342
Fax: 312-226-2114

The Coach Dairy Goat Farm
105 Mill Hill Road
Pine Plains, NY 12567
Phone: 905-629-7570
Fax: 518-398-5329

Colavita USA
Goethals Park
2537 Brusnswick Avenue
Linden, NJ 07036
Phone: 908-862-5454
Fax: 908-862-4382

Consorzio Del Prosciutto Di San Daniele
Via Andreuzzi, 8
San Daniele Del Friuli, UD
Italy 33038
Phone: 39-432-957515
Fax: 39-432-940187

Consorzio Parmigiano Reggiano
Via J. F. Kennedy, 18
Reggio Emilia
Italy 42100
Phone: 39-522-307741
Fax: 39-522-307748

Consorzio Per La Tetela Del Formaggio Pecorino Toscano, D.O.P.
Via Cairoli, 10
Grosseto
Italy 58100
Phone: 39-564-20038
Fax: 39-564-20038

The Culinary Institute of America Campus Store
2555 Main Street
St. Helena, CA 94574-0429
Phone: 707-967-2001
Fax: 707-967-1113

Daniele Prosciutto, Inc.
105 Davis Drive
Pascoag, RI 02859
Phone: 401-568-6228
Fax: 401-568-4778

D'Artagnan
399 St. Paul Avenue
Jersey City, NJ 07306
Phone: 201-792-0194
800-327-8246
Fax: 201-792-6113
E-mail: dartagnanine@worldnet.att.net
Website: http://www.ippi.com/dartagnan.html

Egg Farm Dairy
2 John Walsh Boulevard
Peekskill, NY 10566
Phone: 800-CREAMERY
914-734-7343
Fax: 914-734-9287

Fine Foods of Italy, Inc.
45 Rockefeller Plaza, Suite 3162
New York, NY 10020
Phone: 212-969-1701
800-465-9161
Fax: 212-969-1710

Friedrich Metal Production Company, Inc.
P.O. Box 14069
Greensboro, NC 27415
Phone: 910-375-3067
Fax: 910-621-7901

Gerhard's
901-B Enterprise Way
Napa, CA 94558
Phone: 707-252-4116

Hudson Valley Foie Gras
RR 1, Box 69
Ferndale, NY 12734
Phone: 914-292-2500
Fax: 914-292-3009

Kitchen and Home
64 E. Market Street
Rhinebeck, NY 12572
Phone: 914-876-6900

Mozzarella Company
2944 Elm Street
Dallas, TX 75226
Phone: 800-798-2954
Fax: 214-741-4072
E-mail address: mozzco@aol.com
Website: http://secure.foodwine.com/food/basket/store/50
6/index.html

National Livestock and Meat Board
444 North Michigan Avenue
Chicago, IL 60611
Phone: 312-467-5520
Fax: 312-467-9767

New England Cheesemaking Company
Box 85
Ashfield, MA 01330-0085
Phone: 413-628-3808
E-mail address: info@cheesemaking.com
Website: http://www.cheesemaking.com

Old Chatham Sheepherding Company Inn
Shaker Museum Road
Old Chatham, NY 12136
Phone: 518-794-9774
Fax: 518-794-9779

The Sausagemaker
26 Military Road
Buffalo, NY 14207
Phone: 716-876-5521
Fax: 716-875-0302

Summerfield Farm
1044 James Monroe Highway
Culpepper, VA 22701
Phone: 540-547-9600
Fax: 540-547-9628

Switzerland Cheese Association, Inc.
704 Executive Boulevard
Valley Cottage, NY 10989
Phone: 914-268-2460
Fax: 914-268-2480

Urbani Truffles
29-34 40th Avenue
Long Island City, New York 11101
Phone: 718-392-5050
Fax: 718-392-1704

Vermont Department of Agriculture
116 State Street
Montpelier, VT 15620
Phone: 802-828-3831
Fax: 802-828-3831

Vyse Gelatin
5010 N. Rose Street
Schiller Park, IL 60176
Phone: 800-533-2152
Fax: 847-678-0329

Warren Cutlery
2203 Route 9G
Rhinebeck, NY 12572
Phone: 914-876-3444

Woodsmoke Provisions
1222 Menlo Drive
Atlanta, GA 30318
Phone: 800-883-3747
Fax: 404-350-5850

Recipe Index

D

Q

R

S

T

V

W

Y

Index

G

H

I

J

V

W

Y

Z

Books From The Culinary Institute of America

The Culinary Institute of America (Hyde Park, NY and St. Helena, CA), hailed by *Time* magazine as "the nation's most influential training school for professional cooks," is the author of some of the most significant works for professionals and students.

Garde Manger: The Art and Craft of the Cold Kitchen (0-471-32367-5)
The Culinary Institute of America's complete and contemporary reference to garde manger can help anyone master the art of cold food preparation. Combining clear, illustrated explanations of basic methods in full color with over 400 recipes, it covers sausages, cured and smoked foods, terrines, pâtés, galantines, and roulades as well as sandwiches, salads, cold sauces and soups, hors d'oeuvres, appetizers, and condiments. A separate chapter on cheeses demystifies the unique challenges of cheese selection, preparation, and presentation.

The Professional Chef's Knife Kit (0-471-34997-6)
High quality, well-maintained knives—and the skills to use them properly—are among a chef's most important assets. This book explains how to use and care for these essential tools, and easy-to-follow instructions cover all of the basic knife cuts and techniques. The book also features invaluable information on small tools, such as peelers and zesters, and large equipment such as meat grinders and food processors.

The New Professional Chef, 6th Edition (0-471-28679-6)
This tome offers the most comprehensive and up-to-date information on food identification, preparation, and presentation for both the novice cook and the seasoned chef. It is the most complete culinary encyclopedia of the nineties. *The New Professional Chef* defines the essential ingredients, tools, and techniques of classic and modern cuisine. Detailed charts and step-by-step instructions show how to identify, purchase, and prepare the finest, freshest foods. For easy reference, the recipes—1,000 altogether—are accompanied by display, illustration, and technique photos, and cover a mouthwatering spectrum, from classic to contemporary.

The Professional Chef's Techniques of Healthy Cooking, 2nd Edition (0-471-33269-0)
As lifestyles change and people eat more healthfully, the professional chef and home cook are faced with an ever greater challenge: how to create dramatic, flavorful dishes while limiting the ingredients that aren't good for us. The second edition of *The Professional Chef's Techniques of Healthy Cooking* offers nearly 400 exciting recipes that focus on good nutrition, showing that you don't have to eat tasteless food in order to stay healthy and live longer!

Exploring Wine: The Culinary Institute of America's Complete Guide to Wines of the World (0-471-28626-5)
In this enthralling guide, Steven Kolpan, Brain Smith, and Michael Weiss have thoroughly demystified wine, a topic that can intimidate even the most urbane reader. Whether you've collected books on wine for years, or this is your first, you'll treasure *Exploring Wine.* Its clarity, warmth, practicality, and encyclopedic breadth make it a basic reference for anyone who enjoys wine.

Cooking Essentials for the New Professional Chef (0-471-28717-2)
With *Cooking Essentials*, you can learn the basics of cooking based on the reference that professional chefs have relied on for generations. In addition to providing an excellent foundation in such cooking essentials as raw ingredients, tools, classic techniques, and foundation recipes, this text clarifies every concept with supportive text, step-by-step photos in full color, illustrations, and tables.

From Our Kitchens (0-471-28609-5)
Filled with concisely presented recipes that have been perfected through many hours of testing, *From Our Kitchens* belongs near the stove of every serious home cook. All of these recipes are both sophisticated enough for a restaurant and easy enough to prepare at home. Bon appetit!